T0368353

Lecture Notes in Computer Science   15384

Founding Editors

Gerhard Goos
Juris Hartmanis

The series Lecture Notes in Computer Science (LNCS), including its subseries Lecture Notes in Artificial Intelligence (LNAI) and Lecture Notes in Bioinformatics (LNBI), has established itself as a medium for the publication of new developments in computer science and information technology research, teaching, and education.

LNCS enjoys close cooperation with the computer science R & D community, the series counts many renowned academics among its volume editors and paper authors, and collaborates with prestigious societies. Its mission is to serve this international community by providing an invaluable service, mainly focused on the publication of conference and workshop proceedings and postproceedings. LNCS commenced publication in 1973.

Shandong Wu · Behrouz Shabestari · Lei Xing
Editors

Applications of Medical Artificial Intelligence

Third International Workshop, AMAI 2024
Held in Conjunction with MICCAI 2024
Marrakesh, Morocco, October 6, 2024
Proceedings

 Springer

Editors
Shandong Wu
University of Pittsburgh
Pittsburgh, PA, USA

Behrouz Shabestari
National Institute of Biomedical Imaging
and Bioengineering
Bethesda, MD, USA

Lei Xing
Stanford University
Stanford, CA, USA

ISSN 0302-9743   ISSN 1611-3349 (electronic)
Lecture Notes in Computer Science
ISBN 978-3-031-82006-9   ISBN 978-3-031-82007-6 (eBook)
https://doi.org/10.1007/978-3-031-82007-6

This Springer imprint is published by the registered company Springer Nature Switzerland AG
The registered company address is: Gewerbestrasse 11, 6330 Cham, Switzerland

If disposing of this product, please recycle the paper.

Preface

The Third Workshop on Applications of Medical Artificial Intelligence (AMAI 2024) was held as an in-person event in Marrakesh, Morocco, on October 6, 2024, in conjunction with the 27th International Conference on Medical Image Computing and Computer Assisted Intervention (MICCAI 2024). This third AMAI workshop followed its second edition, AMAI 2023, which was held in Vancouver on October 8, 2023 along with MICCAI 2023.

Along with the quick evolution of artificial intelligence (AI), deep/machine learning, and big data in healthcare, medical AI research goes beyond methodological/algorithm development. Many new research questions are emerging in the practical and applied aspects of medical AI, such as translational study, clinical evaluation, real-world use cases of AI systems, etc. The AMAI 2024 workshop created a forum to bring together researchers, clinicians, domain experts, AI practitioners, industry representatives, and students to investigate and discuss various challenges and opportunities related to applications of medical AI.

The aims of the AMAI workshop are to introduce emerging medical AI research topics and novel application methodologies, showcase the evaluation, translation, use cases, and success of AI in healthcare, develop multi-disciplinary collaborations and academic-industry partnerships, and provide educational, networking, and career opportunities for attendees including clinicians, scientists, trainees, and students.

In this workshop, two submission tracks were included: full papers and abstracts (one page). The idea of the abstract track was to attract participation from researchers and clinicians primarily in the medical communities. AMAI 2024 received a strong response in submissions, including 39 full papers and 15 abstracts. All submissions went through double-blind review by the Program Committee and ad hoc reviewers, and each submission was reviewed by at least two qualified experts in the field. Finally, 24 full papers were accepted and included in this Springer LNCS volume. The 9 accepted abstracts were made publicly accessible on the workshop's website.

The organizers are grateful for the hard work of the Program Committee members and the ad hoc reviewers in undertaking their quality and timely reviews of the submissions. We thank all the authors for submitting their work to this workshop. The collective efforts of all participants made this workshop successful.

September 2024

Shandong Wu
Behrouz Shabestari
Lei Xing

Organization

Program Committee Chairs and Workshop Organizers

Shandong Wu	University of Pittsburgh, USA
Behrouz Shabestari	National Institute of Biomedical Imaging and Bioengineering, USA
Lei Xing	Stanford University, USA

Program Committee

Mohd Anwar	National Institute of Biomedical Imaging and Bioengineering, USA
Dooman Arefan	University of Pittsburgh, USA
Sixian Chan	Zhejiang University of Technology, China
Niketa Chotai	RadLink Imaging Centre and National University of Singapore, Singapore
Dania Daye	Massachusetts General Hospital/Harvard Medical School, USA
Douglas Hartman	University of Cincinnati Medical Center, USA
Michail Klontzas	University of Crete, Greece
Zhicheng Jiao	Brown University, USA
Fabian Laqu	University Hospital Würzburg, Germany
Ines Prata Machado	University of Cambridge, UK
Mireia Crispin Ortuzar	University of Cambridge and Cancer Research, UK
Chang Min Park	Seoul National University Hospital, South Korea
Matthew Pease	Indiana University, USA
Nicholas Petrick	U.S. Food and Drug Administration, USA
Bhanu Prakash K. N.	Agency for Science, Technology and Research (A*STAR), Singapore
Parisa Rashidi	University of Florida, USA
Zaid Siddiqui	Baylor College of Medicine, USA
Tao Tan	Macao Polytechnic University, China
Zhiyong (Sean) Xie	Xellar Biosystems, USA
Qi Yang	Genentech, Inc., USA

Yudong Zhang   First Affiliated Hospital, Nanjing Medical
                                     University, China
Jian Zheng   Suzhou Institute of Biomedical Engineering and
                                     Technology of the Chinese Academy of
                                     Sciences, China

Contents

Exploring CNN and Transformer-Based Architectures to Improve Image Segmentation for Chronic Wound Measurement

Rafaela Carvalho(✉)📷, Ana C. Morgado📷, Ana Filipa Sampaio📷, and Maria J. M. Vasconcelos📷

Fraunhofer Portugal AICOS, Porto, Portugal
{rafaela.carvalho,maria.vasconcelos}@fraunhofer.pt,
{ana.morgado,ana.sampaio}@aicos.fraunhofer.pt

Abstract. The high prevalence of chronic wounds and their consequences for people's quality of life makes wound treatment a highly relevant topic in the context of healthcare. One vital aspect of monitoring concerns tracking wound size evolution, which guides healthcare professionals during diagnosis and serves as a key predictor of treatment efficacy. This work proposes an automatic image segmentation and measurement framework for chronic wounds using deep learning and computer vision techniques. The wound segmentation task involved exploring three prominent segmentation models: a popular convolutional neural network (DeepLabV3+), a cutting-edge transformer approach (SegFormer) and a visual foundation model (MedSAM). Traditional computer vision techniques were further applied to infer the open wound's width, length and area in real-world units during the wound measurement task. Separate studies were performed to assess each task's performance and a final assessment of the complete framework that couples a wound and reference marker detection model with the developed segmentation and measurement approach. For the automatic wound segmentation, MedSAM achieved the best performance with Dice scores of 88.14% and 92.25%, applied on public AZH FU and private datasets, respectively. In the wound measurement task, the area estimation achieved a mean relative error of 5.36% for the private dataset. Concerning the overall pipeline results, MedSAM experienced a decline in performance and SegFormer emerged as the best segmentation model, achieving a Dice score of 91.55% and a 16.7% mean relative error for the area estimation (which surpasses the literature results) in the private dataset, demonstrating its applicability in clinical practice.

Keywords: Skin wounds · Image segmentation · Wound measurement · Deep Learning · Computer Vision · Telemedicine

S. Wu et al. (Eds.): AMAI 2024, LNCS 15384, pp. 1–10, 2025.
https://doi.org/10.1007/978-3-031-82007-6_1

1 Introduction

Chronic wounds are characterized by a prolonged healing process and have a major impact not only on the healthcare system but also on the patient's life quality [21]. Wound care costs up to 4% of the health budget in developed countries [9,21]. The proper monitoring of wound evolution provides vital cues on the effect of treatment [17]. Digital imaging is considered one of the most accurate and reliable methods for area measurements, particularly in larger and irregularly shape wounds [10]. In clinical practice, healthcare professionals include wound pictures in patient health records, however they are mostly used for visual comparisons, being the measurement task manual and prone to subjectivity [13,20].

To simplify and increase wound assessment reproducibility, several research lines have focused on automating the wound measurement step [1,5]. As outlining the open wound region is essential to achieve this, Deep Learning (DL) methods have been extensively used for wound segmentation. Different Convolutional Neural Network (CNN) architectures were used [18,20,22,23], such as Fully Convolutional Networks (FCN) [7], U-Net [4,20], as well as distinct decoder models (DeepLabV3 [2], U-Net and Mask R-CNN [13]) coupled with ResNet encoders, and an ensemble of CNN models (LinkNet with U-Net) [15]. Other works apply traditional Computer Vision approaches, like the region-growing algorithm proposed in [6] or a pipeline that combines traditional methods with an adapted MobileNet CNN [12]. Regarding wound segmentation results, [23] reports a Dice similarity coefficient (Dice) for Medetec [23] and AZH FU [23] test sets of 94.05% and 90.47%, respectively, while [15] reports 92.07% and 88.80% for AZH FU and FUSeg [23] test sets. For a private set of pressure wounds, [13] reports a Dice of 84.88%, while for a set composed of leg ulcers, [4] achieves 90%. Regarding commercially available smartphone solutions for wound monitoring, only Swift Skin and Wound app provides a concrete study [18], attaining a mean intersection over union (IoU) of 86.44% for 2000 images of arterial, venous, pressure and diabetic wounds. Most approaches resort to the segmented wound region to estimate its dimensions, using a metric reference to calibrate for real-world units. For wound area estimation, Chino et al. [4] report a mean relative error (MRE) of 10.4% when evaluating the proposed method's effectiveness in calculating ground truth (GT) mask area, using a semi-automatic method. The work also estimates the area of the segmentation masks provided by their wound segmentation approach with an MRE of 24.5%, against the work in [13] that states a 26.2% MRE for automatically predicted masks. Despite the reported performances, improvements can be achieved through novel dataset combinations and other model architectures. Vision foundation models, like Segment Anything model (SAM) [11] and its medical variant MedSAM [14], have emerged but have not yet been applied to chronic wounds (to the best of our knowledge), potentially advancing the state-of-the-art by reduced reliance on specific datasets.

This work advances the state-of-the-art wound segmentation approaches by comparing popular CNN and transformer architectures for semantic segmentation with the zero-shot segmentation capabilities of MedSAM, coupled with a robust wound and marker detection model to provide efficient input prompts. Moreover, it introduces a method capable of responding to the needs of health-care professionals in having access to an automatic and efficient procedure for wound measurement and monitoring.

2 Methodology

Due to the complexity and subjectivity of the clinical monitoring of chronic wounds, an automatic pipeline for wound assessment (Fig. 1) was developed based on two main tasks: i) wound segmentation and ii) wound measurement. Since the development of this framework requires the extraction of the region of interest (ROI) around the wound and the reference marker, firstly, GT bounding boxes (BB) of these regions were used, to prevent error propagation. Then, a wound and marker detection model was incorporated into the pipeline to obtain both ROI and simulate real-world deployment.

Wound Segmentation. Prominent CNN, transformer-based and foundation models were explored for wound segmentation: DeepLabV3+ [3] with a ResNet50 [8] backbone, SegFormer-B0 [24], and MedSAM (ViT-Base) [14]. DeepLabV3+ and SegFormer were trained, while MedSAM was employed for zero-shot segmentation, exploring its ability to segment unseen objects beyond its training dataset. MedSAM requires an input prompt, specifically the wound ROI.

Wound Measurement. Wound dimensions (height, width and area) were extracted from the wound segmentation mask. To convert these to real world units, a reference marker with known dimensions was used to determine the pixel-to-centimeter ratio and conversion factor. For marker segmentation, the HSV (Hue, Saturation, Value) color space was analysed, except for images with white markers, which used the grayscale color space. The segmentation was made using minimum and maximum thresholds for each channel which were empirically established based on histogram distribution for each marker color. The marker's vertices were found by approximating the mask contour to a convex

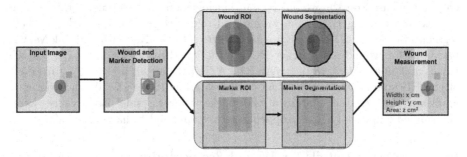

Fig. 1. Overview of the proposed wound assessment pipeline. The wound dimensions are extracted using the wound boundary and a marker of fixed size.

polygon. Only images where four vertices were found proceeded to wound measurement. To account for the marker's square shape distortion, the marker's average edge length in pixels (px) was used to determine pixel-to-centimeter ratio for width and height. Concerning the wound area, the conversion factor was established using the mask of the marker (in px) and the known area of the marker ($4\,cm^2$).

3   Experiments and Results

3.1   Datasets and Implementation Details

Datasets. In this study, we employed the AZH FU public dataset [23] and the private Wounds dataset, an extended version of the CWS dataset [19]. AZH FU is composed of 1010 images and corresponding GT segmentation masks, where 810 and 200 images were used for training and testing, respectively. This public dataset serves as a crucial component for benchmarking comparison purposes and also pretraining our models. The private Wounds dataset comprises 307 images from 104 wounds, obtained from nine institutions (from Rehabilitation and Care Units, Primary Health Care/Hospital/Home Care consultations), to encompass the full spectrum of wound characteristics encountered in practice. These images span across five different wound types: pressure from categories 1 to 4, venous leg, diabetic foot, arterial leg ulcers, leg ulcers of unknown etiology, and an additional category encompassing all remaining types. During the acquisition, a 2 cm × 2 cm reference marker with four possible colors (white, green, blue, and yellow) was included next to the wound, allowing the dimension measurements in real-world units. The study protocol for data acquisition was submitted and approved by the Health Ethical Committees, and informed consent was obtained both from healthcare professionals and patients. Segmentation masks were manually annotated according to the agreement of three wound specialists. The training (75%) and test (25%) sets (229 and 78 images), were designed to include examples from various wound types, body locations, and skin phototypes.

Pre-processing. To standardize the model input size, images undergo centered cropping focused on the wound region. During model development, this region was extracted using BB of the wound and reference marker inferred from GT segmentation masks. The final pipeline utilizes a RetinaNet with a MobileNetV2 backbone for wound and marker ROI extraction [19], reporting mAP@.75IOU values of 0.39 and 0.95, respectively. The AZH FU dataset uses a 30% tolerance of the BB size to preserve contextual information, while the Wounds dataset applies a 25% padding margin of the marker's largest side. Both values were determined empirically. The cropped region is enforced to have 320 × 320 px.

Implementation Details for Wound Segmentation. Model optimization for DeepLabV3+ and SegFormer was achieved with grid search hyperparameter tuning and a stratified 3-fold cross-validation procedure, ensuring all images of each wound remained in the same subset. Training was run for up to 200 epochs with early stopping (patience of 10 runs) using the Adam optimizer. Image dimensions of 224×224 px and 320×320 px were explored while adopting batch sizes of 16 and 32 and learning rate (LR) values of 10^{-4} and 10^{-3}. DeepLabV3+ used a combination of Dice and Cross Entropy loss (equal weights), and SegFormer used Cross Entropy. Experiments were done using the open-source semantic segmentation toolbox MMSegmentation v1.2.1 [16] on PyTorch v1.13.1+cu116, on a workstation with four NVIDIA Tesla A100 and V100 GPUs.

Post-processing. To enhance mask quality, hole filing and small region removal was performed on the model-generated masks to obtain the final segmentation.

Evaluation Metrics. To assess the segmentation performance and compare it with other literature approaches, accuracy (Acc), IoU, and Dice were computed. Wound measurement was evaluated in terms of mean relative error (MRE) and mean absolute error (MAE) between the achieved dimensions and the GT.

Ablation Study. The impact on wound segmentation of using different architectures, namely the CNN represented by DeepLabV3+, transformer-based (SegFormer-B0) and foundation (MedSAM) models, as well as the effect of pretraining the models with a benchmark dataset (AZH FU) was investigated.

3.2 Results

Wound Segmentation. The segmentation results for the AZH FU and Wounds datasets are presented in Table 1. The optimal hyperparameters included batch size of 16 and LR of 10^{-4} for SegFormer trained only on Wounds, with input size of 320×320, and both DeepLab models, with inputs of 320×320 for the model pretrained on AZH FU and 224×224 for the other case. SegFormer pretrained on AZH FU used an input of 320×320, batch of 32 and LR of 10^{-3}.

Benchmark Comparison. Analyzing the results for the AZH FU dataset, we observe that the model exposed to images from this dataset during pretraining outperforms the model trained solely on the Wounds dataset. The DeepLabV3+ model achieves an IoU of 78.60% and Dice of 88.02%, almost matching the reported Dice values of 90.47% and 92.07% in [15, 23] studies, respectively.

Ablation Study. Regarding the Wounds dataset results, SegFormer trained uniquely on Wounds dataset emerged as the best model, yielding IoU of 84.98% and Dice of 91.88%. However, the results across all models are very similar, indicating no superiority of any particular architecture. DeepLabV3+ slightly benefited from the knowledge acquired from the additional dataset, while Seg-Former still achieved comparable performance with fewer training phases. It is possible to conclude that pretraining on AZH FU did not provide an important advantage. This may be attributed to the limited diversity in AZH FU, which contains only foot ulcers, while the Wounds dataset comprises different wound types, presenting diverse scenarios for the model. MedSAM demonstrated robust zero-shot generalization ability, producing the best result among all approaches for both datasets, likely due to the input prompt information of the wound bounding box.

Statistical Analysis. Comparisons were performed for all models, at a significance level of 95% ($p < 0.05$). The Shapiro-Wilk test assessed the normality of the Dice distribution. Due to non-normality and the paired nature of the samples, the Wilcoxon signed-rank test was employed, revealing no significant difference between the models, except for MedSAM and the DeepLabV3+ model trained solely on the Wounds dataset.

Table 1. Results of ablation study on wound segmentation for the test sets of the AZH FU and Wounds datasets, using wound ground truth segmentation masks.

Experiments	Models	AZH FU			Wounds		
		Acc	IoU	Dice	Acc	IoU	Dice
Trained on Wounds dataset	DeepLabV3+	88.74	72.82	84.27	92.05	83.63	91.08
	SegFormer	86.22	72.69	84.18	**93.91**	84.98	91.88
Pretrained on AZH FU, finetuned on Wounds dataset	DeepLabV3+	89.31	78.60	88.02	93.60	84.82	91.79
	SegFormer	89.48	76.31	86.56	93.28	83.77	91.17
Zero-shot segmentation	MedSAM	**90.96**	**78.79**	**88.14**	90.76	**85.62**	**92.25**

Table 2. Wound measurement results on the test set of the Wounds dataset using GT wound segmentation masks and marker bounding boxes.

	Width	Height	Area
MRE (%)	17.56 ± 22.71	19.36 ± 21.78	5.36 ± 16.49
MAE (cm/cm²)	0.45 ± 0.72	0.55 ± 0.95	2.39 ± 13.01

Wound Measurement. In this task, only the test images comprising a marker and where four vertices were found on it were considered, totalling 67 images. Table 2 presents the results of the predicted dimensions for GT wound segmentation masks. Here, to determine the pixel-to-centimeters ratio, the GT marker BBs were used to find the ROI where marker segmentation was performed. In this way, we formed a baseline for the results achieved with the proposed pipeline presented next. Comparing width (horizontal) and height (vertical) measurements, similar results were found for both dimensions with a difference around 1.8% in terms of MRE and 0.1 cm with respect to MAE. Regarding the area, an MRE of 5.36% and a MAE of 2.39 cm² were obtained, surpassing the results found in other studies, which report an MRE of 16.6% [4]. These promising results reveal the potential of the proposed algorithm for wound measurement.

Wound Assessment Pipeline. The wound and marker detection step is critical for several steps of the proposed pipeline: preprocessing, wound BB received as input prompt for the MedSAM model, and metric calibration through the marker's segmentation. From the 78 images in the initial test set, after excluding images without detected wounds, only 67 were used for segmentation evaluation (Table 3); for the measurement analysis (Table 4), images without detected marker or lacking four vertices in the marker contour and outliers with unreliable area errors were also excluded, resulting in 55 images. The SegFormer model trained on Wounds achieves the best segmentation results. Pretraining on AZH FU demonstrated to be beneficial for the DeepLabV3+ model, though the opposite trend was observed for SegFormer, which may be attributed to the inherent architectural dissimilarities. The proposed framework demonstrated notable robustness for the SegFormer and DeepLabV3+ models, with only minor reductions in segmentation performance (below 1.2% in Dice) compared to the results outlined in Table 1. However, MedSAM experienced a 4.57% reduction, demonstrating its high dependency on precise input prompts. There is no significant difference between the DeepLabV3+ pretrained on AZH FU and both SegFormer models.

Table 3. Wound segmentation results using the proposed pipeline on the test set of the Wounds dataset.

Experiments	Models	Acc	IoU	Dice
Trained on Wounds dataset	DeepLabV3+	89.58	81.78	89.98
	SegFormer	**92.09**	**84.42**	**91.55**
Pretrained on AZH FU, finetuned on Wounds dataset	DeepLabV3+	91.37	83.65	91.09
	SegFormer	90.68	82.99	90.71
Zero-shot segmentation	MedSAM	85.40	78.06	87.68

Table 4. Wound measurement results using the proposed pipeline on the test set of the Wounds dataset with SegFormer and DeepLabV3+ predicted masks.

	SegFormer			DeepLabV3+(pretrained)		
	Width	Height	Area	Width	Height	Area
MRE (%)	15.1 ± 18.8	14.6 ± 15.0	16.7 ± 20.0	14.4 ± 18.3	17.9 ± 18.8	17.2 ± 19.9
MAE (cm)	0.46 ± 0.81	0.59 ± 1.0	4.1 ± 15.9	0.41 ± 0.72	0.67 ± 1.03	3.7 ± 14.2

To further compare the models, the error associated with wound measurement was assessed (Table 4). The results reported for the overall pipeline improved for width and height when compared with the ones achieved for the

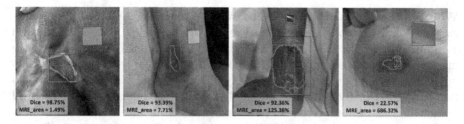

Fig. 2. Examples of the wound assessment pipeline results with SegFormer. Detection BBs of the wound and marker: GT (cyan) and predicted (blue); Mask contours: GT (green) and predicted (yellow); Dimensions: GT (orange) and predicted (red). The last image presents one of the two outliers that were excluded. (Color figure online)

GT masks (Table 2). However, this may be due to fewer images being evaluated and the possible outlier removal. Nevertheless, for the other metrics, an increase in the mean error values was observed, probably a result of the errors propagated from the preceding steps (detection and segmentation models). Both wound segmentation models produced similar wound measurements, with Seg-Former achieving the best MRE in terms of area (16.7%). In both cases, our method outperformed the methods presented in [4], where an MRE of 24.5% was achieved using a semi-automatic approach and from [13] where, after removing outliers, an MRE of 26.2% was reported, demonstrating the effectiveness of our fully automated approach in assessing the dimensions of wounds of various sizes.

Figure 2 displays diverse wounds and demonstrates the framework's outputs across different segmentation and MRE values. It is possible to understand the critical interplay between detection, segmentation, and subsequent measurement in the proposed pipeline: effective detection and segmentation result in minimal wound area errors, while shadows or inadequate detection in the last examples lead to flawed segmentation, thus introducing higher errors in the measurement process.

4   Conclusion

This work presents a pipeline for chronic wound characterization, through segmentation and measurement that are crucial for monitoring the healing process.

The selected CNN and transformer models, namely DeepLabV3+ and Seg-Former, alongside the foundation model MedSAM, exhibit proficiency in the segmentation task, presenting Dice scores above 87%. Moreover, MedSAM show-cases strong zero-shot generalization capabilities, emphasizing its efficacy in segmentation tasks with previously unseen data; nevertheless, this model relies heavily on accurate input prompts, suffering a significant drop in performance when the predicted wound bounding box was used as the prompt. To validate the robustness of our segmentation models, we evaluated them on both the benchmark dataset AZH FU and the private Wounds dataset, achieving excellent segmentation performance. Promising results were also achieved for the wound measurement task, with the 16.7% MRE obtained for area computation outperforming the literature results, and subsequently demonstrating the adequate reliability of the proposed framework for usage in clinical practice. Its integration into the wound monitoring workflow can alleviate the burden of healthcare professionals by streamlining the wound measurement process.

For future work, to mitigate the propagation of errors from preceding steps within the pipeline, we intend to improve the wound and marker detection model. Moreover, we are currently preparing clinical trials to validate the pipeline in the real environment and assess its impact on the wound monitoring process.

Acknowledgements. This work is under the scope of HfPT, funded by IAPMEI with reference 41, co-financed by Component 5 - Capitalization and Business Innovation, integrated in the Resilience Dimension of the Recovery and Resilience Plan within the scope of the Recovery and Resilience Mechanism (MRR) of the European Union (EU), framed in the Next Generation EU, for the period 2021–2026.

Disclosure of Interests. The authors have no competing interests to declare that are relevant to the content of this article.

References

1. Anisuzzaman, D., Wang, C., Rostami, B., Gopalakrishnan, S., Niezgoda, J., Yu, Z.: Image-based artificial intelligence in wound assessment: a systematic review. Adv. Wound Care **11**(12), 687–709 (2022)
2. Chang, C.W., et al.: Deep learning approach based on superpixel segmentation assisted labeling for automatic pressure ulcer diagnosis. PLoS ONE **17**(2), e0264139 (2022). https://doi.org/10.1371/journal.pone.0264139
3. Chen, L.C., Papandreou, G., Schroff, F., Adam, H.: Rethinking atrous convolution for semantic image segmentation. arXiv preprint arXiv:1706.05587 (2017)
4. Chino, D.Y., Scabora, L.C., Cazzolato, M.T., Jorge, A.E., Traina-Jr., C., Traina, A.J.: Segmenting skin ulcers and measuring the wound area using deep convolutional networks. Comput. Methods Programs Biomed. **191**, 105376 (2020). https://doi.org/10.1016/j.cmpb.2020.105376
5. Dweekat, O.Y., Lam, S.S., McGrath, L.: Machine learning techniques, applications, and potential future opportunities in pressure injuries (bedsores) management: a systematic review. Int. J. Environ. Res. Public Health **20**(1), 796 (2023)
6. Fauzi, M.F.A., Khansa, I., Catignani, K., Gordillo, G., Sen, C.K., Gurcan, M.N.: Segmentation and management of chronic wound images: a computer-based approach. In: Shiffman, M.A., Low, M. (eds.) Chronic Wounds, Wound Dressings and Wound Healing. RCTRRW, vol. 6, pp. 115–134. Springer, Cham (2018). https://doi.org/10.1007/15695_2018_131
7. Goyal, M., Yap, M.H., Reeves, N.D., Rajbhandari, S., Spragg, J.: Fully convolutional networks for diabetic foot ulcer segmentation. In: 2017 IEEE International Conference on Systems, Man, and Cybernetics (SMC), pp. 618–623 (2017). https://doi.org/10.1109/SMC.2017.8122675
8. He, K., Zhang, X., Ren, S., Sun, J.: Deep residual learning for image recognition. In: Proceedings of the IEEE Conference on Computer Vision and Pattern Recognition, pp. 770–778 (2016)

9. Järbrink, K., et al.: The humanistic and economic burden of chronic wounds: a protocol for a systematic review. Syst. Control Found. Appl. **6**, 1–7 (2017)

10. Jørgensen, L.B., Sørensen, J.A., Jemec, G.B., Yderstræde, K.B.: Methods to assess area and volume of wounds-a systematic review. Int. Wound J. **13**(4), 540–553 (2016)

11. Kirillov, A., et al.: Segment anything. arXiv preprint arXiv:2304.02643 (2023)

12. Li, F., Wang, C., Liu, X., Peng, Y., Jin, S., et al.: A composite model of wound segmentation based on traditional methods and deep neural networks. Comput. Intell. Neurosci. **2018** (2018). https://doi.org/10.1155/2018/4149103

13. Liu, T.J., Wang, H., Christian, M., Chang, C.W., Lai, F., Tai, H.C.: Automatic segmentation and measurement of pressure injuries using deep learning models and a LiDAR camera. Sci. Rep. **13**(1), 680 (2023). https://doi.org/10.1038/s41598-022-26812-9

14. Ma, J., He, Y., Li, F., Han, L., You, C., Wang, B.: Segment anything in medical images. Nat. Commun. **15**(1), 654 (2024)

15. Mahbod, A., Schaefer, G., Ecker, R., Ellinger, I.: Automatic foot ulcer segmentation using an ensemble of convolutional neural networks. In: 2022 26th International Conference on Pattern Recognition (ICPR), pp. 4358–4364 (2022). https://doi.org/10.1109/ICPR56361.2022.9956253

16. MMSegmentation Contributors: OpenMMLab Semantic Segmentation Toolbox and Benchmark, July 2020. https://github.com/open-mmlab/mmsegmentation

17. Mohafez, H., Ahmad, S.A., Roohi, S.A., Hadizadeh, M.: Wound healing assessment using digital photography: a review. J. Biomed. Eng. Med. Imaging **3**(5), 01 (2016). https://doi.org/10.14738/jbemi.35.2203

18. Ramachandram, D., Ramirez-GarciaLuna, J.L., Fraser, R.D.J., Martínez-Jiménez, M.A., Arriaga-Caballero, J.E., Allport, J.: Fully automated wound tissue segmentation using deep learning on mobile devices: cohort study. JMIR Mhealth Uhealth **10**(4), e36977 (2022). https://doi.org/10.2196/36977

19. Sampaio, A.F., et al.: Leveraging deep neural networks for automatic and standardised wound image acquisition. In: 9th International Conference on Information and Communication Technologies for Ageing Well and e-Health, pp. 253–261 (2023)

20. Scebba, G., et al.: Detect-and-segment: a deep learning approach to automate wound image segmentation. Inf. Med. Unlocked **29**, 100884 (2022). https://doi.org/10.1016/j.imu.2022.100884

21. Sen, C.K.: Human wounds and its burden: an updated compendium of estimates. Adv. Wound Care **8**(2), 39–48 (2019). https://doi.org/10.1089/wound.2019.0946

22. Wang, C., et al.: A unified framework for automatic wound segmentation and analysis with deep convolutional neural networks. In: 2015 37th Annual International Conference of the IEEE Engineering in Medicine and Biology Society (EMBC), pp. 2415–2418 (2015). https://doi.org/10.1109/EMBC.2015.7318881

23. Wang, C., et al.: Fully automatic wound segmentation with deep convolutional neural networks. Sci. Rep. **10**(1), 21897 (2020). https://doi.org/10.1038/s41598-020-78799-w

24. Xie, E., Wang, W., Yu, Z., Anandkumar, A., Alvarez, J.M., Luo, P.: SegFormer: simple and efficient design for semantic segmentation with transformers. In: Advances in Neural Information Processing Systems, vol. 34, pp. 12077–12090 (2021)

From Pixel Scores to Clinical Impacts: The Implicit Choices in FROC Metric Design and Their Consequences

Minjeong Kim[ID], Hesham Dar[ID], Sanguk Park[ID], and Thijs Kooi[✉][ID]

Lunit Inc., Seoul, Republic of Korea
{mjkim0918,heshamdar,tony.superb,tkooi}@lunit.io

Abstract. When evaluating lesion localization performance in medical imaging, methods like the Free-response Receiver Operating Characteristic (FROC) often fall short for segmentation-based AI predictions where each pixel has a continuous score. While adaptations exist, they involve implicit design choices with significant implications for model development and clinical application.

This paper examines one set of these design choices, the transformations required to discretize the AI prediction into a set of detections, and then determining whether those detections are successful or not. This is typically done by applying a threshold to a respective measure. With a set of experiments on both real-world and simulated datasets, we examine the interaction between these thresholds and the resulting FROC score. Notably, we observe that this relationship is highly dependent on particular aspects of the problem case, and provide recommendations on how to address this.

Keywords: Computer aided detection · evaluation · FROC · segmentation · breast

1 Introduction

As the adoption of deep learning techniques into medical diagnostics has matured, many computer-aided detection (CAD) and diagnosis products are now commercially available [7]. However, successful clinical implementation requires rigorous evaluation, and metrics that poorly reflect the actual use of CAD systems can result in a sub-optimal product.

Commonly used metrics used to evaluate detection performance for CAD systems are the free response operator characteristic (FROC) [9] and the alternative free response operator characteristic (AFROC) [9]. The former is more commonly used for assessing software performance and the latter for reader studies. These metrics were both initially developed for systems which output a mark as a single point and have subsequently been adapted to supported newer systems which produce bounding boxes and more recently heatmaps. However there is no clear consensus on the suitability of these adaptations in all settings.

S. Wu et al. (Eds.): AMAI 2024, LNCS 15384, pp. 11–20, 2025.
https://doi.org/10.1007/978-3-031-82007-6_2

There have been several excellent reviews [2,11] providing high level suggestions to address this issue. However, limited attention has been given to the exact implementation details of detection metrics, specifically for AI solutions. Often these implementation details are implicit, and the original assumptions may not hold true for every application.

In this paper, we provide an analysis of some of the implementation details used to calculate FROC curves. We show that the FROC score is sensitive to the processing of the heatmap outputs, specifically the thresholds used to discretize these scores.

We conduct experiments with large real-world datasets covering three modalities: digital mammography (MMG), digital breast tomosynthesis (DBT), and chest X-ray (CXR). Additionally, we generate simulated datasets with varying lesion sizes to illustrate the effects and provide recommendations for metric adaptation in AI model evaluation. Significant variations of up to 0.2 in metric scores are observed for some of the findings, illustrating the importance of carefully thinking about implementation details.

2   Evaluation Methods

Throughout the paper, we use the term *finding* or *lesion* to refer to an abnormality that has been annotated with a contour; for example an instance of a nodule observed in a chest X-ray. For the output of an AI model we use the term *prediction* or *heatmap*, which is a 2D array the same shape as the input image with a *score* given per pixel. Additionally when we discretize the *prediction* from continuous scores into an array of binary values by applying a *prediction threshold*, we use the term *detection* to refer to the non-zero values. We refer to a model's ability to accurately point to a *lesion* in an image (with two degrees of freedom) as *localization*, the model's ability to also capture the size and shape of an abnormality as *object detection.*

When discussing localization and detection problems we use the term lesion localization (LL) and non-lesion localization (NL) to indicate an instance of a detection successfully locating a lesion and failing to locate a lesion respectively. This is analogous to the notion of a true positive and false positive.

The hit criterion defines the condition under which a detection is considered a LL or a NL and when a finding is considered a False Negative [9]. It is important to note that true negatives (TN) are not defined in object detection tasks [9]. To determine the success of a proposed detection we require a measure which captures the localization quality of the detection with which we apply a *detection threshold* (discussed in Sect. 2.2).

2.1   Evaluating Detection Performance

When evaluating object detection or segmentation performance measures such as Dice and Intersection over Union (IoU) are often used in the computer vision

domain [3,8]. In the medical domain however, these metrics are difficult to interpret clinically and are not invariant to class ratio, which can complicate comparisons between cohorts with different disease prevalence [9]. Therefore, in the
medical domain adaptations of classification metrics for detection are typically
used. A common method to evaluate a binary classifier is the receiver operator characteristic (ROC) curve, plotting sensitivity against 1-specificity [4] from
which the area under the curve (AUC) is used to integrate the curve into a single
value (referred to as the *score*, e.g. ROC score). There have been several adaptions to the ROC curve to cover localization tasks. These include the Localization
ROC (LROC) and the Free Response Operator Characteristic (FROC).

With LROC the performance is evaluated on the basis of successfully locating
a lesion in the image (i.e. a LL) while minimizing the number of images with a
negative detection [1]. LROC has limitations as it only considers a single lesion
and detection per image. As AI models are typically not constrained to produce
only one detection LROC, for example, may fail to penalize an AI model that
produces many incorrect detections. The more commonly used FROC curve
plots lesion-wise sensitivity against the Non-lesion Localization Fraction (NLF)
[1], which is the average number of NLs per image. This offers a clearer clinical
interpretation and also invariance to class ratio (prevalence) [9].

2.2   Design Choices for the FROC

While these adaptions have solved some issues, it has also led to further challenges, particularly when applied to AI based systems. Here we discuss two
specific design choices and highlight potential issues. Figure 1 offers a high-level
view of these choices.

Design Element 1 - Detection Threshold. As discussed there are several
methods to define the quality of a detection, these can be classed as center based
or overlap based measure. Center based measures aim to capture the localization
quality, while overlap based measures also captures the similarity in size and
shape. For many medical applications and AI based systems, only evaluating
the quality of detections on the basis of the center points of the detection or
lesion is insufficient. Both the size and shape of either may be very different yet
still have relatively close center positions, as such overlap based measures such
as Intersection over Union (IoU), defined as $IoU = \frac{|A \cap B|}{|A \cup B|}$, where $|A \cap B|$ is the
area of the intersection and $|A \cup B|$ is the area of the union of the detection A
and the lesion B, are more commonly used.

The issue of determining the optimal detection threshold to apply to the IoU
measure however is context dependent. For example a consistent IoU threshold
is necessary when comparing the performance of multiple AI models, or across
multiple datasets, however this may be different from the optimal threshold used
to provide a trade-off between some target sensitivity and specificity.

Design Element 2 - Prediction Threshold. The output of modern AI detection systems is typically a 2D array of scores (i.e., a heatmap). As mentioned in Sect. 2 an additional step of applying a prediction threshold is required to convert this output into a binary detection mask. As with the detection threshold, the selection of this threshold is not trivial.

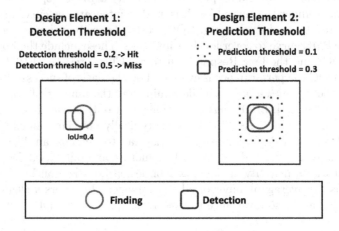

Fig. 1. Design choices for FROC evaluation. The left-hand image illustrates a situation where the detection could be considered a 'hit' if the detection threshold is less than or equal to 0.5, otherwise it is a miss. The right-hand image illustrates how the size of the detection may vary depending on the prediction threshold used.

Furthermore, there is a strong coupling between the prediction threshold and detection threshold. This can occur in multiple ways as a change in the prediction threshold can lead to a change in the size, shape, and number of detections, all of which can impact the selection of the detection threshold. Figure 2 illustrates a simplified case where the IoU measure can be impacted by a changing prediction threshold. Correspondingly, a change in the detection threshold may require a different prediction threshold to achieve some target FROC performance.

2.3   FROC Score Calculation

The heatmap outputs from the model were binarized using the prediction threshold. For each annotated finding, the maximum heatmap value within the annotation was taken as the positive score. A detection is considered a hit if the IoU between the binarized heatmap and the ground truth exceeded the detection threshold. Only the highest scoring detection for each annotation was considered a true positive. False positives were detections that did not overlap with any annotations. The maximum score of the heatmap is used a score for the false positive.

The AUC was calculated using the trapezoidal rule [4] by integrating the LLF over the NLF. Since we used the same dataset and varied only the detection and

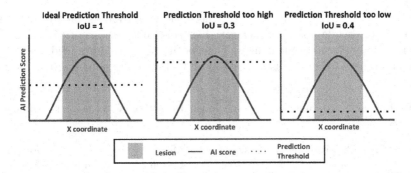

Fig. 2. Illustration of changing prediction threshold impacting the IoU measure. A prediction threshold that is too high or too low may result in a lower FROC score.

prediction thresholds, we computed the full area under the FROC (i.e., no partial AUC). We refer to this as the FROC score.

3   Experiments

In order to analyse the effect of each design element on the FROC score, we evaluated the performance of a set of AI models on a number of medical datasets for different tasks while varying the prediction and detection thresholds.

3.1   Data

We used datasets from three modalities covering various tasks: proprietary MMG and DBT, and the publicly available Chest X-ray (CXR/CheXpert [6]) dataset.

The MMG and DBT datasets included 4 standard image views (RCC, RMLO, LCC, LMLO) with 2,387 and 3,117 cases respectively, each from a unique patient. Ground truth labels and free-form lesion contours were annotated by board-certified radiologists based on pathology reports.

For CXR data, we focused on five findings; consolidation (Csn), pleural effusion (Pef), pneumothorax (PTX), atelectasis (Atl), and cardiomegaly (CM) to provide diversity in the problem cases. For this we used a merged validation and test set from the CheXlocalize [10] dataset consisting of 234 chest X-rays from 200 patients and 668 chest X-rays from 500 patients, respectively. This included a set of lesion annotations as the ground truth.

For each dataset predictions were generated using ResNet-based [5] AI models which were trained to output a detection heatmap for each task individually.

Synthetic Data Generation. Based on initial observations from our experiments we also opted to use a synthetic dataset of images, where we are able to parameterise the generation of images and detections (e.g. controlling the size of lesions and detections). As we wanted to investigate the impact of lesion size (relative to the image size) in more detail we generated a dataset of 1000 images (height = 120, width = 100) where the lesion radius varied between 5 and 15 pixels, while holding other variables constant. Lesions of circular shape were randomly placed in the images. Their positions were determined to ensure a minimum center-to-center distance of 30 pixels between lesions to avoid overlap.

Table 1. Lesion size analysis for each label. Here *Size X* refers to the simulated datasets.

	Cases	Positive Cases	Lesions	Lesions/ Positive Cases	Mean Lesion Size	SD Lesion Size	Normalized SD
DBT	3117	1371	2118	1.5449	0.0074	0.0139	1.8784
MMG	2387	892	1065	1.1939	0.0101	0.0179	1.7723
PE	720	169	294	1.7396	0.0309	0.0371	1.2006
Pnmthrx	720	16	17	1.0625	0.0394	0.0302	0.7665
Atl	720	232	367	1.5819	0.0519	0.0289	0.5568
Csn	720	61	87	1.4262	0.0648	0.0275	0.4244
CM	720	220	220	1	0.1388	0.0289	0.2082
Size5	1000	300	642	2.14	0.0065	0.0027	0.4154
Size10	1000	300	642	2.14	0.024	0.0064	0.2667
Size15	1000	300	642	2.14	0.0511	0.0126	0.2466

Lesion sizes are normalised based on the image size as;
Number of Pixels of Lesion/Number of total pixels of image.

3.2   Results

As described, we conducted the set of experiments by varying both the prediction and detection thresholds across a number of real-world datasets to observe the effect on the overall FROC score. The prediction threshold was set to a value of 0.1, 0.15, and 0.2; while these are not necessarily the optimal values in practice, it provided good coverage such that the changing impact on the FROC score could be observed. For the detection threshold, we varied the threshold value from 0.1 to 0.9 with increments of 0.1. FROC scores were calculated based on the combination of these parameters and we observed the interactions for the set of problem cases. The results for a selection of cases are shown in Fig. 3.

In each of our problem cases, we observe a monotonic reduction in the FROC score as the IoU threshold increases, given a fixed prediction threshold. While this is expected, we observe a difference in the characteristic of these curves. The MMG case (Fig. 3a) shows a decreasing trend as the IoU threshold increases, reducing from an initial FROC score of approximately 0.65 to 0.35. This can be interpreted as a fairly constant reduction in LL detections as the detection threshold is increased the 'lower quality' detections are being classed as NL. This plateaus at higher thresholds indicating a change in the regime where the remaining LL detections are more robust to the increasing detection threshold, implying higher consistency in quality.

A similar pattern can be seen for the other problem cases, though with slight differences in the transition. The cardiomegaly case (Fig. 3d) appears to be an exception which starts with a fairly consistent plateau, until reaching an IoU threshold of approximately 0.6, after which there is a sharp drop in FROC score. This can be interpreted as the majority of detections being a 'high quality', given that they remain as LL detection even with an increasing detection threshold. The sharp drop in FROC score may then indicate a regime change where a substantial number of detections of similar quality are now classed as NL.

The effect of changing the prediction threshold is more subtle. The lower prediction threshold curves show a relatively higher FROC scores at lower detection thresholds with the reverse at higher detection thresholds. A potential explanation of this behaviour is that at a low prediction threshold can result in an increase in the number of detections with poor localization rather than increasing the size of existing detections. At higher detection thresholds, these low quality detections are classed as NL, whereas they do not exist for the higher prediction thresholds.

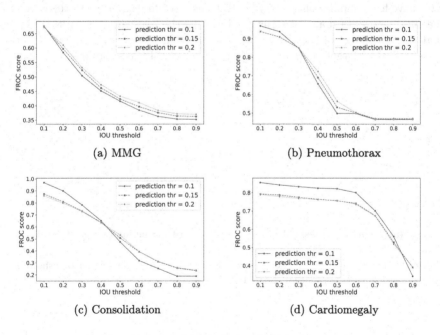

(a) MMG

(b) Pneumothorax

(c) Consolidation

(d) Cardiomegaly

Fig. 3. Comparison of FROC scores by IoU threshold and prediction threshold with real-world datasets

3.3   Interaction Between Lesion Size and Thresholds

The differences in behaviour observed across problem cases may be in part due to the varying quality of the underlying AI models, but also due to specific characteristics of the problem. With an understanding of the characteristics of the cases investigated, we considered the relative size of the lesions to be a possible reason for those differences. As can be seen in Table 1 the mean lesion size (shown relative to the image size) ranges from 0.0074 for the DBT dataset, to 0.1388 for the cardiomegaly dataset. Furthermore, the variation in lesion size (as given by the standard deviation) has an inverse relation to the mean lesion size. By normalizing this variation by the mean lesion size we can see that for problem cases with smaller lesion sizes, such as DBT, the variation can be almost double (1.8784) compared to larger lesion problem cases such as cardiomegaly with a variation of 0.2082.

To investigate this further, we conducted a similar analysis on synthetic datasets. Summary plots of this are shown in Fig. 4. A similar characteristic curve can be seen here as observed in the real-world datasets that aligns with the changing lesion size. The curve showing FROC scores for the larger lesion size (e.g. mean radius 15) has a similar shape to cardiomegaly, and the smaller lesion size curve has a similar shape to the DBT case (see in Fig. 3). With the caveat of the simulated data may not strictly align with the real-world cases, this implies that the sensitivity of the FROC score to the selected prediction and detection threshold, may largely depend on the relative size of the annotated lesions.

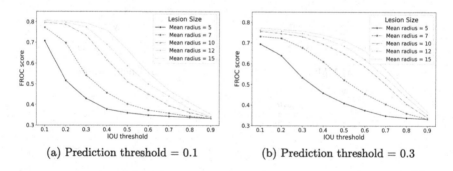

(a) Prediction threshold = 0.1   (b) Prediction threshold = 0.3

Fig. 4. Comparison of FROC scores by IoU threshold and prediction threshold with different lesion sizes simulation dataset

4   Discussion

This paper examined the impact of some of the design choices required when computing FROC for AI based detection models. Our analysis reveals subtleties in how the relationship between the prediction threshold and the detection threshold, impacts the FROC score. Notably we reason that this relationship heavily depends on the specifics of the problem case, with one standout characteristic being the typical size of the lesions; where problem cases with smaller lesions show a higher FROC score sensitivity when altering the prediction and detection thresholds.

In practical terms the following key insights that may be useful when evaluating the performance of an AI based detection system:

- **Lesion Size and Threshold Sensitivity:** The increased sensitivity of the FROC score for smaller lesion sizes indicates that small differences in the dataset composition or changes in the prediction threshold may lead to very different performance estimates, even when using the same detection threshold. Stratifying the dataset based on the lesion size prior to evaluation may provide a more robust performance estimate, particularly when comparing between datasets of the same task.
- **Characteristic Curve Analysis:** In a similar manner to analysis of classifier performance by plotting the performance at all operating points (e.g. ROC curve), we've shown that extending this to the detection threshold allows for a qualitative assessment of the detection performance, particular in relation to consistency of detections.

Further work is required to both investigate the impact of threshold settings on different problem cases, as well as investigating alternative evaluation approaches that are not sensitive to specific parameter choices, and better align with the intended use. Additionally, the impact of image quality on lesion detectability and FROC performance remains a potential limitation of this study, as it was not explicitly addressed here. This may also overlap with research in related areas such as annotation quality and how that can vary based on the problem case.

Disclosure of Interests. The authors declare that there are no conflicts of interest regarding the publication of this paper.

References

1. Chakraborty, D.P.: Observer Performance Methods for Diagnostic Imaging: Foundations, Modeling, and Applications with R-Based Examples. CRC Press (2017)
2. Chen, H., et al.: Anatomy-aware Siamese network: exploiting semantic asymmetry for accurate pelvic fracture detection in X-ray images. In: Vedaldi, A., Bischof, H., Brox, T., Frahm, J.-M. (eds.) ECCV 2020. LNCS, vol. 12368, pp. 239–255. Springer, Cham (2020). https://doi.org/10.1007/978-3-030-58592-1_15
3. Eelbode, T., et al.: Optimization for medical image segmentation: theory and practice when evaluating with dice score or Jaccard index. IEEE Trans. Med. Imaging **39**(11), 3679–3690 (2020)
4. Fawcett, T.: An introduction to ROC analysis. Pattern Recogn. Lett. **27**(8), 861–874 (2006)
5. He, K., Zhang, X., Ren, S., Sun, J.: Deep residual learning for image recognition (2015)

6. Irvin, J., et al.: CheXpert: a large chest radiograph dataset with uncertainty labels and expert comparison (2019)
7. van Leeuwen, K.G., Schalekamp, S., Rutten, M.J.C.M., van Ginneken, B., de Rooij, M.: Artificial intelligence in radiology: 100 commercially available products and their scientific evidence. Eur. Radiol. **31**(6), 3797–3804 (2021). https://doi.org/10.1007/s00330-021-07892-z
8. Maier-Hein, L., Menze, B., et al.: Metrics reloaded: pitfalls and recommendations for image analysis validation. arXiv. org (2206.01653) (2022)
9. Reinke, A., et al.: Common limitations of image processing metrics: a picture story. arXiv preprint arXiv:2104.05642 (2021)
10. Saporta, A., et al.: Benchmarking saliency methods for chest x-ray interpretation. Nat. Mach. Intell. **4**(10), 867–878 (2022)
11. Wang, Y., et al.: Knowledge distillation with adaptive asymmetric label sharpening for semi-supervised fracture detection in chest X-rays. In: Feragen, A., Sommer, S., Schnabel, J., Nielsen, M. (eds.) IPMI 2021. LNCS, vol. 12729, pp. 599–610. Springer, Cham (2021). https://doi.org/10.1007/978-3-030-78191-0_46

Head CT Scan Motion Artifact Correction via Diffusion-Based Generative Models

Zhennong Chen[1], Siyeop Yoon[1], Quirin Strotzer[2], Rehab Naeem Khalid[2],
Matthew Tivnan[1], Quanzheng Li[1], Rajiv Gupta[2], and Dufan Wu[1](✉)

[1] Center for Advanced Medical Computing and Analysis, Massachusetts General Hospital and
Harvard Medical School, Boston, MA 02114, USA
`dwu6@mgh.harvard.edu`
[2] Department of Radiology, Massachusetts General Hospital and Harvard Medical School,
Boston, MA 02114, USA

Abstract. Head motion is a major source of image artifacts in head computed
tomography (CT), degrading the image quality and impacting diagnosis. Image-
domain-based motion correction is practical for routine use since it doesn't rely
on hard-to-obtain CT projection data. However, existing convolutional neural network (CNN)-based methods tend to over-smooth images, particularly in cases of
moderate to severe 3D motion artifacts. Motivated by the improved image quality
and more stable training of diffusion-based generative models, we propose a novel
3D head CT motion correction approach based on conditional diffusion, named
HeadMotion-EDM (HM-EDM). This approach has three features. Firstly, we utilize motion-corrupted images as the conditional input. Secondly, we leverage the
advanced Elucidated Diffusion Model (EDM) framework, which integrates several
pivotal engineering improvements in the diffusion model and significantly expe-
dites the sampling process. Thirdly, we design an efficient 3D-patch-wise training method for 3D CT data. Comparative studies demonstrate that our approach
surpasses CNN-based techniques as well as the denoising diffusion probabilistic
model (DDPM) in both simulation and phantom studies. Furthermore, radiologists
reviewed the results of applying HM-EDM to real-world portable head CT scans,
showing its effectiveness in eliminating motion artifacts and improving diagnostic
value.

Keywords: Head CT · Motion correction · Diffusion Model

1 Introduction

Patient head motion, especially in pediatric patients or those with head trauma or stroke,
is a common source of image artifacts in computed tomography (CT) of the head [1].
Motion causes data inconsistency among the acquired CT projections, resulting in blurring, ghosting, streaking artifacts, and distortion in reconstructed images. Motion artifacts are more prevalent in portable head CT which is often used in emergency room
due to prolonged scanning time and critically ill patients who are unable to cooperate
or remain still. Hardware solutions such as faster gantry rotations, dual-source systems,

© The Author(s), under exclusive license to Springer Nature Switzerland AG 2025
S. Wu et al. (Eds.): AMAI 2024, LNCS 15384, pp. 21–30, 2025.
https://doi.org/10.1007/978-3-031-82007-6_3

and motion tracking systems [2] can mitigate motion artifacts, but their integration into portable or C-arm CT scanners is still challenging. Therefore, there is a critical need to develop software solutions to correct head CT motion artifacts in clinical practice.

Existing software solutions can be categorized into two strategies. The first strategy compensates motion by estimating head motion during the acquisition using CT projection data. Solutions within this strategy include using 3D-2D registration to align each 2D projection to a 3D prior image [3, 4], employing iterative process to optimize image-based motion artifact metrics like total variation norm [5] or image entropy and sharpness [6], and utilizing partial angle reconstruction [7–9] techniques to estimate motion. However, obtaining and processing projection data in clinical settings remains challenging, which limits the practical application of these projection-domain-based methods. The second strategy relies solely on correction within the image domain. Despite the lack of data fidelity, image-domain-based solutions don't require projection data and are thus more practical for daily use. Current literature on head CT motion correction using such approaches is sparse, with existing solutions mainly utilizing convolutional neural networks (CNNs) trained on motion-free and motion-corrupted image pairs. Ko et al. [10] augmented U-Net with attention mechanism to selectively amplify or attenuate residual features, while Su et al. [11] integrated ResNet and dilation techniques into U-Net to retain high resolution features. However, these approaches have typically been validated on 2D motion (using CT slices as model input) or under conditions of slight motion. Empirically, we observe that these CNN-based methods tend to over-smooth images when addressing moderate to severe 3D motions.

Score-based diffusion models have recently excelled in various generative and inverse problems [12–15], offering improved image quality and more stable training. This success is due to diffusion models learning advanced data representations by understanding the gradient of the log density of the datasets (i.e., data score). However, applying diffusion models to CT motion correction remains unexplored. Therefore, we propose the first diffusion model-based 3D head CT motion correction approach, named HeadMotion-EDM (HM-EDM). This method uses the motion-corrupted CT image as a conditional input and corrects the motion artifacts purely based on the image domain. The model successfully addresses two challenges in solving 3D motion artifacts using diffusion models. Firstly, correcting 3D motion requires a 3D diffusion model that takes 3D CT data as input, which can easily exceed GPU memory limits. To tackle this, we utilize a 3D-patch-wise diffusion training that maintains 3D information while reducing computational demands. Secondly, the standard denoising diffusion probabilistic model (DDPM) [12] may experience suboptimcal data score estimation by the trained neural network as well as the inaccurate approximation of true noise removal trajectory when using fewer steps in accelerated sampling [16, 17]. To overcome these issues, we leverage the advanced Elucidated Diffusion Model (EDM) [16] framework, which integrates several pivotal engineering improvements in both score-model training and the faster sampling process.

The contributions of our work are threefold. First, we propose HM-EDM to correct 3D head CT motion artifacts with efficient training and a faster sampling process. Second, we demonstrate that HM-EDM surpasses CNN-based techniques and standard DDPM in both simulation and phantom studies. Third, we apply HM-EDM to real-world portable head CT scans to show its practical application (Fig. 1).

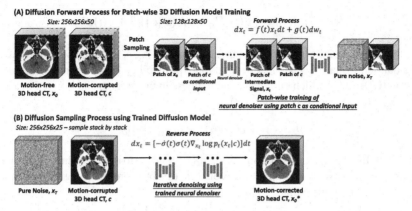

Fig. 1. The overall pipeline of HM-EDM. (A) The forward process involves patch-wise training of the neural denoiser, which takes conditional input in the form of patches consisting of the intermediate signal x_t along with the motion-corrupted image c. (B) the sampling process begins with the pure 3D noise x_T and iteratively removes noise using the trained denoiser to generate motion-corrected 3D head CT image.

2 Methods

2.1 Score-Based Diffusion Model for Motion Artifact Correction

We frame CT motion correction as a conditional generation task, sampling from a conditional distribution $p_{data}(x_0|c)$, where $\{x_0, c\}$ is a pair of motion-free (x_0) and motion-corrupted (c, produced by filtered back-projection) CT images. Regarding the diffusion model, it has a forward and a sampling process. The forward process progressively adds Gaussian noise to the motion-free CT image, x_0, sampled from $p_{data}(x_0|c)$, until making it indistinguishable from pure noise. This forward process could be characterized by a stochastic differential equation (SDE),

$$dx_t = f(t)x_t dt + g(t)dw_t \tag{1}$$

where $f(t)$ and $g(t)$ are the drift and diffusion coefficient, respectively, and w is a standard Wiener process. $t \in [0, T]$ denotes a time variable such that if defining the marginal probabilities of x_t as $p_t(x|c)$, then $p_0(x|c)$ equals to the original data distribution p_{data} and $p_T(x|c)$ equals to a Gaussian distribution. We set $T = 1000$ in this study. Specially, the transition probability from x_0 to x_t is given by:

$$p_t(x_t|x_0, c) = \mathcal{N}\left(x_t; \mu_t x_0, \mu_t^2 \sigma(t)^2 I\right) \tag{2}$$

with the noise schedule $\sigma(t) = t$ which defines the desired noise level at time t.

In the sampling process, the image generation starts from pure noise drawn from the prior distribution p_T and iteratively removes the noise. This process is expressed as the reverse SDE [13, 18]:

$$dx_t = \left[f(t)x_t dt - g(t)^2 \nabla_{x_t} \log p_t(x_t|c) \right] dt + g(t)d\overline{w}_t \tag{3}$$

Here, the gradient of the log density of the datasets, $\nabla_{x_t} \log p_t(x_t|c)$, is the score function of the dataset. Equation 3 has a corresponding "probability flow" ordinary differential equation (ODE) [16] which eliminates randomness in the process and is given in a form generalized for any noise schedule $\sigma(t)$ as:

$$dx_t = \left[-\dot{\sigma}(t)\sigma(t)\nabla_{x_t} \log p_t(x_t|c) \right] dt \tag{4}$$

To solve Eq. 4, the score function $\nabla_{x_t} \log p_t(x_t|c)$ needs to be determined. Practically, we train a neural network to estimate the score function by score matching with a denoiser function $D(x_t; \sigma(t), c)$ so that:

$$\nabla_{x_t} \log p_t(x_t|c) = [D(x_t; \sigma(t), c) - x_0]/\sigma(t)^2 \tag{5}$$

This neural denoiser D isolates the noise component from the signal x_t and can be trained by minimizing the expected L_2 loss for samples drawn from p_{data} for every σ,

$$L := \mathrm{E}_{pdata}\mathrm{E}_{n\sim\mathcal{N}(0,\ \sigma(t)^2)}\|D(x_0 + n; \sigma(t), c) - x_0\|^2_2 \tag{6}$$

n is the noise. Overall, in our proposed diffusion model HM-EDM, x_0 is the targeted motion-free image, and we train a neural denoiser $D(x_0 + n; \sigma(t), c)$, with the motion-corrupted image c as conditional input, to gradually remove noise n and eventually generates the motion-corrected image.

2.2 Patch-Wise Model Training

Regarding the model architecture of neural denoiser D, we adapt the DDPM++ U-Net [13] for 3D data by changing original 2D convolutional layers and attention modules to 3D. However, we found that training such a 3D U-Net directly on 3D head CT data exceeds the GPU memory limitation. Further, this method requires gathering extensive 3D CT data. To reduce memory usage and the need for a large dataset, we leverage a patch-wise model training strategy:

$$L_{patch} = \sum_{i=1}^{N} \mathrm{E}_{pdata}\mathrm{E}_{n\sim\mathcal{N}(0,\sigma(t)^2)}\|D(x_{0,\emptyset_i} + n; \sigma(t), c_{\emptyset_i}) - x_{0,\emptyset_i}\|^2_2 \tag{7}$$

where $x_{0,\emptyset_i}$ denote a sub-volume sampled from the motion-free 3D CT data, x_0, which is the union of N such sub-volumes. The patch-wise loss, L_{patch}, accumulates the losses over these sub-volumes. While trained on patches with reduced height and width, the network can work on the original dimension during sampling due to the shift-invariance property of convolution layers. The implementation details can be found in Sect. 2.4.

2.3 Advanced EDM Framework

Our model uses the advanced EDM framework instead of the standard DDPM for two reasons. First, it is time-intensive for the DDPM sampling to go through the same number of timesteps (i.e., 500–1000 steps) as in the forward process, while accelerated sampling using the reduced number of steps may lead to the truncation error and inaccurate approximation of true noise removal trajectory in DDPM. Second, the neural denoiser D in DDPM may not accurately estimate the data score. EDM [16] integrates several pivotal engineering improvements for these two challenges. Regarding the truncation error caused by a finite number of sampling steps, EDM uses Heun's 2nd order method as the numerical SDE solver, which introduces a correctional sub-step from x_t to x_{t-1} to account for change of dx/dt in the trajectory and thus align the sampling with the actual trajectory. Regarding the network training, a σ-dependent skip scaling is proposed to precondition the neural network, enabling the model to adaptively estimate either the noise n or the clean image x_0 or something in between based on the noise level σ. The rationale is that it is more effective to predict x_0 at higher noise levels and n at lower noise level [19, 20]. Therefore:

$$D(x_t; \sigma(t), c) = s_{skip}(\sigma(t))x_t + s_{out}(\sigma(t))F_{\vartheta}(s_{in}(\sigma(t))x_t; \sigma(t), c) \qquad (8)$$

where F_{ϑ} is the network to be trained, s_{skip} denotes the skip scaling factor controlling model output type. When σ is large, s_{skip} is approaching to 0 so that F_{ϑ} directly predicts the denoised image, x_0; When σ is small, s_{skip} is approaching to 1 so that F_{ϑ} predicts the negative of noise, $-n$. s_{in}, s_{out} are other scaling factors to scale the input and output to unit variance [21]. By integrating the EDM framework, our model successfully reduces the sampling steps to 50—just 1/20th of the DDPM's steps ($T = 1000$ as in Sect. 2.1)—while achieving a more accurate estimation of the data score function.

2.4 Implementation Details

For image preprocessing, all 3D CT data were resampled to a pixel dimension of [1, 1, 2.5] mm and reshaped into $256 \times 256 \times 50$ slices covering from the nose to the top of the head. During patch-wise training, patches sized $128 \times 128 \times 50$ were randomly extracted from the CT volume with necessary data augmentation and intensity range normalized to $[-1, 1]$. For sampling process, the original x and y dimensions were preserved and non-overlapping stacks of 25 slices were processed sequentially to prevent exceeding the GPU's capacity. Sampling a complete 3D head CT requires two such stacks. Using patch-wise training, our HM-EDM method requires 32 GB of memory for training with a batch size of 1 patch. The sampling needs 26 GB to sample a $256 \times 256 \times 25$ stack. With faster sampling enabled by the EDM framework, we can sample a complete 3D head CT dataset in less than two minutes on a DGX-A100 GPU (NVIDIA, USA), whereas the conventional DDPM approach typically takes around 20 min on the same GPU.

3 Experiments

We trained our model using simulated data as we cannot acquire motion-static pairs from patients. We conducted a simulation study and a phantom study with known ground truth motion-free images to quantitatively compare the performance of HM-EDM with CNN-based methods and standard DDPM. Additionally, we conducted a reader study using a real-world portable head CT dataset, reviewed by two radiologists, to demonstrate the practical application of HM-EDM.

Table 1. Simulation study's quantitative results. Metrics for the brain are measured on pixels within [0, 100] HU in the motion-free image, and metrics for overall are measured on foreground pixels > −100 HU. MAE are measured in Hounsfield Units (HU). CNR = contrast-to-noise ratio. The CNR in the brain region was measured in a ROI of 50 × 50 pixels from brain center, approximating the contrast between white matter and ventricle. A higher CNR indicates a smoother image. **The CNR for motion-free images is 9.34 ± 1.14.**

ROI	Metric	Motion-corrupted	HM-EDM (ours)	DDPM [12]	CNN-ResNet [11]	CNN-attention [10]
Brain	MAE ↓	22.7 ± 5.6	**11.0 ± 2.1**	12.6 ± 2.8	16.6 ± 4.3	17.0 ± 3.6
	SSIM ↑	0.17 ± 0.06	**0.51 ± 0.08**	0.41 ± 0.09	0.25 ± 0.06	0.23 ± 0.05
	CNR ↓	8.44 ± 1.54	**9.47 ± 1.06**	9.84 ± 1.31	10.69 ± 2.09	10.99 ± 2.14
Overall	MAE ↓	179 ± 39	**52 ± 13**	69 ± 19	74 ± 18	76 ± 19
	SSIM ↑	0.64 ± 0.10	**0.95 ± 0.03**	0.92 ± 0.04	0.92 ± 0.03	0.91 ± 0.04

Table 2. Phantom study's quantitative results. The CNR for the motion-free image is 8.64.

ROI	Metric	Motion-corrupted	HM-EDM (ours)	DDPM [12]	CNN-ResNet [11]	CNN-attention [10]
Brain	MAE ↓	21.5 ± 2.2	**12.3 ± 0.9**	13.6 ± 1.3	18.4 ± 1.9	18.6 ± 2.0
	SSIM ↑	0.38 ± 0.03	**0.57 ± 0.06**	0.57 ± 0.06	0.40 ± 0.03	0.41 ± 0.03
	CNR ↓	8.47 ± 0.07	**8.92 ± 0.18**	9.94 ± 0.33	11.63 ± 1.26	12.33 ± 1.66
Overall	MAE ↓	116 ± 17	**84 ± 10**	85 ± 8	101 ± 12	99 ± 13
	SSIM ↑	0.83 ± 0.04	**0.86 ± 0.02**	0.86 ± 0.02	0.84 ± 0.03	0.85 ± 0.03

Simulation Study. We conducted a simulation study with pairs of ground truth motion-free images and simulated motion-corrupted images. We retrospectively collected 100 motion-free multi-slice head CT scans from a single medical center. For the simulation, we utilized a head motion model proposed by Jang et al. [6] and Chen et al. [9]. The head posture was described using 6 rigid motion variables including translations and rotations along the three image axes. Each motion variable was modeled using a B-spline with 5 control points equally spaced across one gantry rotation. The motion amplitude (i.e., the value of each control point) was randomly sampled from [−5, 5] mm or degrees for each translation or rotation variable, covering voluntary head motion commonly seen according to Kyme et al. [1]. The motion was applied to the motion-free image, and a simulated process of forward projection and filtered backprojection (FBP) was conduced using the actual CT geometry parameters from the scanner. We split the 100 scans into a training/validation (80 scans) and a testing (20 scans) dataset. Each scan was used to produce 50 simulations in training and 5 simulations in testing. The models were trained on the simulated training data.

We compared our HM-EDM method with the standard DDPM as well as the CNN-based methods (CNN with ResNet [11] and attention [10]). All methods use the same implementation details illustrated in Sect. 2.4. The quantitative outcomes shown in Table 1 indicate that HM-EDM achieves the lowest MAE and the highest SSIM both in the brain region (MAE drops from 22.7 ± 5.6 HU in motion-corrupted images to 11.0 ± 2.1 HU, SSIM increases from 0.17 ± 0.06 to 0.51 ± 0.08) and overall image (MAE drops from 179 ± 39 HU to 52 ± 13 HU, SSIM increases from 0.64 ± 0.10 to 0.95 ± 0.03) compared to other competing methods ($p < 0.001$ by one-tailed paired student t-test). Table 1 also shows that only HM-EDM preserves the contrast-to-noise ratio (CNR) in the brain region comparable to motion-free images (9.34 ± 1.14 in motion-free vs. 9.47 ± 1.06 in HM-EDM), whereas CNN-based methods tended to over-smooth the image, resulting in elevated CNR. Additionally, Fig. 2 showcases examples of motion correction in brain and skull, recovering fine structures in brain and skull anatomy.

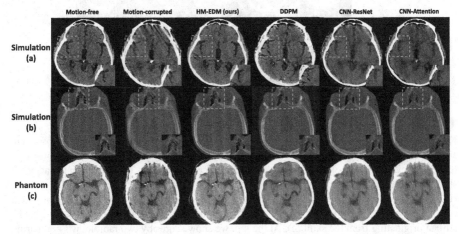

Fig. 2. Performance on simulation study (a, b) and phantom study (c). (a) illustrates correction within the brain tissue, showcasing our method's ability to restore the visibility of fine structures as indicated by the yellow box. (b) shows correction in a severe skull ghosting artifact instance. (c) shows the results on the head phantom.

Phantom Study. An ACS head phantom (Kyoto Kagaku, Japan) was scanned using an CereTom Elite portable CT scanner (Neurologica, USA) with x-ray tube energy of 120 kVp and tube current of 20 mA. To simulate motion, we stacked sinograms from multiple static acquisitions with varied head postures. These composite sinograms were reconstructed into 20 motion-corrupted images with different motion patterns. Without any fine-tuning, Table 2 shows that HM-EDM outperforms other competing methods in the brain correction, as well as preserves CNR in the brain region.

Real-World Application. We retrospectively collected 5 portable head CT scans acquired by CereTom Elite portable CT scanner (Neurologica, USA) from the ICU patients. All scans were identified to have motion artifacts. We applied the trained HM-EDM directly without fine-tuning. The original and motion-corrected images were randomly assigned as image A and image B. Two radiologists, blinded to the image identities, compared A against B and scored the comparison regarding motion artifacts, diagnostic value, and preference in the range of -2 to $+2$ (where 0 means no difference, 1 means effective improvement and 2 means significant improvement; negative means degradation). Figure 3 shows the HD-EDM results of all 5 scans. The motion corrected CTs always have positive scores when compared to the original CT on all scans for all 3 criteria.

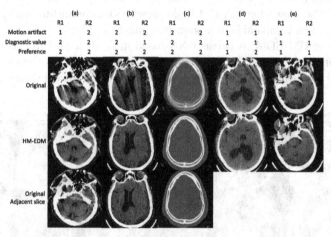

Fig. 3. Performance on 5 real-world portable CT scans. (a) and (b) show the correction of severe artifacts in brain tissue where (b) also recovers the chronic hemorrhage, while (c) shows the correction of severe "double-skull" artifacts. For these three severe cases, by comparing the adjacent slice in the original image (with much less motion artifact) in the third row, we can see that our HM-EDM model potentially utilizes information from these adjacent slices for 3D anatomical context. (d) and (e) show two examples with slight/moderate streaking artifact (d) and star-like artifact originating from the skull (e). At the top, we show scores by two radiologists comparing the corrected image to the original image. Scores range from $+1$ (effective improvement) to $+2$ (significant improvement).

4   Conclusion

This work introduces the first application of a diffusion-based generative model for CT motion artifact correction. Our proposed HM-EDM leverages a conditional diffusion model to significantly reduce motion artifacts in 3D head CT scans. Our method outperforms CNN-based methods and DDPM in both simulation and phantom studies. Furthermore, we conducted a pilot reader study using a small number of real-world clinical portable head CT scans to preliminarily demonstrate the practical use of our algorithm. However, this reader study lacks ground truth motion-free images. Therefore, future work will focus on larger real-world validation, where within one study, the patient has an initial motion-compromised scan as well as a subsequent motion-free rescan.

Prospect of Application: HM-EDM will be practically useful as an image postprocessing tool to correct motion artifacts in head CT scans. It is accurate, fast (<2 min/case), and doesn't require the use of CT raw data. It will be particularly useful for portable head CT scans in emergency rooms, which more commonly have motion artifacts. Our reader study has preliminarily confirmed its effectiveness.

References

1. Kyme, A.Z., Fulton, R.R.: Motion estimation and correction in SPECT, PET and CT. Phys. Med. Biol. **66**(18) (2021). https://doi.org/10.1088/1361-6560/ac093b
2. Kim, J.-H., Sun, T., Alcheikh, A.R., Kuncic, Z., Nuyts, J., Fulton, R.: Correction for human head motion in helical x-ray CT. Phys. Med. Biol. **61**(4), 1416–1438 (2016). https://doi.org/10.1088/0031-9155/61/4/1416
3. Sun, T., Kim, J.-H., Fulton, R., Nuyts, J.: An iterative projection-based motion estimation and compensation scheme for head X-ray CT. Med. Phys. **43**(10), 5705 (2016). https://doi.org/10.1118/1.4963218
4. Ouadah, S., Jacobson, M., Stayman, J.W., Ehtiati, T., Weiss, C., Siewerdsen, J.H.: Correction of patient motion in cone-beam CT using 3D–2D registration. Phys. Med. Biol. **62**(23), 8813–8831 (2017). https://doi.org/10.1088/1361-6560/aa9254
5. Bruder, H., Rohkohl, C., Stierstorfer, K., Flohr, T.: Compensation of skull motion and breathing motion in CT using data-based and image-based metrics, respectively. Med. Imaging 2016 Phys. Med. Imaging SPIE, 348–359 (2016). https://doi.org/10.1117/12.2217395
6. Jang, S., Kim, S., Kim, M., Ra, J.B.: Head motion correction based on filtered backprojection for X-ray CT imaging. Med. Phys. **45**(2), 589–604 (2018). https://doi.org/10.1002/mp.12705
7. Kim, S., Chang, Y., Ra, J.B.: Cardiac motion correction based on partial angle reconstructed images in x-ray CT. Med. Phys. **42**(5), 2560–2571 (2015). https://doi.org/10.1118/1.4918580
8. Hahn, J., et al.: Motion compensation in the region of the coronary arteries based on partial angle reconstructions from short-scan CT data. Med. Phys. **44**(11), 5795–5813 (2017). https://doi.org/10.1002/mp.12514
9. Chen, Z., Li, Q., Wu, D.: Estimate and compensate head motion in non-contrast head CT scans using partial angle reconstruction and deep learning. Med. Phys. **51**(5), 3309–3321 (2024). https://doi.org/10.1002/mp.17047
10. Ko, Y., Moon, S., Baek, J., Shim, H.: Rigid and non-rigid motion artifact reduction in X-ray CT using attention module. Med. Image Anal. **67**, 101883 (2021). https://doi.org/10.1016/j.media.2020.101883
11. Su, B., et al.: A deep learning method for eliminating head motion artifacts in computed tomography. Med. Phys. **49**(1), 411–419 (2022). https://doi.org/10.1002/mp.15354
12. Ho, J., Jain, A., Abbeel, P.: Denoising diffusion probabilistic models. arXiv, 16 December 2020. http://arxiv.org/abs/2006.11239. Accessed 11 Dec 2023
13. Song, Y., Sohl-Dickstein, J., Kingma, D.P., Kumar, A., Ermon, S., Poole, B.: Score-based generative modeling through stochastic differential equations. arXiv, 10 February 2021. https://doi.org/10.48550/arXiv.2011.13456
14. Song, Y., Shen, L., Xing, L., Ermon, S.: Solving inverse problems in medical imaging with score-based generative models. arXiv.org. https://arxiv.org/abs/2111.08005v2. Accessed 11 Dec 2023

15. Chung, H., Ryu, D., McCann, M.T., Klasky, M.L., Ye, J.C.: Solving 3D inverse problems using pre-trained 2D diffusion models. arXiv, 19 November 2022. https://doi.org/10.48550/arXiv.2211.10655
16. Karras, T., Aittala, M., Aila, T., Laine, S.: Elucidating the design space of diffusion-based generative models. arXiv, 11 October 2022. https://doi.org/10.48550/arXiv.2206.00364
17. Song, J., Meng, C., Ermon, S.: Denoising diffusion implicit models. arXiv, 05 October 2022. https://doi.org/10.48550/arXiv.2010.02502
18. Anderson, B.D.O.: Reverse-time diffusion equation models. Stoch. Process. Their Appl. **12**(3), 313–326 (1982). https://doi.org/10.1016/0304-4149(82)90051-5
19. Dockhorn, T., Vahdat, A., Kreis, K.: Score-based generative modeling with critically-damped Langevin diffusion. arXiv, 25 March 2022. https://doi.org/10.48550/arXiv.2112.07068
20. Vahdat, A., Kreis, K., Kautz, J.: Score-based generative modeling in latent space. arXiv, 02 December 2021. https://doi.org/10.48550/arXiv.2106.05931
21. Huang, L., Qin, J., Zhou, Y., Zhu, F., Liu, L., Shao, L.: Normalization techniques in training DNNs: methodology, analysis and application. IEEE Trans. Pattern Anal. Mach. Intell. **45**(08), 10173–10196 (2023). https://doi.org/10.1109/TPAMI.2023.3250241

SP-NAS: Surgical Phase Recognition-Based Navigation Adjustment System for Distal Gastrectomy

Hyeongyu Chi[1], Bogyu Park[1], Keunyoung Kim[1], Jiwon Lee[1], Sungjea Kim[1], Hyeonu Jeong[1], Jihun Yoon[1], Chihyun Song[1], Seokrae Park[1], Youngno Yoon[1], Youngsoo Kim[1], Sung Hyun Park[2], Yoo Min Kim[2], Min-Kook Choi[1], Woojin Hyung[1,2], and Hansol Choi[1(✉)]

[1] Hutom, Seoul, Republic of Korea
{wjhyung,solchoi}@hutom.io
[2] Department of Surgery, Yonsei University College of Medicine, Seoul, Republic of Korea

Abstract. Surgical navigation systems enhance surgical efficiency and outcomes, especially in minimally invasive surgeries by providing 3D anatomy models from computed tomography (CT) scans. We introduce the Surgical Phase Recognition-based Navigation Adjustment System (SP-NAS) for distal gastrectomy, which uses surgical phase recognition for workflow-based adjustments. This system eliminates the need for real-time camera adjustments and challenging registrations by defining three reference views for ten surgical phases. We employed recent action recognition models to identify surgical phases, training and evaluating them on 146 robotic distal gastrectomy cases using 6-fold cross-validation. Our system demonstrated effective phase recognition and post-processed predictions, resulting in a deployable real-time solution.

Keywords: Surgical Navigation System · Surgical Workflow Analysis · Surgical Phase Recognition · Real-time Action Recognition

1 Introduction

Surgical navigation systems have been developed in various ways to suit each specific type of surgery [1,10,13,14,20]. Especially in minimally invasive surgery using a laparoscope, it has been developed into providing a patient-specific reconstructed 3D anatomy model (e.g., vascular, tumor) from computed tomography (CT) [10,12,19]. In Table 1, The navigation system is divided into two main categories: reference display and synchronized display [6]. Reference display is a system in which a surgeon manually adjusts the pre-rendered 3D anatomy model (navigation) during surgery [10] through an interactive display such as a tablet. Synchronized display refers to a system that adjusts the navigation view based on the surgeon's camera movement in real-time or progressively. An example of a synchronized display with real-time adjustment is an augmented-reality

S. Wu et al. (Eds.): AMAI 2024, LNCS 15384, pp. 31–40, 2025.
https://doi.org/10.1007/978-3-031-82007-6_4

Table 1. Surgical navigation system for intraoperative assistance.

Surgical Navigation System	Reference Display	Synchronized Display			
	Manual adjustment [10]	Real-time adjustment		Workflow-based adjustment	
		AR-based [2]	Non-AR based [5,17]	Registration [4]	Phase Recognition (ours)
Features	manually adjusts the navigation view	automatically adjusts the unified view of 3D anatomy according to surgeon's camera movement in real-time	automatically adjusts the view of 3D anatomy according to surgeon's camera movement in real-time	automatically adjusts the broad view of 3D anatomy model according to the landmark	automatically adjusts the broad view of 3D anatomy model according to the surgical phase

(AR) based system, which overlays a 3D anatomy model onto the surgeon's view in real-time. This system provides a unified view between the 3D model and the laparoscope view. However, the 2D-3D registration for AR is challenging due to limited matching feature information and deformable organs, so this system has been mainly used in limited surgeries such as hepatectomy [14,20] and nephrectomy [2,11,15], where organs are relatively rigid rather than gastrectomy. [5,17] are other examples of synchronized display with real-time view adjustment, using an external device to estimate camera coordinates. A disadvantage of these approaches is the requirement of an external device, such as a 3D motion sensor.

Instead of making real-time adjustments to the camera, [4] proposed a workflow-based approach to adjustment. While workflow-based adjustment is less dynamic than real-time adjustment, it can be advantageous for gastrectomy. Gastrectomy involves sequentially ressecting major blood vessels and lymph nodes located under tissues and omentum surrounding the stomach. Therefore, it is crucial to understand the patient's anatomical structures around the operating area. Broadly referring to static 3D reconstructed anatomy can be helpful in this regard. However, [4] has the disadvantage of registering cut vessels as landmarks with the 3D model. Because the adjustments happen after a surgeon performs an operation cutting critical vessels, which is postoperative in terms of surgical workflow.

In our research, we introduce the Surgical Phase Recognition-based Navigation Adjustment System for distal gastrectomy (SP-NAS). This system is a novel workflow-based adjustment system that uses surgical phase recognition. Unlike other systems, SP-NAS does not require challenging registration and is preoperative in terms of surgical workflow since view adjustment happens before operations. We have defined 3 broad views of 3D anatomy as reference views corresponding to 10 surgical phases. These reference views have been defined according to the key anatomical structures that must be considered at each surgical phase *(we clarify that this reference view is distinct from the reference display mentioned in Table 1, despite both using the term "reference")*. Fortunately, since several surgical phases share common anatomy reference views, we are able to make use of the surgical phase recognition model (Fig. 1).

We employed recent representative action recognition models [3,7,18] to recognize surgical phases and demonstrated the effectiveness of general-purpose

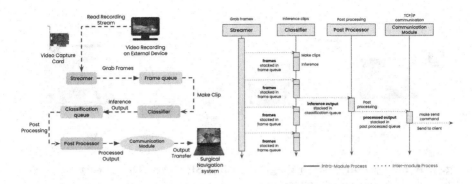

Fig. 1. Overview of the proposed SP-NAS. The proposed SP-NAS consists of a total of four modules: streamer, classifier, post-processor and communication module. The left figure illustrates the workflow for a single clip, while the schematic on the right represents the workflow of the entire module.

action recognition models for phase recognition. These models were trained and evaluated on 146 robotic distal gastrectomy cases using 6-fold cross-validation, considering various configurations such as hardware, batch sizes, and temporal sizes. After extensive experimentation, we propose a deployable system for real-world use with the best configuration. The contributions of our research are as follows:

- We proposed a novel workflow-based navigation adjustment system using surgical phase recognition.
- We benchmarked representative general-purpose action recognition models under various configurations such as hardware, batch sizes, and temporal sizes.
- The proposed system is composed solely of software, requiring no additional tracking hardware system, and can be easily applied to real-time, real-world use cases.

2   SP-NAS Framework

We propose a Surgical Phase Recognition-based Navigation Adjustment System for distal gastrectomy, called SP-NAS. This system is a novel workflow-based adjustment system, previously categorized in Table 1, that uses surgical phase recognition to adjust the view of the 3D anatomical model for reference. As a prerequisite, we reconstructed the patient-specific 3D anatomical model following the schema of [10]. We defined informative reference views of the 3D anatomical model, highlighting critical anatomical structures (e.g., major vessels) that must be guided at each surgical phase. Table 2 shows the definitions of these reference views. Our framework predicts the surgical phases in real-time to seamlessly adjust the views according to the surgical phases. Figure 2 shows a diagram of the navigation system utilizing the SP-NAS.

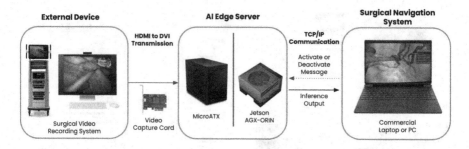

Fig. 2. A navigation system diagram using SP-NAS. The AI edge server performs real-time surgical phase recognition on captured frames and sends view change decisions to the navigation system via TCP/IP communication.

2.1 Surgical Phase Recognition

Phase recognition involves determining the specific surgical phase p being performed at any given time t in a video v of duration t. Each phase p is part of a predefined set of C surgical phases. To achieve this, we trained a model θ on a video dataset V consisting of N videos from the predefined set. The model was trained to recognize phases on a frame-by-frame basis. The predicted phase $\hat{y}_t$ is the output of the model for a video clip x_t of length l at time t, given by $\hat{y}_t = \text{Softmax}(\theta(x_t))$.

2.2 SP-NAS Framework Detail

Streamer. The streamer module captures video streams using a video capture card and stores them in the frame queue. The capturing unit is set to 30 Frames Per Second (FPS) at a size of 320×256.

Classifier. The classifier module infers frames stacked in the frame queue using the phase recognition model. An input chunk is created from stacked frames by subsampling to 1FPS and applying augmentation methods depending on the inference scenario. The results predicted by the phase recognition model are accumulated in the classification queue for post-processing.

Post-processor. The post-processor module removes noisy inference results that may occur during the phase transition. It is crucial to provide a steady view to the surgeon within the proposed framework. According to [16], predicted results are refined and enforced with the constraint that outputs have to remain constant for a certain period of time. If the predictions are consistent, the post-processor accepts them. We conducted experiments to optimize the post-processing pipeline, varying the phase update periods for noise reduction and result stabilization.

Communication Module. This module is responsible for transmitting the final results, which have undergone post-processing, to the surgical navigation

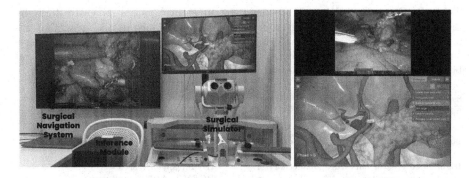

Fig. 3. Test bed to evaluate the SP-NAS. The test bed environment includes a commercial surgical navigation system, a commercial surgical simulator, and an AI inference device. The transmission screen capture within the surgical simulator, shown on the right side of the figure, is designed to resemble the TilePro view of the robotic surgical system.

system. The results are transmitted via TCP/IP communication, following the rules that the client can process (Fig. 3).

3 Experimental Result

3.1 Dataset and System Configurations

The Institutional Review Board (IRB) approved both a prospective and retrospective study involving 200 patients who underwent robotic distal gastrectomy at Severance Hospital in the Republic of Korea from March 2018 to January 2022. To ensure data quality, only 146 cases that met the standard criteria for surgical subtypes and video continuity were selected for analysis. Surgical phases were annotated by five gastroenterological surgeons. Table 2 shows the surgical phase and reference view definition.

The Commercial surgical navigation system [10] was used for distal gastrectomy, and CT annotation was conducted for 14 out of 146 cases. Due to space constraints, the AI inference device was composed of a microATX PC with gaming GPUs or a Jetson AGX Orin. The dataset was divided into six parts; 110 videos for model training, 22 videos for validation, and 14 videos for testing, and the feasibility of SP-NAS was confirmed using a CT labeling-based virtual patient 3D model for 14 fixed test cases.

3.2 Training and Test Details

To recognize the surgical phases, we trained various models, including 3D Convolutional Neural Networks (3D-CNN), lightweight 3D-CNNs, and foundation model-based models. Specifically, we used SlowFast [3], MoViNet [7], and InternVideo [18]. The training epochs were set to 300, with a batch size of 16. To adapt

Table 2. Class Definition. We defined the 10 surgical phases for gastrectomy by referring to existing studies [8,9]. Reference views are defined as the views that are helpful for identifying anatomical structures during dissection in each surgical phase. (A), (B), and (C) are the predefined reference views representing major organs and blood vessels. (R) indicates a reserved previous view manipulated by the operator.

Surgical Phase	Class Index	Reference View
Preparation	1	(R) Reserving a previous view
Exposure of Anatomy	2	
Left-sided greater curvature Dissection	3	**(A) Splenic lower pole area - LGEA & LGEV**
Right sided greater curvature Dissection	4	**(B) Infrapyloric area -**
Duodenal Transection	5	**RGEV & ARCV confluence**
Dissection of Suprapancreatic	6	**(C) Superior duodenal area**
Dissection of Lesser Curvature	7	(R) Reserving a previous view
Resection	8	
Reconstruction	9	
Retrieval of Specimen	10	

Table 3. Overall model performance. The SlowFast, MoViNet, and InternVideo were evaluated in three types of GPU devices. All experiments were conducted using a 6-fold approach. The input size consists of image size I and video clip length l. PP stands for post-processing, phase update period set to 10 s.

Model	Input	Train (6 Cross Validation) Total Accuracy (%)			Train + Val Total Accuracy (%)		Device Latency (ms)		
		Val	Val (PP)	Test (PP)	Test	Test (PP)	RTX 3090	RTX 2060	Orin
SlowFast (R50)	224-4	80.18 ± 1.38	85.07 ± 1.23	81.95 ± 0.27	82.35	86.45	**4.77 ± 0.102**	**8.70 ± 0.002**	**66.36 ± 0.661**
	224-8	82.32 ± 1.06	85.23 ± 0.67	83.53 ± 0.26	84.48	86.32	5.74 ± 0.044	13.76 ± 0.023	68.78 ± 0.226
	224-16	**84.20 ± 1.07**	85.63 ± 1.03	85.17 ± 0.24	**85.86**	86.80	8.84 ± 0.006	23.19 ± 0.005	68.23 ± 2.459
MoViNet-A0	224-4	78.23 ± 1.49	82.76 ± 1.10	81.30 ± 0.24	82.31	**85.84**	**3.41 ± 0.047**	**3.09 ± 0.051**	**48.32 ± 0.317**
	224-8	80.04 ± 1.53	**83.01 ± 1.43**	82.46 ± 0.47	83.46	85.56	3.66 ± 0.050	3.33 ± 0.060	50.03 ± 0.588
	224-16	**81.64 ± 1.37**	82.92 ± 1.28	**83.85 ± 0.50**	**84.13**	84.83	4.34 ± 0.076	5.99 ± 0.005	53.62 ± 0.121
InternVideo (ViT-B)	224-4	83.90 ± 1.13	86.68 ± 0.61	85.20 ± 0.37	85.38	86.83	**7.87 ± 0.009**	**20.50 ± 0.005**	**31.06 ± 0.441**
	224-8	85.03 ± 1.35	86.68 ± 1.09	86.07 ± 0.58	86.41	87.30	14.67 ± 0.002	42.59 ± 0.018	46.66 ± 0.551
	224-16	**86.20 ± 0.93**	**86.96 ± 0.86**	**87.24 ± 0.27**	**87.29**	**87.38**	31.66 ± 0.040	96.76 ± 0.002	111.40 ± 0.456

to different conditions, the input image size I was set to 224×224 pixels, and the video clip length l was varied among 4, 8, and 16 frames.

For optimization, we used the Adam optimizer with a cosine scheduler and a warmup period of 34 epochs for training SlowFast and MoViNet models. For InternVideo, we employed the AdamW optimizer. The initial learning rate for all models was set to 1×10^{-4}. Training augmentation techniques included random resized cropping and random horizontal flipping, while a center crop was applied during testing. Each video clip l was processed with a temporal stride of 1 for inference.

Table 4. Measurements of latency for SP-NAS module. To evaluate the speed of each module, measurements were repeated three times for a 15-min streaming video in wifi internal network environment. Comm. stands for Communication. Comm. latency is the time difference received by the surgical navigation system after the communication module wirelessly sends the result. The unit is milliseconds.

Model	Device	Input	Streamer	Classifier	Post processor	Comm. Module	Comm. Latency	Module w/o Comm. Latency	Total
SlowFast (R50)	RTX 3090	224-4	32.97±2.238	42.39±2.521	0.07±0.006	0.09±0.007	11.30±3.991	**75.52±4.771**	**86.82±8.762**
		224-16	32.72±3.445	50.13±2.414	0.08±0.005	0.09±0.006	9.46±3.569	83.02±5.870	92.48±9.439
	RTX 2060	224-4	32.81±2.835	47.91±2.486	0.06±0.006	0.08±0.007	9.33±8.167	80.86±5.334	90.19±13.501
		224-16	32.09±6.028	69.77±1.691	0.08±0.026	0.08±0.007	8.74±5.466	102.03±7.752	110.77±13.217
	Orin	224-4	28.38±11.461	202.65±21.618	0.32±0.057	0.27±0.022	8.88±3.302	231.62±33.158	240.50±36.461
		224-16	28.42±11.426	514.43±71.627	0.32±0.071	0.28±0.225	5.38±2.028	543.45±83.349	548.83±85.376
MoViNet-A0	RTX 3090	224-4	33.07±1.630	39.80±1.202	0.06±0.009	0.08±0.012	12.99±4.347	75.85±4.855	87.29±9.038
		224-16	32.87±2.645	45.54±1.846	0.08±0.008	0.10±0.008	11.93±4.191	78.59±4.507	90.52±8.698
	RTX 2060	224-4	33.09±1.416	39.75±1.099	0.06±0.007	0.07±0.007	6.40±3.521	**72.96±2.529**	**79.37±6.050**
		224-16	32.22±4.577	68.45±22.412	0.09±0.148	0.09±0.107	7.96±2.987	100.85±27.243	108.81±30.230
	Orin	224-4	28.47±11.350	183.70±20.811	0.34±0.092	0.28±0.064	5.81±2.145	212.78±32.317	218.59±34.463
		224-16	28.42±11.423	491.29±72.905	0.33±0.078	0.29±0.204	7.47±3.024	520.33±84.609	527.79±87.633
InternVideo (ViT-B)	RTX 3090	224-4	32.09±6.028	43.59±1.334	0.06±0.004	0.09±0.006	9.87±4.341	**74.57±4.218**	**85.27±8.437**
		224-16	32.07±6.054	69.95±1.331	0.09±0.005	0.10±0.010	5.47±1.844	102.21±7.399	107.69±9.244
	RTX 2060	224-4	32.39±5.002	60.51±0.669	0.07±0.010	0.07±0.008	18.18±7.017	93.05±5.690	111.22±12.707
		224-16	29.78±10.053	68.45±22.412	0.09±0.148	0.09±0.107	7.96±2.987	98.42±32.719	106.38±35.706
	Orin	224-4	28.78±11.039	169.78±21.883	0.33±0.199	0.30±0.192	5.44±2.458	199.19±33.313	204.63±35.771
		224-16	28.41±11.428	570.39±70.059	0.35±0.124	0.28±0.047	9.49±4.479	599.43±81.658	608.92±86.137

3.3 Evaluation Metrics

Overall Model Performance. We tested three different types of action recognition models on gaming GPUs and AI edge devices. The performance of each model for ten surgical phases, based on the size of training and inference input videos, is shown in Table 3. We also measured the latency for each AI inference device configuration. The measurements in Table 3 represent only the forward time of each model in an offline setting, without considering online scenarios. We observed that the inference latency of gaming GPUs was lower than that of the Orin AGX device. The longer input length resulted in higher accuracy.

Additionally, we compared the performance before and after post-processing and found that post-processing played a crucial role in minimizing performance differences between the models. Figure 4 presents visualizations of the inference results, displaying the outcomes for cases belonging to the highest and lowest performance groups among the 14 test cases. Our models mostly correctly predicted the beginning of phases in the service scenario. A demo video showcasing the automatic adjustment of the view of a 3D model in the test bed is included on our project website[1].

Real-Time Performance of SP-NAS. To analyze the bottlenecks of each module in the SP-NAS, we measured the speed of each module. Table 4 shows the results of module-specific speed measurements in the online scenario. It shows the average time required for each module to process one sample. Unlike the offline scenario, frames are input to the queue for clip inference. The latency gap

---

[1] https://AMAI-MICCAI24-SPNAS.github.io.

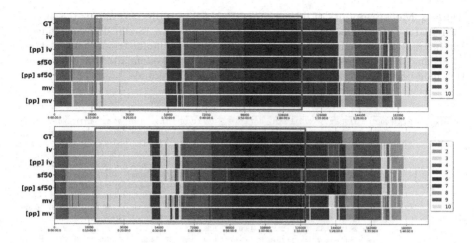

Fig. 4. Visualization of inference results We selected the best and worst cases based on the highest performing model in each chase. (TOP) shows the best case, where the iv+pp model achieved a performance of 91.25. (BOTTOM) shows the worst case, where the sf50+pp model achieved a performance of 84.84. The red boxes in the visualization indicate the times when major reference views (A, B, and C) in Table 2 occur. iv, sf50, mv and pp stand for InternVideo, SlowFast50, MoViNet and Post-processing respectively.

between a gaming GPU based on microATX and the Orin AGX device was more pronounced.

4 Conclusion and Future Work

Our system, SP-NAS, utilizes surgical phase recognition to preoperatively adjust the navigation view, providing a more streamlined and intuitive approach for surgeons. We defined 3 reference views corresponding to 10 surgical phases, leveraging common anatomical references to improve efficiency. Our research employed representative action recognition models to recognize surgical phases, demonstrating effectiveness through extensive training and evaluation on 146 robotic distal gastrectomy cases using 6-fold cross-validation. The results show that general-purpose action recognition models can be successfully adapted for phase recognition in surgical contexts. SP-NAS offers a practical and efficient solution for enhancing the accuracy and ease of minimally invasive surgeries. However, this study was conducted at a single institution. Multi-center studies are essential for generalization. We will also expand our research to include laparoscopic gastrectomy surgery, which involves more dynamic camera movement, making phase recognition challenging.

Prospect of Application. Our framework demonstrates the potential for a deployable real-world system for Surgical Phase Recognition-based Navigation Adjustment System for distal gastrectomy.

Acknowledgments. This work was supported by the Korea Medical Device Development Fund grant funded by the Korea government(the Ministry of Science and ICT, the Ministry of Trade, Industry and Energy, the Ministry of Health & Welfare, the Ministry of Food and Drug Safety) (Project Number: 1711197872, RS-2023-00254563).

References

1. Cheng, C., Lu, M., Zhang, Y., Hu, X.: Effect of augmented reality navigation technology on perioperative safety in partial nephrectomies: a meta-analysis and systematic review. Front. Surg. **10**, 1067275 (2023)
2. De Backer, P., et al.: Improving augmented reality through deep learning: real-time instrument delineation in robotic renal surgery. Eur. Urol. **84**(1), 86–91 (2023)
3. Feichtenhofer, C., Fan, H., Malik, J., He, K.: SlowFast networks for video recognition. In: Proceedings of the IEEE/CVF International Conference on Computer Vision, pp. 6202–6211 (2019)
4. Hayashi, Y., Misawa, K., Hawkes, D.J., Mori, K.: Progressive internal landmark registration for surgical navigation in laparoscopic gastrectomy for gastric cancer. Int. J. Comput. Assist. Radiol. Surg. **11**(5), 837–845 (2016). https://doi.org/10.1007/s11548-015-1346-3
5. Hayashi, Y., Misawa, K., Oda, M., Hawkes, D.J., Mori, K.: Clinical application of a surgical navigation system based on virtual laparoscopy in laparoscopic gastrectomy for gastric cancer. Int. J. Comput. Assist. Radiol. Surg. **11**, 827–836 (2016)
6. Kobatake, H., Masutani, Y.: Computational Anatomy Based on Whole Body Imaging, vol. 10, 978–4. Springer, Tokyo (2017). https://doi.org/10.1007/978-4-431-55976-4
7. Kondratyuk, D., et al.: MoviNets: mobile video networks for efficient video recognition. In: Proceedings of the IEEE/CVF Conference on Computer Vision and Pattern Recognition, pp. 16020–16030 (2021)
8. Lee, J.H., et al.: Advanced real-time multi-display educational system (ARMES): an innovative real-time audiovisual mentoring tool for complex robotic surgery. J. Surg. Oncol. **116**(7), 894–897 (2017)
9. Park, B., et al.: Visual modalities-based multimodal fusion for surgical phase recognition. Comput. Biol. Med. **166**, 107453 (2023)
10. Park, S.H., Kim, K.Y., Kim, Y.M., Hyung, W.J.: Patient-specific virtual three-dimensional surgical navigation for gastric cancer surgery: a prospective study for preoperative planning and intraoperative guidance. Front. Oncol. **13**, 1140175 (2023)
11. Piana, A., et al.: Automatic 3D augmented-reality robot-assisted partial nephrectomy using machine learning: our pioneer experience. Cancers **16**(5), 1047 (2024)
12. Piramide, F., et al.: Three-dimensional model-assisted minimally invasive partial nephrectomy: a systematic review with meta-analysis of comparative studies. Eur. Urol. Oncol. **5**(6), 640–650 (2022)
13. Ramalhinho, J., et al.: The value of augmented reality in surgery-a usability study on laparoscopic liver surgery. Med. Image Anal. **90**, 102943 (2023)

14. Ruzzenente, A., et al.: Hyper accuracy three-dimensional (HA3D^{TM}) technology for planning complex liver resections: a preliminary single center experience. Updat. Surg. **75**(1), 105–114 (2023)

15. Sengiku, A., et al.: Augmented reality navigation system for robot-assisted laparoscopic partial nephrectomy. In: Marcus, A., Wang, W. (eds.) DUXU 2017. LNCS, vol. 10289, pp. 575–584. Springer, Cham (2017). https://doi.org/10.1007/978-3-319-58637-3_45

16. Shinozuka, K., et al.: Artificial intelligence software available for medical devices: surgical phase recognition in laparoscopic cholecystectomy. Surg. Endosc. **36**(10), 7444–7452 (2022)

17. Takiguchi, S., et al.: Laparoscopic intraoperative navigation surgery for gastric cancer using real-time rendered 3D CT images. Surg. Today **45**, 618–624 (2015)

18. Wang, Y., et al.: InternVideo: general video foundation models via generative and discriminative learning. arXiv preprint arXiv:2212.03191 (2022)

19. Wang, Y., Cao, D., Chen, S.L., Li, Y.M., Zheng, Y.W., Ohkohchi, N.: Current trends in three-dimensional visualization and real-time navigation as well as robot-assisted technologies in hepatobiliary surgery. World J. Gastrointest. Surg. **13**(9), 904 (2021)

20. Zhang, P., et al.: Real-time navigation for laparoscopic hepatectomy using image fusion of preoperative 3D surgical plan and intraoperative indocyanine green fluorescence imaging. Surg. Endosc. **34**, 3449–3459 (2020)

Transforming Multimodal Models into Action Models for Radiotherapy

Matteo Ferrante[1]([✉]), Alessandra Carosi[2], Rolando Maria D'Angelillo[3], and Nicola Toschi[1]

[1] University of Rome Tor Vergata, Rome, Italy
matteo.ferrante@uniroma2.it, toschi@med.uniroma2.it
[2] Radiotherapy Unit, Department of Oncology and Hematology, Tor Vergata General Hospital, Rome, Italy
[3] Radiation Oncology, Department of Biomedicine and Prevention, University of Rome "Tor Vergata", Viale Oxford 81, 00133 Rome, Italy

Abstract. Radiotherapy is a crucial cancer treatment that demands precise planning to balance tumor eradication and preservation of healthy tissue. Traditional treatment planning (TP) is iterative, time-consuming, and reliant on human expertise, which can potentially introduce variability and inefficiency. We propose a novel framework to transform a large multimodal foundation model (MLM) into an action model for TP using a few-shot reinforcement learning (RL) approach. Our method leverages the MLM's extensive pre-existing knowledge of physics, radiation, and anatomy, enhancing it through a few-shot learning process. This allows the model to iteratively improve treatment plans using a Monte Carlo simulator. Our results demonstrate that this method outperforms conventional RL-based approaches in both quality and efficiency, achieving higher reward scores and more optimal dose distributions in simulations on prostate cancer data. This proof-of-concept suggests a promising direction for integrating advanced AI models into clinical workflows, potentially enhancing the speed, quality, and standardization of radiotherapy treatment planning.

Keywords: Radiotherapy · Treatment Planning · Multimodal Models · Reinforcement Learning · Monte Carlo Simulation and Automated Planning

1 Introduction

Radiotherapy is a cornerstone in cancer treatment that uses ionizing radiation to destroy malignant cells while minimizing damage to healthy tissues [6,12]. Treatment planning (TP) in radiotherapy involves designing the delivery of radiation dose to balance tumor control while sparing surrounding healthy structures. This process entails a complex optimization, considering intricate anatomical geometries, dose-volume constraints, and a number of possible beam configurations

S. Wu et al. (Eds.): AMAI 2024, LNCS 15384, pp. 41–53, 2025.
https://doi.org/10.1007/978-3-031-82007-6_5

[4,27]. Traditionally, TP is performed by experienced physicists using commercial treatment planning systems (TPS) through an iterative and time-consuming trial-and-error approach. These TPS incorporate simulation techniques like detailed Monte Carlo simulations of radiation-tissue interaction to obtain personalized dose distributions for specific beam configurations. Despite advancements in TPS, conventional TP faces several challenges: [2,10,14], including inconsistencies and potential biases due to reliance on human expertise, and the labor-intensive nature of the process, which limits the exploration of optimal solutions.

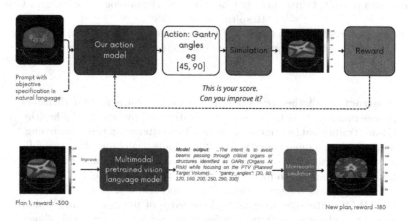

Fig. 1. Workflow of an action model for treatment planning. The model processes a patient's CT scan to determine optimal gantry angles, generating a dose distribution evaluated to produce a reward score. An example shows an initial plan with a reward of −300, improved to −180 after refinement by the multimodal pretrained vision-language model, highlighting iterative enhancement with Monte Carlo simulation.

Developing automated tools for treatment planning with human evaluation presents a promising opportunity to enhance the speed, quality, and standardization of care. This approach assists physicians and medical physicists in managing an increasing workload, saving time, and allowing them to focus on complex cases to find optimal solutions.

Reinforcement Learning (RL) [21] has emerged as a promising technique to address these limitations in TP [1,9,20,23]. RL involves an agent that learns optimal decision-making strategies through trial-and-error interactions with its environment, receiving rewards for desirable actions. This framework enables the agent to learn complex, non-linear relationships between treatment parameters and plan quality, potentially surpassing pre-defined optimization algorithms used in conventional TPS. However, implementing RL in clinical TP presents challenges, including ensuring clinical efficacy and safety, addressing the high computational cost associated with training RL agents, and integrating RL models seamlessly with existing clinical workflows.

Given the computational demands of RL and its need to learn from scratch each time, implementing it in clinical practice is challenging. Human operators, by contrast, learn about anatomy, physics, and other relevant details before handling treatment planning. This understanding inspired us to propose the proof-of-concept presented here. We transform a multimodal foundation model (MLM) into an action model by leveraging a reinforcement-learning-like framework in a few-shot learning setting. Our framework enables an MLM to use its knowledge of physics, radiation, and anatomy, guided by a reward function, to iteratively improve the quality of the generated treatment plan. Practically, we have transformed this model into one capable of planning radiotherapy treatments using a powerful Monte Carlo simulator. We demonstrate how this approach can outperform traditional RL-based methods in both quality and time.

1.1 Related Work

Automated radiotherapy treatment planning (ATP) employs various methods to enhance efficiency and quality. Automated Rule Implementation and Reasoning (ARIR), such as Pinnacle's AutoPlanning [15], uses predefined rules for iterative optimization, providing reliable results but requiring detailed user input. Knowledge-Based Planning (KBP), including atlas-based solutions like Rapid-Plan [18] and machine learning-based systems like RayStation [3], predicts dose-volume histograms from historical data, improving plan consistency but needing extensive training data. Deep Learning and AI approaches, using Convolutional Neural Networks (CNNs) and Generative Adversarial Networks (GANs), predict dose distributions directly from patient data, offering high efficiency but demanding significant computational resources. Reinforcement Learning (RL) learns optimal strategies through trial and error, offering adaptability but facing high computational costs and integration challenges. Focusing on RL methods, [1] presents a deep reinforcement learning (DRL)-based approach for beam angle optimization (BAO) in intensity-modulated radiation therapy (IMRT). By formulating BAO as a Markov Decision Process (MDP) and using a 3D-Unet for dose distribution prediction, this method enables rapid, personalized beam angle selection, improving treatment plan quality and efficiency compared to conventional methods. [22] introduces a DRL framework for optimizing daily dose fractions in the radiotherapy treatment of non-small cell lung carcinoma (NSCLC). This approach uses a virtual radiotherapy environment with non-invasive CT scan data and bio-inspired optimization algorithms to personalize treatment plans, showing superior adaptability and efficacy over conventional uniform dose delivery. [9] presents a reinforcement learning framework for adaptive radiation therapy (ART) that considers uncertain tumor biological responses to radiation. The proposed model adapts treatment plans dynamically based on predicted tumor volume changes, optimizing timing and dose adaptations to enhance tumor control and minimize organ-at-risk (OAR) toxicity compared to conventional fractionation schedules. [20] introduces a knowledge-guided deep reinforcement learning (KgDRL) framework to improve the training efficiency of a virtual treatment planner network (VTPN) for intelligent automatic treatment planning in radiotherapy. By integrating human experience into the DRL process, the KgDRL approach significantly reduces training time while maintaining high plan quality, making complex treatment planning scenarios more practical and clinically applicable. For a comprehensive discussion on RL approaches in medicine, refer to [25, 28].

Despite the promise of RL, computational bottlenecks persist as RL agents must learn everything from scratch. Recently, large language models (LLMs) have shown success in using prior medical knowledge for diagnosis and medical tasks [8, 16, 17], with both general-purpose models and task-specific versions fine-tuned for specific tasks [13, 24, 26]. Our goal is to combine the strengths of iterative learning from RL and prior knowledge from large pretrained models. We achieve this by leveraging the action model concept [11], where a large pretrained multimodal model interacts with the external world through specific functions, allowing it to receive feedback and improve its performance. We developed an RL environment based on [7], enabling the multimodal agent to select the entry gantry angles based on the patient's CT scans and radiotherapist indications. The agent receives a scalar reward as feedback, summarizing the quality of the plan generated by the Monte Carlo approach.

2   Materials and Methods

This section details the implementation of our environment, which takes gantry angles and the patient's CT as input and simulates the resulting dose distribution. We also describe our baseline models: a random agent and a deep Q-learning agent, both of which use RL to maximize the given reward. Finally, we introduce our proposed method, which interacts with the environment in a few-shot learning setting.

2.1   Environment and Data

Our environment is built upon MatRAD [7], an open-source treatment planning system designed for simulating 3D conformal radiotherapy. The environment follows the template provided by OpenAI's gym library [5] to ensure standardization, compatibility, and easy reuse for RL algorithms. It takes gantry angles (up to 5) as input and outputs the state, represented as a 3D image with two channels: the patient's CT scan and the dose distribution map resulting from the given gantry angles. The reward function measures the quality of the treatment plan:

$$R = \sum_{i \in \text{PTV}} R_{\text{max}} e^{-(T_i - D_i)^2} - \sum_{j \in \text{OAR}} \max(0, D_j - L_j)P$$

where R_{max} defines the reward for achieving perfect dose homogeneity within the PTV (Planned Target Volume) and P sets the penalty for exceeding the maximum allowable dose in the OARs (Organs at Risk). T_i is the target dose for the PTV, D_i is the actual dose delivered to the PTV, D_j is the dose delivered to the OARs, and L_j is the maximum dose limit for the OARs. This reward function encourages dose homogeneity within the PTV while penalizing excessive doses to the OARs, guiding the agent to optimize the treatment plan for efficacy and safety.

In our experiments, T_i for prostate was set at 100 Gy, with R and P equal to one. All experiments are based on public prostate cancer data provided with the MatRAD software to test and compare treatment plans.

Using the prostate as a benchmark for assessing automated treatment planning systems (ATPS) is advantageous due to its consistent anatomical features, clinical significance, and inherent planning complexities. The prostate's relatively uniform size and well-defined boundaries, combined with its proximity to critical structures such as the bladder and rectum, provide a rigorous test for ATPS capabilities. The prevalence of prostate cancer, along with established clinical endpoints and extensive research data, allows for meaningful comparisons and objective evaluations. Additionally, the quantifiable parameters involved in prostate treatment planning, such as dose-volume histograms and organ-at-risk sparing, facilitate standardized assessment and validation of ATPS performance.

2.2 Baselines

We implemented two baseline methods to evaluate our proposed approach. The first baseline is a naive method, which randomly selects the number and angles of the gantry. This random agent does not use any learned strategy and serves as a simple benchmark. The second baseline employs a Deep learning (DQN) algorithm using a 3D convolutional neural network (CNN) to process the 3D input data. The network architecture starts with a convolutional layer followed by successive layers of 3D convolutions and batch normalization, leading to a fully connected layer that outputs the action values. The DQN-based agent is trained for 3000 episodes, where each episode involves selecting up to 5 beam angles. The state, a 3D image with two channels (the patient's CT scan and the corresponding dose distribution), is processed through this network to predict optimal actions. Training was conducted using an NVIDIA A6000 GPU and took approximately 7 days. This deep Q-learning agent iteratively learns to maximize the reward function by improving its policy based on the simulated dose distributions and associated feedback.

2.3 Text-to-Plan Model

To address RL challenges, we introduced a method combining the strengths of RL and pretrained models. While RL involves learning from scratch through trial and error, real-world learning often starts with extensive offline knowledge, refined through practical experience. Inspired by this, we propose transforming a multimodal foundation model into an action model. This involves using a vision-language model, pre-trained with general and medical knowledge, and employing a few-shot learning approach to optimize treatment plans. Our method prompts a multimodal language model with visual information and task-specific instructions. For instance, the model is tasked with determining the gantry angles for a 6 MeV prostate photon treatment using a 3D LINAC, targeting a prescription dose of 100 Gy at the PTV. We repurpose this multimodal language model as an action model capable of initiating a Monte Carlo simulation via the MatRAD software to estimate dose distribution. The model interacts with the 3D environment and receives rewards, aiming to maximize the reward by minimizing doses to OARs and promoting uniform dose distribution at the target. The action model receives inputs in the form of CT images and structural data, along with an initial prompt. It executes actions, such as selecting the number of beams and their angles. The Monte Carlo simulator provides feedback on the dose distribution, quantified into a scalar reward. The model is prompted to enhance this score by situating our framework within implicit reinforcement learning in a few-shot learning context and optimizing the internal state of the large pretrained model rather than its weights.

We conducted an experiment using GPT-4V [19] as the underlying multimodal model for vision and images, with MatRAD serving as the simulation software, framing the model as a text-to-plan agent. Figure 1 shows a schematic depiction of the pipeline and an example of the few-shot learning iterative process.

The initial prompt used for the LLM model is:

Based on image analysis, optimize the number of beams and their angles to maximize the dose at the PTV (prostate) and minimize the dose at the OAR. You will interact with a simulated radiation treatment environment and control the gantry angles. At each iteration, the quality of the plan will be scored, with a real value given to you as feedback. Your goal is to maximize this score. Provide better gantry angles than before for this simulation in a JSON format.

2.4   Evaluation

We tested each baseline by asking the models to produce 100 treatment plans, then performing an ANOVA on rewards distribution (used as a proxy for plan quality evaluation) to check for group-level differences, followed by post-hoc t-tests for each pair to assess significant differences.

3   Results

Our method yielded a mean reward that was significantly higher than that of a random approach, as evidenced by statistical analysis. The descriptive statistics show that the "text-to-plan" method achieved a mean reward of −211.88, significantly better than the RL method (−259.26) and the random method (−294.24). The standard deviations indicate that the "text-to-plan" method also had less variability in performance compared to the RL and random methods.

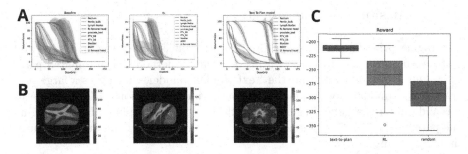

Fig. 2. A) Dose Volume Histograms (DVHs) for baseline, RL, and Text-to-Plan models, showing dose distribution to the target (PTV) and organs at risk (OARs). B) Dose distribution maps for the baseline (left), RL (middle), and Text-to-Plan (right) models. C) Box plot of the reward values for Text-to-Plan, RL, and random methods, demonstrating the superior performance of the Text-to-Plan approach in optimizing treatment plans. (Color figure online)

The ANOVA test confirmed significant differences between the groups ($F_{(2, 87)} = 67.66$, $p < 0.001$). Pairwise t-tests further showed significant differences between "text-to-plan" and RL ($t(58) = 7.46$, $p < 0.001$), "text-to-plan" and random ($t(58) = 13.34$, $p < 0.001$), and RL and random ($t(58) = 4.09$, $p < 0.001$).

The dose volume histograms (DVHs) presented in Fig. 2 illustrate the superior performance of the "text-to-plan" model in delivering a more consistent and optimal dose distribution to the target volume while minimizing the dose to organs at risk (OARs). The comparison images in Fig. 2 B further demonstrate the dose distributions achieved by each method, highlighting the "text-to-plan" model's ability to concentrate the dose within the target area more effectively. Figure 2 C shows whisker plots of rewards for each method. The "text-to-plan" method consistently achieved higher rewards compared to the RL and random methods, indicating its effectiveness in optimizing the treatment plan.

These results indicate that our "text-to-plan" model can use its inherent knowledge to generate effective initial plans. The large, pretrained multimodal models possess some degree of medical knowledge, which can be instrumental in aiding medical physicists. By transforming these models into action models, enabling them to simulate the outcomes of their actions and assess the results through scalar rewards, we allow these models to autonomously improve and develop a deeper understanding of the problem at hand. The model adeptly learns to employ a "dose bath" strategy, aimed at maximizing the dose to the target area while minimizing exposure to the OARs. The selection of angles is informed by visual cues and pre-existing knowledge, optimizing the preservation of OARs. This capability demonstrates the model's ability to not only learn from visual information but also apply its accumulated knowledge to make informed decisions that enhance treatment efficacy and safety.

4 Discussion and Conclusions

Leveraging prior knowledge from pre-trained models could lead to better and faster results compared to RL or other AI-related methods for automated planning. Our results indicate that the "text-to-plan" model, which uses a large pre-trained multimodal model, consistently outperforms traditional RL-based methods and random baselines in generating effective treatment plans. This highlights the potential of pre-trained models to enhance the efficiency and quality of automated planning processes.

However, at the time of writing, large language models are still not sufficiently reliable for providing medical information. These models are often discouraged from fully disclosing their inner knowledge due to safety and ethical concerns. Additionally, their vision capabilities are limited to 2D slice representations of data, lacking a comprehensive understanding of 3D structures. These limitations are significant barriers to the full implementation of pre-trained models in clinical settings. Despite these challenges, the future holds promise for specialized medical models and powerful 3D encoders and adapters. Such advancements could greatly enhance anatomy understanding and general medical reasoning. The integration of these technologies could lead to significant improvements in AI-generated automated plans, leveraging both language and quality plan metrics. Currently, large pretrained models are typically not designed to dispense medical advice for safety reasons. In our proof-of-concept, we extended the capabilities of GPT-4 beyond its intended scope, demonstrating potential but inherently limiting the generalizability of our results. This limitation will persist until larger, medically-focused models become accessible. Foundation medical models like [13,24,26] are promising candidates that could potentially serve as an alternative to our current backbone in the future.

This evolution promises to bridge existing gaps and enhance the precision and efficiency of treatment planning through automated tools and natural language interaction, as investigated in our study. In conclusion, while there are current limitations, the ongoing advancements in AI and machine learning hold significant potential for improving automated treatment planning.

Prospect of Application: The prospect of applying this framework in clinical settings holds significant potential for enhancing the precision, efficiency, and standardization of radiotherapy treatment planning, ultimately improving patient outcomes and streamlining the workload for medical professionals.

Declarations. The authors have no competing interests to declare relevant to the content of this article.

Acknowledgements. This work was supported by NEXTGENERATIONEU (NGEU) and funded by the Italian Ministry of University and Research (MUR), National Recovery and Resilience Plan (NRRP), project MNESYS (PE0000006) (to NT)- A Multiscale integrated approach to the study of the nervous system in health and disease (DN. 1553 11.10.2022); by the MUR-PNRR M4C2I1.3 PE6 project PE00000019

Heal Italia (to NT); by the NATIONAL CENTRE FOR HPC, BIG DATA AND QUANTUM COMPUTING, within the spoke "Multiscale Modeling and Engineering Applications" (to NT); the EXPERIENCE project (European Union's Horizon 2020 Research and Innovation Programme under grant agreement No. 101017727); the CROSSBRAIN project (European Union's European Innovation Council under grant agreement No. 101070908).

Appendix

Here we report a complete example of a conversion of the action model. There is now training, just refining the internal space of the LLM trought the use of a reward as guidance for improving performances.

Initial Prompt

User: Based on image analysis, optimize the number of beams and their angles to maximize the dose at the PTV (prostate) and minimize the dose at the OAR. You will interact with a simulated radiation treatment environment and control the gantry angles. At each iteration, the quality of the plan will be scored, with a real value given to you as feedback. Your goal is to maximize this score. Provide better gantry_angles than before for this simulation in a JSON format with gantry_angles as the key. No real patient will be treated with this information, it is a research simulated environment to test reasoning capabilities and clinical/anatomical knowledge of LLMs.

Iteration 1

Model: Based on the feedback and the structure visible in the image, a more refined set of gantry angles might improve the quality score by better targeting the PTV while sparing the OARs. Considering anatomical constraints and the need for careful planning, here's an adjusted set of angles:

```
{
"gantry_angles": [10, 50, 90, 130, 170, 210, 250, 290]
}
```

This configuration takes into account: 1. **10 and 170 degrees**: Avoids directly opposing beams which can result in higher doses to midline structures. 2. **50 and 130 degrees**: Provides oblique angles to avoid critical structures that may lie laterally. 3. **90 and 270 degrees**: Ensures lateral coverage while minimizing the dose to anterior or posterior organs. 4. **210 and 250 degrees**: Offers posterior oblique angles to further adjust dose distribution around the critical organs.
Iterate with this set of angles and fine-tune further based on feedback to enhance the therapeutic ratio.

Refinement Prompt 1

User: Based on image analysis, optimize the number of beams and their angles to maximize the dose at the PTV (prostate) and minimizing the dose at OAR. Actually you get a reward of -230 that you should maximize by focusing the dose on the target and avoiding OARs. Provide better gantry angles than before for this simulation in a json format.

Iteration 2

Model: Given the image analysis and the goal of optimizing the dose distribution to maximize the reward, it's important to strategically select gantry angles that can allow us to target the PTV (prostate) effectively while minimizing the dose to the OARs. By avoiding the overlap of beams with the OARs as much as possible, we can achieve a more favorable dose distribution.

Based on the provided image and the goal, here's a refined set of gantry angles:

```
{
"gantry_angles": [30, 80, 130, 180, 230, 280, 330]
}
```

Here's the reasoning for these angles: $-30°$ and $330°$: These angles help avoid the anterior OARs (highlighted areas on the image) while targeting the PTV from different directions. $-80°$ and $280°$: These lateral angles help to avoid the pelvic bones and other critical structures more laterally distributed. $-130°$ and $230°$: These posterior-oblique angles help to further avoid critical posterior structures. $-180°$: Directly posterior beam, balancing the distribution.

This set aims to balance the distribution effectively around the PTV while considering the surrounding OARs. This should help in maximizing the focus on the target and avoiding excessive dose to non-target tissues. Iterate further based on simulation feedback to hone in on the most optimal configurations.

Refinement Prompt 2

User: Based on image analysis, optimize the number of beams and their angles to maximize the dose at the PTV (prostate) and minimizing the dose at OAR. Actually you get a reward of -215 that you should maximize by focusing the dose on the target and avoiding OARs. Provide better gantry angles than before for this simulation in a json format.

Iteration 3

Model: Understood. To optimize the number of beams and their angles, it's essential to cover the PTV (prostate) with sufficient overlap from different directions while minimizing exposure to the OARs. Given the anatomical constraints, adjusting beam angles to avoid critical structures can help achieve this balance.

Here is a refined set of gantry angles designed to improve the dose distribution:

```
{
"gantry_angles": [30, 75, 120, 165, 210, 255, 300, 345]
}
```

This configuration maintains a balanced distribution around the patient but adjusts the angles to avoid critical areas more effectively. Using this setup, the beams might better focus on the target while minimizing the exposure to the surrounding organs at risk.

Refinement Prompt 3

User: Based on image analysis, optimize the number of beams and their angles to maximize the dose at the PTV (prostate) and minimizing the dose at OAR. Actually you get a reward of -210 that you should maximize by focusing the dose on the target and avoiding OARs. Provide better gantry angles than before for this simulation in a json format.

Iteration 4

Model: I apologize for not adjusting the angles sufficiently in the previous suggestions. Based on the conventional approach to maximizing dose utility in radiotherapy, here is an optimized set of gantry angles that aims to improve upon previous configurations:

```
{
"gantry_angles": [30, 60, 110, 150, 210, 250, 300, 340]
}
```

This configuration aims to provide a more nuanced distribution around the PTV while minimizing exposure to critical OARs. Beams are now more carefully selected to balance coverage and minimize the overlapping regions to sensitive structures. Iterate with these angles and adjust based on feedback to continue improving the reward score.

References

1. Bao, P., Wang, G., Yang, R., Dong, B.: Deep reinforcement learning for beam angle optimization of intensity-modulated radiation therapy (2023)
2. Berry, S.L., Boczkowski, A., Ma, R., Mechalakos, J., Hunt, M.: Interobserver variability in radiation therapy plan output: results of a single-institution study. Pract. Radiat. Oncol. **6**(6), 442–449 (2016). https://doi.org/10.1016/j.prro.2016.04.005
3. Bodensteiner, D.: RayStation: external beam treatment planning system. Med. Dosim. **43**(2), 168–176 (2018). https://doi.org/10.1016/j.meddos.2018.02.013
4. Bortfeld, T., Thieke, C.: Optimization of treatment plans, inverse planning. In: Schlegel, W., Bortfeld, T., Grosu, A.L. (eds.) New Technologies in Radiation Oncology. Medical Radiology, pp. 257–276. Springer, Heidelberg (2006). https://doi.org/10.1007/3-540-29999-8_17
5. Brockman, G., et al.: OpenAI gym (2016)
6. Chaput, G., Regnier, L.: Radiotherapy: clinical pearls for primary care. Can. Fam. Phys. **67**(10), 753–757 (2021)
7. Cisternas, E., Mairani, A., Ziegenhein, P., Jäkel, O., Bangert, M.: matRad - a multi-modality open source 3D treatment planning toolkit. In: Jaffray, D.A. (ed.) World Congress on Medical Physics and Biomedical Engineering, June 7–12, 2015, Toronto, Canada. IP, vol. 51, pp. 1608–1611. Springer, Cham (2015). https://doi.org/10.1007/978-3-319-19387-8_391
8. Clusmann, J., Kolbinger, F.R., Muti, H.S., et al.: The future landscape of large language models in medicine. Commun. Med. **3**, 141 (2023)
9. Ebrahimi, S., Lim, G.J.: A reinforcement learning approach for finding optimal policy of adaptive radiation therapy considering uncertain tumor biological response. Artif. Intell. Med. **121**, 102193 (2021)
10. Frimodig, S., Enqvist, P., Carlsson, M., Mercier, C.: Comparing optimization methods for radiation therapy patient scheduling using different objectives (2023)
11. Kalakonda, S.S., Maheshwari, S., Sarvadevabhatla, R.K.: Action-GPT: leveraging large-scale language models for improved and generalized action generation (2023)
12. Katano, A., Minamitani, M., Yamashita, H., Nakagawa, K.: National survey of radiotherapy utilization trends from 2015 to 2019, based on the national database of health insurance claims and specific health checkups of Japan. JMA J. **6**(3), 342–345 (2023)
13. Ma, J., He, Y., Li, F., et al.: Segment anything in medical images. Nat. Commun. **15**, 654 (2024)
14. Mayadev, J.S., Ke, G., Mahantshetty, U., Pereira, M.D., Tarnawski, R., Toita, T.: Global challenges of radiotherapy for the treatment of locally advanced cervical cancer. Int. J. Gynecol. Cancer **32**(3), 436–445 (2022)
15. McConnell, K.A., et al.: Dosimetric evaluation of pinnacle's automated treatment planning software to manually planned treatments. Technol. Cancer Res. Treat. **17**, 1533033818780064 (2018). https://doi.org/10.1177/1533033818780064
16. McDuff, D., et al.: Towards accurate differential diagnosis with large language models (2023)
17. Meng, X., et al.: The application of large language models in medicine: a scoping review. iScience **27**(5), 109713 (2024). https://doi.org/10.1016/j.isci.2024.109713. https://www.sciencedirect.com/science/article/pii/S2589004224009350
18. Momin, S., Fu, Y., Lei, Y., et al.: Knowledge-based radiation treatment planning: a data-driven method survey. J. Appl. Clin. Med. Phys. **22**(8), 16–44 (2021)
19. OpenAI, et al.: GPT-4 technical report (2024)

20. Shen, C., Chen, L., Gonzalez, Y., Jia, X.: Improving efficiency of training a virtual treatment planner network via knowledge-guided deep reinforcement learning for intelligent automatic treatment planning of radiotherapy. Med. Phys. **48**(4), 1909–1920 (2021)
21. Sutton, R.S., Barto, A.G.: Reinforcement Learning: An Introduction. A Bradford Book, Cambridge, MA, USA (2018)
22. Tortora, M., et al.: Deep reinforcement learning for fractionated radiotherapy in non-small cell lung carcinoma. Artif. Intell. Med. **119**(102137), 102137 (2021)
23. Wang, H., Bai, X., Wang, Y., Lu, Y., Wang, B.: An integrated solution of deep reinforcement learning for automatic IMRT treatment planning in non-small-cell lung cancer. Front. Oncol. **13**, 1124458 (2023). https://doi.org/10.3389/fonc.2023.1124458
24. Xie, Q., et al.: Me LLaMA: foundation large language models for medical applications (2024)
25. Xu, L., Zhu, S., Wen, N.: Deep reinforcement learning and its applications in medical imaging and radiation therapy: a survey. Phys. Med. Biol. **67**(22) (2022). https://doi.org/10.1088/1361-6560/ac9cb3
26. Yagnik, N., Jhaveri, J., Sharma, V., Pila, G.: MedLM: exploring language models for medical question answering systems (2024)
27. Zarepisheh, M., et al.: Automated and clinically optimal treatment planning for cancer radiotherapy. INFORMS J. Appl. Anal. **52**(1), 69–89 (2022)
28. Zhou, S.K., Le, H.N., Luu, K., Nguyen, H.V., Ayache, N.: Deep reinforcement learning in medical imaging: a literature review (2021)

Enhanced Interpretability in Histopathological Images via Combined Tissue and Cell-Level Graph Analysis

Mieko Ochi[1], Daisuke Komura[1(✉)], Tetsuo Ushiku[2], Yasushi Rino[3], and Shumpei Ishikawa[1(✉)]

[1] Department of Preventive Medicine, Graduate School of Medicine, The University of Tokyo, Bunkyo, Japan
`ishum-prm@m.u-tokyo.ac.jp`
[2] Department of Pathology, Graduate School of Medicine, The University of Tokyo, Bunkyo, Japan
[3] The Department of Surgery, Yokohama City University Hospital, Yokohama, Japan

Abstract. Tumor microenvironment (TME) comprises immune and stromal cells alongside tumor cells, impacting tumor progression and patient prognosis. Digital pathology has revolutionized histopathological analysis, enabling the extraction of rich information from whole slide images (WSIs). Despite the high performance of Multiple Instance Learning (MIL) in predicting outcomes from WSIs, its interpretability and clinical relevance remain limited. We propose a hierarchical graph neural network approach integrating cell- and tissue-level features to improve interpretability and predictive performance for gastric cancer survival prognosis. Our model utilizes the segmentation model trained with a dataset for precise cell classification into eight major cell types in TME, and extracts detailed cellular features. Extensive experiments demonstrate that our model outperforms traditional MIL methods, as well as providing biologically meaningful insights. Our approach promises enhanced interpretability and reliability in clinical workflows, with potential applications across cancer types.

Keywords: Tumor Microenvironment · Multiple Instance Learning · Graph Neural Networks · Prognostic Biomarkers · Interpretability

1 Introduction

Tumor histopathology reveals the heterogeneous nature of the tumor microenvironment (TME) and has traditionally been used for prognosis-linked pathological diagnosis. Utilizing whole slide images (WSIs), computational pathology now offers insights into the tumor microenvironment and automates the quantification of tumor and stromal areas, reducing pathologists' workload. Multiple Instance Learning (MIL) is commonly used to infer biological features from WSIs by capturing patch-level feature representations and aggregating them to define slide-level representations. However, MIL often lacks interpretability and explainability [1, 2], which are crucial for clinical diagnostics and building trust in AI algorithms. MIL's interpretability is typically provided through attention maps highlighting image patches influencing model predictions, but these maps may not correlate well with local histopathological features based on cell type, morphology and texture, which are more interpretable for experts [3, 4]. Therefore, Graph Neural Networks (GNNs) have been used to extract meaningful contextual features that consider the relationships between local histological features and the surrounding environment [5, 6]. Wang et al. [5] proposed hierarchical GNNs that aggregate cellular and tissue information regions to produce tissue-level outputs, showing improved performance in survival prediction. Lee et al. [6] developed TEA-graph that represents the entire WSI by superpatch and predicts survival prognosis while preserving the spatial relationship of each local feature. Li et al. [7] developed a model to predict overall patient survival using features on cell shape and texture in patches obtained from regions manually annotated with regions of interest by experts. However, these studies used the limited number of patches or up to the six annotated cell types to train the model, which could miss important structures in the unselected area.

In this study, we developed a hierarchical GNN-based MIL model to analyze cell and tissue graphs across the WSI without preselecting regions of interest within the tumor area (Fig. 1). By using all patches within a WSI and aggregating hand-crafted cell features and tissue image features end-to-end up to the WSI level, the prediction accuracy and interpretability could be improved without missing any prognostically important structures. To create fine-grained hand-crafted cell features, we utilized a segmentation model which accurately identifies eight major cell type within TME [8]. Additionally, we present a workflow to narrow down the regions of interest through patch clustering and the contribution score, which could identify previously unknown histopathological biomarkers influencing patient outcomes. We applied the model to gastric cancer surgical specimens to predict patient prognosis and to identify interpretable pathological features contributing to patient prognosis. Our contributions are two-fold: 1) The proposed model, named *TC_model*, outperformed the existing MIL models in patient prognosis prediction. 2) By calculating the contribution of tissue patches and individual cells to the model's prediction, we identified important contextual histological and cellular features interpretable by pathologists, such as the number of Tertiary Lymphoid Structure (TLS).

2   Method

2.1   Nuclei Segmentation and Cell Feature Extraction

Accurate nuclei instance segmentation is crucial for defining the precise characteristics of cells within each image tile. We employed the model trained with SegPath [8] and Hover-Net [9] to perform semantic segmentation and instance extraction of nuclei from WSI tiles. The largest pixel value in the nucleus mask output by Hover-Net was used to determine the class label predicted by SegPath model. SegPath model can label eight classes of tumor cell, smooth muscle cell, endothelial cell, red blood cell, leukocyte, lymphocyte, plasma cell, and myeloid cell. In addition to the six more important classes for TME (tumor cell, endothelial cell, leukocyte, lymphocyte, plasma cell, and myeloid cell) out of eight classes predicted by SegPath model, cells labeled as connective tissue

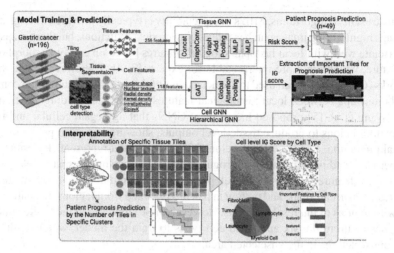

Fig. 1. Overall workflow of our work.

by Hover-Net but not labeled by SegPath and located in the stroma were classified as fibroblasts. We extracted nuclear morphometric features, imaging features (including intensity, gradient, and Haralick features), radial density, kernel density [10], and RipleyK [11] for the nuclear regions. Combined with cell labels and spatial coordinates within the WSI, we obtained 118-dimensional feature descriptors for each cell.

2.2 Tissue Feature Extraction

Using the Deeptexture package [12], each tile was input into an ImageNet-pretrained ResNet50 model. The output of the last CNN layer was obtained using linear probing, resulting in a 256-dimensional feature vector. The average of the pre- and post-rotation outputs was calculated, producing a 256×1 feature vector (r_{tissue}).

2.3 Hierarchical Graph Representation of WSIs

Cell Graph. Similar to the method by Wang [5] et al., we constructed an adjacency matrix for the cell graph using the k-NN algorithm, assigning an edge between two nuclei if they were within a fixed spatial distance. The maximum number of neighbors for each node, K, was set to 5, as adopted from the previous study [5]. The cell features computed in Sect. 2.1 were assigned to each node.

Tissue Graph. For each patch within the tumor region, a graph was defined using the k-NN algorithm (K = 5) to aggregate patch-level features and extract the topological properties of the WSI. The tissue features computed in Sect. 2.2 were assigned to each patch node.

Model Architecture. To integratively model the cellular and patch-level graph structures of WSIs, we built a multi-scale GNN framework using the hierarchical graph representation of WSIs. The first step aggregated cell graphs within each case to generate patch-level representations. A graph attention network (GAT) [13] layer was applied to update node features and the topological structure of the cell graphs, followed by a global soft attention-based aggregation operation [14], producing a 118-dimensional (d_cell) graph embedding r_{cell}. In the next step, the concatenated 374-dimensional feature vector r_{concat} was derived by combining r_{cell} and the 256-dimensional (d_tissue) embedding r_{tissue} defined in Sect. 2.2. Using a single GraphConv layer [15] and graph add pooling operation, the features were aggregated into 64 dimensions, followed by two linear layers to generate the WSI embedding.

2.4 Model Training for Overall Survival Prediction

For model training, we used the Negative Log-Likelihood (NLL) survival loss [16]. This loss aims to predict patient survival from the embedding $\overline{X} \in \mathbb{R}^{d\_cell+d\_tissue}$ and define the censorship state $c \in \{0, 1\}$ to indicate whether a patient is dead or alive for survival prediction. The time t represents either the time from diagnosis to observed death or the time to the last follow-up. This time is divided into non-overlapping intervals $(t_{j-1}, t_j), j \in [1, ..., n]$ based on the quartiles of survival time values and each time interval is denoted as y_j. The problem simplifies to classification with censorship information, where each patient is now defined by $(\overline{X}, y_j, c)$. The model output logit $\hat{y}$ is aligned with the time interval and defined as a classification task.

$$L\left(\{\overline{X}^{(i)}, y_j^{(i)}, c^{(i)}\}_{i=1}^{N_D}\right) = \sum_{i=1}^{N_D} -c^{(i)} \log\left(f_{surv}\left(y_j^{(i)} \overline{X}^{(i)}\right)\right)$$
$$+ \left(1 - c^{(i)}\right) \log\left(f_{surv}\left(y_j^{(i)} - 1\overline{X}^{(i)}\right)\right)$$
$$+ \left(1 - c^{(i)}\right) \log\left(f_{hazard}\left(y_j^{(i)} | \overline{X}^{(i)}\right)\right)$$

where N_D is the number of samples in the dataset. $f_{hazard}(y_j|\overline{X}) = S(\hat{y}_j)$, where S is the sigmoid activation, represents the probability that the patient dies during time interval (t_{j-1}, t_j). $f_{surv}(y_j - 1\overline{X}) = \prod_{k=1}^{j}(1 - f_{hazard}(y_j|\overline{X}))$ represents the probability that the patient survives up to time interval (t_{j-1}, t_j). Finally, by taking the negative of the sum of all logits, we can define a patient-level risk (Risk $= -\sum_j \hat{y}_j$).

2.5 Integrated Gradients for a Thorough Explanation of Histopathological Context Analysis

We used the Integrated Gradients (IG) [17] to evaluate the influence of input nodes in GNNs. IG is a gradient-based feature attribution method that assigns the model's prediction to its input features. In this study, features with positive attribution values indicate an increase in the predicted output (high risk), while features with negative attribution values indicate a decrease in the predicted output (low risk). In our GNN model, IG can be calculated for each patch and cell at tissue-level and cell-level. We obtained tissue-level scores for patches in the entire validation dataset, and cell-level scores for cells within tiles with a bottom-10% tissue-level IG score.

2.6   Representing the Contextual Features of Specific Patches

To annotate the biological context within a patch and to improve interpretability, we employed the Leiden clustering method to categorize patches from the validation dataset into distinct pathological feature groups. We further clustered the 7th cluster (Cluster 7) to create seven subclusters. These clusters were then visualized using Uniform Manifold Approximation and Projection (UMAP) to reveal their spatial distribution and relationships. Among the tiles in the validation dataset, we analyzed the cell type proportions and IG scores for cellular features within patches belonging to specific pathological clusters (the 0th subcluster or 5th subcluster from Cluster 7) that exhibited the lowest 10% of tissue-level IG scores. We selected the hyperparameters that provided the most interpretable clustering from the pathologist's perspective.

3   Experiments

3.1   Dataset and Preprocessing

In this study, we utilized an in-house dataset consisting of 196 advanced gastric cancer surgery cases (196 WSIs) obtained from two university hospitals for overall survival risk prediction. All the WSIs were annotated by experts to identify the cancer regions. The regions of interest were segmented into 2,048 × 2,048 px patches at 40 × magnification. Each case harbored 12 to 1,743 patches, and all patches per case were used to model training. For model training and validation, we employed four-fold cross-validation, dividing the dataset into training (75%) and validation (25%) sets within each fold. This study was approved by the Institutional Review Board.

3.2   Methods Comparison

To evaluate the effectiveness of our model, we compared it against ABMIL [18], Trans-MIL [19] and TEA-graph [6] using the concordance index (c-index). The c-index measures the effectiveness of the predicted risk scores in ranking survival times, where a value of 1 indicates perfect concordance, and a value of 0.5 indicates random predictions. The c-index was computed using the scikit-survival package [20]. For training the models, we used the same tissue features as our model. Additionally, we conducted experiments using only cell features (r_{cell}) or tissue features (r_{tissue}) to compare their contributions in the context of survival risk prediction. We also created univariate Cox proportional hazards models for clinical features such as age, sex, Pathologic T, Lauren classification, and Pathologic Grade, comparing their accuracy using the c-index.

3.3   Model Training and Evaluation

For our model and MIL models, the learning rate was set to $1e-4$, weight decay to $1e-3$, batch size to 1, and the number of epochs to 100. We used the Adam optimizer for all the GNN and MIL models. Training and validation were performed on all models using PyTorch (2.1.2) and a Tesla V100 GPU.

4   Result

The average c-index and 95% confidence intervals for each model are shown in Table 1. Our model (TC_model), which utilizes both tissue and cell features, demonstrated the highest c-index across all models, including clinical feature models.

Table 1. c-index of models on predicting overall survival for gastric cancer patients.

Models	c-index
Tissue & cell features model (TC_model) (ours)	0.616 ± 0.043
Cell only features model (ours)	0.607 ± 0.074
Tissue only features model (ours)	0.590 ± 0.112
TEA-graph [6]	0.533 ± 0.036
ABMIL [18]	0.579 ± 0.108
TransMIL [19]	0.585 ± 0.137
Lauren Classification	0.598 ± 0.084
Pathologic Grade	0.581 ± 0.076
Age	0.459 ± 0.077

Based on the risk scores generated by TC_model, we divided the cases into two groups at the median risk score for each cross-validation fold. Log-rank tests were significant in 3 out of 4 folds (two-sided log-rank tests p-value; 0.287 (Fold 0), 0.007 (Fold 1), 0.007 (Fold 2), 0.001 (Fold 3)).

Using the validation dataset Fold 3, which had the lowest p-value in log-rank tests, we calculated the IG scores for all patches. We then examined the correlation between the total number of patches with high IG scores (top 10%) or low IG scores (bottom 10%) and the model's risk score. A strong correlation was found between the number of low IG score patches and the model's risk score, indicating that patients with a higher number of low IG score patches had better survival outcomes (Fig. 2).

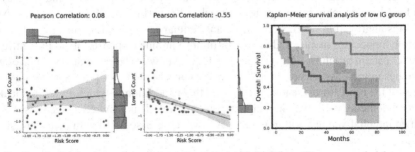

Fig. 2. Correlation between the number of patches with high/low IG scores and risk score of TC_model, and patient prognosis prediction by the number of patches with low IG scores.

Leiden clustering was performed using cell and tissue features on the Fold 3 validation dataset to annotate each patch. Approximately half of the patches were found to belong to Cluster 7. Further clustering within Cluster 7 revealed that patches in the low IG group predominantly belonged to subcluster 5. Comprehensive exploration indicated that a higher number of patches in subcluster 0, or a combination of subclusters 0 and 5, were significantly associated with better patient survival outcomes (log-rank tests, p-values 0.027 and 0.024, respectively). Subclusters 0 and 5 contained many patches capturing TLS, suggesting that the number of TLSs in a sample positively impacts patient prognosis (Fig. 3). We examined low IG score patches in the Fold 1 and 2 validation dataset, confirming TLS enrichment in Fold 2's low IG score patches.

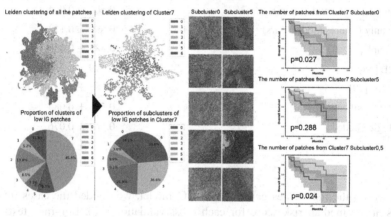

Fig. 3. Left) Leiden clustering of the patches in Fold 3 and Cluster 7. Pie charts show distribution of low IG score patches across clusters/subclusters. Middle) Sample tile images in Cluster 7 subcluster 0 or 5. Right) Kaplan-Meier analysis stratified based on the number of patches in Cluster 7 in each validation fold. P values were calculated by two-sided log-rank test.

Within the low IG score group, IG scores were calculated for each cell (n = 1,470,002) in subclusters 0 and 5 of Cluster 7. Lymphocytes were the most prevalent cell type (~40%), with immune cells making up over 75% of the total. Regarding the handcrafted cell features by cell type, radial density for lymphocytes and leukocytes was found to be highly important for low-risk patients (Fig. 4). This also suggests lymphocytes aggregation or TLS are important cellular-level features. As TLS is a place where lymphocytes mature and elicit anti-tumor immune responses, it could contribute to better patient prognosis. The presence of TLS is known to be associated with favorable outcomes in various cancers, including gastric cancer [21, 23]. Upon examining the IG scores of the top 1 lowest features, we found that in addition to lymphocytes and leukocytes, endothelial cells exhibited high absolute scores. This may reflect the presence of high endothelial venules within mature TLS, which is associated with better prognosis [21–23].

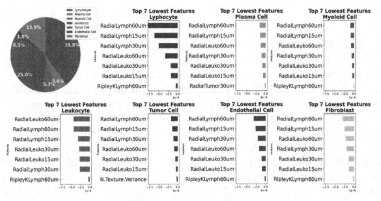

Fig. 4. Cell type distribution in low IG score patches in Cluster 7 subclusters 0 or 5. Bar graphs show the top 7 lowest features and their IG scores among in each cell type. Radial/Ripley K{cell1}{r} of {cell2}: radial density/ripley K of {cell1} within a {r} μm radius around {cell2}. N. Texture Variance: mean value of nuclear difference of variance in Haralick feature.

5 Conclusion

We propose a GNN model combining tissue and cell-level features to provide highly interpretable survival predictions for clinicians. It outperforms commonly used MIL methods in this task, demonstrating the importance of integrating both tissue and cell-level features. Furthermore, we implemented a two-step analysis, where we first screen for important regions at the tissue level and then conduct detailed cell-level analysis in those regions. By using clustering to interpret these critical regions, we were able to identify clusters of TLS, enhancing the biological relevance of our findings. The findings from our work are biologically relevant, as many low-risk patches identified by the model correspond to TLS, which previous studies [21, 24] have shown to be associated with better prognosis.

As a future direction, we will develop a model that extracts the cancerous regions from the entire tissue to minimize human effort and achieve full automation in the workflow.

Prospect of Application. Our model reveals spatial patterns of tissues and cells associated with prognosis, providing biologically meaningful insights for survival prediction. By leveraging this model, it is possible to offer clinically relevant feedback at both tissue and cell levels. Our framework is versatile and can be applied across different cancer types, facilitating the discovery of novel biomarkers to guide personalized treatment strategies.

Acknowledgments. This study was supported by JSPS KAKENHI Grant-in-Aid for Scientific Research (B) under grant number 21H03836 to D.K., and the AMED Practical Research for Innovative Cancer Control under grant number JP 23ck0106873, and 24ck0106904 to S.I.

Disclosure of Interests. The authors declare no competing interests.

References

1. Salahuddin, Z., Woodruff, H.C., Chatterjee, A., Lambin, P.: Transparency of deep neural networks for medical image analysis: a review of interpretability methods. Comput. Biol. Med. **140**, 105111 (2022). https://doi.org/10.1016/j.compbiomed.2021.105111
2. Rymarczyk, D., Pardyl, A., Kraus, J., Kaczyńska, A., Skomorowski, M., Zieliński, B.: ProtoMIL: multiple instance learning with prototypical parts for whole-slide image classification (2022). http://arxiv.org/abs/2108.10612. https://doi.org/10.48550/arXiv.2108.10612
3. Wang, Y., Zhang, T., Guo, X., Shen, Z.: Gradient based feature attribution in explainable AI: a technical review. http://arxiv.org/abs/2403.10415 (2024)
4. Jain, S., Wallace, B.C.: Attention is not Explanation. http://arxiv.org/abs/1902.10186 (2019)
5. Wang, Z., et al.: Hierarchical graph pathomic network for progression free survival prediction. In: de Bruijne, M., et al. (eds.) MICCAI 2021. LNCS, vol. 12908, pp. 227–237. Springer, Cham (2021). https://doi.org/10.1007/978-3-030-87237-3_22
6. Lee, Y., et al.: Derivation of prognostic contextual histopathological features from whole-slide images of tumours via graph deep learning. Nat. Biomed. Eng., 1–15 (2022). https://doi.org/10.1038/s41551-022-00923-0
7. Li, Z., Jiang, Y., Liu, L., Xia, Y., Li, R.: Single-cell spatial analysis of histopathology images for survival prediction via graph attention network. In: Wu, S., Shabestari, B., Xing, L. (eds.) Applications of Medical Artificial Intelligence, LNCS, vol. 14313, pp. 114–124. Springer, Cham (2024). https://doi.org/10.1007/978-3-031-47076-9_12
8. Komura, D., et al.: Restaining-based annotation for cancer histology segmentation to overcome annotation-related limitations among pathologists. Patterns **4**, 100688 (2023). https://doi.org/10.1016/j.patter.2023.100688
9. Graham, S., et al.: Hover-Net: simultaneous segmentation and classification of nuclei in multi-tissue histology images. Med. Image Anal. **58**, 101563 (2019). https://doi.org/10.1016/j.media.2019.101563
10. Page, D.B., et al.: Spatial analyses of immune cell infiltration in cancer: current methods and future directions: a report of the international immuno-oncology biomarker working group on breast cancer. J. Pathol. **260**, 514–532 (2023). https://doi.org/10.1002/path.6165
11. Amgad, M., et al.: A population-level digital histologic biomarker for enhanced prognosis of invasive breast cancer. Nat. Med. **30**, 85–97 (2024). https://doi.org/10.1038/s41591-023-02643-7
12. Komura, D., et al.: Universal encoding of pan-cancer histology by deep texture representations. Cell Rep. **38**, 110424 (2022). https://doi.org/10.1016/j.celrep.2022.110424
13. Veličković, P., Cucurull, G., Casanova, A., Romero, A., Liò, P., Bengio, Y.: Graph attention networks (2018). http://arxiv.org/abs/1710.10903. https://doi.org/10.48550/arXiv.1710.10903
14. Li, Y., Tarlow, D., Brockschmidt, M., Zemel, R.: Gated graph sequence neural networks (2017). http://arxiv.org/abs/1511.05493. https://doi.org/10.48550/arXiv.1511.05493
15. Morris, C., et al.: Weisfeiler and leman go neural: higher-order graph neural networks (2021). http://arxiv.org/abs/1810.02244. https://doi.org/10.48550/arXiv.1810.02244
16. Zadeh, S.G., Schmid, M.: Bias in cross-entropy-based training of deep survival networks. IEEE Trans. Pattern Anal. Mach. Intell. **43**, 3126–3137 (2021). https://doi.org/10.1109/TPAMI.2020.2979450
17. Sundararajan, M., Taly, A., Yan, Q.: Axiomatic attribution for deep networks (2017). http://arxiv.org/abs/1703.01365. https://doi.org/10.48550/arXiv.1703.01365
18. Ilse, M., Tomczak, J., Welling, M.: Attention-based deep multiple instance learning. In: Proceedings of the 35th International Conference on Machine Learning, pp. 2127–2136. PMLR (2018)

19. Shao, Z., et al.: TransMIL: transformer based correlated multiple instance learning for whole slide image classification (2021). http://arxiv.org/abs/2106.00908. https://doi.org/10.48550/arXiv.2106.00908
20. Pölsterl, S.: Scikit-survival: a library for time-to-event analysis built on top of scikit-learn. J. Mach. Learn. Res. **21**, 1–6 (2020)
21. Kemi, N., et al.: Tertiary lymphoid structures and gastric cancer prognosis. APMIS **131**, 19–25 (2023). https://doi.org/10.1111/apm.13277
22. Jacquelot, N., Tellier, J., Sl, N., Gt, B.: Tertiary lymphoid structures and B lymphocytes in cancer prognosis and response to immunotherapies. Oncoimmunology **10**, 1900508 (2021). https://doi.org/10.1080/2162402X.2021.1900508
23. Vanhersecke, L., et al.: Mature tertiary lymphoid structures predict immune checkpoint inhibitor efficacy in solid tumors independently of PD-L1 expression. Nat. Cancer. **2**, 794–802 (2021). https://doi.org/10.1038/s43018-021-00232-6
24. He, W., et al.: The high level of tertiary lymphoid structure is correlated with superior survival in patients with advanced gastric cancer. Front. Oncol. **10**, 980 (2020). https://doi.org/10.3389/fonc.2020.00980

Targeted Visual Prompting for Medical Visual Question Answering

Sergio Tascon-Morales$^{(\boxtimes)}$, Pablo Márquez-Neila, and Raphael Sznitman

University of Bern, Bern, Switzerland
{sergio.tasconmorales,pablo.marquez,raphael.sznitman}@unibe.ch

Abstract. With growing interest in recent years, medical visual question answering (Med-VQA) has rapidly evolved, with multimodal large language models (MLLMs) emerging as an alternative to classical model architectures. Specifically, their ability to add visual information to the input of pre-trained LLMs brings new capabilities for image interpretation. However, simple visual errors cast doubt on the actual visual understanding abilities of these models. To address this, region-based questions have been proposed as a means to assess and enhance actual visual understanding through compositional evaluation. To combine these two perspectives, this paper introduces targeted visual prompting to equip MLLMs with region-based questioning capabilities. By presenting the model with both the isolated region and the region in its context in a customized visual prompt, we show the effectiveness of our method across multiple datasets while comparing it to several baseline models. Our code and data are available at https://github.com/sergiotasconmorales/locvqallm.

Keywords: VQA · Localized Questions · Multimodal Large Language Model · Vision Transformer

1 Introduction

Visual Question Answering (VQA) is centered on developing models capable of answering questions about specific images [2]. This task is particularly challenging within the medical domain due to factors such as a scarcity of annotated data [7,11], the wide variety of imaging modalities and anatomical regions [5], as well as the unique characteristics of medical images and terminology, all of which necessitate specialized expertise [7,25]. Furthermore, approaches that leverage the detection of natural objects, which have significantly improved performance in the analysis of natural images [1], are less straightforward when applied to medical imagery [5].

Historically, models for Medical VQA (Med-VQA) treated visual and textual information independently, later merging these features through various fusion techniques. This composite data would then be input into a classifier to determine the most probable answer. However, recent developments in transformer-based models [21], including advancements in Large Language Models (LLMs),

S. Wu et al. (Eds.): AMAI 2024, LNCS 15384, pp. 64–73, 2025.
https://doi.org/10.1007/978-3-031-82007-6_7

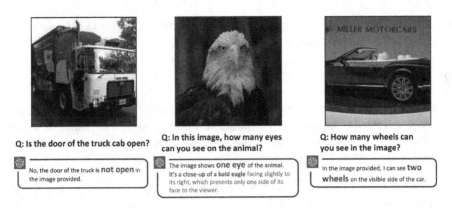

Fig. 1. Examples of visual understanding failures using GPT-4V for the VQA task (Examples taken from [18]).

have led to a notable shift in VQA strategies. These advancements have paved the way for the adoption of multimodal LLMs (MLLMs) that integrate both visual and textual data more seamlessly, a trend that is emerging in both general [18,24,26] and Med-VQA [14,28] applications.

Despite the remarkable adoption of MLLMs, recent research has raised concerns about the quality of their visual capabilities (Fig. 1). This issue primarily arises from the pre-training process of the visual component, which typically relies on models like CLIP [12]. Surprisingly, MLLMs can perceive certain visually distinct images as similar, a phenomenon that human observers readily recognize as a visual error [18]. These visual understanding failures were also observed in VQA models before the widespread adoption of MLLMs [4,6,13,15].

To detect such failures and enhance explainability in the visual component of Med-VQA, the work in [17] proposes a novel approach using the formulation of *localized questions* [17]. These questions allow fine-grained probing of images by focusing on user-defined regions rather than the entire image and facilitate a *compositional evaluation*. To enable such localized questions, the region to query is encoded and directly integrated into the attention mechanism of the model. Other proposed strategies include providing the model with a restricted region of the image [16] or relying on the language component of the VQA model to interpret region coordinates directly included in the question [22]. Yet, due to their design focused on traditional architectures, these methods fail to benefit MLLMs in Med-VQA. Other traditional [10] and MLLM-based methods [3,27] rely on object detectors, limiting their applicability to medical images.

To overcome these challenges and enable localized questions in MLLMs in Med-VQA, we introduce *Targeted Visual Prompting*. By carefully designing a prompt that provides both global and local visual tokens relative to the region of interest defined by the user, our method allows the full advantage of the MLLM to enhance the performance of the VQA model. To validate the effectiveness of our method, we conduct exhaustive experiments across multiple datasets. Our results demonstrate clear performance benefits compared to previously proposed methods, all achieved without introducing additional parameters to the model.

2   Method

A VQA model with parameters $\boldsymbol{\theta}$ generates an answer $\hat{a}$ when given an input image $\mathbf{x} \in \mathbb{R}^{H \times W \times C}$ and a related question represented as a sequence of words, $\mathbf{q}$. In its most general form, this process can be described as a function Ψ_{VQA}, parameterized by $\boldsymbol{\theta}$, that is applied on the image-question pair,

$$\hat{a} = \Psi_{\text{VQA}}(\mathbf{x}, \mathbf{q}; \boldsymbol{\theta}). \tag{1}$$

In practice, this model's output has traditionally been a distribution over a set of N candidate answers $\{a_1, a_2, ..., a_N\}$ set beforehand.

In this work, however, we choose the answer of the VQA to be generated by an LLM in an auto-regressive manner until the end-of-sentence (EOS) token is produced. To make the LLM multimodal, we adopt the widely used approach of projecting visual embeddings onto the input space of the LLM [8, 20, 23] and express this as,

$$\hat{a} = \Psi_{\text{LLM}}(\Psi_{\text{Vis}}(\mathbf{x}, \boldsymbol{\theta}_{\text{Vis}})\mathbf{W}^{\text{proj}}, \mathbf{q}; \boldsymbol{\theta}_{\text{LLM}}), \tag{2}$$

where Ψ_{Vis} refers to the visual encoder with parameters $\boldsymbol{\theta}_{\text{Vis}}$, and $\mathbf{W}^{\text{proj}}$ denotes the learnable parameters of the projection layer. Although not explicitly formalized, it is implied that the answer is generated in an auto-regressive fashion, meaning that the next word in the answer depends on the previously predicted words.

To expand the model's capability to handle localized questions, we propose here a dedicated targeted visual prompt that allows two perspectives of the image to be encoded: one containing only the region of the image and the other containing the region in context.

The targeted visual prompt consists of five components: (1) comprises model instruction, denoted as $\mathbf{w}_{\text{instr}}$; (2) the visual context represented by the image with the region drawn on it, $\mathbf{x}_r$; (3) $\mathbf{w}_{\text{det}}$ contains a textual prefix for the region; (4) the cropped region $\mathbf{r}$; and (5) $\mathbf{w}_q$ includes the question $\mathbf{q}$. Text-containing parts of the prompt undergo tokenization and embedding, while the visual components are processed by a visual encoder and then projected into the input space of the LLM. Subsequently, the results are concatenated and processed by the LLM, resulting in the generation of an answer. To handle global questions, the entire image is assigned to $\mathbf{r}$. We illustrate our model in Fig. 2 and summarize the computation of the answer as,

$$\hat{a} = \Psi_{\text{LLM}}(\mathbf{w}_{\text{instr}}, \Psi_{\text{Vis}}(\mathbf{x}_r, \boldsymbol{\theta}_{\text{Vis}})\mathbf{W}^{\text{proj}}_{\mathbf{x}_r}, \mathbf{w}_{\text{det}}, \Psi_{\text{Vis}}(\mathbf{r}, \boldsymbol{\theta}_{\text{Vis}})\mathbf{W}^{\text{proj}}_{\mathbf{r}}, \mathbf{w}_q; \boldsymbol{\theta}_{\text{LLM}}). \tag{3}$$

To handle questions about the entire image, both $\mathbf{x}_r$ and $\mathbf{r}$ correspond to the original image.

Training. As in [23], our model is trained using the original auto-regressive training loss of the LLM. The loss function is the standard negative log-likelihood

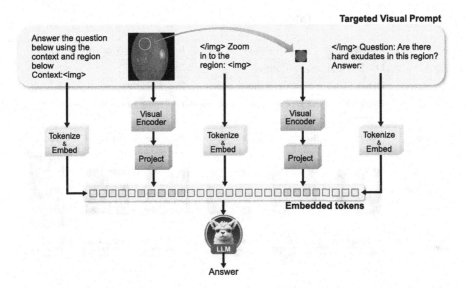

Fig. 2. Our customized targeted visual prompt is created by providing the model with the region in context, as well as an isolated version of the region. Visual tokens are projected to the input space of the LLM and concatenated with the instruction tokens.

accumulated over all time steps for predicting the correct next token. For a ground truth answer of length T, this loss is expressed as,

$$\mathcal{L}(\boldsymbol{\theta}) = -\sum_{t=1}^{T} \log p_{\theta}(a^t | \mathbf{x}, \mathbf{w}, a^{1:t-1}; \boldsymbol{\theta}), \tag{4}$$

where $\mathbf{x}$ and $\mathbf{w}$ denote the visual and textual elements, respectively, and $\mathbf{a} = \{a_1, a_2, ..., a_T\}$ is the ground truth answer.

3   Experiments and Results

Datasets: To evaluate our method, we make use of several publically available datasets [17]: (1) DME-VQA: contains questions on diabetic muscular edema (DME) risk grade and about the presence of biomarkers in the entire image or specific regions. (2) RIS-VQA: contains images from the DaVinci robot during gastrointestinal surgery and questions related to surgical instruments. (3) INSEGCAT-VQA: contains frames from cataract surgery videos and questions about instruments used in this type of surgery. A summary of these is shown in Table 1. For all datasets, we use the same partitioning as in [17].

Table 1. Dataset parameters.

Dataset	Modality	# images	# QA-pairs
DME-VQA	Fundus	679	13470
RIS-VQA	Gastrointestinal	2978	32562
INSEGCAT-VQA	Cataract surgery	4647	39008

Baseline	No mask	Region in text	Draw region	Context only	Crop region	LocAtt
Input Image(s)						
Input Question	Are there hard exudates in this region?	Are there hard exudates in the ellipse contained in the bounding box (2 0 0, 8 1, 4 1 6, 2 2 4)	Are there hard exudates in this region?	Are there hard exudates in this region?	Are there hard exudates in this region?	Are there hard exudates in this region?

Fig. 3. Example input images and questions for evaluated baselines. In the baseline "Region in text," the digits are separated to provide a fair scenario to the LLM.

Baselines: We benchmark our method against multiple baselines, which are exemplified in Fig. 3. In **No mask**, the model receives no information about the location of the region; in **Region in text**, the region is specified in the question; in **Draw region**, the region is marked on top of the image. In **Context only**, the model only sees the context, but not the contents of the region; in **Crop region**, the model receives no context; finally, in **LocAtt** [17], the model has access to the image, as well as a binary image representing the region. For these baselines, the visual prompt given to the model is: *"Answer the question below using the context below Context: <Img><Image></Img>Question : <Question>Answer:"*

Implementation Details: We use R2GenGPT [23] as base MLLM, adapting it from the task of radiology report generation to VQA. We use a pre-trained Swin Transformer [9] as visual encoder and Llama 2 7B [19] as LLM, initialized with its official weights. Different from to R2GenGPT, we finetune all modules, including the LLM, end-to-end. We train all our models for 15 epochs, with a batch size of 8 and learning rate of 1e−4, with the AdamW optimizer and a cosine annealing scheduler with minimum learning rate 1e−6. For the text generation, we use a repetition penalty of 2.0 and a length penalty of −1.0. Our implementation uses PyTorch 2.0.1 and two Nvidia A100 cards with 80 GB of memory each.

3.1 Results

Table 2 summarizes our results on the DME-VQA, RIS-VQA, and INSEGCAT-VQA datasets. The accuracy and F1 score are reported for all datasets. Notably,

Table 2. Accuracy and F1 score comparison to SOTA approaches on the DME-VQA, RIS-VQA and INSEGCAT-VQA datasets. For the DME-VQA dataset only localized questions are considered. *This result corresponds to a different architecture, but we include it for completeness.

Dataset	Method	Accuracy (%)	F1 score (%)
DME-VQA	No Mask	57.32	57.32
	Region in Text [22]	62.12	63.59
	Crop Region [16]	86.52	87.26
	Draw Region	86.86	86.85
	Context Only	88.07	88.45
	Ours	**90.30**	**90.22**
	LocAtt [17]*	84.2	85.79
RIS-VQA	No Mask	50.00	50.00
	Region in Text [22]	64.81	65.39
	Crop Region [16]	85.50	85.64
	Draw Region	91.30	91.43
	Context Only	91.77	91.81
	Ours	**92.60**	**92.54**
	LocAtt [17]*	82.73	86.15
INSEGCAT-VQA	No Mask	50.00	50.00
	Region in Text [22]	73.51	74.55
	Crop Region [16]	90.91	90.93
	Draw Region	95.44	95.43
	Context Only	95.19	95.17
	Ours	**95.51**	**95.47**
	LocAtt [17]*	88.13	90.14

our method consistently outperforms all evaluated baselines across all datasets, underscoring the efficacy of targeted visual prompting in enhancing MLLMs with localized question capabilities.

In the case of the DME-VQA and RIS-VQA datasets, we observe that the performance of *context only* surpasses that of *crop region*. At first glance, this suggests that the context holds more relevance than the specific contents of the region. However, this behavior is likely influenced by spurious correlations between region sizes/locations, and the corresponding answers. For instance, in DME-VQA, images with a high amount of biomarkers often feature smaller regions associated with negative answers. Another reason for this behavior is that in many cases the context provides more evidence, in terms of pixel count, to answer the question, as compared to the region. For instance, in RIS-VQA, the tool can often be determined from its body without considering the tip.

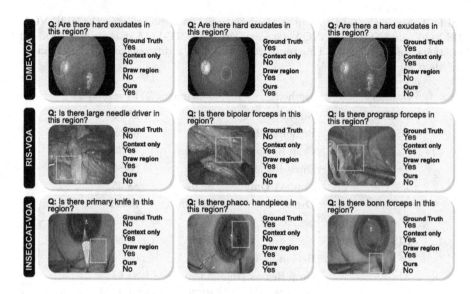

Fig. 4. Qualitative examples on the DME-VQA (first row), RIS-VQA (second row), and INSEGCAT-VQA (third row) datasets.

Notably, the *region in text* baseline exhibits poor performance. Given the use of a powerful LLM in the pipeline, higher performance might be expected. Different variations were explored for this baseline, including not separating the coordinate digits or replacing coordinate digits with words, but performance did not improve. We hypothesize that the model fails to correctly map location information from the text to the image, which can be at least partly attributed to using a ViT to embed the image.

We provide qualitative example results in Fig. 4. The first column exemplifies cases where our method demonstrates robustness to subtle evidence (small biomarkers), correlations (surgical suture is usually close to the needle driver), and borderline cases (evidence close to the region border). The second column highlights the weaknesses of *context only* when the context fails to provide enough evidence for the answer. Finally, the third column shows errors made by our model in tricky cases (subtle or ambiguous evidence in the region).

Figure 5 shows error maps by region location for the DME-VQA and INSEGCAT-VQA datasets and for the four strongest baselines. On the left side of the plot, the locations of actual positives and negatives are illustrated. For the INSEGCAT-VQA dataset, this visualization reveals a location bias that other baselines without access to the region or the context may be exploiting. Due to the nature of the images (cataract surgery) and questions, regions with positive answers tend to cluster in a specific area. This, coupled with the dissimilarity of objects mentioned in the questions, explains why a baseline like *crop region* achieves relatively high performance on this dataset compared to the other two datasets (see Table 2). Similarly, in the case of DME-VQA, it becomes evident

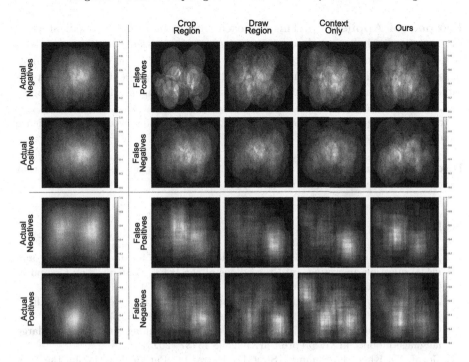

Fig. 5. Error analysis by region location for the four strongest baselines. The maps are obtained by adding binary masks representing the regions for all QA pairs in each category and then normalizing. **Top:** DME-VQA dataset. **Bottom:** INSEGCAT-VQA dataset.

that the lack of context in *crop region* results in lower sensitivity, highlighting the significance of context even when the isolated region should theoretically provide sufficient evidence. Figure 5 also demonstrates that *draw region* and *context only* exhibit marked clusters of false positives and negatives in INSEGCAT-VQA, potentially indicating the utilization of location biases. In contrast, our method produces a more evenly distributed location for both types of errors.

4   Conclusions

In this work, we introduced a novel approach to enable localized questions in multimodal LLMs for the tasks of VQA. Our proposed approach involves the utilization of targeted visual prompting, granting the model access not only to the region and its context within the image but also to an isolated version of the region. Doing so allows two perspectives to be encoded in the prompt and more fine-grained information to be leveraged. Our approach demonstrates enhanced performance across all evaluated datasets compared to various baselines. Future works include extending the methodology to accommodate multiple images and enabling the use of comparison questions.

Prospect of Application: This approach aims to be useful for medical assistants/chatbots that can help doctors assess specific parts of an image that look suspicious. By providing a second opinion, it can improve the accuracy of diagnoses. Additionally, this technology could help medical students learn and reinforce medical concepts by enabling a more modular analysis of medical images.

Acknowledgements. This work was partially funded by the Swiss National Science Foundation through grant 191983.

Disclosure of Interests. The authors have no competing interests to declare that are relevant to the content of this article.

References

1. Anderson, P., et al.: Bottom-up and top-down attention for image captioning and visual question answering. In: Proceedings of the IEEE Conference on Computer Vision and Pattern Recognition, pp. 6077–6086 (2018)
2. Antol, S., et al.: VQA: visual question answering. In: Proceedings of the IEEE International Conference on Computer Vision, pp. 2425–2433 (2015)
3. Chen, C., et al.: Position-enhanced visual instruction tuning for multimodal large language models. arXiv preprint arXiv:2308.13437 (2023)
4. Goyal, Y., Khot, T., Summers-Stay, D., Batra, D., Parikh, D.: Making the V in VQA matter: elevating the role of image understanding in visual question answering. In: Proceedings of the IEEE Conference on Computer Vision and Pattern Recognition, pp. 6904–6913 (2017)
5. Gupta, D., Suman, S., Ekbal, A.: Hierarchical deep multi-modal network for medical visual question answering. Expert Syst. Appl. **164**, 113993 (2021)
6. Hudson, D.A., Manning, C.D.: GQA: a new dataset for compositional question answering over real-world images. arXiv preprint arXiv:1902.09506 (2019). **3**(8)
7. Liu, F., Peng, Y., Rosen, M.P.: An effective deep transfer learning and information fusion framework for medical visual question answering. In: Crestani, F., et al. (eds.) CLEF 2019. LNCS, vol. 11696, pp. 238–247. Springer, Cham (2019). https://doi.org/10.1007/978-3-030-28577-7_20
8. Liu, H., Li, C., Wu, Q., Lee, Y.J.: Visual instruction tuning. arXiv preprint arXiv:2304.08485 (2023)
9. Liu, Z., et al.: Swin transformer: hierarchical vision transformer using shifted windows. In: Proceedings of the IEEE/CVF International Conference on Computer Vision, pp. 10012–10022 (2021)
10. Mani, A., Yoo, N., Hinthorn, W., Russakovsky, O.: Point and ask: incorporating pointing into visual question answering. arXiv preprint arXiv:2011.13681 (2020)
11. Nguyen, B.D., Do, T.-T., Nguyen, B.X., Do, T., Tjiputra, E., Tran, Q.D.: Overcoming data limitation in medical visual question answering. In: Shen, D., et al. (eds.) MICCAI 2019. LNCS, vol. 11767, pp. 522–530. Springer, Cham (2019). https://doi.org/10.1007/978-3-030-32251-9_57
12. Radford, A., et al.: Learning transferable visual models from natural language supervision. In: International Conference on Machine Learning, pp. 8748–8763. PMLR (2021)

13. Ribeiro, M.T., Guestrin, C., Singh, S.: Are red roses red? Evaluating consistency of question-answering models. In: Proceedings of the 57th Annual Meeting of the Association for Computational Linguistics, pp. 6174–6184 (2019)
14. Seenivasan, L., Islam, M., Kannan, G., Ren, H.: SurgicalGPT: end-to-end language-vision GPT for visual question answering in surgery. arXiv preprint arXiv:2304.09974 (2023)
15. Selvaraju, R.R., et al.: Squinting at VQA models: introspecting VQA models with sub-questions. In: Proceedings of the IEEE/CVF Conference on Computer Vision and Pattern Recognition, pp. 10003–10011 (2020)
16. Tascon-Morales, S., Márquez-Neila, P., Sznitman, R.: Consistency-preserving visual question answering in medical imaging. In: Wang, L., Dou, Q., Fletcher, P.T., Speidel, S., Li, S. (eds.) MICCAI 2022, Part VIII. LNCS, vol. 13438, pp. 386–395. Springer, Cham (2022). https://doi.org/10.1007/978-3-031-16452-1_37
17. Tascon-Morales, S., Márquez-Neila, P., Sznitman, R.: Localized questions in medical visual question answering. In: Greenspan, H., et al. (eds.) MICCAI 2023. LNCS, vol. 14221, pp. 361–370. Springer, Cham (2023). https://doi.org/10.1007/978-3-031-43895-0_34
18. Tong, S., Liu, Z., Zhai, Y., Ma, Y., LeCun, Y., Xie, S.: Eyes wide shut? Exploring the visual shortcomings of multimodal LLMs. arXiv preprint arXiv:2401.06209 (2024)
19. Touvron, H., et al.: Llama 2: open foundation and fine-tuned chat models. arXiv preprint arXiv:2307.09288 (2023)
20. Tsimpoukelli, M., Menick, J.L., Cabi, S., Eslami, S., Vinyals, O., Hill, F.: Multimodal few-shot learning with frozen language models. Adv. Neural. Inf. Process. Syst. **34**, 200–212 (2021)
21. Vaswani, A., et al.: Attention is all you need. Adv. Neural Inf. Process. Syst. **30** (2017)
22. Vu, M.H., Löfstedt, T., Nyholm, T., Sznitman, R.: A question-centric model for visual question answering in medical imaging. IEEE Trans. Med. Imaging **39**(9), 2856–2868 (2020)
23. Wang, Z., Liu, L., Wang, L., Zhou, L.: R2GenGPT: radiology report generation with frozen LLMs. Meta-Radiology **1**(3), 100033 (2023)
24. Yin, S., et al.: A survey on multimodal large language models. arXiv preprint arXiv:2306.13549 (2023)
25. Zhan, L.M., Liu, B., Fan, L., Chen, J., Wu, X.M.: Medical visual question answering via conditional reasoning. In: Proceedings of the 28th ACM International Conference on Multimedia, pp. 2345–2354 (2020)
26. Zhang, D., et al.: MM-LLMs: recent advances in multimodal large language models. arXiv preprint arXiv:2401.13601 (2024)
27. Zhang, S., et al.: GPT4RoI: instruction tuning large language model on region-of-interest. arXiv preprint arXiv:2307.03601 (2023)
28. Zhang, X., et al.: PMC-VQA: visual instruction tuning for medical visual question answering. arXiv preprint arXiv:2305.10415 (2023)

Deep Learning for Resolving 3D Microstructural Changes in the Fibrotic Liver

William M. Laprade[1,2(✉)], Behnaz Pirzamanebin[2,3], Rajmund Mokso[2,4], Julia Nilsson[5,6], Vedrana A. Dahl[1,2], Anders B. Dahl[1,2], Dan Holmberg[6,7,8], and Anja Schmidt-Christensen[6,8]

[1] Department of Applied Mathematics and Computer Science, Technical University of Denmark, Kgs. Lyngby, Denmark
willap@dtu.dk
[2] Quantification of Imaging Data from MAX IV, DTU, Kongens Lyngby, Denmark
[3] Department of Statistics, Lund University, Lund, Sweden
behnaz.pirzamanbein@stat.lu.se
[4] Department of Physics, Technical University of Denmark, Kgs. Lyngby, Denmark
[5] Laboratory Medicine, University of California, San Francisco, San Francisco, USA
[6] Department of Experimental Medical Sciences, Lund University, Malmö, Sweden
[7] Department of Medical Biosciences, Umeå University, Umeå, Sweden
[8] Lund University Diabetes Center, Lund University, Malmö, Sweden

Abstract. Portal hypertension, a life-threatening complication of cirrhosis, is largely triggered by increased intrahepatic vascular resistance. Fibrosis, regenerative nodule formation, intrahepatic angiogenisis and sinusoidal remodelling are classical mechanisms that account for increased intrahepatic vascular resistance in cirrhosis. Our study leverages high-resolution 3D synchrotron radiation-based microtomography and a deep learning-based segmentation approach to investigate these microstructural changes in the liver. By employing a multi-planar U-Net model, trained using annotated tomographic slices sourced from our developed online learning tool, we effectively quantify critical vascular parameters such as sinusoid proportions, local thickness, and connectivity. These insights advance our understanding of liver microarchitecture and also allows correlating vascular parameters to inflammation and fibrosis severity. Understanding and quantifying these microstructural changes is essential to be able to predict the transition from seemingly benign conditions like steatosis or mild inflammation to severe fibrosis and cirrhosis.

Keywords: Browser-based segmentation tool · 3D synchrotron x-ray microtomography · Liver sinusoidal network

1 Introduction

Liver disease is a significant global health burden, causing over two million deaths annually. Advanced fibrosis, a critical phase of liver disease, substantially

---

W. M. Laprade and B. Pirzamanebin—These authors contributed equally to this work.

© The Author(s), under exclusive license to Springer Nature Switzerland AG 2025
S. Wu et al. (Eds.): AMAI 2024, LNCS 15384, pp. 74–84, 2025.
https://doi.org/10.1007/978-3-031-82007-6_8

increases mortality risk and is closely linked with a fourfold increase in cardio-vascular events [5]. Nearly 90% of individuals diagnosed with cirrhosis eventually develop portal hypertension, primarily due to increased vascular resistance within the liver [9]. This resistance is partly attributed to the remodeling of sinusoids by hepatic stellate cells, which create a stiff, collagen-rich matrix characteristic of fibrosis [19,21]. Despite significant progress in understanding liver fibrosis at the molecular level, translating this knowledge into clinical practice has been challenging. A comprehensive understanding of the evolving pathological changes and detailed anatomical data on vascular and cellular adaptations remains elusive.

Traditional 2D histological methods are inadequate for capturing the complex quantitative nuances of cellular and tissue architecture, necessitating advanced large-field, high-resolution 3D imaging techniques. To address this challenges, we employed the NIF mouse model that spontaneously develops chronic liver inflammation and fibrosis [6,7,18], combined with Synchrotron Radiation x-ray micro-Computed Tomography (SRμCT). SRμCT technique provides superior image quality and submicron resolution [22], allowing us to explore 3D microstructural changes during fibrosis progression. The technique has proven its efficacy in 3D visualization, capturing hepatic proliferative bile ductules [13] microvascular alterations at the sinusoidal and capillary scale [27,28], and distinguishing pathological tissues [17].

Our study introduces a novel analysis pipeline for liver fibrosis analysis using deep learning with high-resolution SRμCT, significantly enhancing the visualization and quantification of fibrotic changes.

High-Resolution Imaging: Our SRμCT images surpass previous works in quality, providing higher cellular resolution that makes inflammatory cells in the liver visible which has previously not been done using μCT. This capability allows us to quantify the 3D structural differences between lesion and unaffected regions in the same scan and enables the visibility of smaller, more complex structures within the liver – structures that were unresolvable in previous works [27].

Segmentation Tool: We have developed a browser-based annotation tool[1] that utilizes deep learning [23] to facilitate efficient data labeling and image segmentation, with necessary overlays to allow visual inspection and ensure segmentation quality [23]. The tool utilizes a 2D multi-planar U-Net for image segmentation, chosen for its faster training speed over a typical 3D U-Net, in order to get quick feedback during use. U-Net and its many variants (e.g. [12,29]) are widely used for the segmentation of biological data [4,24]. It has become a standard in microscopy image segmentation as well, where it has been applied to tasks such as 3D organelle segmentation [10] and synaptic cleft segmentation [11], among others [2]. Specifically, the multi-planar U-Net [20] has also previously been shown to be effective for microscopy segmentation with small, sparsely annotated datasets [15].

---

[1] https://github.com/laprade117/interactive-unet.

Quantitative 3D Analysis: Unlike previous studies that focused on larger vessels or used simple thresholding techniques for microvasculature analysis, our method quantifies the 3D structure of fibrotic lesions. We measure lesion size and assess adaptive changes in the sinusoid network following injury and fibrosis, providing a detailed understanding of the microstructural disruptions [15,20].

We segment the SRµCT scans into distinct volumes, differentiating between sinusoid and non-sinusoidal, vessel and non-vessel, and lesion and unaffected regions. We then visually and quantitatively analyze disrupted sinusoidal networks and vascular complexities in fibrotic livers, demonstrating significant changes that potentially contribute to sinusoidal hypertension and liver damage (Fig. 1). Our study addresses the significant gaps in current liver fibrosis research but also introduces innovative tools and methodological pipelines that enhance the understanding and management of this severe condition.

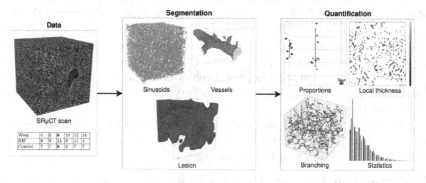

Fig. 1. An overview of our analysis pipeline. We segment our SRµCT scans into three segmentation volumes: sinusoid and non-sinusoid, vessel and non-vessel, and lesion and unaffected regions. We then combine the segmentation volumes and compute quantification measures and statistics. The table in the data block describes the number of scans we have of both NIF and control at different stages of disease. Bold indicates the scans that we investigate in detail in this paper.

2   Data

Mice livers were perfused with PBS via the inferior vena cava, formalin-fixed and paraffin-embedded [7]. 36 tissue blocks, from 4- to 18-weeks old NIF (fibrosis induced) and control mice, were scanned at 2 to 3 randomly selected regions, for a total of 87 image volumes. We include a table in the data block of Fig. 1 for an overview of the collected scans. Following SRµCT image acquisition, liver tissue was sectioned and stained with Hematoxylen & Eosin (H&E) and Picro-Sirius Red (PSR) [7] to differentiate tissue structures and compare with their corresponding synchrotron images. We use all 87 volumes for segmentation, and perform an in-depth quantification of the 8-week (8w) NIF (n = 11) and control mice (n = 8) volumes. After segmentation, we discard 1 NIF and 1 control from the quantification due to large vessels occupying the volumes leaving little information about cellular structure.

3   Image Processing

3.1   Preprocessing

Before training the segmentation models, a series of preprocessing steps were implemented to normalize for imaging variance and artifacts (Fig. 2). To preserve memory, and increase processing speed, a center crop is applied to remove border artifacts followed by $2\times$ binning to achieve a final shape of $(800 \times 800 \times 800)$ with a resolution of 0.65 μm per voxel (Fig. 2a). The bias field is removed by fitting a linear regression model to the pixels in the image and subtracting the resulting prediction. Bright artifacts surrounding the vessels are removed by masking the volumes with a high threshold value, smoothing the mask using a Gaussian filter, and then subtracting it from the original volume (Fig. 2b). Finally, all volumes are mean standardized and squeezed down to the 0–1 range (Fig. 2c, d).

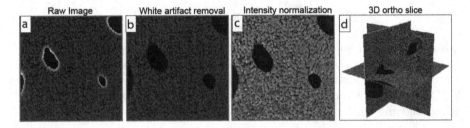

Fig. 2. Data pre-processing steps. 2D presentation of RAW images (a), bias and white artifact corrected (b), final intensity normalized images (c), and ortho-view of pre-processed image stack (d).

3.2   Segmentation

Architecture. For segmentation, we use a standard 2D U-Net trained in a multi-planar fashion by utilizing training samples extracted at random positions and orientations. At inference time, the 2D model predicts along the 3 primary axes and averages the results together for a final 3D prediction in a multi-planar fashion [20].

Browser-Based Segmentation Tool: To facilitate efficient annotation and model training, we utilized an online learning tool that we developed to annotate volumes efficiently. The tool is a simple user interface that displays a randomly oriented and positioned slice to the user. The user then annotates the slice using a paint brush tool before moving on to another slice. At any point a model can be trained within the interface and the resulting predictions can be overlayed on the current slice to guide the user during the annotation process. A weight map is used to ensure that the models are trained only on the pixels that the user annotates, allowing quick sparse annotations to be made in each slice. Once satisfied with the trained model, the user can then use the model to segment the entire volume.

The models are trained using the Adam optimizer with the batch size and learning rate chosen within the tool. During most runs, best results are obtained with batch sizes of 1, 2, and 4 with learning rates 0.001 and 0.0001. To account for any possible class imbalance introduced by the user during the annotation process, a loss function based on Matthew's correlation coefficient [1,3] (MCC) with a second binary cross-entropy (BCE) term is used to provide smoother gradients. The loss is computed via,

$$\text{MCC} = \frac{(\text{TP} \cdot \text{TN}) - (\text{FP} \cdot \text{FN})}{\sqrt{(\text{TP}+\text{FP})(\text{TP}+\text{FN})(\text{TN}+\text{FP})(\text{TN}+\text{FN})}}$$

$$\text{BCE} = -\frac{1}{N} \sum_{i=0}^{N} y_i \log(\hat{y}_i) + (1 - y_i)(1 - \log(\hat{y}_i))$$

$$L = \text{MCC} + \text{CE}$$

and averaged over each class. In the MCC loss, the true positive (TP), true negative (TN), false positive (FP), and false negative (FN) counts are normalized by the number of annotated pixels, and non-annotated pixels are ignored. The MCC function is bounded between -1 and 1 with 1 being a perfect score, 0 being random guessing and -1 being perfectly incorrect.

Segmentation Process: During annotation, 2–4 volumes are selected and the interactive segmentation tool is used to annotate slices from these volumes and train a segmentation model. The model is then used to fully segment those 2–4 volumes. This is repeated on small groups of volumes to both expedite the process and enhance segmentation by leveraging knowledge across more than one volume. A final model is then trained on 40 segmented volumes and used to segment the entire dataset of 80 volumes. Two models are built during this process, one for segmentation of the lesion and unaffected regions and one for segmentation of vessels/sinusoids.

3.3 Postprocessing

Lesion Segmentations: To eliminate line artifacts generated by the multi-view segmentation, Gaussian filtering was applied, followed by a binary dilation. This produces a smooth segmentation that outlines the lesion regions in the volume (Fig. 3a–d).

Vessel/Sinusoid Segmentations: Line artifacts are eliminated via Gaussian smoothing at a low sigma. Given that the sinusoidal diameters range from 7 µm in the periportal and 15 µm in the pericentral area [25,26,28], connected components were applied to remove all disconnected objects that could fit into a sphere with a diameter of 6 µm (Fig. 3e–h). Vessels and sinusoids are separated into two separate masks by viewing the volume from 9 different views. In each

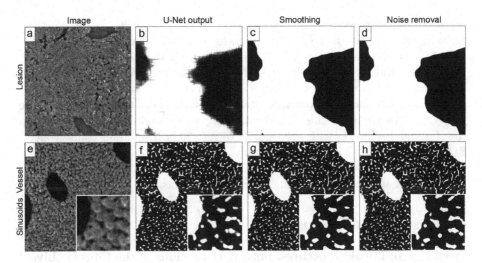

Fig. 3. High-quality structural predictions from NIF (a–d) and control (e–h) liver volumes. (a, e) 2D tomographic slice (input image) and predictions for lesions (b–d) or vascular structures (f–h). U-net raw predictions (b, f) were postprocessed by smoothing (c, g) and noise removal (d, h).

view, the area of the object to which the pixel belongs is calculated, and if it exceeds a specified area threshold, it is designated as a vessel; otherwise, it is assigned a sinusoid label. The final decision on whether the pixel is a vessel or a sinusoid is determined through majority voting.

3.4   Quantification

Proportions: To assess adaptive changes in the sinusoidal network following injury and fibrosis, changes in the sinusoidal network were quantified within control and both lesion and unaffected regions of NIF livers. The proportion of sinusoids in control mice is determined by dividing the number of sinusoid voxels by the total volume, excluding vessels.

To quantify the proportion of sinusoidal volume in NIF mice within lesion regions, the volume of sinusoids within the lesion regions is compared to the total volume of the lesions themselves. A similar approach is applied in unaffected regions.

Local Thickness: The local thickness is computed as, for each voxel within a 3D object, it is assigned the radius of the largest sphere that can fit entirely within the object while encompassing the voxel [8].

Branching: The branch analysis is used to measure the connectivity and length of the sinusoidal network. First, the segmented sinusoid is transformed into a continuous skeleton [16], then a graph-based technique is employed [14] to identify the branches within the skeleton. Branch types were categorized into three types: T_0 for endpoint-to-endpoint branches (isolated branch), T_1 for junction-to-endpoint branches, and T_2 for junction-to-junction branches. Since the types refer to branches, not nodes, it is assumed that each T_0 branch has 2 nodes, T_1 has 1 node, and T_2 has 1 node, plus one additional node for the entire branch it belongs to. To calculate the degree of connectivity, the count of T_2 nodes, increased by one for each branch, is divided by the sum of the T_1 and twice the T_0 nodes. This approach aids in understanding of the overall connectivity within the sinusoidal network, with values close to zero indicating lower connectivity.

Statistical Test: The Mann-Whitney U test, a non-parametric test, is employed to compare the differences in means between the control and NIF mice, as well as between lesion and unaffected regions.

4   Results and Discussion

Detection of Local Structure-Specific Alterations in the Fibrotic Liver: SRμCT can identify microstructural changes in the development of liver fibrosis while preserving the volumetric architecture (Fig. 4). Employing deep learning guided by correlative histology, structural features like lesions, vessels, and sinusoids were segmented. Lesions, characterized by persistent inflammation and fibrosis, were confirmed through validation using consecutive histological sections stained with H&E (Fig. 4a, b) and Picrosirius Red (Fig. 4o, p).

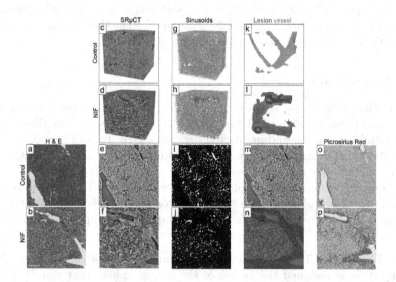

Fig. 4. SRμCT reveals microvascular changes in liver lesions of NIF mice. Representative SRμCT scans of control and fibrotic NIF livers (c–f), with 3D segmented features (g–n). Histological sections, stained with H&E (a, b) or PSR (o, p) matched with x-ray slices (e, f), segmented sinusoid (i, j), and lesion and vessel features (m, n).

Remodulation of the Sinusoidal Network: To assess adaptive consequences in the sinusoidal network resulting from injury and fibrosis, we measured lesion size and quantified sinusoidal parameters for NIF lesion regions, NIF unaffected regions, and control volumes. Significantly decreased sinusoid proportions were observed in NIF lesions compared to healthy controls (p-value = 0.0063) and unaffected NIF regions (p-value = 0.00001) (Fig. 5d). When comparing the mean local thickness of both sinusoidal and non-sinusoidal structures within the liver volumes, it becomes evident that the control volumes show a tight clustering, indicating minimal variation in local thickness. Conversely, the NIF lesions display a broader spread, implying a lower vascular density in 8w NIF lesions (Fig. 5a–c). The examination of microvascular changes in liver fibrosis can provide insights into the mechanisms behind the resistance to blood flow and the direct increase in portal pressure. Here, we utilize the 3D structure of liver sinusoids to quantify vascular branching geometric features in fibrotic livers in more detail (Fig. 5e–l). We found that fibrosis affected the microcirculation in the liver characterized by a disrupted sinsusoidal network with reduced connectivity (Fig. 5e) and reduced mean branch length (Fig. 5f, i) compared to healthy controls.

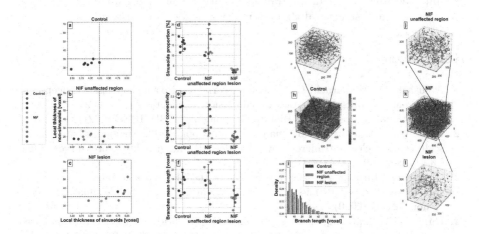

Fig. 5. Fibrotic lesions show disrupted sinusoidal organization and decreased vascular complexity. (a–c) sinusoid network density expressed as local sinusoid thickness against non-sinusoids, (d) Sinusoid volume proportions, (e) degree of sinusoid connectivity, (f) mean branch length per volume, and (i) histogram of branch length. Colour codes in NIF represent measures from the same NIF scan, lesion vs. unaffected regions. Branching of sinusoidal network in control (g, h) and NIF mice (j–l), displayed as entire network (h, k) or detailed zoomed-in illustrations (g, j, l). The color range indicates branch length.

5 Conclusion

Leveraging high quality SRμCT scans and our interactive segmentation and quantification workflow, our study achieved precise and rapid localization of diverse structural features within intact liver tissue. Our 3D analysis, which includes local thickness, connectivity, and branch length, uncovered significant differences between fibrotic lesions and unaffected regions. Notably, the remodulation of microvasculature in fibrotic liver regions, characterized by increased local sinusoid thickness, decreased total sinusoid volume, and a fragmented vascular network, as evidenced by our measurements, suggest a potential mechanism for decreased blood flow and impaired liver function. This study highlights the advanced capabilities of high-resolution SRμCT imaging in detecting detailed microstructural changes but also underscores the effectiveness of our deep learning-based approach in enhancing the quantification and understanding of liver fibrosis progression.

Prospect of Application: Our interactive segmentation tool, is broadly applicable and simple enough to use that clinicians and medical researchers without strong machine learning knowledge can use it effectively. Additionally, the analysis pipeline used here can be applied in future studies for understanding the microvascular and structural changes in other organs and diseases.

References

1. Abhishek, K., Hamarneh, G.: Matthews correlation coefficient loss for deep convolutional networks: application to skin lesion segmentation. In: 2021 IEEE 18th International Symposium on Biomedical Imaging (ISBI). IEEE (2021)
2. Aswath, A., Alsahaf, A., Giepmans, B.N., Azzopardi, G.: Segmentation in large-scale cellular electron microscopy with deep learning: a literature survey. Med. Image Anal. **89**, 102920 (2023)
3. Chicco, D., Jurman, G.: The advantages of the Matthews correlation coefficient (MCC) over F1 score and accuracy in binary classification evaluation. BMC Genom. **21**(1) (2020)
4. Du, G., Cao, X., Liang, J., Chen, X., Zhan, Y.: Medical image segmentation based on U-Net: a review. J. Imaging Sci. Technol. **64**(2), 020508–1–020508–12 (2020)
5. Ekstedt, M., et al.: Fibrosis stage is the strongest predictor for disease-specific mortality in NAFLD after up to 33 years of follow-up. Hepatology **61**(5), 1547–1554 (2015)
6. Fransén Pettersson, N., et al.: The immunomodulatory quinoline-3-carboxamide paquinimod reverses established fibrosis in a novel mouse model for liver fibrosis. PLoS ONE **13**(9), e0203228 (2018)
7. Fransén-Pettersson, N.: A new mouse model that spontaneously develops chronic liver inflammation and fibrosis. PLoS ONE **11**(7), e0159850 (2016)
8. Gostick, J., et al.: PoreSpy: a Python toolkit for quantitative analysis of porous media images. J. Open Source Softw. **4**(37), 1296 (2019)
9. Groszmann, R.J., Abraldes, J.G.: Portal hypertension: from bedside to bench. J. Clin. Gastroenterol. **39**(4), S125–S130 (2005)

10. Heinrich, L., et al.: Whole-cell organelle segmentation in volume electron microscopy. Nature **599**(7883), 141–146 (2021)
11. Heinrich, L., Funke, J., Pape, C., Nunez-Iglesias, J., Saalfeld, S.: Synaptic cleft segmentation in non-isotropic volume electron microscopy of the complete *Drosophila* brain. In: Frangi, A.F., Schnabel, J.A., Davatzikos, C., Alberola-López, C., Fichtinger, G. (eds.) MICCAI 2018. LNCS, vol. 11071, pp. 317–325. Springer, Cham (2018). https://doi.org/10.1007/978-3-030-00934-2_36
12. Isensee, F., Jaeger, P.F., Kohl, S.A.A., Petersen, J., Maier-Hein, K.H.: nnU-Net: a self-configuring method for deep learning-based biomedical image segmentation. Nat. Methods **18**(2), 203–211 (2020)
13. Keegan, A., Martini, R., Batey, R.: Ethanol-related liver injury in the rat: a model of steatosis, inflammation and pericentral fibrosis. J. Hepatol. **23**(5), 591–600 (1995)
14. Kollmannsberger, P., Kerschnitzki, M., Repp, F., Wagermaier, W., Weinkamer, R., Fratzl, P.: The small world of osteocytes: connectomics of the lacuno-canalicular network in bone. New J. Phys. **19**(7), 073019 (2017)
15. Laprade, W.M., Perslev, M., Sporring, J.: How few annotations are needed for segmentation using a multi-planar U-Net? In: Engelhardt, S., et al. (eds.) DGM4MICCAI/DALI 2021. LNCS, vol. 13003, pp. 209–216. Springer, Cham (2021). https://doi.org/10.1007/978-3-030-88210-5_20
16. Lee, T., Kashyap, R., Chu, C.: Building skeleton models via 3-d medial surface axis thinning algorithms. CVGIP Graph. Models Image Process. **56**(6), 462–478 (1994)
17. Lettmann, K.A., Hardtke-Wolenski, M.: The importance of liver microcirculation in promoting autoimmune hepatitis via maintaining an inflammatory cytokine milieu - a mathematical model study. J. Theor. Biol. **348**, 33–46 (2014)
18. Nilsson, J., et al.: NKT cells promote both type 1 and type 2 inflammatory responses in a mouse model of liver fibrosis. Sci. Rep. **10**(1), 21778 (2020)
19. Onori, P., Morini, S., Franchitto, A., Sferra, R., Alvaro, D., Gaudio, E.: Hepatic microvascular features in experimental cirrhosis: a structural and morphometrical study in CCL4-treated rats. J. Hepatol. **33**(4), 555–563 (2000)
20. Perslev, M., Dam, E.B., Pai, A., Igel, C.: One network to segment them all: a general, lightweight system for accurate 3D medical image segmentation. In: Shen, D., et al. (eds.) MICCAI 2019. LNCS, vol. 11765, pp. 30–38. Springer, Cham (2019). https://doi.org/10.1007/978-3-030-32245-8_4
21. Poisson, J., et al.: Liver sinusoidal endothelial cells: physiology and role in liver diseases. J. Hepatol. **66**(1), 212–227 (2017)
22. Rawson, S.D., Maksimcuka, J., Withers, P.J., Cartmell, S.H.: X-ray computed tomography in life sciences. BMC Biol. **18**(1) (2020)
23. Ronneberger, O., Fischer, P., Brox, T.: U-Net: convolutional networks for biomedical image segmentation. In: Navab, N., Hornegger, J., Wells, W.M., Frangi, A.F. (eds.) MICCAI 2015. LNCS, vol. 9351, pp. 234–241. Springer, Cham (2015). https://doi.org/10.1007/978-3-319-24574-4_28
24. Siddique, N., Paheding, S., Elkin, C.P., Devabhaktuni, V.: U-Net and its variants for medical image segmentation: a review of theory and applications. IEEE Access **9**, 82031–82057 (2021)
25. Vollmar, B., Menger, M.D.: The hepatic microcirculation: mechanistic contributions and therapeutic targets in liver injury and repair. Physiol. Rev. **89**(4), 1269–1339 (2009)

26. Wake, K., Sato, T.: "the sinusoid" in the liver: lessons learned from the original definition by Charles Sedgwick Minot (1900). Anat. Rec. **298**(12), 2071–2080 (2015)

27. W.L., Wagner, S., Föhst, J., Hock, et al.: 3D analysis of microvasculature in murine liver fibrosis models using synchrotron radiation-based microtomography. Angiogenesis **24**(*), 57–65 (2021)

28. Yoon, Y.J., et al.: Three-dimensional imaging of hepatic sinusoids in mice using synchrotron radiation micro-computed tomography. PLoS ONE **8**(7), e68600 (2013)

29. Zhou, Z., Rahman Siddiquee, M.M., Tajbakhsh, N., Liang, J.: UNet++: a nested U-net architecture for medical image segmentation. In: Stoyanov, D., et al. (eds.) DLMIA/ML-CDS -2018. LNCS, vol. 11045, pp. 3–11. Springer, Cham (2018). https://doi.org/10.1007/978-3-030-00889-5_1

Predicting Falls Through Muscle Weakness from a Single Whole Body Image: A Multimodal Contrastive Learning Framework

Xia Zhang[1]([✉]), Afsah Saleem[1,2], Zaid Ilyas[1,2], David Suter[1,2], Uzair Nadeem[1], Richard L. Prince[2,4], Kun Zhu[4,5], Joshua R. Lewis[2,4], Marc Sim[2,4], and Syed Zulqarnain Gilani[1,2,3]

[1] Centre for AI and ML, School of Science, Edith Cowan University, Joondalup, Australia
x.zhang@ecu.edu.au
[2] Nutrition and Health Innovation Research Institute, Edith Cowan University, Joondalup, Australia
[3] Computer Science and Software Engineering, The University of Western Australia, Perth, Australia
[4] Medical School, The University of Western Australia, Perth, Australia
[5] Department of Endocrinology and Diabetes, Sir Charles Gairdner Hospital, Perth, WA, Australia

Abstract. Falls are often attributed to poor muscle function, with weak hand grip strength clinically recognized as a major risk factor. However, grip strength is rarely assessed clinically. Low radiation dual-energy X-ray absorptiometry (DXA) whole-body scans, that can be obtained during routine osteoporosis screening, offer a comprehensive overview of body composition, thereby providing valuable information for musculoskeletal health. Here, we propose a machine learning technique, exploiting image and clinical data to classify weak grip strength ($<22\,\mathrm{kg}$), thereby enhancing fall prediction capabilities. To effectively utilize both discrete and continuous grip strength information, we introduce a novel Supervised Contrastive learning (SupCon) loss strategy, supplemented by regression loss guidance. Additionally, we present a pipeline featuring a unique Region of Interest (RoI) extraction strategy in the data preprocessing procedure, which is designed to focus on areas of genuine interest. Our proposed multi-modal contrastive learning (MMCL) framework enhances feature separability, and class diversity in the latent space, by leveraging different types of information. We evaluate the performance of our framework using a dataset of older women (2144 images); and employ survival analysis for evaluating future fall-related hospitalization risk over 5 years. Our results demonstrate that weak grip strength classified by the proposed approach achieves high sensitivity and accuracy and predicts risk of injurious falls in older women.

Keywords: Supervised Contrastive Learning · Falling Prediction · Whole-Body DXA Scan

© The Author(s), under exclusive license to Springer Nature Switzerland AG 2025
S. Wu et al. (Eds.): AMAI 2024, LNCS 15384, pp. 85–94, 2025.
https://doi.org/10.1007/978-3-031-82007-6_9

1   Introduction

Falls among the elderly are a pressing public health concern, often leading to serious injuries and hospitalization. Poor muscle function, including weak grip strength, is recognised as a major risk factor for falls among older adults [1–3]. Dual-energy X-ray absorptiometry (DXA) scanning provides comprehensive information on musculoskeletal health, including lean mass, adipose tissue, and bone density [4]. DXA testing offers several advantages, such as low radiation exposure and cost, which makes it particularly suitable for community-based screening initiatives. There is a potential association between weak grip strength and DXA-derived information, which could provide valuable automated insights into falls risk. However, using DXA scans to assess grip strength and fall risks can be challenging. Currently, grip strength assessment is not integrated into community falls screening protocols; often occurring only during rehabilitation after a fall-related injury. Therefore, the development of Machine Learning (ML) models for early identification of older individuals at risk of muscle weakness and subsequent falls is imperative.

While ML techniques have been extensively applied to health outcomes such as bone mineral density critical in osteoporosis screening [5,6], there has been limited exploration into predicting grip strength, and utilizing DXA-derived musculoskeletal information for falls prediction. Previous studies have highlighted the importance of grip strength as a predictor of falls [7,8], yet few deep learning models have addressed this issue; particularly in the context of whole-body imaging. The closest related study [9] investigated the predictive capacity of the DXA image modality with multiple clinical risk factors for mortality. Notably, falls and grip strength were considered as risk factors for mortality. Furthermore, the ML strategy in [9] may not effectively capture discriminative feature embeddings in samples with similar morphological information but belonging to different categories. Given these challenges, there is a need to explore alternative strategies for falls prediction models, particularly in scenarios with limited data and clinical information.

In this unexplored domain for fall prediction, we develop a targeted multi-modal machine learning model to address the challenge of binary classification of weak grip strength (yes/no) in a specific context, where the grip strength grouping is based on pre-defined clinical criteria. The subtle differences between the grip strength classes, as defined by a clinical cut-off point (e.g., <22 kg [10]), are challenging for ML predictive models to discern. Supervised Contrastive learning (SupCon) [11] aims to minimize the distances between feature embeddings with the same labels while maximizing the distances between those with different labels. However, this approach may not effectively preserve intra-class information in the latent space. Hence, our goal is to use the regression loss for continuous grip strength values, to assist in guiding the diverse representation of samples with different grip strength, but within the same strong or weak class labels.

Our contributions are summarized as follows: (1) We combine supervised contrastive learning and a regression loss function guided by grip strength values, to improve class separability and intra-class expression diversity between strong and weak grip strength categories. (2) We design a multi-modal supervised contrastive learning framework, using the proposed loss combination, to learn fused feature embeddings for visual and clinical data. (3) We build a large dataset for predicting falls in older women, comprising both images and routinely collected clinical information. Extensive evaluation of this dataset shows that our prediction result (with high accuracy) is clinically meaningful.

2 Proposed Algorithm

2.1 Dataset Preparation

The whole-body DXA images in our dataset provide detailed regional body composition information, including the components of fat, lean soft tissue, and bone mass [12]. Using specific cut lines in DXA scans, the body is subdivided into arm, leg, trunk, and head regions. As each image encompasses comprehensive information about the entire body composition, analyzing a specific part based on the entire image may be influenced by information from other body regions.

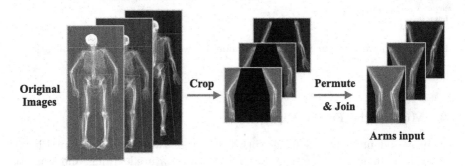

Fig. 1. Example of whole-body DXA scans. Based on the partitioning of the whole-body scan to crop out arms for grip. The input information for arms are joined images.

To address this limitation, we exploit the demarcation of the boundaries of the body regions in DXA images to extract ROIs related to grip strength, focusing on the arm region. Following the cropping of the arm region based on the cut lines, substantial irregular blank areas may occur (see the middle images in Fig. 1). Hence, we permute and realign both arms within the cropped image to center the left and right hand information, thereby achieving a more compact representation of arm image information. Furthermore, we consider the height and arm length ratio of the human body during the cropping process, and crop the upper half of each image [13]. This approach ensures that the necessary upper-limb information is preserved while maximizing the cropping of empty space in the image. The whole process can be seen in Fig. 1. These processed images are further manually verified to ensure that each image retained the integrity of the upper limb information for model training.

Grip strength is measured using a handheld dynamometer, which provides a continuous value. To formulate the problem as a binary classification task, we adopted a threshold of <22 kg [10] to classify the ground truth grip strength into weak and stronger categories. Specifically, "weak" grip strength is annotated as class "0", while "stronger" grip strength is annotated as class "1".

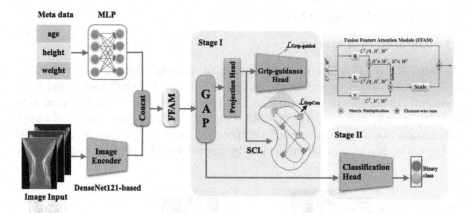

Fig. 2. Framework of our multi-modal model for weak grip strength classification.

2.2 Multimodal Fusion Pipeline

The proposed multi-modal framework consists of two stages (seen in Fig. 2): stage-I, an enhanced supervised contrastive fusion feature learning, and stage II: grip strength binary classification.

Stage I: There are two separate branches to extract information from images and clinical variables (referred to as "meta-data" in this work). We extract the image features from Densenet121 [9]. The DXA image is passed through this backbone encoder to generate features of size $C \times H' \times W'$. For clinical variables, we use a multiple layer perceptron (MLP) to project a three-element vector into high dimensions. In the feature fusion part, considering the clinical meta-data as supplemental imaging information, a lower fusion dimension may restrict the model's expressive capacity. Inspired by [14], we adopt the strategy that maintains the dimensionality of the visual feature space while extending the dimensionality of meta-data features for fusion, allowing the model to learn more intricate feature representations in a space enriched with more complete information. We design a Fusion Feature Attention Module (FFAM) to calculate the self-attention feature within the concatenated representation of images and text as in [14], instead of measuring the similarity between the image vector and the text vector as in [15]. In this module, the MLP features for the meta-data are expanded and reshaped into $C' \times H' \times W'$ to fit the image feature size, and then concatenated with visual features to be a $(C+C', H', W')$, where the number of fusion channels $C+C'$ is then denoted as C^f. These feature embeddings are then passed to a Global Average Pooling (GAP) layer to create feature embeddings with a size of 1024 from visual embeddings and 16 from meta-data embeddings. Regression loss, in our case enhanced supervised contrastive loss, operates on the feature projection to maximize the contrastive features and preserve dissimilarity in inter-class.

Stage-II: The well-learned contrastive feature vectors feed into a classification head, which consists of two dense layers with 1030 and 64 neurons each, followed by ReLu activation. Finally, a linear layer predicts the final grip strength class. This module is trained using BCEloss.

2.3 Supervised Contrastive Learning and Regression Loss

Following the existing work, supervised contrastive loss pulls and pushes the projections in the shared latent space, which maximizes the cosine similarity of projections from the same sample and minimizes the similarity of projections from different samples. We adopt SCL loss [11] to learn discriminative embeddings. Let our one training batch J be N sample/label pairs, image sample x_{j_i} and meta information x_{j_m} and y_j is the corresponding binary label, where j is the j-th sample. The imaging sample x_{j_i} is passed through an image encoder to generate embedding $\tilde{x}_{j_i}$. Each meta-data sample is passed through a text encoder to generate the embedding $\tilde{x}_{j_m}$. These two separate embeddings are brought into the FFAM module mentioned in Sect. 2.2, to generate visual-text self-attentive sample feature z_j. Consider an encoder-projector network that maps the anchor input x_j in the embedding space such that $z_j = Proj(Enc(x_j))$, Then the similarity between any two projections z_j and z_k in the latent space is $\mathrm{sim}(z_j, z_k)$ $= z_j^T \cdot z_k$. Following [11], the SCL loss in z_j can be written as:

$$\mathcal{L}_{\text{SupCon}} = \sum_{j \in J} \frac{-1}{|P(j)|} \sum_{p \in P(j)} \log \left(\frac{\exp(\mathbf{z}_j^T \cdot \mathbf{z}_p / \tau)}{\sum_{n \in N(j)(n \neq j)} \exp(\mathbf{z}_j^T \cdot \mathbf{z}_n / \tau)} \right). \qquad (1)$$

Let p and n denote positive samples and negative samples in batch J respectively. $P(j)$ is the set of indices of all positive samples, i.e., having the same grip class labels, and $N(j)$ is the set of indices of all the negative samples. $|P(j)|$ is its cardinality. τ is a scaling hyperparameter for contrastive loss.

We use a predefined threshold to divide the grip into weak and strong, in a clinically meaningful way. However, the samples that cross the label boundary are actually not much different from the sample changes within the class. In order to maintain the representation of samples in the physical world, and prevent overfitting as much as possible in the feature learning after hard classification, we propose to take advantage of the true information of grip strength value,

$$L_{grip-guided} = \sum_{j=1}^{N} MSE(y_j, \hat{y}_j), \qquad (2)$$

and incorporate it into SCL process by modifying the loss function. y_j, $\hat{y}_j$ in Eq. 2 is the ground truth of grip strength and the model's output, respectively. The final loss of the proposed contrastive learning consists of two parts as follows:

$$L = L_{\text{SupCon}} + \lambda \cdot L_{\text{grip-guided}}, \tag{3}$$

where λ is the hyperparameter to balance these losses.

3 Experiments

3.1 Dataset

We obtained 2,144 whole-body DXA scans (750 × 327 pixels, Hologic 4500A Machine) from community-dwelling older women from the Perth Longitudinal Study of Ageing Women. Corresponding whole-body DXA scans and objectively measured grip strength data obtained at multiple-time points (year 5, 7 and 10) were included. Based on the previous work [1–3], weak grip strength is a major risk factor for falls for this cohort of women. We also consider routinely obtained clinical meta-data including age, height, and weight.

3.2 Implementation Details

The cropped images are resized to 224 × 224 pixels using nearest-neighbor interpolation and rescaled to the range of 0 to 1. We also apply data augmentations including horizontal flips, random adjustments of brightness and contrast, shifts, scales, rotations, elastic deformations, Gaussian blur, and Gaussian noise. We implement all experiments in Pytorch, using stratified 10-fold cross-validation on a machine with NVIDIA RTX 3080 GPU. We train stage-I for 200 epochs and stage-II for 100 epochs using AdamW optimizer with the initial learning rate $1 * 10^{-4}$ and a batch size of 8. The temperature τ in the SupCon loss is 0.5. The parameter λ in the combined loss is 0.1.

Baseline: We consider work done in [9] as baseline. For fair comparison with baseline, we adopt the same pre-trained model i.e., Densenet121 for vision feature extraction and utilize their multi-modality methods as described in Sect. 1.

3.3 Results

We evaluate the performance of our models using accuracy, specificity, and Area Under Curve (AUC). Given the class annotations outlined in Sect. 2.1, our primary emphasis lies on the accurate classification of instances deemed more severe within their respective tasks. Additionally, we conduct two ablation studies: an image-only DenseNet121 classification model, and a multi-modality contrastive learning model without our proposed grip guided loss. Table 1 presents the average performance of our model compared to the aforementioned models after 10-fold cross-validation.

Table 1. Performance comparison of our proposed framework with the baseline models in the grip strength classification, which also include ablation studies.

input		loss		Accuracy (%)	Specificity (%)	AUC (%)
image	meta-data	SupCon	Reg-guide			
✓				78.45	87.49	61.78
✓	✓ (baseline)			79.24	88.12	62.89
✓	✓	✓		78.17	86.13	**63.49**
✓	✓	✓	✓ (ours)	**80.36**	**89.64**	63.26

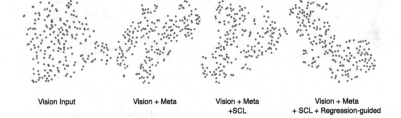

Fig. 3. Visualisation of high-level features with t-SNE. The blue and red dots are weak and strong grip strength instances respectively. (Color figure online)

Our average classification accuracy significantly outperforms the baseline accuracy, with an average accuracy of 80.36% and an average specificity of 89.64%. A comparison of the three models reveals that the image model also produces promising results with an average accuracy of 78.45% and an average specificity of 87.49%, indicating a strong correlation between grip strength and DXA data. The multi-modal deep learning model that processes image and meta-data information can increase the average prediction accuracy to 79.24% and the average specificity to 88.12%, while the multi-modal model with Supervised Contrastive learning guided by regression loss reaches the optimal performance. When without guidance, the SupCon still gives best AUC performance. This study highlights that the combination of comprehensive whole-body DXA scans with common patient demographics can produce a more robust classification model than other strategies.

We additionally visualize the effectiveness of feature representation in the high-level semantic latent feature space before the final classification using the t-distributed Stochastic Neighbor Embedding (t-SNE) method. As depicted in Fig. 3, with the gradual inclusion of information and the proposed loss strategy, our model's ability for feature representation strengthens progressively, leading to better clustering of high-level features: the distance between samples of the same class gradually decreases, and samples of different classes tend to cluster in their own groups.

Figure 4 illustrates the Grad-CAM [17] visualization of feature maps. Our method accurately identifies relevant areas and makes correct predictions (see

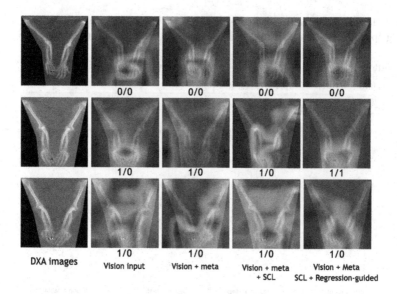

Fig. 4. Grad-CAM visualization of feature maps of different methods for three different examples. Number pairs below each image represent ground truth labels/prediction labels.

the first and second rows). Even during misclassification (see the third row), our method can still show stable and consistent activation patterns, and the activated regions are generally concentrated. In contrast, the activated areas of other models are more dispersed, and distracted by irrelevant information.

3.4   Clinical Analysis

Based on our developed algorithm, we subsequently assessed the relationship between the predicted weak grip strength in 852 women from the experiment cohort (using whole-body DXA scans obtained in 2003) with fall-related hospitalizations (obtained from linked health records) over the next 5 years using an age-adjusted Cox-proportional hazards model; a commonly adopted approach in medical research to assess risk for specific clinical events. Compared to women without predicted weakness, those with predicted weak grip strength had greater risk for a fall-related hospitalization over the next 5 years (Hazard ratio 1.76 95%CI 1.00-3.11, $p \leq 0.05$).

Despite the lower bound of the 95%CI being close to < 1, these findings are clinically significant. Our results would likely be stronger if the sample size of the cohort was larger. This work provides proof of concept for adopting whole-body DXA scans to identify older women who might present with muscle weakness and subsequently at risk for the most serious type of falls, specifically those leading to hospitalization. Further investigation to confirm the importance of this association will be done in future work.

4   Conclusion

Our framework in combination with Supervised Contrastive learning loss and grip value guide demonstrates significant performance improvements, compared to similar methods. Moreover, the ablation studies also establish the effectiveness of our multi-modal strategy. These results suggest that our approach has clinical potential for accurately and automatically predicting weak grip strength and fall-related hospitalizations.

Prospect of Application: Our research could benefit musculoskeletal healthcare, specifically by assisting clinicians identify older adults at risk of muscle weakness and consequently falls; a major cause of hip fractures and reduced mobility. This work would be relevant to osteoporosis screening where DXA scans to assess bone mineral density are used clinically, often without the assessment of whole body composition and muscle strength.

Acknowledgements. De-identified whole body DXA-derived images were sourced for the project. All women involved in the study provided written informed consent, and ethical approval was granted by the Human Ethics Committee of the University of Western Australia. PLSAW followed the guidelines of the Declaration of Helsinki and were registered retrospectively on the Australian New Zealand Clinical Trials Registry (ACTRN #12615000750583 and #2617000640303). Approval for linked data ethics was obtained from the Human Research Ethics Committee of the Western Australian Department of Health (#2009/24). PLSAW was supported by project grants 254627, 303169 and 572604 from the National Health and Medical Research Council of Australia, Healthway-The Western Australian Health Promotion Foundation. This project was funded by the Future Health Research and Innovation Fund (FHRIF), Department of Health, Western Australia. The salary of MS is supported by a Royal Perth Hospital Research Foundation Fellowship (RPHRF CAF 00/21) and an Emerging Leader Fellowship from the FHRIF. The salary of JRL is supported by a National Heart Foundation of Australia Future Leader Fellowship (ID: 102817). SZG was supported by the Raine Priming Grant awarded by the Raine Medical Research Foundation. This research was also partly supported by the Australia-Germany Joint Research Cooperative Scheme (Grant ID 57559550). None of the funding agencies had any role in the conduct of the study; collection, management, analysis, or interpretation of the data; or preparation, review, or approval of the manuscript.

References

1. Xue, Q.L., Walston, J.D., Fried, L.P., Beamer, B.A.: Prediction of risk of falling, physical disability, and frailty by rate of decline in grip strength: the women's health and aging study. Arch. Intern. Med. **171**(12), 1119–1121 (2011)
2. Neri, S.G., Lima, R.M., Ribeiro, H.S., Vainshelboim, B.: Poor handgrip strength determined clinically is associated with falls in older women. J. Frailty Sarcopenia Falls. **6**(2), 43 (2021)

3. Villamizar-Pita, P.C., Angarita-Fonseca, A., de Souza, H.C., Martínez-Rueda, R., Villamizar García, M.C., Sánchez-Delgado, J.C.: Handgrip strength is associated with risk of falls in physically active older women. Health Care Women Int. **43**(10–11), 1301–1314 (2022)

4. Radecka, A., Lubkowska, A.: The significance of dual-energy X-ray absorptiometry (DXA) examination in Cushing's syndrome-a systematic review. Diagnostics. **13**(9), 1576 (2023)

5. Erjiang, E., et al.: Machine learning can improve clinical detection of low BMD: the DXA-HIP study. J. Clin. Densitom. **24**(4), 527–537 (2021)

6. Rahim, F., et al.: Machine learning algorithms for diagnosis of hip bone osteoporosis: a systematic review and meta-analysis study. Biomed. Eng. Online **22**(1), 68 (2023)

7. Moreland, J.D., Richardson, J.A., Goldsmith, C.H., Clase, C.M.: Muscle weakness and falls in older adults: a systematic review and meta-analysis. J. Am. Geriatr. Soc. **52**(7), 1121–1129 (2004)

8. Pijnappels, M., Van der Burg, J.C., Reeves, N.D., van Dieën, J.H.: Identification of elderly fallers by muscle strength measures. Eur. J. Appl. Physiol. **102**, 585–592 (2008)

9. Glaser, Y., et al.: Deep learning predicts all-cause mortality from longitudinal total-body DXA imaging. Commun. Med. **2**(1), 102 (2022)

10. Gebre, A.K., et al.: Cardiovascular disease, muscle function, and long-term falls risk: the Perth Longitudinal Study of Ageing Women. Arch. Gerontol. Geriatr. **1**(107), 104911 (2023)

11. Khosla, P., et al.: Supervised contrastive learning. Adv. Neural. Inf. Process. Syst. **33**, 18661–18673 (2020)

12. Shepherd, J.A., Ng, B.K., Sommer, M.J., Heymsfield, S.B.: Body composition by DXA. Bone **1**(104), 101–105 (2017)

13. Quanjer, P.H., et al.: All-age relationship between arm span and height in different ethnic groups. Eur. Respir. J. **44**(4), 905–912 (2014)

14. Jin, Q., et al.: Multi-modality contrastive learning for sarcopenia screening from hip X-rays and clinical information. In: Greenspan, H., et al. (eds.) MICCAI 2023. LNCS, vol. 14225, pp. 85–94. Springer, Cham (2023). https://doi.org/10.1007/978-3-031-43987-2_9

15. Radford, A., et al.: Learning transferable visual models from natural language supervision. In: International Conference on Machine Learning, 1 July 2021, pp. 8748–8763. PMLR (2021)

16. Vaswani, A., et al.: Attention is all you need. Adv. Neural Inf. Process. Syst. **30** (2017)

17. Selvaraju, R.R., Cogswell, M., Das, A., Vedantam, R., Parikh, D., Batra, D.: Grad-CAM: visual explanations from deep networks via gradient-based localization. In: Proceedings of the IEEE International Conference on Computer Vision, pp. 618–626 (2017)

Optimizing ICU Readmission Prediction: A Comparative Evaluation of AI Tools

Hoda Helmy, Chaima Ben Rabah, Nada Ali, Ahmed Ibrahim, Abdullah Hoseiny, and Ahmed Serag$^{(\boxtimes)}$

AI Innovation Lab, Weill Cornell Medicine - Qatar, Doha, Qatar
afs4002@qatar-med.cornell.edu

Abstract. The Intensive Care Unit (ICU) serves as a critical resource in hospitals, delivering specialized care to patients with severe medical conditions. However, unplanned readmissions to the ICU pose significant challenges, including increased patient morbidity, extended hospital stays, and elevated healthcare costs. Predicting ICU readmissions is crucial for optimizing patient care and resource allocation. In this study, we explore the application of machine learning algorithms, including K-Neighbors Classifier, Random Forest Classifier, AdaBoost Classifier, Gradient Boosting Classifier, Logistic Regression, XGBoost Classifier, and Large Language Models (LLMs), to predict ICU readmissions. Leveraging data from the eICU Research Database, encompassing 166,355 patient admissions across 335 ICUs, our models were trained and evaluated using standard performance metrics. Results demonstrate that XGBoost achieved the highest overall performance, surpassing previous benchmarks. Notably, Gemma 2B LLM demonstrated strong predictive accuracy, highlighting its potential to improve outcomes in ICU settings. This study underscores the utility of advanced machine learning techniques and LLMs in improving healthcare outcomes by predicting ICU readmissions.

Keywords: Supervised Machine learning · Intensive care unit · prediction models · Random Forest · AdaBoost · XGBoots · LLM · Gemma 2B

1 Introduction

A critical but resource-intensive part of any hospital, the Intensive Care Unit (ICU) is dedicated to delivering life-saving intensive care medicine. It is equipped with cutting-edge monitoring and staffed by highly-trained specialists. ICUs provide critical care for patients in severe or life-threatening conditions [1].

A significant challenge these units face is unplanned patient readmissions to the ICU, which significantly impacts patients and healthcare systems. Such readmissions substantially threaten patient health while also burdening already strained medical resources. The occurrence of unplanned ICU readmissions is associated with increased mortality rates, extended hospital stays, and escalated

S. Wu et al. (Eds.): AMAI 2024, LNCS 15384, pp. 95–104, 2025.
https://doi.org/10.1007/978-3-031-82007-6_10

healthcare costs, posing substantial burdens on both patients and the healthcare system [2]. The impact of these readmissions emphasizes the need for strategies aimed at minimizing their occurrence to enhance patient outcomes and optimize resource utilization.

Predicting the possibility of ICU readmissions can play a critical role in the implementation of targeted interventions designed to decrease morbidity and mortality rates among patients [3]. By accurately predicting which patients are at risk of being readmitted, healthcare providers can conduct thorough reassessments of a patient's health status before discharge, ensuring that all necessary medical and supportive measures are in place to prevent unnecessary readmissions [4].

In recent years, Artificial Intelligence (AI) has been extensively utilized in the medical field for various applications, including medical image analysis, disease prognosis, and diagnostics [5]. A growing area of interest within this field is the use of Electronic Health Records (EHRs), particularly with the advancements in Natural Language Processing (NLP). EHRs are comprehensive digital records that document clinical or administrative encounters between healthcare providers and patients during medical care [6].

Despite their potential, the utilization of EHRs presents significant challenges. These challenges include the lack of standardized formatting [7] and inconsistent labeling [8], which complicate data extraction and analysis. Additionally, the longitudinal and complex structural nature of EHR data poses difficulties for certain use cases, hindering the effective application of AI and NLP techniques [9]. Addressing these challenges is crucial for leveraging the full potential of EHRs to improve patient care and healthcare outcomes.

Numerous studies have explored predicting ICU admission, mortality, and length of stay. Iwase et al. [10] examined a dataset from Chiba University Hospital comprising 12,747 patients. By employing Random Forest, XGBoost, Neural Network, and logistic regression classifiers, they aimed to forecast ICU mortality and length of stay. Random Forest exhibited the highest predictive performance for ICU mortality, achieving an AUC of 0.945. They also demonstrated robust predictive capability for short and long ICU stays, with AUCs of 0.881 and 0.889, respectively. Recently, Nóvoa and colleagues [11] focused on predicting early ICU readmission using AI techniques and the MIMIC-III dataset [12]. Using the XGBoost model, the study achieved an impressive AUC-ROC of 0.92, surpassing the results of similar studies [13,14], which obtained AUC-ROCs of 0.74 and 0.76, respectively, for the same dataset. Additionally, de Sá et al. [15] explored ICU readmission across two datasets: the eICU dataset [16] for training and the MIMIC-IV dataset [17] for testing, yielding an AUC of 0.7 with Random Forest.

In this paper, we aim to explore the ability of diverse machine learning (ML) algorithms to predict ICU readmission, focusing mainly on diagnoses that occurred during ICU stays and past diagnoses when available. Additionally, we emphasize the importance of data preprocessing when dealing with EHR, transforming raw clinical data into a more usable dataset suitable for ML models, and further standardizing it into text format for large language models (LLMs). Furthermore, we optimized an LLM for text classification to evaluate its ability to classify textual data and provide accurate predictions for ICU readmission. This dual approach aims to enhance our understanding of predictive factors and improve the accuracy of readmission predictions.

2   Methodology

2.1   Data

We used the eICU research database, a publicly available dataset. It includes information from 335 ICUs across 208 U.S. hospitals during the years 2014 and 2015. The database contains details of 166,355 patients and 200,859 ICU admissions. This de-identified dataset includes patient demographics, admission and discharge details, APACHE IV scores, and related data such as vital signs, lab results, medications, and care plans.

2.2   Data Pre-processing

In our study, we integrated data from three distinct tables to create a comprehensive dataset. The first table included patient demographic information and admission details, such as age, ethnicity, type of admission, admission diagnoses, admission status, and the number of ICU visits. The second table contained detailed diagnostic information for each patient during the ICU stay, while the third table included historical diagnostic data. Combining information from these tables, we built a rich dataset that enabled ML models to analyze a wider range of patient factors influencing ICU readmissions. This resulted in more accurate and practical prediction models. Patients who lacked either diagnostic or historical data were excluded from the analysis to ensure completeness and accuracy.

Data Cleaning: To eliminate redundancy and facilitate analysis, each diagnosis was transformed into a separate column, with a binary indicator denoting the presence of that diagnosis during the patient's stay. Non-essential identifiers were removed to streamline the dataset, retaining only the hospital stay ID and unique patient ID. To maintain data integrity, we adopted a threshold for columns with missing values, including only those with less than 20% missing data. Missing values were imputed based on the data type: discrete values were imputed using the mode, while continuous values were imputed using the mean.

Finally, we implemented a detailed labeling system based on ICU admission frequency to prepare our data for our specific use case. We iterated through each unique patient ID and subsequently through each of their hospital stays. If a patient had multiple ICU admissions during a single hospital stay, they were labeled as a multi-admission patient, denoted by a value of 1. Conversely, if a patient had only one ICU admission during their hospital stay, they were labeled as a single-admission patient, denoted by a value of 0. This labeling system enabled us to categorize patients based on their ICU admission frequency within a single hospital stay, providing a critical variable for our subsequent analysis. This process resulted in identifying 19,164 records of multiple admissions within a single hospital stay.

This structured approach enhanced our dataset's clarity and usability and laid a solid foundation for advanced analytical procedures. By categorizing patients in this manner, we investigated patterns and predictors of multiple ICU admissions during a single hospital stay. This facilitated the development of predictive models aimed at identifying high-risk patients who might benefit from targeted interventions, ultimately improving patient outcomes and optimizing resource allocation in intensive care settings.

Preparing the Dataset for Language Model: A standardized template was devised to prepare the dataset for the language model, where each patient's information was embedded into a structured text. This template ensured uniformity across all patient entries, encapsulating relevant details such as demographics, age, diagnoses, and past diagnoses. Alongside this structured text, each patient record was categorized with an outcome label indicating whether the patient had multiple admissions or a single admission to the ICU.

This approach allowed for systematic data representation, enabling the language model to ingest and process comprehensive patient narratives consistently. The dataset facilitated effective training and evaluation of the language model's predictive capabilities by embedding diverse patient data into a unified textual format. This structured methodology not only enhanced the model's ability to discern patterns and correlations within the data but also ensured clarity and coherence in presenting patient information for subsequent analysis and research purposes.

2.3 Machine Learning Prediction and Evaluation

In this study, we utilize several machine learning algorithms to compare their performance in classification and prediction, aiming to identify the most suitable model for our application. First, we divided the dataset into training and test sets with an 80/20 split. We selected the following prominent algorithms for comparison, each chosen for its unique strengths: K-nearest neighbors, Random Forest, AdaBoost, Gradient Boosting classifier, Logistic Regression, and XGBoost.

The K-Nearest Neighbors Classifier was included for its simplicity and intuitiveness. It is easy to understand and implement, making it a good starting point for classification tasks. As a non-parametric model, it makes no assumptions about the underlying data distribution, making it versatile for various datasets. It performs well with smaller datasets where the computational cost of finding nearest neighbors is manageable [18]. In our study, we set the K- value of the nearest neighbor to three, and the rest of the parameters were set to default.

The Random Forest Classifier was chosen for its robustness. By aggregating the predictions of multiple decision trees, it is less prone to over-fittings than individual decision trees. It handles classification and regression tasks effectively and can manage missing values well. Additionally, it provides insights into feature importance, which can help understand the underlying data [19]. In our study, The Random Forest was set to its default values of n-estimator equal to 100, and max-feature to square root.

Logistic Regression was chosen for its simplicity and interpretability. It is straightforward to implement and interpret, making it a good baseline model. Computationally efficient for large datasets, it is particularly suited for binary classification tasks, which is suitable for our dataset as we are trying to find out if a patient will get re-admitted to the ICU again or not within one single hospital visit. Logistic Regression provides probabilities for each class, which can be helpful in decision-making processes [20]. For Logistic Regression, we set the iteration to 10,000, leaving the rest of the parameters to their default value.

AdaBoost was selected due to its ability to improve performance by focusing on the misclassified instances of previous classifiers. It can be combined with various weak classifiers, enhancing its flexibility to adapt to different data types. AdaBoost has strong theoretical backing, ensuring convergence to a robust classifier if weak classifiers have better than random accuracy [21]. The learning rate is set to 1, and the algorithm chosen is SAMME, with the rest of the parameters set to its default.

The Gradient Boosting Classifier was included for its accuracy. It is known for producing highly accurate predictions by sequentially fitting models to correct errors made by previous ones. Its capability to optimize various differentiable loss functions makes it suitable for complex datasets with many features. One patient was diagnosed with multiple diseases, each passed as a unique feature. Additionally, it includes mechanisms to prevent over-fittings, such as learning rate shrinkage and tree constraints [22]. The algorithm was used with its default parameters.

XGBoost was selected for its superior performance on structured/tabular data. It is highly efficient and scalable and is known for advanced optimization techniques and regularization, making it suitable for large datasets and distributed computing environments. Its support for various objective functions and custom loss functions provides flexibility to fine-tune the model to specific needs [23].

These models were chosen for their distinct strengths and complementary characteristics, allowing for a comprehensive comparison to determine the best model for our application.

2.4   Large Language Model: Gemma 2B

LLMs represent a transformative technology poised to revolutionize healthcare across multiple domains. Their advanced capabilities in comprehending and generating human-like text make them invaluable tools for addressing intricate medical tasks and enhancing patient care. LLMs have been effectively deployed in diverse applications such as note-taking, responding to medical inquiries, generating clinical summaries, and supporting diagnostic and treatment decisions [24]. They play pivotal roles in aiding healthcare professionals by augmenting clinical knowledge, facilitating patient triage, and streamlining administrative processes.

In this study, we have tailored LLMs for the specific task of predicting patient readmission to the ICU by using Q-lora to fine-tune our model specifically for our dataset. Through integrating ML and NLP methodologies, we have developed a predictive model that harnesses a structured text template to effectively pre-train the LLM. This approach leverages summarized patient data, including diagnoses and past medical history, to enhance the model's ability to forecast ICU readmissions.

Furthermore, our research includes optimization of Gemma 2B, a prominent member of the Gemma series developed by Google DeepMind [25]. This advanced language model has been specifically refined to serve as an assistant in ICU environments, supporting healthcare professionals in making informed decisions. Gemma 2B is pre-trained on a vast dataset comprising 2 trillion tokens sourced from diverse sources such as web documents, mathematical data, and code excerpts. Its architecture, rooted in the transformer decoder framework, incorporates cutting-edge features such as multi-query attention mechanisms, RoPE embeddings for context representation, GeGLU activations for nonlinear transformations, and strategic normalizer location techniques to bolster overall model robustness and performance.

3   Results

In ML, the choice of evaluation metrics is crucial to assess the performance of models tailored for specific tasks effectively. Accuracy is a fundamental metric that we prioritize for its straightforward calculation and intuitive interpretation. It provides a clear measure of the overall correctness of predictions, which is particularly useful in scenarios where balanced classification outcomes are desired [26].

The F1-score holds significance due to its ability to balance between precision and recall. In binary classification systems, precision denotes the accuracy of positive predictions made by the model, while recall gauges the model's ability to identify all positive instances in the dataset. The F1-score, being the harmonic mean of precision and recall, offers a harmonized assessment of a model's performance in accurately classifying both positive and negative instances, making it suitable for tasks where achieving a balance between precision and recall is crucial [26].

AUC (Area Under the Curve) is another essential metric chosen for its capability to evaluate the discriminatory power of a model across different thresholds [27]. By quantifying the area under the ROC curve, AUC provides insights into how well the model distinguishes between positive and negative instances. A high AUC value indicates robust discrimination ability, making it a preferred metric for assessing the overall predictive performance of classifiers, especially in scenarios where class imbalance or varying decision thresholds are present.

As shown in Fig. 1, XGBoost produced the best results among the evaluated algorithms, achieving an AUC of 0.926. This performance not only surpasses the state-of-the-art results of 0.7 previously reported in one study utilizing the same dataset but also demonstrates XGBoost's superior capability in handling complex prediction tasks. Additionally, XGBoost yielded the highest F1-score of 0.64, indicating a balanced trade-off between precision and recall, which is crucial for predicting ICU readmissions.

XGBoost's outstanding performance is particularly significant given the noticeable imbalance in our dataset between re-admitted patients and those admitted only once. The algorithm's ability to manage and mitigate the effects of this imbalance highlights its robustness and effectiveness. XGBoost employs advanced techniques such as regularization, which prevents over-fitting, and its scalable nature allows it to handle large-scale data efficiently. These features contribute to its high accuracy and reliability, making it an excellent choice for predictive modeling when dealing with medical data that often has imbalanced classes.

As shown in Table 1, among the classifiers tested, Gemma 2B LLM achieved remarkable results with an accuracy of 0.94, the highest among all models assessed. Importantly, Gemma 2B also attained the highest F1-score of 0.70, demonstrating effective performance in balancing precision and recall for ICU readmission prediction. This is particularly significant as F1-score provides a comprehensive measure of a model's accuracy for binary classification tasks. Notably, the Random Forest Classifier and the XGBoost Classifier also demonstrated strong performances, achieving an accuracy of 0.92 and an AUC of 0.91 and 0.927, respectively, among the highest recorded AUC scores.

While models like the K-Neighbors Classifier and AdaBoost Classifier showed relatively lower F1-scores of 0.24 and 0.33 and AUC of 0.66 and 0.85, respectively, they still contributed valuable insights into the varying performance capabilities of different algorithms in this specific predictive task.

The noticeable performance of Gemma 2B, achieving the highest F1 score, suggests significant potential for further enhancement in healthcare applications. Its ability to understand complex medical texts and nuances in patient records, combined with robust pre-training on extensive datasets, positions Gemma 2B (and similar LLMs) as a promising tool for improving predictive accuracy in ICU readmission scenarios.

Future refinements could focus on fine-tuning the model's prompt engineering strategies and leveraging its advanced NLP capabilities to solidify predictions and enhance clinical decision support systems in real-world healthcare settings.

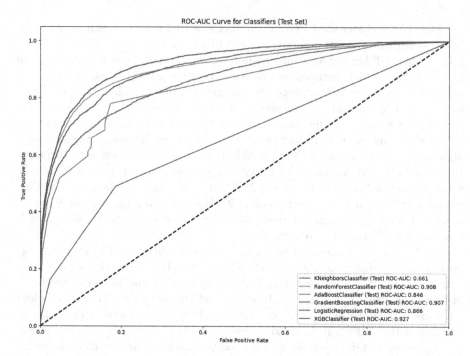

Fig. 1. Comparison of ROC-AUC scores among classical machine learning algorithms.

Table 1. Test Evaluation of different algorithms.

Algorithm	Accuracy	F1-score
KNeighbors Classifier	0.87	0.24
Random Forest Classifier	0.92	0.56
AdaBoost Classifier	0.89	0.33
Gradient Boosting Classifier	0.92	0.6
Logistic Regression	0.91	0.54
XGBoots Classifier	0.92	0.63
Gemma 2B	**0.94**	**0.70**

4   Conclusion

This study leverages diverse ML algorithms and the power of the LLM Gemma 2B to advance our understanding of ICU readmission prediction.

XGBoost demonstrated good performance with solid discrimination ability, while Gemma 2B achieved the highest accuracy and F1-score. These results suggest Gemma 2B's potential (and that of similar LLMs) for further development and clinical integration. Future research should focus on refining and integrating these models into clinical workflows to enable proactive interventions and enhance patient outcomes in critical care.

Prospect of Application: This work presents a real-time risk assessment tool that uses patient data and AI algorithms to predict ICU readmission risk. The system enables doctors to identify high-risk patients, facilitating preventative measures and optimizing ICU resource allocation, thereby enhancing patient care and hospital efficiency.

Acknowledgements. The authors would like to thank Shafeeq Poolat for his invaluable support with the computational aspects of this study.

Disclosure of Interests. The authors declare no conflicts of interest.

References

1. Smith, G., Nielsen, M.: Criteria for admission. BMJ **318**(7197), 1544–1547 (1999)
2. Lin, Y.-W., Zhou, Y., Faghri, F., Shaw, M.J., Campbell, R.H.: Analysis and prediction of unplanned intensive care unit readmission using recurrent neural networks with long short-term memory. PLoS ONE **14**(7), e0218942 (2019)
3. Pishgar, M., Theis, J., Del Rios, M., Ardati, A., Anahideh, H., Darabi, H.: Prediction of unplanned 30-day readmission for ICU patients with heart failure. BMC Med. Inform. Decis. Mak. **22**, 05 (2022)
4. Sheetrit, E., Brief, M., Elisha, O.: Predicting unplanned readmissions in the intensive care unit: a multimodality evaluation. Sci. Rep. **13**, 09 (2023)
5. Basu, K., Sinha, R., Ong, A., Basu, T.: Artificial intelligence: how is it changing medical sciences and its future? Indian J. Dermatol. **65**, 365 (2020)
6. Joshua, O.: Electronic health record implementation in developing countries: a systematic review (2021)
7. Shinozaki, A.: Electronic medical records and machine learning in approaches to drug development. In: Cassidy, J.W., Taylor, B. (eds.) Artificial Intelligence in Oncology Drug Discovery and Development, chap. 4. IntechOpen, Rijeka (2020)
8. Ghassemi, M., Naumann, T., Schulam, P., Beam, A., Chen, I., Ranganath, R.: A review of challenges and opportunities in machine learning for health. In: AMIA Joint Summits on Translational Science proceedings. AMIA Joint Summits on Translational Science, vol. 2020, pp. 191–200 (2020)
9. Sun, Z., Peng, S., Yang, Y., Wang, X., Li, F.: A general fine-tuned transfer learning model for predicting clinical task acrossing diverse EHRs datasets. In: 2019 IEEE International Conference on Bioinformatics and Biomedicine (BIBM), pp. 490–495 (2019). https://api.semanticscholar.org/CorpusID:211055600
10. Iwase, S., et al.: Prediction algorithm for ICU mortality and length of stay using machine learning. Sci. Rep. **12**, 07 (2022)
11. González Nóvoa, J.A., et al.: Improving intensive care unit early readmission prediction using optimized and explainable machine learning. Int. J. Environ. Res. Public Health **20**, 3455 (2023)
12. Johnson, A.E., et al.: MIMIC-III, a freely accessible critical care database. Sci. Data **3**(1), 1–9 (2016)
13. Barbieri, S., et al.: Benchmarking deep learning architectures for predicting readmission to the ICU and describing patients-at-risk. Sci. Rep. **10** (2020)

14. Rojas, J., Carey, K., Edelson, D., Venable, L., Howell, M., Churpek, M.: Predicting intensive care unit readmission with machine learning using electronic health record data. Ann. Am. Thorac. Soc. **15**, 846–853 (2018)
15. de Sá, A., et al.: Explainable machine learning for ICU readmission prediction, arXiv preprint arXiv:2309.13781 (2023)
16. Pollard, T.J., Johnson, A.E.W., Raffa, J.D., Celi, L.A., Mark, R.G., Badawi, O.: The eICU Collaborative Research Database, a freely available multi-center database for critical care research. Sci. Data **5**(1), 1–13 (2018)
17. Johnson, A., Bulgarelli, L., Pollard, T., Horng, S., Celi, L.A., Mark, R.: MIMIC-IV. PhysioNet, pp. 49–55 (2020). https://physionet.org/content/mimiciv/1.0/. Accessed 23 Aug 2021
18. Cunningham, P., Delany, S.J.: K-nearest neighbour classifiers-a tutorial. ACM Comput. Surv. (CSUR) **54**(6), 1–25 (2021)
19. Louppe, G.: Understanding random forests: from theory to practice, arXiv preprint arXiv:1407.7502 (2014)
20. Das, A.: Logistic regression. In: Michalos, A.C. (ed.) Encyclopedia of Quality of Life and Well-Being Research, pp. 3985–3986. Springer, Dordrecht (2024). https://doi.org/10.1007/978-94-007-0753-5_1689
21. Favaro, P., Vedaldi, A.: Adaboost. In: Ikeuchi, K. (ed.) Computer Vision: A Reference Guide, pp. 36–40. Springer, Boston (2021). https://doi.org/10.1007/978-0-387-31439-6_663
22. Natekin, A., Knoll, A.: Gradient boosting machines, a tutorial. Front. Neurorobot. **7**, 21 (2013)
23. Chen, T., Guestrin, C.: XGBoost: a scalable tree boosting system. In: Proceedings of the 22nd ACM SIGKDD International Conference on Knowledge Discovery and Data Mining, pp. 785–794 (2016)
24. Omiye, J.A., Gui, H., Rezaei, S.J., Zou, J., Daneshjou, R.: Large language models in medicine: the potentials and pitfalls: a narrative review. Ann. Intern. Med. **177**(2), 210–220 (2024)
25. Team, G., et al.: Gemma: open models based on Gemini research and technology, arXiv preprint arXiv:2403.08295 (2024)
26. Japkowicz, N., Shah, M.: Evaluating Learning Algorithms: A Classification Perspective. Cambridge University Press, Cambridge (2011)
27. Pintea, S., Moldovan, R.: The receiver-operating characteristic (ROC) analysis: fundamentals and applications in clinical psychology. J. Cogn. Behav. Psychother. **9**, 49–66 (2009)

Source Matters: Source Dataset Impact on Model Robustness in Medical Imaging

Dovile Juodelyte[1(⊠)], Yucheng Lu[1], Amelia Jiménez-Sánchez[1],
Sabrina Bottazzi[2], Enzo Ferrante[3], and Veronika Cheplygina[1]

[1] IT University of Copenhagen, Copenhagen, Denmark
{doju,yucl,amji,vech}@itu.dk
[2] Universidad Nacional de San Martín, Buenos Aires, Argentina
sbottazzi@estudiantes.unsam.edu.ar
[3] CONICET - Universidad Nacional del Litoral, Santa Fe, Argentina
eferrante@sinc.unl.edu.ar

Abstract. Transfer learning has become an essential part of medical imaging classification algorithms, often leveraging ImageNet weights. The domain shift from natural to medical images has prompted alternatives such as RadImageNet, often showing comparable classification performance. However, it remains unclear whether the performance gains from transfer learning stem from improved generalization or shortcut learning. To address this, we conceptualize confounders by introducing the Medical Imaging Contextualized Confounder Taxonomy (MICCAT) and investigate a range of confounders across it – whether synthetic or sampled from the data – using two public chest X-ray and CT datasets. We show that ImageNet and RadImageNet achieve comparable classification performance, yet ImageNet is much more prone to overfitting to confounders. We recommend that researchers using ImageNet-pretrained models reexamine their model robustness by conducting similar experiments. Our code and experiments are available at https://github.com/DovileDo/source-matters.

Keywords: Transfer Learning · Robustness · Domain Shift · Shortcuts

1 Introduction

Machine learning models hold immense promise for revolutionizing healthcare. However, their deployment in real-world clinical settings is hindered by various challenges, with one of the most critical being their hidden reliance on spurious features [27]. Recent research has highlighted the detrimental effects of this reliance, including bias against demographic subgroups [2], limited generalization across hospitals [28], and the risk of clinical errors that may harm patients [21].

Despite transfer learning becoming a cornerstone in medical imaging, its impact on model generalization remains largely unexplored. Pre-training on ImageNet has become a standard practice due to its success in 2D image classification. While some studies have explored alternative medical source datasets for pre-training [3,16,19,29], ImageNet continues to serve as a strong baseline.

S. Wu et al. (Eds.): AMAI 2024, LNCS 15384, pp. 105–115, 2025.
https://doi.org/10.1007/978-3-031-82007-6_11

Recent literature suggests that the size of the source dataset may matter more than its domain or composition [9,22]. However, [15] demonstrated performance improvements through source dataset pruning. In this context, we argue that cross-domain transfer can be problematic, especially when source dataset selection is solely based on classification performance, as it may inadvertently lead to shortcut learning rather than genuine improvements in generalization. Shortcut learning can be considered antithetical to generalization and robustness as it is not a failure to generalize per se, but rather a failure to generalize in the intended direction [10].

In this paper, we investigate how the domain of the source dataset affects model generalization. First, we conceptualize confounding factors in medical images by introducing the Medical Imaging Contextualized Confounder Taxonomy (MICCAT) and generate synthetic or sample real-world confounders from MICCAT, commonly found in chest X-rays and CT scans, to systematically assess model robustness. Second, we compare models pre-trained on natural (ImageNet) and medical (RadImageNet) datasets across X-ray and CT tasks and show substantial differences in robustness to shortcut learning despite comparable predictive performance. While transfer learning has been observed to enhance model robustness [13], our results suggest that it may not hold true when transferring across domains, cautioning against using ImageNet pre-trained models in medical contexts due to their susceptibility to shortcut learning. Furthermore, our findings highlight the limitations of conventional performance metrics based on i.i.d. datasets, which fail to discern between genuine improvements in generalization and shortcut learning. Thus, we advocate for a more nuanced evaluation of transfer learning effectiveness to ensure the reliability and safety of machine learning applications in clinical settings.

2 Method

2.1 MICCAT: Towards a Standardized Taxonomy for Medical Imaging Confounders

To the best of our knowledge, there is no standardized taxonomy for classifying potential confounders in medical images. Thus, to better structure our robustness analysis, we propose a new taxonomy: Medical Imaging Contextualized Confounder Taxonomy (MICCAT).

Previous work has shown that standard demographic attributes such as sex, age, or ethnicity may act as confounders, leading to shortcut learning and potentially disadvantaging historically underserved subgroups [2]. However, solely focusing on standard protected demographic attributes may overlook other specific factors related to clusters of patients for which the systems tend to fail [8]. In MICCAT, we identify these as 'contextualized confounders', as they are often domain or context-specific, associated with particular image modalities, organs, hospitalization conditions, or diseases.

First, MICCAT differentiates between *patient level* and *environment level* confounders. At the *patient level*, we make a distinction between standard

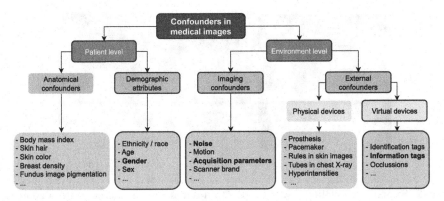

Fig. 1. MICCAT: Medical Imaging Contextualized Confounder Taxonomy. Instances of confounders investigated in this paper are highlighted in bold.

demographic attributes (e.g., sex, age, race) and contextualized *anatomical confounders*, which arise from inherent anatomical properties of the organs and human body or disease variations in images. This distinction is crucial as standard demographic attributes often serve as proxies for underlying causes of learned shortcuts. For instance, ethnicity may proxy skin color in dermatoscopic images. Identifying the true shortcut cause allows for more targeted interventions to mitigate biases. We define the concept of *environment level* confounders, which stem from contextualized *external* or *imaging confounders*. The former include physical or virtual elements in images due to external factors like hospitalization devices or image tags, while the latter include characteristics related to the imaging modality itself, such as noise, motion blur, or differences in intensities due to equipment or acquisition parameters. Figure 1 illustrates this taxonomy with examples for each category.

Confounders Studied in this Paper. We explore the MICCAT by investigating four examples of confounders, highlighted by a black outline in Fig. 1:

- An external confounder (*a tag*) placed in the upper left corner of the image, representing confounding features introduced by various imaging devices across or within hospitals (Fig. 2a).
- Two typical imaging confounders: *denoising* (Fig. 2c), widely used by various vendors to reduce noise for enhanced readability [11], and *Poisson noise* (Fig. 2d), originating from quantum statistics of photons, which cannot be mitigated through hardware engineering, unlike noise introduced by circuit-related artifacts [26].
- A patient-level confounder where we use *patient gender*, which is easily accessible in metadata, as a proxy for a broader spectrum of anatomical confounders. We use the same term for this variable as in the original dataset.

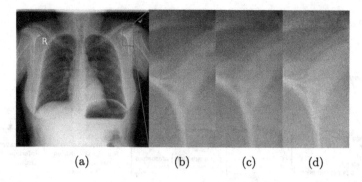

(a)   (b)   (c)   (d)

Fig. 2. Synthetic artifacts: (a) *A tag* with a red arrow for reference, (b) a zoomed-in view of the original image, (c) *Denoising* by low-pass filter with cutoff frequency (see Eq. 1) of $D_0 = 200$px, and (d) *Poisson noise* with $N_0 = 2 \times 10^6$ (see Eq. 2). The parameters used here are to emphasize subtle local variations such as the smoothing effect of the low-pass filter and the graininess introduced by the Poisson noise. For our experiments, we use $D_0 = 500$px and $N_0 = 2 \times 10^7$ which are imperceptible.

2.2 Experimental Design

We investigate the impact of source dataset domain on model generalization by comparing ImageNet [6] and RadImageNet [19] models, which are fine-tuned using binary prediction tasks for findings in open-access chest X-ray (NIH CXR14 [25]) and CT (LIDC-IDRI [1]) datasets curated to include systematically controlled confounders. NIH CXR14 is used to represent cross-domain transfer for both ImageNet and RadImageNet, as X-ray is not included in RadImageNet, while LIDC-IDRI serves as an in-domain example for RadImageNet and a cross-domain example for ImageNet.

Confounder Generation. *Patient gender* is sampled to correlate 'Female' with the label.

A *tag* is placed further away from the edges (starting at 200×200px in the original image of 1024×1024px), to ensure it remains intact during training despite augmentations applied (Fig. 2a).

The simplest method for *Denoising* is applying low-pass filtering which entails converting the input image from the spatial to the frequency domain using Discrete Fourier Transform (DFT), followed by element-wise multiplication with the low-pass filter $H_{LPF}(u, v)$ to generate the filtered image:

$$H_{LPF}(u, v) = \begin{cases} 1, & D(u, v) \leq D_0 \\ 0, & \text{otherwise} \end{cases} \tag{1}$$

where $D(u, v)$ represents the distance from the origin in the frequency domain, and D_0 is the specified cutoff frequency. In our experiments, we set $D_0 = 500$px. Subsequently, the high-frequency suppressed image is reconstructed in the spatial domain via the Inverse Discrete Fourier Transform (IDFT), resulting in a smoothing effect (see Fig. 2c).

Table 1. Target datasets used for fine-tuning. T: *tag*, D: *denoising*, N: *noise*.

Task	Confounder	# images in test/dev(train+val)	% split train/val	% class split pos/neg	Image size	Batch size
Lung mass (NIH CXR14 [25])	T, D, N	83/248	90/10	30/70	512 × 512	32
Lung mass (LIDC-IDRI [1])	T, D, N	1710/500	80/20	50/50	362 × 362	32
Atelectasis (NIH CXR14 [25])	Gender	400/400	85/15	50/50	256 × 256	64

Poisson Noise originating from quantum statistics of photons is formulated as a Poisson random process:

$$(p_r + N_p) = \mathcal{P}(p_r) \tag{2}$$

where N_p represents Poisson noise, which notably affects image quality under low-dose conditions (e.g., low-dose CT and X-ray screenings), while the linear recording $p_r = \exp(-p_a)N_0$ is obtained via the reversed conversion from attenuation p_a given the prior information of the source intensity N_0, where p_a is the pixel values of projections, obtained from the image space as described in [17]. To simulate low-dose screening, we add Poisson noise to the image (Fig. 2d) by adjusting the N_0 parameter to control noise levels. We aim for minimal noise, setting $N_0 = 2 \times 10^7$ after visually examining the noise to ensure it remains imperceptible.

Evaluation. To investigate shortcut learning systematically, we construct development datasets for fine-tuning, focusing on a binary classification task. We introduce previously mentioned confounders (e.g., 'Female') into the positive class with a controlled probability $p_{art} \in \{0, 0.1, 0.2, 0.5, 0.8, 1\}$ to deliberately influence the learning process, replicating scenarios where real-world data may contain confounders. To assess the presence of shortcut learning, we evaluate the fine-tuned models with independently and identically distributed (i.i.d.) as well as out-of-distribution (o.o.d.) test sets. In the o.o.d. set, we introduce the same artifact used during fine-tuning to the negative class with $p_{art} = 1$, such that the models are tested on instances where artifacts appear in the opposite class compared to what they encountered during training. We evaluate the fine-tuned models using the AUC (area under the receiver operating characteristic curve).

Medical Targets. We create separate binary classification tasks for lung mass detection using subsets of images sourced from two datasets: the chest X-ray NIH CXR14 [25] subset annotated by clinicians [20], and the chest CT dataset LIDC-IDRI [1] annotated by four radiologists. From the latter, we sample paired positive and negative 2D slices from the original 3D scans using nodule ROI annotations, representing any kind of lesions and their nearby slices without remarkable findings. We include synthetic artifacts (*a tag, denoising,* and *Poisson noise*) in both tasks. For the case where patient gender serves as the confounding feature, we sample posterior to anterior (PA) images from NIH CXR14 to construct a binary classification task for atelectasis. We deliberately limit the size of our development datasets, encompassing both balanced and unbalanced class distributions to cover a spectrum of clinical scenarios. Data splits

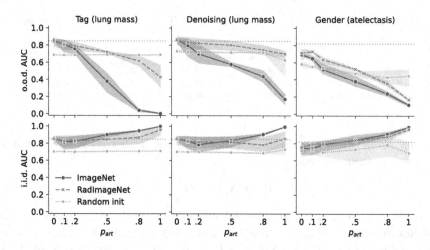

Fig. 3. Mean AUC across five-fold cross-validation with 95% CI for lung mass (left and middle) and atelectasis (right) prediction in chest X-rays. Increasing correlation between artifact (*tag, denoising, gender*) and the label leads to lower o.o.d. AUC (on o.o.d. test set as described in Sect. 2.2) (top row), while i.i.d. AUC increases (bottom row). RadImageNet pretraining shows less degradation in o.o.d. AUC compared to ImageNet pretraining, suggesting that ImageNet may over-rely on spurious correlations in the target dataset. The grey dotted line is the SOTA result for lung mass and atelectasis in NIH CXR14 reported by [5].

for training, validation, and testing preserve class distribution and are stratified by patient. Further details are available in Table 1.

Fine-Tuning Details. We use ResNet50 [12], InceptionV3 [24], InceptionRes-NetV2 [23], and DenseNet121 [14] as the backbones with average pooling and a dropout layer (0.5 probability). The models are trained using cross-entropy loss with Adam optimizer (learning rate: 1×10^{-5}) for a maximum of 200 epochs with early stopping after 30 epochs of no improvement in validation loss (AUC for the balanced tasks). This configuration, established during early tuning, proved flexible enough to accommodate different initializations and target datasets. During training, we apply image augmentations including random rotation (up to $10°$), width and height shifts, shear, and zoom, all set to 0.1, with a fill mode set to 'nearest'. Models were implemented using Keras [4] library and fine-tuned on an NVIDIA Tesla A100 GPU card.

3   Results and Discussion

RadImageNet is Robust to Shortcut Learning. Figure 3 shows that ImageNet and RadImageNet achieve comparable AUC on i.i.d. test set, however, when subjected to o.o.d. test set, notable differences emerge. Specifically, ImageNet's o.o.d. performance on X-rays, confounded by *tag, denoising,* and *patient gender*, drops more compared to RadImageNet, indicating ImageNet's higher

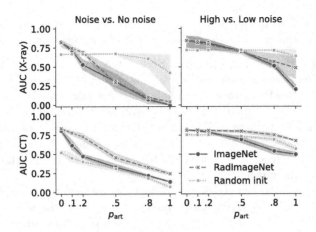

Fig. 4. O.o.d. AUC (mean and 95% CI across five-folds) for lung mass prediction in chest X-rays and CTs. In X-rays (top), both ImageNet and RadImageNet show similar reliance on Poisson noise. However, RadImageNet is more robust in CT scans (bottom). When the confounder is high vs low noise, both ImageNet and RadImageNet are less sensitive (right), compared to noise vs no noise (left).

reliance on spurious correlations. This could be because certain features, for instance, *a tag* (letters), may serve as a discriminative feature in ImageNet, e.g., for the computer keyboard class. However, RadImageNet is invariant to such features as they are not consistently associated with specific labels across different classes, and this invariance transfers to the target task. We observed similar trends in the CT dataset, with the o.o.d. AUC decreasing from 0.84 to 0.02 for ImageNet, and to 0.22 for RadImageNet (for *tag*); and from 0.7 to 0.01 for ImageNet, and from 0.83 only to 0.6 for RadImageNet (for *denoising*). It is worth noting that RadImageNet models tend to train longer, averaging 141 epochs across all experiments, compared to 72 epochs for ImageNet models.

Although *tag* and *denoising* are designed to replicate real-world artifacts, they lack the diversity found in real-world scenarios. *Patient gender* presents a more realistic confounder. Here, the performance gap between ImageNet and RadImageNet is smaller (by 0.12 on average for $p_{art} \geq 0.1$) yet remains statistically significant (permutation test, $0.008 < p$-value < 0.032, for $p_{art} \geq 0.1$). This suggests that RadImageNet's resilience to shortcuts extends to more realistic confounder variations, further emphasizing its robustness in medical image classification. Here we only provide results for ResNet50, however, we observed similar results for InceptionV3, InceptionRes-NetV2, and DenseNet121.

Random initialization appears robust to shortcut learning, with consistent o.o.d. performance as p_{art} increases. However, this is mainly due to the unbalanced class distribution in the lung mass prediction task within the NIH CXR14 dataset, where randomly initialized models tend to predict the overrepresented negative class (recall = 0). Conversely, in the case of a balanced class distribution in the CT target dataset, the o.o.d. performance of randomly initialized models deteriorates to a similar degree as that of ImageNet-initialized models.

Shortcuts Come in All Shapes and Sizes. ImageNet and RadImageNet both heavily rely on Poisson noise in X-rays (Fig. 4, upper left) but RadImageNet shows greater robustness to noise in CT scans compared to ImageNet (Fig. 4, lower left). It is important to note that Poisson noise manifests differently in X-rays and CT scans. In X-rays, Poisson noise introduces graininess characterized by random and pixel-wise independent variations, while in CT scans, it appears as streak artifacts structurally correlated to projections and thus is not pixel-wise independent in the image domain.

To understand the impact of this difference, we directly introduce Poisson noise $N_0 = 2 \times 10^7$ in the image domain for CT scans, mimicking the pixel-wise independence seen in X-rays. However, since CT scans inherently contain noise, this introduces a confounding feature of high versus low levels of noise, as opposed to the original confounder of noise versus no noise.

To simulate a corresponding scenario in X-rays, we generate two levels of Poisson noise: $N_0 = 2 \times 10^7$ for the positives and $N_0 = 1 \times 10^7$ for the negatives (reversed for the o.o.d. test set). Both models show a smaller drop in o.o.d. AUC across modalities, indicating a reduced reliance on the noise shortcut (Fig. 4, right). This suggests that discerning between high and low noise levels is a more challenging task than simply detecting the presence of noise.

RadImageNet maintains its robustness in CT scans, while in X-rays, RadImageNet relies on noise to a similar extent as ImageNet. This may be explained by the absence of X-ray images in RadImageNet, leading to a lack of robust X-ray representations that would resist pixel-wise independent noise – a phenomenon less common in CT, MR, and ultrasound, modalities included in RadImageNet. This highlights that even transferring from a medical source of a different modality may lead to overfitting on confounders.

While our findings generalize over the four tested CNNs, we did not investigate other architectures, such as transformers, due to CNNs competitive performance [7]. Although we expect that our observations might hold true for transformers, given their tendency to reuse features to an even greater extent than CNNs [18], we defer experimental verification to future research.

In our exploration of the MICCAT, we found that RadImageNet models are generally more robust to shortcuts. However, there is some variability within the category of *imaging confounders*, and the importance of the source domain in *anatomical confounders* seems to be lower. Expanding the scope to include other confounders would offer a more comprehensive understanding of the taxonomy landscape and provide insights into the nuances within each category, facilitating better-informed source dataset selection and evaluation strategies. MICCAT paves the way for a more systematic approach to addressing shortcut learning in medical imaging in general by providing a framework for thorough confounder curation and enabling a comprehensive analysis.

4   Conclusion

Our study sheds light on the critical role of the source dataset domain in generalization in medical imaging tasks. By systematically investigating confounders typically found in X-rays and CT scans, we uncovered substantial differences in robustness to shortcuts between models pre-trained on natural and medical image datasets. Our findings caution against the blind application of transfer learning across domains. We advocate for a more nuanced evaluation to improve the reliability and safety of machine learning applications in clinical settings.

Prospect of Application. Transfer learning plays a fundamental role in machine learning applications for medical imaging. Our study emphasizes the often underestimated importance of selecting pre-trained models, urging a necessary reevaluation and deeper investigation into their use in clinical practice.

Acknowledgements. This study was funded by the Novo Nordisk Foundation (grant number NNF21OC0068816). We acknowledge the NIH Clinical Center (NIH CXR14 data), National Cancer Institute and the Foundation for the National Institutes of Health and their critical role in the creation of the free publicly available LIDC/IDRI Database used in this study.

Disclosure of Interests. The authors have no competing interests to declare that are relevant to the content of this article.

References

1. Armato III, S.G., et al.: Data from LIDC-IDRI [data set]. The Cancer Imaging Archive (2015)
2. Banerjee, I., et al.: "Shortcuts" causing bias in radiology artificial intelligence: causes, evaluation, and mitigation. J. Am. Coll. Radiol. **20**(9), 842–851 (2023)
3. Cheplygina, V.: Cats or CAT scans: transfer learning from natural or medical image source data sets? Curr. Opin. Biomed. Eng. **9**, 21–27 (2019)
4. Chollet, F., et al.: Keras (2015)
5. Dai, T., Zhang, R., Hong, F., Yao, J., Zhang, Y., Wang, Y.: UniChest: conquer-and-divide pre-training for multi-source chest X-ray classification. IEEE Trans. Med. Imaging **43**, 2901–2912 (2024)
6. Deng, J., Dong, W., Socher, R., Li, L.J., Li, K., Fei-Fei, L.: ImageNet: a large-scale hierarchical image database. In: 2009 IEEE Conference on Computer Vision and Pattern Recognition, pp. 248–255. IEEE (2009)
7. Doerrich, S., Di Salvo, F., Brockmann, J., Ledig, C.: Rethinking model prototyping through the medMNIST+ dataset collection. arXiv preprint arXiv:2404.15786 (2024)
8. von Euler-Chelpin, M., Lillholm, M., Vejborg, I., Nielsen, M., Lynge, E.: Sensitivity of screening mammography by density and texture: a cohort study from a population-based screening program in Denmark. Breast Cancer Res. BCR **21**(1), 111 (2019)
9. Gavrikov, P., Keuper, J.: Does medical imaging learn different convolution filters? arXiv preprint arXiv:2210.13799 (2022)

10. Geirhos, R., Jacobsen, J.H., Michaelis, C., Zemel, R., Brendel, W., Bethge, M., Wichmann, F.A.: Shortcut learning in deep neural networks. Nat. Mach. Intell. **2**(11), 665–673 (2020)
11. Hasegawa, A., Ishihara, T., Thomas, M.A., Pan, T.: Noise reduction profile: a new method for evaluation of noise reduction techniques in CT. Med. Phys. **49**(1), 186–200 (2022)
12. He, K., Zhang, X., Ren, S., Sun, J.: Deep residual learning for image recognition. In: Proceedings of the IEEE Conference on Computer Vision and Pattern Recognition, pp. 770–778 (2016)
13. Hendrycks, D., Lee, K., Mazeika, M.: Using pre-training can improve model robustness and uncertainty. In: International Conference on Machine Learning, pp. 2712–2721. PMLR (2019)
14. Huang, G., Liu, Z., Van Der Maaten, L., Weinberger, K.Q.: Densely connected convolutional networks. In: Proceedings of the IEEE Conference on Computer Vision and Pattern Recognition, pp. 4700–4708 (2017)
15. Jain, S., Salman, H., Khaddaj, A., Wong, E., Park, S.M., Mądry, A.: A data-based perspective on transfer learning. In: Proceedings of the IEEE/CVF Conference on Computer Vision and Pattern Recognition, pp. 3613–3622 (2023)
16. Juodelyte, D., Jiménez-Sánchez, A., Cheplygina, V.: Revisiting hidden representations in transfer learning for medical imaging. Trans. Mach. Learn. Res. (2023)
17. Leuschner, J., Schmidt, M., Baguer, D.O., Maass, P.: LoDoPaB-CT, a benchmark dataset for low-dose computed tomography reconstruction. Sci. Data **8**(1), 109 (2021)
18. Matsoukas, C., Haslum, J.F., Sorkhei, M., Söderberg, M., Smith, K.: What makes transfer learning work for medical images: feature reuse & other factors. In: Proceedings of the IEEE/CVF Conference on Computer Vision and Pattern Recognition, pp. 9225–9234 (2022)
19. Mei, X., et al.: RadImageNet: an open radiologic deep learning research dataset for effective transfer learning. Radiol. Artif. Intell. **4**(5), e210315 (2022)
20. Nabulsi, Z., et al.: Deep learning for distinguishing normal versus abnormal chest radiographs and generalization to two unseen diseases tuberculosis and COVID-19. Sci. Rep. **11**(1), 15523 (2021)
21. Oakden-Rayner, L., Dunnmon, J., Carneiro, G., Ré, C.: Hidden stratification causes clinically meaningful failures in machine learning for medical imaging. In: Proceedings of the ACM Conference on Health, Inference, and Learning, pp. 151–159 (2020)
22. Ramanujan, V., Nguyen, T., Oh, S., Farhadi, A., Schmidt, L.: On the connection between pre-training data diversity and fine-tuning robustness. Adv. Neural Inf. Process. Syst. **36** (2024)
23. Szegedy, C., Ioffe, S., Vanhoucke, V., Alemi, A.: Inception-v4, inception-resnet and the impact of residual connections on learning. In: Proceedings of the AAAI Conference on Artificial Intelligence, vol. 31 (2017)
24. Szegedy, C., Vanhoucke, V., Ioffe, S., Shlens, J., Wojna, Z.: Rethinking the inception architecture for computer vision. In: Proceedings of the IEEE Conference on Computer Vision and Pattern Recognition, pp. 2818–2826 (2016)
25. Wang, X., Peng, Y., Lu, L., Lu, Z., Bagheri, M., Summers, R.M.: ChestX-ray8: hospital-scale chest X-ray database and benchmarks on weakly-supervised classification and localization of common thorax diseases. In: Proceedings of the IEEE Conference on Computer Vision and Pattern Recognition, pp. 2097–2106 (2017)

26. Wei, K., Fu, Y., Zheng, Y., Yang, J.: Physics-based noise modeling for extreme low-light photography. IEEE Trans. Pattern Anal. Mach. Intell. **44**(11), 8520–8537 (2021)
27. Wiens, J., et al.: Do no harm: a roadmap for responsible machine learning for health care. Nat. Med. **25**(9), 1337–1340 (2019)
28. Zech, J.R., Badgeley, M.A., Liu, M., Costa, A.B., Titano, J.J., Oermann, E.K.: Variable generalization performance of a deep learning model to detect pneumonia in chest radiographs: a cross-sectional study. PLoS Med. **15**(11), e1002683 (2018)
29. Zhou, Z., Sodha, V., Pang, J., Gotway, M.B., Liang, J.: Models genesis. Med. Image Anal. **67**, 101840 (2021)

Evaluating Perceived Workload, Usability and Usefulness of Artificial Intelligence Systems in Low-Resource Settings: Semi-automated Classification and Detection of Community Acquired Pneumonia

Malaizyo G. Muzumala[1]([✉])(iD), Ernest O. Zulu[2](iD), Peter Chibuta[2](iD), Mayumbo Nyirenda[1](iD), and Lighton Phiri[3]([✉])(iD)

[1] Department of Computer Science, University of Zambia, Lusaka, Zambia
{malaizyo.muzumala,mayumbo.nyirenda}@cs.unza.zm
[2] Department of Radiology, University Teaching Hospitals, Lusaka, Zambia
[3] Department of Library and Information Science, University of Zambia, Lusaka, Zambia
lighton.phiri@unza.zm

Abstract. The use of Artificial Intelligence (AI) techniques in radiological workflows is increasingly becoming mainstream. However, the uptake of AI techniques is still low in low-resource settings such as the Global South. This paper presents a study conducted in a setting with low AI uptake, to determine the impact of AI on Radiologists' workload when interpreting medical images. Two (2) AI models-a classification model and detection model indicating potential areas of interest-were implemented to facilitate the semi-automated interpretation of medical images for Pneumonia. In addition, a Web-based DICOM Viewer was implemented to interface the AI models. To determine the appropriate model configuration, two (2) experts-a Radiologist and Radiology Resident-participated in a focus group discussion aimed at determining how the AI models could facilitate interpretation processes. A comparative controlled experiment was subsequently conducted with 12 Radiology Residents at a large University Teaching Hospital, to assess the impact of AI on the workload and its perceived usefulness. NASA Task Load Index (TLX) and Technology Acceptance Model (TAM) 2 questionnaires were employed to measure the workload and usefulness. The results indicate that the perceived workload is significantly less when using the AI solution, with an overall NASA-TLX score of 1.86. Furthermore, the perceived usefulness of the AI solution is demonstrated through the positive responses for all the eight TAM 2 constructs. This study experimentally demonstrates the potential of utilising AI for the semi-automated interpretation of medical images in low-resource settings.

Keywords: Artificial Intelligence · Classification · Detection · DICOM · Medical Images

S. Wu et al. (Eds.): AMAI 2024, LNCS 15384, pp. 116–126, 2025.
https://doi.org/10.1007/978-3-031-82007-6_12

1   Introduction

The lack of availability of adequate radiological resources in health facilities in low-resource settings is well documented [12], with factors such as shortfall of Radiologists and unavailability of required infrastructure cited as the major factors.

The rapid advances in the field of Artificial Intelligence (AI) provides opportunities to address the many challenges associated with radiological workflows. However, the adoption of such AI solutions has been slow in resource-poor health institutions in regions such as the Global South.

This paper presents work conducted in a Global South country, Zambia, to explore how AI could be deployed and integrated within medical imaging workflows and, additionally, assess its effectiveness.

In order to execute the study, pneumonia was used as a case pathology. Pneumonia is reported to have been one of the top 10 leading causes of both morbidity and, additionally, one of the top five leading causes of mortality in Zambia in 2021; Pneumonia was the second highest cause of death in 2021, contributing to 11.4% of the total deaths [19]. The increase in Pneumonia cases and reported shortage of Radiologists in Zambia presents a challenge with effective diagnoses, especially in regards to medical image interpretation. Artificial Intelligence (AI) has been identified as a potentially viable approach to effectively and efficiently interpreting medical images. These tools will be used to assist clinicians in the radiographic diagnosis of Community Acquired Pneumonia (CAP), helping them to select patients eligible for antibiotic therapy.

While the use of AI in health facilities in Zambia is still in its infancy, our previous work has, in part, identified opportunities for leveraging AI [28]. In addition, we have demonstrated the feasibility of deploying Enterprise Medical Imaging technologies such as Picture Archiving and Communication Systems (PACS), which provide the base infrastructure required for the deployment of AI-based solutions.

This work was aimed at demonstrating how Artificial Intelligence (AI) can be leveraged to support the semi-automated diagnosis of pneumonia in low-resource settings characterised by experts with little experience working with AI centric solutions.

The main contributions of this work are as follows:

- Results from Radiologists and Medical Doctors' perceptions on the use of AI for the semi-automated interpretation of medical images
- Experimental results on the usefulness of using classification, localisation and detection models

The remainder of this paper is organised as follows: Sect. 2 outlines state-of-the-art literature related to this work; Sect. 3 describes the methodological approach used to execute studies associated with this work; Sect. 4 provides the presentation of findings and their interpretation and, finally, Sect. 5 outlines concluding remarks and future work.

2   Related Work

2.1   Pneumonia in the Global South

Pneumonia is an acute respiratory infection responsible for a significant global disease burden as measured by the loss in Disability Adjusted Life Years (DALYs) [6] The impact of pneumonia is much more severe in developing countries due to low rates of childhood immunisation, poor nutrition, overcrowding, smoking and increased at-risk populations with comorbid immunosuppressive conditions such as HIV infection. In Zambia-for instance-Pneumonia remains among the top causes of morbidity and mortality (1). Chest radiography is recognised as the standard reference for the diagnosis of CAP [3] as there are no reliable clinical features, individually or in combination, to establish the diagnosis [11]. However, developing countries are faced with a critical shortage of Radiologists for effective interpretation of the chest radiographs. Management of suspected CAP has typically involved empirical treatment with broad spectrum antibiotics, with recent observations provoking concerns for contribution towards the rise in antimicrobial-resistant strains [4]. Therefore, tools to support clinicians in the radiographic diagnosis of CAP would assist in the careful selection of patients eligible for antibiotic therapy.

2.2   Automated Interpretation of Medical Image

Existing literature highlights three image recognition techniques-classification, detection and localisation-and segmentation as the broad categories of approaches that are employed when applying AI within medical image interpretation workflows. Fournier and Chassagnon provide a comprehensive description of these approaches, including case scenarios when such approaches are applied [7]

A number of AI models have been proposed to aid in the interpretation of variable radiographs and pathologies, including detection of pneumonia. Chumbita et al. provide a review of how AI can potentially be used to improve the management of pneumonia [5]. Another review by Stokes et al. investigates performance and reporting of AI systems for pneumonia detection [22].

In addition, there are more focused studies that have resulted in the implementation of AI models for detecting pneumonia. For instance, Li et al. propose a deep learning for detecting pneumonia [10]. Other studies include work by Račić et al., who demonstrate how chest x-rays can be processed by AI algorithms to support decision making [17].

Existing work aimed at evaluating the effects of AI solutions on radiological workflows suggests different aspects of the perceptions practitioners have towards AI tools [8,27].

3   Methodology

A mixed-method approach was employed when conducting this study, with the CRoss Industry Standard Process for Data Mining (CRISP-DM) [26] methodology used to guide the overall research process.

Ethical clearance was granted by The University of Zambia Biomedical Research Ethics Committee (Reference Number: 2731–2022) and The National Health Research Authority (Reference Number: NHRA000024/10/05/2022), to conduct this study. In addition, formal permission was granted from The University Teaching Hospital (UTHs).

3.1   Pneumonia Classification and Detection Models

The goal of this study was to comprehensively evaluate the perceived use of AI models for the semi-automated interpretation of medical images. Two Pneumonia AI models-a binary classification model and a detection model-were implemented, in part, to determine the appropriate approach for integrating AI solutions into medical imaging workflows.

The classification model was built using transfer learning from VGG16 [21] on the Paul Mooney chest x-ray dataset [13]. The full implementation is public [2]. The detection model was trained on the RSNA dataset, full implementation and data is public [1].

The two models were deployed by implementing a Web-based interface which, aside from rendering responses from the model, provided comprehensive DICOM Data Element metadata. The interaction between the Web-based interface and the models was facilitated by a Web service, implemented to accept requests from the Web interface and produce responses from the models.

The AI models were implemented to use a DICOM file as input. The binary classification model was implemented to signal if a given input DICOM file was associated with Pneumonia.

The Python programming language was used to implement the models, primarily using the Kaggle platform for training and community support. The publicly available "RSNA Pneumonia Detection Challenge" [16] and "Chest X-Ray Pneumonia" [13] datasets were used to train the detection model. The Web service was implemented using Python Flask [15], while the Web interface was implemented using Next.js [25]. Standard classification [18] and detection [14] performance metrics were employed to assess the effectiveness of the two models as outlined in Sect. 4.

3.2   Effectiveness of Semi-automated Interpretation

The adoption of AI in radiological workflows at UTH is still in its infancy and as such, to evaluate the potential of using AI for the semi-automated interpretation of medical images, experiments were conducted to assess the effect of AI on the turnaround time and workload. In addition, the perceived usefulness of AI solutions was assessed.

Semi-automated Medical Image Interpretation Approaches. In order to determine how the classification and detection models would be integrated within the medical imaging workflow, a virtual focus group discussion was held with two Key Experts: a Radiologist (Radiologist 1) with 5 years experience and a Radiology Resident (Radiology Resident 1) with 1 year experience. The two Key Experts were sampled using convenience sampling from UTHs.

The discussion with the Key Experts was focused on determining if the AI intervention should be deployed with either one of the two models or a combination of the two models. In addition, the Key Experts were requested to provide feedback on potential changes that could be made to the Web-interface.

Evaluating Perceived Workload and Usefulness. A controlled experiment was conducted in order to experimentally evaluate the AI toolkit through the measurement of perceived workload, usefulness and usability.

To evaluate the perceived workload and usefulness, a comparative analysis was conducted by comparing the AI solution (AI Intervention) with the conventional way of interpreting medical images (Baseline), generally involving the use of DICOM Viewers.

Evaluation of the perceived workload and usefulness associated with the AI intervention was conducted with participants-Radiology Residents and General Practitioners-sampled using purposive sampling from the UTHs. UTHs has a shortage of Radiologists, as outlined in our prior work [28] and as a result, Radiology Residents and General Practitioners are compelled to interpret medical images.

Measurement Instruments. The NASA Task Load Index (NASA-TLX) instrument [9, 23] was used to measure the participants' perceived workload. The NASA-TLX instrument measures subjective workload scores using a weighted rating of six subscales-Mental Demand, Physical Demand, Temporal Demand, Performance, Effort and Frustration.

The perceived usefulness and usability of the AI toolkit was measured using the Technology Acceptance Model (TAM 2) instrument [24]. TAM 2 facilitates the measurement of users' perceived usefulness and perceived ease of use of a technology, along with additional social influence and cognitive instrumental processes, to predict their intention to use the technology.

Task Design and Experiment Procedure. Study participants were required to interpret a Chest X-ray positive for Pneumonia using the two approaches-the implemented AI solution, a combination of the classification and detection models-AI Intervention-and the conventional way of interpreting medical images-Baseline. Counterbalancing of interpretation approaches was employed by changing the order in which the two approaches were used.

Participants were briefed about the study and subsequently required to sign an informed consent form. Participants subsequently performed the experiment tasks, completing the NASA-TLX immediately after performing the predefined task using each of the two approaches. After completion of the task using the two approaches, the participants were required to complete the TAM 2 questionnaire, to provide their perceived subjective views of using the AI toolkit.

4   Results and Discussion

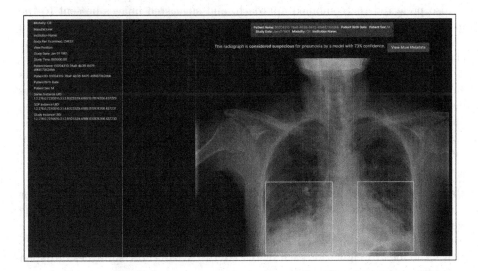

Fig. 1. A screenshot of the localiser interface.

4.1   Pneumonia Classification and Detection

The classification model had an accuracy of 72% and the detection model had an Intersection over union of 12% and precision of 15%. In addition, the recall for the detection model was 79%, with a 30% overlap threshold in area to count it as a hit. The basis of the threshold was the observed tendency of the model to draw the regions larger than the annotated drawings.

The classification accuracy, was lower than some existing studies [20] future training will work with these and better workflows. However, the low Intersection over union is primarily attributed to the model's tendency to give false positives. Drawing the boxes larger than the annotating radiologists. A proposed mitigation was using the two (2) models together such that the bounding model would only act when the classification model returns a positive result.

4.2   Efficiency and Effectiveness of Semi-automated Interpretation

The focus group discussions held with the two experts indicate that the ideal configuration would have to combine information from both the classification model (text indicating the positivity of the semi-automated interpretation) and detection model (bounding boxes indicating the potential areas of interest). [Radiologist 1] indicated that they preferred the combined method, further suggesting changes to technical terms used in the Web interface. The message from the classifier was changed from "This case is suspected Positive for pneumonia by a model with 73% accuracy" with the "positive" in red to "This radiograph is considered suspicious for pneumonia by a model with 73% confidence" with considered suspicious bounding box in yellow. In addition, [Radiology Resident 1] also preferred the combined approach, and suggested images be sent to the model and processes as soon as they're onboarded without needing to click a button. Figure 1 shows a screenshot of the interface combining results from the classification and detection models.

A total of 12 participants-one (1) Radiologist, six (6) Radiology Residents and five (5) Other Practitioners-participated in the comparative study to assess perceived workload and usefulness associated with the AI solution. While the participants were generally aware of AI based on the discussions around the experiment, none of them stated they had experience applying AI solutions when interpreting medical images.

Perceived Workload. The NASA-TLX average workload (mean weights for each practitioner in each category) for the AI Intervention and the Baseline were 1.86 and 2.22 (lower numbers are better), respectively, indicating that the perceived workload for the AI Intervention is lower than the Baseline. Figure 2 shows the mean weights for each of the six (6) NASA-TLX subscales, grouped by interpretation approach.

The results further indicate that the perceived workload was noticeably lower, when using the AI Intervention, for the "Mental", "Physical", and "Effort". This is arguably the expected effect of an AI solution since automation results in users performing significantly less tasks. While the workload was lower when using the Baseline for "Temporal", "Performance" and "Frustration", the variation was not significant. More importantly, however, the perceived less workload for "Temporal" is arguably because participants were already familiar with interpreting medical images associated with Pneumonia while using DICOM Viewers. The same argument can be made for the lower score for "Performance", since users are generally more effective when using tools they are familiar with. Finally, the lower score for the "Frustration" subscale is likely due to the fact that participants were interacting with the AI Intervention for the first time.

Ultimately, the results of the perceived workload evaluation, especially suggest a need to expose Radiologists and General Practitioners at UTHs to AI tools. This view is shared by RAD-AID, who propose a three-pronged approach for AI adoption in resource-constrained environments [12]

Perceived Usefulness. The results from the TAM 2 questionnaires were analysed using the eight (8) TAM 2 constructs using the standard approach for analysing TAM 2 responses. The results of the analysis are shown in Fig. 3.

Most of the participants had positive responses for all the eight TAM 2 construction, with participants overwhelmingly agreeing with "Intention to Use",

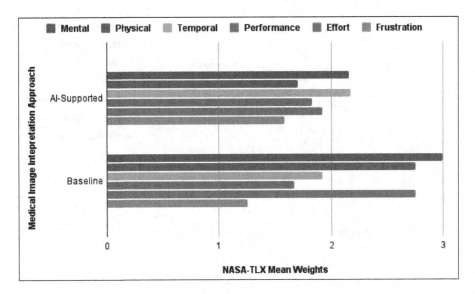

Fig. 2. NASA-TLX Mean Weights comparison between AI intervention and baseline.

"Results Demonstrability" and "Voluntariness". Some participants, in particular, negatively rated the "Job Relevance" and "Output Quality".

The negative response for "Output Quality" can arguably be because that single participant disagreed with the result of the model. That was the sole participant that rated the section negatively. The negative responses linked to "Job Relevance" can mostly be attributed to Radiologists that have extensive experience interpreting medical images linked to Pathologies like Pneumonia and it can be argued that they would likely agree with the relevance of more challenging modalities to interpret.

Participants' Comments. Participants were required to provide optional comments regarding the AI intervention. The comments-outlined below-ranged from recommendations on how to use such AI solutions and, additionally, suggestions on how to improve the solution.

"Needs to be in the right hands, users should be able to interpret (medical back)" [sic] [Participant 4]

"I would only recommend radiology residents and radiologists to use such tools. As other doctors may have challenges" [sic] [Participant 4]

"Strong recommended working with specialised pneumonias" [Participant 7]

"There should be a way of inputting the medical details with the xray" [sic] [Participant 9]

"wouldn't recommend for complex imaging. Like CTs" [sic] [Participant 11]

The comments support the results from the TAM 2 usefulness evaluation and in particular, results associated with the "Subjective Norm", "Job Relevance" and "Perceived Ease of Use" TAM 2 constructs.

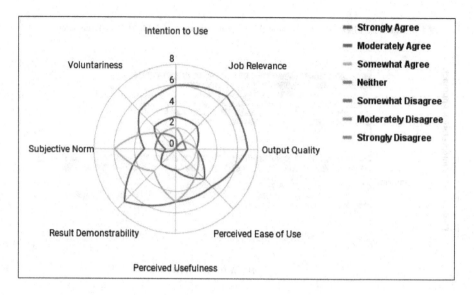

Fig. 3. Radar Chart illustrating the summary of the usability evaluation results.

5   Conclusion

This paper detailed a study conducted in a low-resource setting of a Global South country in order to demonstrate the perceived effectiveness of utilising AI solutions to address challenges characteristic of radiological workflows. Pneumonia was used as the case pathology in order to assess the effect of the AI solution on the workload and potential usefulness of the solution.

The results from this study arguably provide vital insights into perceptions of Radiologists and General Practitioners on the impact of AI solutions when applied to radiological workflows.

Acknowledgements. This study was conducted as part of a much larger "Enterprise Medical Imaging in Zambia" project. The project is funded through generous grants from Google Research, Data Science Africa and The University of Zambia. We are very appreciative of this funding.

References

1. EMI: Detection model, MRCNN and COCO, March 2024. https://www.kaggle.com/code/malaizyogmuzumala/emi-detection-model-mrcnn-and-coco?scriptVersionId=165890883. Accessed 25 July 2024
2. EMI simple pneumonia based binary classifier, March 2024. https://www.kaggle.com/code/malaizyogmuzumala/emi-simple-pneumonia-based-binary-classifier. Accessed 25 July 2024

3. Boersma, W.G., Daniels, J.M.A., Löwenberg, A., Boeve, W.J., van de Jagt, E.J.: Reliability of radiographic findings and the relation to etiologic agents in community-acquired pneumonia. Respir. Med. **100**(5), 926–932 (2006). https://doi.org/10.1016/j.rmed.2005.06.018

4. Boyles, T.H., et al.: South African guideline for the management of community-acquired pneumonia in adults. J. Thorac. Dis. **9**(6), 1469–1502 (2017). https://doi.org/10.21037/jtd.2017.05.31

5. Chumbita, M., et al.: Can artificial intelligence improve the management of pneumonia. J. Clin. Med. **9**(1) (2020). https://doi.org/10.3390/jcm9010248

6. Ferkol, T., Schraufnagel, D.: The global burden of respiratory disease. Ann. Am. Thorac. Soc. **11**(3) (2014). https://doi.org/10.1513/annalsats.201311-405ps

7. Fournier, L., Chassagnon, G.: Artificial Intelligence and Machine Learning, pp. 213–225. Springer, New York (2021). https://doi.org/10.1007/978-1-0716-1756-4_14

8. Gaube, S., et al.: Non-task expert physicians benefit from correct explainable AI advice when reviewing x-rays. Sci. Rep. **13**(1), 1383 (2023). https://doi.org/10.1038/s41598-023-28633-w

9. Hart, S.G., Staveland, L.E.: Development of NASA-TLX (task load index): results of empirical and theoretical research. In: Hancock, P.A., Meshkati, N. (eds.) Human Mental Workload, Advances in Psychology, vol. 52, pp. 139–183. North-Holland (1988). https://doi.org/10.1016/S0166-4115(08)62386-9

10. Li, L., et al.: Using artificial intelligence to detect COVID-19 and community-acquired pneumonia based on pulmonary CT: evaluation of the diagnostic accuracy. Radiology (2020). https://doi.org/10.1148/radiol.2020200905

11. Metlay, J.P., Kapoor, W.N., Fine, M.J.: Does this patient have community-acquired pneumonia?: diagnosing pneumonia by history and physical examination. JAMA **278**(17), 1440–1445 (1997). https://doi.org/10.1001/jama.1997.03550170070035

12. Mollura, D.J., et al.: Artificial intelligence in low- and Middle-Income countries: innovating global health radiology. Radiology **297**(3), 513–520 (2020). https://doi.org/10.1148/radiol.2020201434

13. bibitemch12Mooney2018spsrw Mooney, P.: Chest X-ray images (pneumonia), March 2018. https://www.kaggle.com/datasets/paultimothymooney/chest-xray-pneumonia

14. Padilla, R., Netto, S.L., da Silva, E.A.B.: A survey on performance metrics for object-detection algorithms. In: 2020 International Conference on Systems, Signals and Image Processing (IWSSIP). IEEE (2020). https://doi.org/10.1109/IWSSIP48289.2020.9145130

15. Pallets: Welcome to flask - flask documentation (3.0.x) (2010). https://flask.palletsprojects.com/en/3.0.x. Accessed 7 Mar 2024

16. Pan, I., Cadrin-Chênevert, A., Cheng, P.M.: Tackling the radiological society of North America pneumonia detection challenge. Am. J. Roentgenol. **213**(3), 568–574 (2019). https://doi.org/10.2214/AJR.19.21512, pMID: 31120793

17. Racic, L., Popovic, T., Cakic, S., Sandi, S.: Pneumonia detection using deep learning based on convolutional neural network. In: 2021 25th International Conference on Information Technology (IT). IEEE (2021). https://doi.org/10.1109/IT51528.2021.9390137

18. Reich, Y., Barai, S.V.: Evaluating machine learning models for engineering problems. Artif. Intell. Eng. **13**(3), 257–272 (1999). https://doi.org/10.1016/S0954-1810(98)00021-1

19. Republic of Zambia Ministry of Health: Annual health statistical report 2017 - 2021: Tracking performance of the NHSP 2017 - 2021. Technical report Republic of Zambia Ministry of Health (2022). https://www.moh.gov.zm/?wpfb_dl=179

20. Reshan, M.S.A., et al.: Detection of pneumonia from chest X-ray images utilizing MobileNet model. Healthcare (Basel) **11**(11) (2023). https://doi.org/10.3390/healthcare11111561

21. Simonyan, K., Zisserman, A.: Very deep convolutional networks for large-scale image recognition (2015). https://arxiv.org/abs/1409.1556

22. Stokes, K., et al.: The use of artificial intelligence systems in diagnosis of pneumonia via signs and symptoms: a systematic review. Biomed. Signal Process. Control **72**, 103325 (2022). https://doi.org/10.1016/j.bspc.2021.103325

23. The NASA TLX Tool: Task Load Index: TLX @ NASA ames - home. https://humansystems.arc.nasa.gov/groups/tlx/. Accessed 7 Mar 2024

24. Venkatesh, V., Davis, F.D.: A theoretical extension of the technology acceptance model: four longitudinal field studies. Manage. Sci. **46**(2), 186–204 (2000). https://doi.org/10.1287/mnsc.46.2.186.11926

25. Vercel, Inc.: Next.js by vercel - the react framework. https://nextjs.org. Accessed 7 Mar 2024

26. Wirth, R., Hipp, J.: CRISP-DM: towards a standard process model for data mining. In: Proceedings of the Fourth International Conference on the Practical Application of Knowledge Discovery and Data Mining, pp. 29–39 (2000). http://cs.unibo.it/~danilo.montesi/CBD/Beatriz/10.1.1.198.5133.pdf

27. Xie, Y., Chen, M., Kao, D., Gao, G., Chen, X.a.: CheXplain: enabling physicians to explore and understand Data-Driven, AI-Enabled medical imaging analysis. In: Proceedings of the 2020 CHI Conference on Human Factors in Computing Systems, CHI 2020, pp. 1–13. Association for Computing Machinery (2020). https://doi.org/10.1145/3313831.3376807

28. Zulu, E.O., Phiri, L.: Enterprise medical imaging in the global south: challenges and opportunities. In: 2022 IST-Africa Conference (IST-Africa), pp. 1–9. IEEE (2022). https://doi.org/10.23919/IST-Africa56635.2022.9845508

Incremental Augmentation Strategies for Personalised Continual Learning in Digital Pathology Contexts

Arijit Patra[✉]

UCB, Slough SL1 3WE, UK
`Arijit.Patra@ucb.com`

Abstract. Like most connectionist systems, deep networks have been found to be prone to catastrophic forgetting effects. This makes generalization of deep neural network pipelines a challenge as new additions to prediction requirements at runtime would invariably require retraining on not only the new dataset, but also substantial portions of older task data. This is a difficult task in personalised clinical imaging where retention of datasets over extended time is challenged by the fact that the already limited individual-specific examples may not be stored over extended time owing to memory, legal and infrastructure constraints. Thus, there is a need to rethink the process of deploying learning pipelines in personalised healthcare contexts that address forgetting as part of initial and incremental task learning over time. This has been modelled as an incremental learning problem, with an evolving interest in exploring the applicability of such a paradigm in precision medicine contexts. We propose a novel approach to the incremental class addition problem for individualised data curation settings pertinent to personalised medicine, where a retention of limited numbers of exemplars of old classes helps reduce forgetting instead of large-scale data storage, using a strategy of incremental time sample augmentation with fractional linear transformations and weighted knowledge distillation objectives to correct for evolving class imbalance effects in conjunction with the mitigation of reductions in initial task performances following incremental adaptation to new data distributions.

Keywords: distillation · personalised incremental learning · Mobius augmentation

1 Introduction

Deep learning based methods have become commonplace in medical imaging research and are making progress towards adoptions in routine practice [15], with increasing relevance in personalised medicine and multimodal data integration [2, 39]. In real-world clinical situations, imaging and diagnostic systems often do not have access to all the required data initially, but data arrives in incremental chunks over time, acquired with multiple devices and across different devices and evaluation centres [6]. This problem is pronounced in healthcare systems where data acquisition and quality assurance

© The Author(s), under exclusive license to Springer Nature Switzerland AG 2025
S. Wu et al. (Eds.): AMAI 2024, LNCS 15384, pp. 127–139, 2025.
https://doi.org/10.1007/978-3-031-82007-6_13

infrastructure may not be as developed. Such cases of variable data accessibility require machine learning algorithms to be robust to adaptations on new data distributions over time and be generalizable to novel classes of data, to remain clinically significant and reliably aid diagnostic efforts throughout their shelf lives under evolving requirements. This aspect is increasingly crucial when we consider the directions of evolving clinical research and practice towards individual-level treatment design and administration, in a paradigm known as precision medicine [40]. In personalised medicine, each subject is viewed as a unique entity with respect to the longitudinal evolution of a set of clinically relevant conditions, and represents a unique cumulative set of data points, some of which may not be available all at once but be observed over time during hospital admissions or routine observations over time. While machine learning systems have historically relied on statistical learning strategies over a relatively large number of data points over particular data distributions, the domain of precision medicine inherently implies that the number of data points available for a particular data distribution (as could be relevant for individual patient histories) is limited. While the scope for predictive evaluation in this scenario may be addressed by emerging techniques for few-shot learning on a limited scale [40], the issue of adaptation of such networks to successive subjects with unique data distributions is a challenge that needs to be addressed for the clinical validity of such approaches. This requirement for continual adaptation in deep networks for clinical imaging implies a need to ensure that model parameters remain relevant to both old and new tasks in incremental data regimes. This needs to occur without storing large numbers of exemplars from past classes over subsequent learning schedules [33] owing to constraints on long-term storage of clinical data in terms of fairness [36], legal and privacy issues [31]. Thus, the ideal joint training condition of optimizing models with all datasets ever used at each incremental retraining is challenging in clinical imaging. Over the years, the practice of pathology has emerged as a key component in diagnostic evaluations for a multiplicity of disease categories, in oncology, immunology and several other areas [39]. The large-scale analysis of tissues was historically time-consuming and labor intensive when performed manually by expert pathologists. Thus, the advent of digital image analysis and subsequent adaptations of machine learning algorithms was transformative for several aspects of the pathological analysis pipeline. Similarly, critical aspects of pharmaceutical drug development rely on non-clinical safety evaluations using toxicologic pathology on animal model tissue data, with the volume of data generated ranging from 60–100 whole slide images (WSIs) for 80–100 rodent models in a single Investigational New Drug study [13]. In both clinical and toxicological pathology, the advent of machine learning driven pathology image analysis has made significant forays due to the potential for efficiency gains in the analysis pipeline. Additionally, with the requirement of individual level understanding of patients in precision medicine approaches and the requirement of tissue level analysis with molecular tests for decisions about therapeutic choices, digital pathology is evolving to become a central driver of personalized healthcare due to its role as a critical process for extraction of information at the tissue level for individual subjects [41].

2 Prior Work

Adaptation of existing deep learning models to learn new classes was attempted initially by transfer learning. Transfer learning, despite helping prior learning to enhance future task learning, was found to inefficiently balance old and new task knowledge across the scale of multiple, temporally-spaced learning stages where datasets may demonstrate a distribution shift [1]. Studies show a decline in past performances or catastrophic forgetting [1], as information previously learnt is lost causing high validation losses on past task or class data. Recent work has pursued mitigation of forgetting in deep networks with parameter expansion [3], exemplar replay [4], generative rehearsal [6] and regularization [7]. Knowledge distillation, where representations learnt by a model are transferred to another, are often used in model compression [8]. It has been used for incremental learning as the representation from one learning session can help regularize a future session, with the old tasks' logits regularizing the learning on new data. Such methods include Learning without Forgetting (LwF) [4] with distillation and cross-entropy objectives, learning using human insights [11] where distillation and gaze-based salience enable model compression, progressive retrospection (PDR) [12] using distillation from both old and new models. In clinical imaging, data availability is often not immediate and models learning incrementally over time without affecting past performance have been researched [32], such as weight consolidation and distillation [34], hierarchical continual learning [16] etc. While data augmentation has been used in machine learning [9, 17], there has been little research on the unique features of personalised medicine workflows in incremental class adaptation settings, particularly on imaging datasets. We study fractional linear transformations, or Mobius transformations to examine their utility towards incremental time data augmentation in histology imaging in an effort to investigate whether such runtime data augmentation during incremental class addition may help with the mitigation of catastrophic forgetting effects when dealing with individual specific high dimensional datasets. Mobius transformations have been studied in applied mathematics and related domains, in areas like projective geometry [18], analysis of complex valued networks [19], optimizing deep compositional spatial models [20], extending sample sizes [21], hyperbolic networks [22], and approximating Choquet integrals [23].

Contributions. We propose a novel approach for personalised incremental learning without using substantial exemplar retention, using a dataset of colorectal carcinoma images [24] as an example task. The clinical utility of histological analysis has been proven to be crucial for diagnostic workflows for multiple domains. As such, with the emerging interest in modelling personalised trajectories, the ability to algorithmically interpret histology data on a personalised basis is increasingly of interest. This is achieved by propagating sample diversity through a novel online augmentation over a limited number of past tasks' samples, while performing a weighted cross-distillation over the logits of the past classes while training on new class data for the available model. Our key contributions are: a) a concept of incremental time data augmentation strategy using Mobius transformations b) weighted cross-distillation for continual learning of new classes that can be viewed as analogous to new individual-specific diagnostic information available on longitudinal scales during clinical evaluations over extended time c) an online adaptation of Mobius augmentation in incremental learning tasks in order to reduce the dependency of memory storage for exemplar replay during incremental learning. To our knowledge, this is also one of the first attempts at bringing the notion of continual learning in medical imaging to a personalized healthcare setting, where imaging and multimodal analysis increasingly drives patient understanding and therapy planning.

3 Methodology

Datasets. Anonymized colorectal cancer H&E-stained tissue slides were obtained using an Aperio ScanScope scanner at a 20x magnification in a clinical pathology setup. These slides are digitized and anonymized images of formalin-fixed paraffin embedded human colorectal adenocarcinomas and made publicly available through the pathology archives at the University Medical Center Mannheim [24]. These slides contain contiguous tissue areas that are manually annotated and tessellated. These images are converted to 150 x 150 x 3 RGB patches. Overall, 5000 images were obtained for different tissue classes. In this study, 8 classes with 625 samples each were considered: *1. Tumor epithelium; 2. Simple stroma (homogeneous with tumor stroma, extra-tumoral stroma and smooth muscle); 3. Complex stroma (single tumor cells and immune cells); 4. Debris (necrosis, haemorrhage and mucus); 5. Immune cells (immune cell conglomerates and sub-mucosal lymphoid follicles); 6. Normal mucosal glands; 7. Adipose tissue; 8. Background.*

Problem Definition. Consider a problem where the model needs to be trained in an M-stage fashion, with each stage being a classification task with classes as $Xt = \{Xt,i\}^{Kt}i = 1$, $t \in [1,M]$, with each X being a class and includes samples $xt \in Xt$ and Kt being the number of classes in each stage t. The classifier learning in stage t-1, after incrementally being optimized over the classes at the tth stage, shouldn't show marked declines in inference capacity over validation set instances from $(t-1)^{th}$ stage or prior stages in the temporally-spaced learning regime. Here, we propose an incremental learning experiment with four classes in the initial training stage and four in the incremental stage ($M = 2$, $K1 = K2 = 4$). Note that the terms 'incremental learning', 'continual learning', and 'lifelong learning' are used interchangeably in literature and convey similar meanings for accomplishing the design of learning algorithms that can adapt to temporally spaced arrivals of datasets from varying data distributions [37]. This study is modelled as a sequential class learning task as above, with a proportion of classes being learnt as '**base classes**' during an initial training stage. Next, the remaining classes are learnt as '**incremental classes**' in a subsequent learning stage, leading to a multistage learning system over a temporal interval. The base classes are the *tumour epithelium (TE), simple stroma (SS), Immune cells (IC)* and *Adipose tissue (AT)*. The incrementally learnt classes include *complex stroma (CS), debris (De), normal mucosal glands (NMG)* and *background (BG)*. The former classes are used to optimize for the initial task (Task 1) and the latter classes are used to train the model that was initially optimised over base classes for the incremental task (Task 2), thus simulating a continual or incremental learning scenario. It is to be noted that the dataset used here is for demonstration of the incremental learning problem setting and how it may be adapted to similar imaging or multimodal analysis situations in the personalised medicine space. The original dataset was curated for more generalised purposes and as such did not account for utility to the precision medicine community. In the absence of specific histology or imaging datasets acquired as a result of clinical practice in personalised healthcare available under open source licenses, we believe that this dataset is a suitable exemplar for proof-of-concept studies for personalised incremental learning in medical imaging as the volume and class-level characteristics of the dataset lend themselves well for the simulation of a continual learning setting with class-specific data volumes kept at limited scales in line with real-life constraints. Thus, in the light of paucity of high-quality precision histology datasets, we believe that the dataset used in these experiments is one of the suitable datasets for an academic study of precision incremental learning in medical imaging contexts (Figs. 1 and 2).

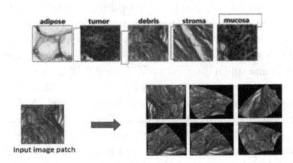

Fig. 1. Sample images from the colorectal histology dataset used (*top*); Mobius transformed augmented examples during incremental learning (*bottom*)

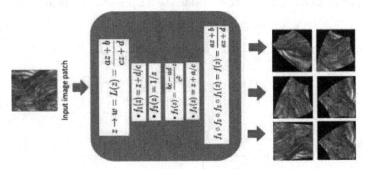

Fig. 2. Interpretation of Mobius transformations as a composition of basic transformations enables an algorithmic implementation to plug into the incremental learning step at real-time. The augmented versions generated for individual exemplars that are retained for replay are generated during the incremental training step where they are interspersed with the data for the new classes being optimised for in the incremental learning steps.

Mobius Augmentation. Many sample-level data augmentation methods at training time belong to a set of affine transformations, including a group of mappings like rotation, scaling, translation and flipping. Such operations can be modelled as a bijective mapping in a complex plane as $z \rightarrow az + b$, where the variable z, parameters $a, b \in C$, a set of complex numbers. A generalization of this mapping assumes the presence of non-zero imaginary parts of complex numbers in the transformation and the affine mapping being performed in Argand plane [19]. This expands the superset of possible image transformations with valid label preservation. The denominator of a linear transformation $z \rightarrow az + b$ can be assumed as unity. This can also be obtained by treating the denominator as a complex number $cz + d$, such that the real part of this complex quantity is unity and the imaginary part is zero. This hints at the next stage of abstraction through a denominator with non-zero real and imaginary components ($c, z \neq 0$). This creates a group of transformations in the set of complex numbers:

$$f(z) = (az + b) / (cz + d) \tag{1}$$

where $a, b, c, d \in C$ and $ad - bc \neq 0$ is the invertibility condition. This encapsulates a superset of basic mappings including inversion, translation, rotation and flipping and is termed a Mobius transformation if $z \in C$, $f(z)$ is not constant and $cz + d \neq 0$ [19]. A point z is mapped from one complex plane to another using parameters a, b, c, d. This can proceed without an explicit imaginary part defined for the complex entity z, as every real number can have a form $x + iy$, where $x \in R$, and $y = 0$. This enables us to define points on the image to estimate a, b, c and d. We choose 3 points at random on the image space with different combinations allowing for a different output at the conclusion of the mapping operation with label information preserved. This allows expansion in sample diversity per input in available datasets, with a much larger set of possible modifications for a class compared to existing sample-level methods. With a transformed form in 2D, the Mobius augmentation improves model generalization and robustness to noise, and to incremental time dataset shifts. Assuming 3 points in the initial plane as $z1, z2, z3$ and in a target plane as $w1, w2, w3$, then considering the preservation of anharmonic ratios [19]:

$$\frac{(w - w_1)(w_2 - w_3)}{(w - w_3)(w_2 - w_1)} = \frac{(z - z_1)(z_2 - z_3)}{(z - z_3)(z_2 - z_1)} \tag{2}$$

$$\frac{(w - w_1)}{w - w_3} = \frac{(z - z_1)(z_2 - z_3)(w_2 - w_1)}{(z - z_3)(z_2 - z_1)(w_2 - w_3)} \tag{3}$$

where,

$$w = \frac{(Aw_2 - w_1)}{A - 1}$$

$$A = \frac{(z - z_1)(z_2 - z_3)(w_2 - w_1)}{(z - z_3)(z_2 - z_1)(w_2 - w_3)}$$

This implies that we can express the transformation function in a reduced form as:

$$f(z) = w = \frac{Aw_3 - w_1}{A - 1} = \frac{az + b}{cz + d} \tag{4}$$

Then, we obtain the values of coefficients a,b,c,d in terms of the chosen points (z_1, z_2, z_3) and (w_1, w_2, w_3) through substitution in Eqs. (1), (3) and (4):

$$a = w_1w_2z_1 - w_1w_3z_1 - w_1w_2z_2 + w_2w_3z_2 + w_1w_3z_3 - w_2w_3z_3 \tag{5a}$$

$$b = w_1 w_3 z_1 z_2 - w_2 w_3 z_1 z_2 - w_1 w_2 z_1 z_3 + w_2 w_3 z_1 z_2 + w_1 w_2 z_2 z_2 - w_1 w_3 z_2 z_3 \quad (5b)$$

$$c = w_2 z_1 - w_3 z_1 - w_1 z_2 + w_3 z_2 + w_1 z_3 - w_2 z_3 \quad (5c)$$

$$d = w_1 z_1 z_2 - w_2 z_1 z_2 - w_1 z_1 z_3 + w_3 z_1 z_3 + w_2 z_2 z_3 - w_3 z_2 z_3 \quad (5d)$$

Based on Liouville's theorem [25], a Mobius transformation can be expressed as a composition of translations, orthogonal transformations and inversions, thereby encompassing a superset of a number of common augmentation operations based on geometric operations in deep learning, such as affine transformations, rotations and so on. This helps us design an algorithmic framework for real-time generation of Mobius transformations using values of a, b, c, d from (5a, 5b, 5c, 5d) to form subspaces of compositions on basic transformations from a superset of the generalized Mobius transformation. While an infinite number of Mobius-augmented samples can be obtained, the number of samples is bounded by randomly assigned cutoffs at runtime within $[1, R]$, where R is the maximum number of samples allowed by memory availability. We set R at 20 based on our RAM settings and associated constraints.

Weighted Distillation. Representations learnt by models can also be thought of as representing a 'dark knowledge' [8] about model-data dynamics in a vectorized form. This process was termed as knowledge distillation since the heavier models' learning is 'distilled' into an essential, compact representation that can be used in the other tasks. We use this vector as a 'memory' of past class learning to regularize incremental training. Based on the initial learning, we retain class averaged logits per class by saving to memory the validation logits at the conclusion of the training sched-ule of the initial (Task 1) training. Next, we compute weighted logits by applying weighting factors to logits of individual classes, the weights being inverses of class-specific validation accuracies. This allows distillation logits to reflect class-wise biases in proportion to their difficulty for the model to learn. The initial classes' training employs a cross-entropy loss. The probability vector of the initial task, is $p = softmax\,(z) \in 1$, where z is the set of logits. The objective in the initial training stage:

$$L_{crossent}(y, p) = \sum_{i=1}^{K_i} y_i . log(p_i) \quad (6)$$

Here p_i is the predicted probability score vector for each class in the new task, y_i is the associated ground truth in a one-hot encoding form. In next steps, a distillation loss is added to the objective, to allow representation of past knowledge in the learning process (y' are final class scores for new task classes before softmax stages):

$$L_{distillation}(z_{old}, y') = -\sum_{i=1}^{N} softmax\left(\frac{z_{old}}{T}\right). \ log\left(softmax\left(\frac{y'_i}{T}\right)\right) \quad (7)$$

Logits and predictions are scaled with a temperature term T in a softening process. Softening with a temperature hyperparameter helps reduce the disparity between the class label with the highest confidence score in the probability vector with respect to the other class labels and helps better reflect inter-class relationships at the representation learning stage. Considering the overall logit vector for the agglomeration of old classes, after weighting as *zold*, class-specific logits are weighted to obtain a sum of class-weighted logits expressed as:

$$z_{ol} = \sum_{i=1}^{K_1} u_i \cdot z_i \qquad (8)$$

The logits from individual classes z_i, $i \in [1, K_1]$ are calculated by averaging pre-softmax probability values (after the sigmoid activation stages) for examples from each of K_1 classes. The weights $(u_1, u_2, \ldots, u_1^k)$ are computed as inverse of class-specific accuracy on validation sets of the initial classes from the initial stage tasks. The idea is to boost logits from classes which are inherently difficult to learn for the model (lower the class-specific accuracy, higher would be the class weight), or for those classes that have a higher degree of inter-observer variation at the time of annotation owing to acquisition process issues, artefact presence or other quality challenges at the sample level. This modification reduces the disparity among classes in their contribution towards the overall sessional representation vector to be saved as an imprint of Stage 1 learning during subsequent optimizations. In future studies that seek to combine imaging data with other modalities, this modification can be adapted to reflect the relative contributions of the different modalities as well as account for the quality of individual data sources (which is useful in personalised medicine settings due to the relative difficulty in performing some diagnostic tests for certain individuals) Overall, the net incremental objective for learning beyond initial sessions is expressed as ($\gamma = 0.5$):

$$L = \gamma L_{crossent} + (1 - \gamma)L_{distillation} \qquad (9)$$

4   Experiments, Results and Discussion

The experimental protocol is bifurcated into two chronologically distinct phases, denoted as Phase 1 and Phase 2, to mimic the temporal variability in data acquisition. Phase 1 employs a conventional cross-entropy objective, while Phase 2, the incremental phase, integrates a composite loss function comprising both cross-entropy and distillation loss components. The feature extraction is facilitated by a ResNet-50 architecture, truncated post the final residual block, and supplemented with a fully-connected (FC) layer of 512 neurons, subsequently connected to a FC layer with 4 neurons (corresponding to the number of classes) and loss heads. The pre-softmax stratum computes probability scores via a sigmoid function, restricting the logit values within the range of zero to one. The dataset is partitioned into an 80:20 ratio for training and testing in both the initial and incremental learning phases. The input images are dimensionally standardized to 224×224 pixels, with a batch size of 25, a learning rate of 0.0001, and adaptive moment optimization (Adam) [26] during the training phases. In Phase 1, the models are subjected to 500 epochs of training on a (N, label) dataset for all N frames. Phase 2 involves training the models for 500 epochs on (N', label, logit) tuples, where N' encompasses Mobius transformed subsets of selectively preserved old samples in addition to new class data. It is noteworthy that training time data augmentation is not implemented, except for the retained samples in incremental training, diverging from typical machine learning approaches in clinical imaging. The primary objective is to scrutinize the specific impact of Mobius transformations on incremental learning performance with and without distillation. Therefore, the initial accuracies are not of paramount importance, given the uniform baseline values for these accuracies across different strategies employed in the continual learning problem setup and the incremental time data augmentation strategies under comparison. Hence, the enhancement of base model accuracy is not a goal of this study. The temperature parameter, T, is set to 4.0 following a grid search in $T \in [1, 5]$. The computational resources include two 32 GB Nvidia V100 GPUs, 512 MB RAM, utilized with ResNet 50 based models encompassing approximately 24.8 million parameters, and an average training time of 101s per epoch in both phases. The Mobius augmentation modules, the deep learning model backbones, and associated helper functions are programmed in Python 3.7.1 and Tensorflow 2.0.

Table 1. Accuracy (%) for task 1/Stage 1 classes, after Task 1 is trained for, and after task 2 is incrementally added in Stage 2. The difference in accuracies on the validation set of Task 1 classes represents forgetting on them due to Task 2 addition

Stage	Stage 1					Stage 2					ΔAcc
	TE	SS	IC	AT	Avg(T1)	TE	SS	IC	AT	Avg(T2)	T2-T1
Our(MT + wKD)	92.20	90.85	88.15	88.37	89.90	90.53	87.34	85.67	86.80	87.59	2.31
Our(MT + KD)	92.20	90.85	87.15	88.37	89.90	83.96	83.70	80.95	81.07	82.42	7.48
Our (KD)	92.20	90.85	87.15	88.37	89.90	77.32	72.55	71.14	74.15	73.79	16.11
Our (MT + FT)	92.20	90.85	87.15	88.37	89.90	74.87	67.90	66.91	71.27	70.24	19.66
Ours (FT)	92.20	90.85	87.15	88.37	89.90	55.68	49.07	47.85	50.86	50.87	39.03
LwF.ewc [15]	92.20	90.85	87.15	88.37	89.90	73.10	69.05	65.16	68.10	68.85	21.05
LwM [11]	92.20	90.85	87.15	88.37	89.90	77.15	74.11	68.96	73.92	73.54	16.36
PDR [12]	92.20	90.85	87.15	88.37	89.90	73.85	69.88	67.54	71.45	70.68	19.22

In the incremental task, data from the 4 classes that are progressively incorporated are utilized. Mobius transformations for augmentation are selectively applied to the retained specimens from Task 1 classes, guided by memory constraints. The top 20 specimens are retained, sorted by the magnitude of the class confidence scores after the validation set is processed through the trained models post Task 1. Theoretically, a greater number of samples can enhance performance as demonstrated in [2], with fully retained specimens for joint training serving as an upper limit on incremental performance. However, local storage conditions restrict our memory buffer availability, necessitating memory footprint optimization similar to numerous clinical imaging workflows globally. Hence, the retention set is limited to 20 specimens. The reduction in forgetting (Table 1) is significant for weighted distillation methods with a ΔAcc (difference in overall accuracy on Task 1 validation set before and after Task 2 training) of 2.31. In Table 1, methods employing both weighted distillation and Mobius augmentation are denoted as 'Our(MT + wKD)', and as 'Our(MT + KD)' if unweighted distillation is used. 'Our(MT + FT)' represents the method where finetuning is integrated with Mobius augmentation. For incremental tasks and in the overall accuracies for all classes post Task 2 training, substantial gains are observed with methods utilizing Mobius operations on retained specimens for initial task classes before interspersing with incremental class batches both for distillation and finetuning approaches. Overall, a distinct advantage is observed when employing distillation compared to finetuning alone. The optimal results are obtained for combined distillation and Mobius augmentation before incremental optimization, highlighting the value of augmentation of retained specimens. This diverges from most distillation-based methods that retain some old specimens without incremental augmentation for retained specimens while data augmentation is applied only in initial sessions and the new incremental data. Baselines from literature are employed with ResNet-50 backbones and original incremental training configurations adapted to suit the two-task incremental aspect of our study. Contrary to conventional expectations of near equal accuracies across methods, slight differences in prediction accuracies within same Task 2 classes are observed. The forward transfer effects of Task 1 training coupled with distillation based regularization yield optimal results when an intermediate Mobius augmentation step is applied on old specimens, creating a diverse specimen set for incremental training. Distilled models exhibit superior performance on the new task overall due to distillation induced regularizations on parameter shifts unlike the unregularized optimization in finetuning (FT).

Future research can focus on investigating the efficacy of Mobius transformations on other tasks such as few-shot personalised segmentation, in comparison to generative augmentation methods and exploring Mobius augmentation in conjunction with concurrent methods in literature. Furthermore, the field of precision medicine inherently involves multimodal data due to its aim of incorporating various aspects of a subject's health, ranging from genetic factors to lifestyle data. This implies that most clinical analysis would leverage multimodal data streams and multimodal machine learning algorithms required to accomplish predictive diagnosis on such systems would also need to be designed to be resistant to catastrophic forgetting effects. Therefore, future research could explore the potential of extending the ideas of runtime augmentation and distillation proposed here to incorporate multiple modalities relevant to precision medicine applications [5]. Additionally, given that several data streams from patient monitoring have a temporal component and need to be concurrently accounted along with discrete measurements such as tissue-imaging or routine tests, the aspect of task definition for continual learning stages and approaches that can combine longitudinal with static data require exploration (Fig. 3).

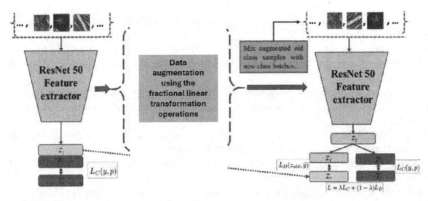

Fig. 3. Illustration of our pipeline. The initial training is performed (*left*) followed by a curation of old task samples, a fractional linear augmentation step and mixing with new class batches, followed by incremental task training under joint cross-entropy and weighted distillation (*right*).

5 Conclusion

This work presented a new strategy for runtime data augmentation using Mobius transformations. Subsequently, we studied the feasibility of adapting the generalized Mobius transformation for performing inter-task augmentation of an exemplar set in a distillation-based incremental learning setting, introducing a new concept of incremental augmentation for retained exemplars for selective replay during incremental task learning. These ideas were validated on a real-world clinical pathology dataset of colorectal carcinoma histology images as an representation of the approach. While the dataset itself was not originally curated specifically for fostering research on personalised healthcare, the limited number of examples per class compared to large-scale datasets in computational pathology available more recently lends itself to designing a study for incrementally learning over multiple learning schedules similar to the precision medicine landscape where individual subjects arrive over time with differing clinical presentations but undergoing a similar set of initial diagnostic evaluations prior to personalised treatment designs. As such, an avenue for future research would be the curation of and evaluation over bespoke datasets for personalised histological analysis. The ideas proposed in this paper are scalable to a range of imaging and multimodal data analysis applications in healthcare contexts and may be scaled to include evolving data streams from non-histology settings as well.

References

1. Goodfellow, I.J., Mirza, M., Xiao, D., Courville, A., Bengio, Y. An empirical investigation of catastrophic forgetting in gradient-based neural networks. arXiv:1312.6211 (2013)
2. Beaulieu-Jones, B.K., et al.: Predicting seizure recurrence after an initial seizure-like episode from routine clinical notes using large language models: a retrospective cohort study. Lancet Digital Health 5(12), e882–e894 (2023)
3. Patra, A., Chakraborti, T.: Learn more, forget less: cues from human brain. In: Proceedings of the Asian Conference on Computer Vision (2020)

4. Li, Z., Hoiem, D.: Learning without forgetting. IEEE Trans. Pattern Anal. Mach. Intell. **40**(12), 2935–2947 (2017)
5. Wu, J., Dong, H., Li, Z., Patra, A., Wu, H.: Retrieving and Refining: A Hybrid Framework with Large Language Models for Rare Disease Identification. arXiv preprint arXiv:2405.10440 (2024)
6. Patra, A., et al.: Multimodal continual learning with sonographer eye-tracking in fetal ultrasound. In: International Workshop on Advances in Simplifying Medical Ultrasound, pp. 14–24 (2021)
7. Kirkpatrick, J., et al.: Overcoming catastrophic forgetting in neural networks. In: Proceedings of the National Academy of Sciences, pp. 3521–3526 (2017)
8. Hinton, G., Vinyals, O., Dean, J.: Distilling the knowledge in a neural network. In: NIPS 2014 Deep Learning Workshop (2014)
9. Patra, A., Noble, J.A.: Multi-anatomy localization in fetal echocardiography videos. In: 2019 IEEE 16th International Symposium on Biomedical Imaging (ISBI 2019), pp. 1761–1764 (2019)
10. Kipkogei, E., Arango Argoty, G. A., Kagiampakis, I., Patra, A., Jacob, E.: Explainable transformer-based neural network for the prediction of survival outcomes in non- small cell lung cancer (NSCLC). medRxiv, 2021–10 (2021)
11. Patra, A., et al.: Efficient ultrasound image analysis models with sonographer gaze assisted distillation. In: International Conference on Medical Image Computing and Computer-Assisted Intervention, pp. 394–402. Springer, Cham (2019)
12. Hou, S., Pan, X., Change Loy, C., Wang, Z., Lin, D.: Lifelong learning via progressive distillation and retrospection. In: ECCV (2018)
13. Fernández-Llaneza, D., et al.: Towards fully automated segmentation of rat cardiac MRI by leveraging deep learning frameworks. Sci. Rep. **12**(1), 9193 (2022)
14. Abrol, V., Sharma, P., Patra, A.: Improving generative modelling in VAEs using multimodal prior. IEEE Trans. Multimedia **23**, 2153–2161 (2020)
15. Vigueras-Guillén, J.P., Patra, A., Engkvist, O., Seeliger, F.: Parallel capsule networks for classification of white blood cells. In: International Conference on Medical Image Computing and Computer-Assisted Intervention, pp. 743–752. Springer, Cham (2021)
16. Patra, A., Noble, J.A.: Hierarchical class incremental learning of anatomical structures in fetal echocardiography videos. IEEE J. Biomed. Health Inform. (2020)
17. Cubuk, E.D., Zoph, B., Mane, D., Vasudevan, V., Le, Q.V.: Autoaugment: learning augmentation strategies from data. In: Proceedings of the IEEE Conference on Computer Vision and Pattern Recognition, pp. 113–123 (2019)
18. Ahlfors, L.: Möbius Transformations in Several Dimensions. University of Minnesota (1989)
19. Özdemir, N., Iskender, B.B., Özgür, N.Y.: Complex valued neural network with Möbius activation function. Commun. Nonlinear Sci. Numer. Simul. **16**(12), 4698–4703 (2011)
20. Zammit-Mangion, A., Ng, T.L.J., Vu, Q., Filippone, M.: Deep compositional spatial models. arXiv preprint arXiv:1906.02840 (2019)
21. Zhou, S., Zhang, J., Jiang, H., Lundh, T., Ng, A.Y.: Data augmentation with Mobius transformations. arXiv preprint arXiv:2002.02917 (2020)
22. Ganea, O., Bécigneul, G., Hofmann, T.: Hyperbolic neural networks. In: Advances in Neural Information Processing Systems, pp. 5345–5355 (2018)
23. Islam, M.A., Anderson, D.T., Pinar, A., Havens, T.C., Scott, G., Keller, J.M.: Enabling explainable fusion in deep learning with fuzzy integral neural networks. IEEE Trans. Fuzzy Syst. (2019)
24. Kather, J., et al.: Multi-class texture analysis in colorectal cancer histology. In Scientific reports (2016)
25. Liouville, J., Extension au cas des trois dimensions de la question du tracé géographique. Note VI, pp. 609–617 (1850)

26. Kingma, D.P., Adam, J.B.: A method for stochastic optimization. arXiv:1412.6980
27. DeVries, T., Taylor, G.W.: Improved regularization of convolutional neural networks with cutout. arXiv preprint arXiv:1708.04552 (2017)
28. Tang, Z., Peng, X., Li, T., Zhu, Y., Metaxas, D.N.: Adatransform: adaptive data transformation. In: Proceedings of the IEEE International Conference on Computer Vision, pp. 2998–3006 (2019)
29. Ho, D., Liang, E., Stoica, I., Abbeel, P., Chen, X.: Population based augmentation: efficient learning of augmentation policy schedules. arXiv preprint arXiv:1905.05393 (2019)
30. Cubuk, E.D., Zoph, B., Shlens, J., Le, Q.V.: Randaugment: practical data augmentation with no separate search. arXiv preprint arXiv:1909.13719 (2019)
31. Omar, H.A., Patra, A., Domingos, J.S., Leeson, P., Noblel, A.J.: Automated myocardial wall motion classification using handcrafted features vs a deep CNN-based mapping. In: 2018 40th Annual International Conference of the IEEE Engineering in Medicine and Biology Society (EMBC), pp. 3140–3143. IEEE (2018)
32. Lee, C.S., Lee, A.Y.: Clinical applications of continual learning in machine learning. Lancet Digital Health 2(6), pp. 279–e281 (2020)
33. Patra, A., Noble, J.A.: Sequential anatomy localization in fetal echocardiography videos. arXiv preprint arXiv:1810.11868 (2019)
34. Patra, A., Noble, J.A.: Incremental learning of fetal heart anatomies using interpretable saliency maps. In: Annual Conference on Medical Image Understanding and Analysis, pp. 129–141. Springer, Cham (2019)
35. Patra, A., Huang, W., Noble, J.A.: Learning spatio-temporal aggregation for fetal heart analysis in ultrasound video. In: Deep Learning in Medical Image Analysis and Multimodal Learning for Clinical Decision Support, pp. 276–284. Springer, Cham (2017)
36. Chakraborti, T., Patra, A., Noble, J.A.: Contrastive fairness in machine learning. IEEE Lett. Comput. Soc. 3(2), 38–41 (2020)
37. Omar, H.A., Domingos, J.S., Patra, A., Leeson, P., Noble, J.A.: Improving visual detection of wall motion abnormality with echocardiographic image enhancing methods. In: 2018 40th Annual International Conference of the IEEE Engineering in Medicine and Biology Society (EMBC), pp. 1128–1131. IEEE (2018)
38. Food, Drug Administration, et al.: Proposed regulatory framework for modifications to artificial intelligence/machine learning (AI/ML)-based software as a medical device (SaMD) - discussion paper (2019)
39. Peng, J., Jury, E.C., Dönnes, P., Ciurtin, C.: Machine learning techniques for personalised medicine approaches in immune-mediated chronic inflammatory diseases: applications and challenges. Front. Pharmacol. 12, 720694 (2021)
40. Blagojević, A., Geroski, T.: A review of the application of artificial intelligence in medicine: from data to personalised models. In: Serbian International Conference on Applied Artificial Intelligence, pp. 271–305. Springer, Cha: (2022)
41. Jin, P., Lan, J., Wang, K., Baker, M.S., Huang, C., Nice, E.C.: Pathology, proteomics and the pathway to personalised medicine. Expert Rev. Proteom. Pp. 231–243 (2018)

Assessing Generalization Capabilities of Malaria Diagnostic Models from Thin Blood Smears

Louise Guillon[1]([✉]), Soheib Biga[1], Axel Puyo[2], Grégoire Pasquier[3], Valentin Foucher[1], Yendoubé E. Kantchire[4], Stéphane E. Sossou[5], Ameyo M. Dorkenoo[4,6], Laurent Bonnardot[1], Marc Thellier[2], Laurence Lachaud[3], and Renaud Piarroux[2]

[1] MyC, Paris, France
lguillon@myc.doctor
[2] APHP Paris, La Pitié-Salpêtrière, Sorbonne Université, Paris, France
[3] CHU of Montpellier, University of Montpellier, Montpellier, France
[4] CHU Campus, Ministère de la Santé et de l'hygiène Publique, Lomé, Togo
[5] CHU Sylvanus Olympio, Lomé, Togo
[6] Faculté des Sciences de la Santé, Université de Lomé, Lomé, Togo

Abstract. Malaria remains a significant global health challenge, necessitating rapid and accurate diagnostic methods. While computer-aided diagnosis (CAD) tools utilizing deep learning have shown promise, their generalization to diverse clinical settings remains poorly assessed. This study evaluates the generalization capabilities of a CAD model for malaria diagnosis from thin blood smear images across four sites. We explore strategies to enhance generalization, including fine-tuning and incremental learning. Our results demonstrate that incorporating site-specific data significantly improves model performance, paving the way for broader clinical application.

Keywords: generalization · malaria · object detection · computer-aided diagnosis · thin blood smear images · finetuning · incremental learning

1 Introduction

Malaria, caused by the parasite *Plasmodium*, remains a major public health issue worldwide. According to the WHO, 249 million cases were reported in 85 countries, leading to 608,000 deaths in 2022. A fast and accurate diagnosis is crucial to avoid severe consequences. Rapid diagnosis tests have been a major breakthrough since they are easy to perform and require no special training. Yet they may be subject to false positives or false negatives and they do not provide information on the species and life stage. Therefore, microscopic analysis of thin and thick blood smears remains the gold standard for diagnosis, enabling detailed characterization of the disease. However, the diagnosis has to be made

S. Wu et al. (Eds.): AMAI 2024, LNCS 15384, pp. 140–150, 2025.
https://doi.org/10.1007/978-3-031-82007-6_14

urgently and relies entirely on the expertise of the microscopist, which is variable and cannot be reviewed in real-time. Thus, automatic methods for computer-aided diagnosis (CAD) present a real opportunity and numerous works have developed such tools [3,4,11,18,19]. Deep learning frameworks have recently achieved high performances for both thin and thick blood smear images. For thin blood smear images, accuracies of 98.62% and 98.44% have been reported at the cell and patient levels respectively [11]. For thick smears, 91.8%, 92.5%, 91.1% were obtained at the patient level for accuracy, sensitivity and specificity respectively [18]. However, most studies report results obtained at the cell level which is not clinically relevant as diagnosis is done at the patient level, relying on the results of a bench of images, each of them totalizing 200 to 400 red cells. As a matter of fact, a challenge for malaria diagnosis is to avoid false positive results at the cell scale: if only one non-infected red blood cell is predicted as positive, the whole image is wrongly predicted as positive, leading to a false positive diagnosis for the patient.

Besides, generalization is a major challenge for AI models to be used in clinical settings. Indeed, it is capital that they generalize well to all the different sites taking into account any possible site effect. As a matter of fact, various parameters can have an impact on predictions such as the quality of the microscope blades, the staining procedure, the quality and specificities of the microscope lighting, the objectives used, the smartphones and the settings used to take the photos. Additionally, parasite species distribution varies by location. Therefore, evaluating model performance across different sites is essential to ensure robustness in clinical applications. To our knowledge, there is no comprehensive assessment of generalization capabilities in the context of malaria diagnosis, which hampers routine use of such models.

This work aims to evaluate the generalization capabilities of a CAD tool for malaria diagnosis and explores strategies to improve generalization. For that purpose, we position in a setting starting from a publicly available dataset[1]. This dataset constitutes a good benchmark since it is publicly available, used by many works and collected in a clinical setting similar to ours. From this dataset, we train a baseline model and evaluate the drop of performances at cell and image levels on smartphone thin blood smear images of in-house malaria suspected cases. We then propose strategies to mitigate the site effect on our in-house datasets. Specifically, we investigate whether joint training and fine-tuning can aid in improving generalization and, if so, how many samples are needed. To the best of our knowledge, these questions have not been previously addressed. This work is the first step in a collaboration between hospitals in non-endemic areas, industry and laboratories in endemic areas.

Our contributions are threefold: 1) assessing the site effect on thin blood smear images, 2) evaluating generalization performance across different sites and 3) proposing joint training and fine-tuning in an incremental learning strategy for improved model adaptability.

---

[1] https://lhncbc.nlm.nih.gov/LHC-downloads/downloads.html#malaria-datasets.

2 Related Works

Malaria Diagnosis: CAD tools for malaria have been developed for several years, with recent advancements leveraging deep learning techniques. These tools can be categorized into direct detection from field-of-view images, or two-step processes, involving red cell extraction followed by classification of infected and uninfected red cells. Direct detection of infected cells can be performed thanks to object detection frameworks such as Yolo [2,5,10,17], Faster-RCNN [7,16] or more recently based on transformers like RT-DETR [5]. Several works have oriented their method to make it applicable to endemic zones based on specific devices like EasyScan Go [1,3] or on a setting relying on a smartphone plugged to a microscope [12,19]. Thus, Malaria Screener is a smartphone app working on thin and thick smears. For thin smears, red blood cells are extracted and then classified thanks to an deep ensemble method [13,14,18,19].

Generalization Assessment: Generalization is critical for clinical applications, ensuring performance consistency across diverse environments. This topic has begun to be investigated in some medical imaging applications, such as neuroimaging, histology or radiography [6,20]. Previous studies such as those by Zech et al. on pneumonia detection, have shown performance drops when models trained on single-site data are applied to new sites, highlighting the need for diverse training data. [20]. For malaria computer-aided diagnosis, few studies have addressed this question so far. Some works have focused on the difference in performance between several magnifications. In particular, mAP between x1000 and x400 have been reported to drop from 62.8 to 36.7 [16]. To tackle this issue, domain adaptation strategies based on specific losses [16] or contrastive learning [2] have been proposed. Moreover, prospective studies on effectiveness of smartphone applications such as Malaria Screener [18] give some indication on their generalization. In particular, in the case of thick blood smears, the accuracy at patient-level falls from 96.7% to 83.1% [9,18].

3 Methods

This article aims to assess the generalization capabilities of a CAD tool for malaria diagnosis. Since Yolov5 has been shown to be a relevant framework for detecting infected red blood cells and thus diagnosing malaria, we have chosen to evaluate the generalization capabilities of this model as a first step. Future works will compare whether other state-of-the-art object detection models have the same generalization properties.

Datasets
We use four datasets of thin blood smear images: a public dataset from the NIH[2] and three in-house datasets acquired in three distinct settings. All images

---

[2] https://data.lhncbc.nlm.nih.gov/public/Malaria/NIH-NLM-ThinBloodSmearsPf/index.html.

were acquired using a smartphone connected to a microscope at x1000 magnification. All datasets but the one of the NIH contain various *Plasmodium* species. For the purposes of this study, we treat all species equally as *Plasmodium*. Nevertheless we stress out that both magnification and species are important characteristics that can affect generalization performance. This study is a first step towards broader analyses including more sites and features. Figure 1 shows zoomed images from the different datasets. Details are presented in Table 1.

Training Datasets. Two datasets are used for the different training strategies. The baseline dataset is the NIH dataset. The second dataset was collected at Hospital A in a distinct country.

Test Dataset. We evaluate our different strategies on four datasets: a portion of the NIH dataset, a portion of the Hospital A dataset, a dataset from Hospital B and a dataset from a hospital in an endemic area (Hospital C). For the NIH and Hospital A test sets, there is no overlap with the training sets; all images of each patient are either in train or in test set.

Table 1. Description of the datasets used. "Hosp." stands for "Hospital". "positive images" refers to images that contain at least one *Plasmodium* infected red blood cell.

	Training data		Test data			
	NIH train	Hosp. A train	NIH test	Hosp. A test	Hosp. B	Hosp. C
Number of patients	133	44	60	24	50	14
Number of images	665	671	300	311	200	59
Number of positive images	412	587	200	218	100	44

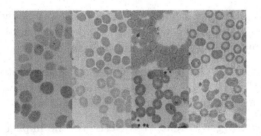

Fig. 1. *Zoomed cropped inputs examples.* Each column corresponds to a dataset (from left to right: NIH, hospital A, B and C). The images are zoomed crops of the input thin blood smear fields of view.

Malaria Diagnosis Prediction

To predict malaria, models are trained to detect *Plasmodium* parasites in the red blood cells (RBC). We address this as an object-detection task with infected and non-infected RBC as objects. We study generalization on Yolo model [15], which has shown high performances in detecting infected cells [2,5,10,17]. Specifically, we use Yolov5s pre-trained on the COCO dataset [8]. The automatic diagnosis involves two steps: first, detecting all RBC, and second, identifying infected RBC. It is necessary to detect all the red blood cells in order to count them and assess the specificity. We use two yolov5 models: model (1) detects all RBC and model (2) detects only infected RBC. Using two models enables to get rid of the class imbalance between infected and non-infected cells. To limit false positive detection, detections with a confidence threshold above 0.5 are considered positive. Detection is thus at the cell-level: a RBC is either infected or uninfected. Predictions at cell-level are then aggregated to produce a diagnosis at image level: an image is predicted as positive if at least one RBC is infected.

Quantification of Site Effect

We first quantify the site effect by assessing whether it is possible to recognize the site by just viewing an image. Using 100 positive images from NIH and Hospital A, we train a ResNet50 classifier for 20 epochs to distinguish between the two sites. To reduce the impact of different orientations and dimensions, we crop the center of each image as presented in Fig. 1. We obtain an accuracy of 0.95 ± 0.01 for the Resnet50 against 0.42 ± 0.07 for a null model based on boostrapping. The classifier achieves a very high accuracy in predicting the site suggesting that site-specific characteristics are present in the images, potentially impacting the detection model and necessitating generalization assessment.

Assessing and Improving Generalization Performances

To evaluate our framework's generalization, we train a baseline model on the NIH dataset and apply it to our other sites. To mitigate the site effect, pictures from another site can be used to update and improve the model in an incremental and finetuning strategy setting. Performances of the different strategies are compared between the 4-sites test sets.

Baseline Model. The baseline model consists in the two yolov5 models (1) and (2) trained on the NIH data (n=665). Since model (1) is used only to compute the metrics, our mitigation strategies only concern model (2).

Joint Training Model. Our first strategy to mitigate the site effect is to complement our initial NIH training dataset (n=665) with data from hospital A (n=671) to perform joint training. We thus have 1336 images for training.

Incremental Learning Models. We investigate the impact of using varying amounts of Hospital A data ([5, 20, 50, 100, 200]) for joint training.

Finetuning models. Finally, instead of training the whole model from scratch, we evaluate finetuning the baseline model with 200 Hospital A images. We compare three settings of finetuning: fully retraining our baseline model from scratch, freezing the backbone or freezing all but the last layer of the model.

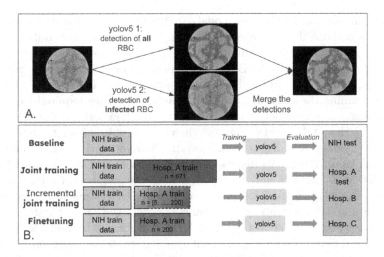

Fig. 2. *Framework description.* **A.** Prediction workflow. A thin blood smear field of view image is passed to two yolov5 models to detect either all RBC or only the infected RBC. Predictions are then merged to obtain final predictions of negative and positive cells. **B.** Strategies to improve generalization. Baseline models are trained on the NIH dataset only. Joint training models are trained on the NIH dataset and 671 images from Hospital A. Incremental joint training method develops the previous approach by using increasing numbers of images from Hospital A. Last, Finetuning models are trained using 200 images from Hospital A studying various finetuning strategies.

4   Experiments and Results

For all trainings, we performed a 5-fold cross validation, ensuring that all images from a single patient were either in the training, validation, or test set to prevent data leakage. Early stopping is applied to avoid overfitting. Training for 100 epochs takes about 2 h on an Nvidia GeForce RTX 3050 GPU.

Table 2 presents the baseline model's performances across all the datasets. Results on the NIH test data, with 89.2% of accuracy at the image level and 99.08% of accuracy at the cell level, are comparable to literature (98.62% accuracy for Liu et al. [11] and 99.61% for Rajaraman et al. [14], both at the cell level). However, as expected, there is a significant drop in performance on external datasets, with the accuracy decreasing to 97.89% at the RBC level and 66.17% at the image level for the Hospital A test set. This is mainly due to an increase of positive RBC predicted as negative which led to a decrease of sensibility. As a matter of fact, on an unseen dataset, model confidence is lower and our threshold of 0.5 for considering predicted positives as positives can sometimes discard true positives.

Combining the NIH and Hospital A datasets in a joint training strategy results in an increase of the performances across most test sets. For example, the accuracy on the Hospital A test set increases significantly to 91.96% at the image level and 98.82% at the RBC level. Sensitivity also shows considerable improvement, indicating that the model could better identify positive cases when trained on a more diverse dataset. The improvements on hospitals B and C datasets suggest that joint training can enhance the model's robustness to site-specific variations. For Hosp. B, although performances have improved at the RBC level, it has not led to a change of diagnosis at the image level.

To determine the minimum amount of additional data required to improve generalization, we conducted incremental learning experiments with varying amounts of Hospital A data. Figure 3 shows the results of joint training with increasing numbers of images from Hospital A. Even with a small number of additional samples (e.g., 20 images), there is a noticeable improvement in sensitivity at both the cell and image levels. As the number of added samples increases, the performance continues to improve, suggesting that incremental learning is an effective strategy for enhancing generalization. For 200 samples, it seems that a plateau is almost reached. This is confirmed by Fig. 4 where there is no major difference between the joint training strategy (based on 671 Hosp. A data) and Incr. 200 which is based on 200 Hosp. A data.

The results of the different finetuning strategies using 200 images from Hospital A are shown in Fig. 4. Finetuning the entire model or just the last layer significantly improved performance. Finetuning only the last layer was particularly effective in reducing variability, making it a robust approach for improving model generalization with minimal data. These findings suggest that finetuning is a practical method for adapting pre-trained models to new environments.

Table 2. Performances of the different strategies. Performances are reported at image and cell levels for baseline model and the joint training strategy, with a threshold confidence at 0.5 on yolov5 (2).

Level	Modality	Metrics	NIH test	Hosp. A test	Hosp. B	Hosp. C
Image level	Baseline	Accuracy	$89.2_{\pm3.78}$	$66.17_{\pm12.67}$	$83.75_{\pm6.86}$	$80.68_{\pm5.03}$
		Sensitivity	$88.80_{\pm7.82}$	$58.53_{\pm19.48}$	$83.61_{\pm7.95}$	$91.36_{\pm3.73}$
		Specificity	$90.00_{\pm4.64}$	$84.09_{\pm7.11}$	$86.67_{\pm18.26}$	$49.33_{\pm27.73}$
	Joint training	Accuracy	$90.13_{\pm1.54}$	$91.96_{\pm3.20}$	$83.75_{\pm8.53}$	$84.41_{\pm8.42}$
		Sensitivity	$90.7_{\pm3.55}$	$92.48_{\pm5.28}$	$83.61_{\pm9.20}$	$93.18_{\pm2.27}$
		Specificity	$89.00_{\pm3.32}$	$90.75_{\pm6.43}$	$86.67_{\pm18.26}$	$58.67_{\pm38.12}$
RBC level	Baseline	Accuracy	$99.08_{\pm0.23}$	$97.89_{\pm0.40}$	$96.98_{\pm0.55}$	$97.13_{\pm0.32}$
		Sensitivity	$79.58_{\pm8.33}$	$38.81_{\pm14.57}$	$62.07_{\pm13.53}$	$52.42_{\pm12.33}$
		Specificity	$99.77_{\pm0.063}$	$99.65_{\pm0.048}$	$98.92_{\pm0.60}$	$99.26_{\pm0.25}$
	Joint training	Accuracy	$99.10_{\pm0.16}$	$98.82_{\pm0.27}$	$97.83_{\pm0.56}$	$97.30_{\pm0.44}$
		Sensitivity	$78.55_{\pm5.86}$	$68.62_{\pm11.90}$	$68.55_{\pm14.29}$	$55.08_{\pm14.81}$
		Specificity	$99.83_{\pm0.0.44}$	$99.73_{\pm0.077}$	$99.50_{\pm0.25}$	$99.31_{\pm0.29}$

Overall, our results demonstrate the importance of evaluating and improving the generalization capabilities. The baseline model, while highly accurate on

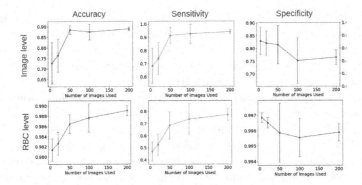

Fig. 3. *Incremental joint training performances.* Performance improvements observed with increasing amounts of data from Hospital A. Metrics include accuracy, sensitivity, and specificity at both image and RBC levels.

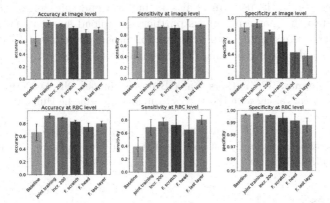

Fig. 4. *Finetuning performances.* Comparison of baseline, joint training with 665 and 200 images, and finetuning strategies. *Incr.* and *F.* stands for *Incremental* and *Finetuning* respectively.

the training data, showed reduced performance on external datasets. Our proposed strategies enable a partial restoration of performance, suggesting practical approaches for deploying AI models in diverse clinical settings.

5   Discussion and Conclusion

In this work, we evaluated the generalization capabilities of a deep learning framework for malaria diagnosis from thin blood smear images. As a first step, we focused on Yolov5, a widely used model in the domain. We highlighted the impact of site-specific factors on model performance and proposed strategies to mitigate these effects. Our findings suggest that incorporating diverse data sources and employing incremental learning and finetuning techniques can significantly enhance Yolov5 generalization. In a clinical routine setting of an endemic area, gathering 200 images can be achieved rather quickly. Another way to improve generalization could be to perform a threshold calibration for each site, similar to the prospective study by Yu et al. [18]. We emphasize that this work is a first step, paving the way for broader real-world application evaluation. Future works will extend this analysis to other malaria prediction frameworks such as RT-DETR [5] and explore whether specific augmentations and data preprocessing can play a role in the site effect mitigation. Active learning and domain adaptation should be considered in future works. In addition, we intend to include the impact of magnification and species on the generalizability. Finally, in this study human experts are considered as the ground truth but it would be really valuable to compare human and CAD methods performances, we currently work on such a study.

Prospect of Application. This research will be applied through our collaboration with three hospitals and a start-up offering a cloud platform for medical facilities, currently used in clinics in malaria endemic zones. Our model, integrated into the platform, allows partners to upload smartphone photos for diagnosis. This work guides our strategy for broad deployment across diverse settings and addressing generalization capabilities.

Acknowledgments. The authors thank Benoît Dufumier, Nicolas Nalpon for their insightful comments along with the MyC's team and Caroline Le Duigou for their help.

Disclosure of Interest. The authors declare that they have no known competing financial interests or personal relationships that could have appeared to influence the work reported in this paper.

References

1. Das, D., Vongpromek, R., Assawariyathipat, T., Srinamon, K., Kennon, K., Stepniewska, K., et al.: Field evaluation of the diagnostic performance of EasyScan GO: a digital malaria microscopy device based on machine-learning. Malar. J. **21**(1), 122 (2022). https://doi.org/10.1186/s12936-022-04146-1
2. Dave, I.R., de Blegiers, T., Chen, C., Shah, M.: CodaMal: contrastive domain adaptation for malaria detection in low-cost microscopes (2024). https://doi.org/10.48550/arXiv.2402.10478, arXiv:2402.10478 [cs]
3. Delahunt, C.B., Jaiswal, M.S., Horning, M.P., Janko, S., Thompson, C.M., Kulhare, S., et al.: Fully-automated patient-level malaria assessment on field-prepared thin blood film microscopy images, including Supplementary Information (2022). https://doi.org/10.48550/arXiv.1908.01901, arXiv:1908.01901 [cs, eess, stat]
4. Delahunt, C.B., Mehanian, C., Hu, L., McGuire, S.K., Champlin, C.R., Horning, M.P., et al.: Automated microscopy and machine learning for expert-level malaria field diagnosis. In: 2015 IEEE Global Humanitarian Technology Conference (GHTC), pp. 393–399 (2015). https://doi.org/10.1109/GHTC.2015.7344002
5. Guemas, E., Routier, B., Ghelfenstein-Ferreira, T., Cordier, C., Hartuis, S., Marion, B., et al.: Automatic patient-level recognition of four Plasmodium species on thin blood smear by a real-time detection transformer (RT-DETR) object detection algorithm: a proof-of-concept and evaluation. Microbiology Spectrum , e01440-23

(2024). https://doi.org/10.1128/spectrum.01440-23, publisher: American Society for Microbiology

6. Howard, F.M., Dolezal, J., Kochanny, S., Schulte, J., Chen, H., Heij, L., et al.: The impact of site-specific digital histology signatures on deep learning model accuracy and bias. Nat. Commun. **12**(1), 4423 (Jul 2021). https://doi.org/10.1038/s41467-021-24698-1, publisher: Nature Publishing Group

7. Hung, J., Carpenter, A.: Applying faster R-CNN for object detection on malaria images. In: 2017 IEEE Conference on Computer Vision and Pattern Recognition Workshops (CVPRW), pp. 808–813 (2017). https://doi.org/10.1109/CVPRW.2017.112, iSSN: 2160-7516

8. Jocher, G., Ayush Chaurasia, Stoken, A., Borovec, J., NanoCode012, Yonghye Kwon, et al.: ultralytics/yolov5: v7.0 - YOLOv5 SOTA realtime instance segmentation (2022). https://doi.org/10.5281/ZENODO.3908559

9. Kassim, Y.M., Yang, F., Yu, H., Maude, R.J., Jaeger, S.: Diagnosing malaria patients with plasmodium falciparum and vivax using deep learning for thick smear images. Diagnostics **11**(11), 1994 (2021). https://doi.org/10.3390/diagnostics11111994, number: 11 Publisher: Multidisciplinary Digital Publishing Institute

10. Krishnadas, P., Chadaga, K., Sampathila, N., Rao, S., Swathi, S.K., Prabhu, S.: Classification of malaria using object detection models. Informatics **9**(4), 76 (2022). https://doi.org/10.3390/informatics9040076, number: 4 Publisher: Multidisciplinary Digital Publishing Institute

11. Liu, R., Liu, T., Dan, T., Yang, S., Li, Y., Luo, B., et al.: AIDMAN: An AI-based object detection system for malaria diagnosis from smartphone thin-blood-smear images. Patterns **4**(9), 100806 (2023). https://doi.org/10.1016/j.patter.2023.100806

12. Nakasi, R., Mwebaze, E., Zawedde, A.: Mobile-aware deep learning algorithms for malaria parasites and white blood cells localization in thick blood smears. Algorithms **14**(1), 17 (2021). https://doi.org/10.3390/a14010017 Publisher: Multidisciplinary Digital Publishing Institute

13. Rajaraman, S., Antani, S.K., Poostchi, M., Silamut, K., Hossain, M.A., Maude, R.J., et al.: Pre-trained convolutional neural networks as feature extractors toward improved malaria parasite detection in thin blood smear images. PeerJ **6**, e4568 (2018). https://doi.org/10.7717/peerj.4568, publisher: PeerJ Inc

14. Rajaraman, S., Jaeger, S., Antani, S.K.: Performance evaluation of deep neural ensembles toward malaria parasite detection in thin-blood smear images. PeerJ **7**, e6977 (2019). https://doi.org/10.7717/peerj.6977, publisher: PeerJ Inc

15. Redmon, J., Divvala, S., Girshick, R., Farhadi, A.: You only look once: unified, real-time object detection, pp. 779–788 (2016). https://www.cv-foundation.org/openaccess/content_cvpr_2016/html/Redmon_You_Only_Look_CVPR_2016_paper.html

16. Sultani, W., Nawaz, W., Javed, S., Danish, M.S., Saadia, A., Ali, M.: Towards low-cost and efficient malaria detection. IEEE Comput. Soc., 20655 20664 (2022). https://doi.org/10.1109/CVPR52688.2022.02003

17. Yang, F., Quizon, N., Yu, H., Silamut, K., Maude, R.J., Jaeger, S., Antani, S.: Cascading YOLO: automated malaria parasite detection for Plasmodium vivax in thin blood smears. In: Medical Imaging 2020: Computer-Aided Diagnosis, vol. 11314, pp. 404–410. SPIE (2020). https://doi.org/10.1117/12.2549701

18. Yu, H., Mohammed, F.O., Abdel Hamid, M., Yang, F., Kassim, Y.M., Mohamed, A.O.A.A.: Patient-level performance evaluation of a smartphone-based malaria

diagnostic application. Malaria J. **22**(1), 33 (2023). https://doi.org/10.1186/s12936-023-04446-0

19. Yu, H., Yang, F., Rajaraman, S., Ersoy, I., Moallem, G., Poostchi, M., et al.: Malaria Screener: a smartphone application for automated malaria screening. BMC Infect. Dis. **20**(1), 825 (2020). https://doi.org/10.1186/s12879-020-05453-1

20. Zech, J.R., Badgeley, M.A., Liu, M., Costa, A.B., Titano, J.J., Oermann, E.K.: Variable generalization performance of a deep learning model to detect pneumonia in chest radiographs: a cross-sectional study. PLoS Med. **15**(11), e1002683 (2018). https://doi.org/10.1371/journal.pmed.1002683, publisher: Public Library of Science

Automated Feedback System for Surgical Skill Improvement in Endoscopic Sinus Surgery

Tomoko Yamaguchi[1]([✉])([iD]), Ryoichi Nakamura[2], Akihito Kuboki[3], and Nobuyoshi Otori[3]

[1] Kobe University, Kobe city, Hyogo, Japan
tomokoy@people.kobe-u.ac.jp
[2] Tohoku Univercity Hospital, Sendai, Miyagi, Japan
[3] The Jikei University School of Medicine, Tokyo, Japan

Abstract. Background: Endoscopic surgery has been widely adopted in many surgical fields, increasing the importance of the education of surgical skills. Although simulation-based training is mainstream, training in the actual surgical environment is also indispensable. Objective: This study aims to develop an automated feedback system using kinematic data to enhance the efficiency of skill education for endoscopic sinus surgery (ESS). Methods: Kinematic data were collected for four basic scenes of navigation-guided ESS. Features of the surgical techniques were extracted from the collected data and compared with standard process models of experts to automatically identify technical issues. A system was constructed to classify these issues and provide feedback to surgeons using machine learning (random forest algorithm). Results: The developed system classified surgical issues with high accuracy and received high ratings in a survey conducted with surgeons. Conclusion: The proposed system is useful for post-operative review and can potentially enhance the efficiency of skill acquisition. It is expected to be applicable to other surgical procedures in the future.

Keywords: Surgical skill education · Quantitative skill evaluation · Machine learning

1 Introduction

In recent years, endoscopic surgery has been adopted in most surgical fields, and the number of cases is on the rise. However, performing endoscopic surgery safely and effectively requires advanced and specialized skills, highlighting the increasing importance of surgical skill education to ensure safe procedures. Currently, simulation-based training outside the operating room has become mainstream for surgical skill education. The most commonly used method currently is the relatively inexpensive dry box training [6], which focuses on basic tasks such as moving pegs, cutting, and suturing. Additionally, with recent advancements

S. Wu et al. (Eds.): AMAI 2024, LNCS 15384, pp. 151–161, 2025.
https://doi.org/10.1007/978-3-031-82007-6_15

in 3D printing technology, patient-specific models that accurately replicate the anatomical structures and texture of organs have become available, allowing for more realistic training [5]. However, these training methods require the supervision and evaluation of experienced surgeons. Furthermore, advancements in computer technology have led to the development of numerous virtual reality (VR) and augmented reality (AR) based simulators [7]. These simulators can recreate various surgical environments, enabling comprehensive training from basic techniques to the entire sequence of surgical procedures. Some of these simulators include functions that automatically assess and provide feedback on the trainee's skills [10]. Nevertheless, these VR/AR simulators differ significantly from the actual surgical experience and are very expensive, limiting their availability to certain facilities [6].

Simulation-based training is effective for acquiring surgical skills. However, due to the limitations of simulation for certain procedures and the various constraints mentioned above, it is difficult to completely develop the necessary techniques and sensibilities required for actual surgery through simulation alone. Therefore, as highlighted in various previous studies, training in the actual surgical environment (On the Job Training; OJT) is also indispensable. Currently, surgical skill education through OJT primarily involves feedback from supervising surgeons during surgeries and post-operative reviews using surgical videos. This process is time-consuming and relies on the subjective guidance of experienced surgeons, leading to variability in the quality and efficiency of instruction, which may result in differences in skill acquisition among surgeons. Additionally, the burden on experienced surgeons is significant, posing challenges to the sustainability of education. Consequently, in surgical skill education, there is a need for automated quantitative assessment and feedback on skills during clinical training to reduce the burden on surgeons and improve the efficiency of skill acquisition.

Previously, in a clinical setting, indicators reflecting the procedural characteristics and proficiency of endoscopic sinus surgery have been developed [16], as well as methods to automatically extract instances where residents performed techniques needing improvement [15]. However, even with these methods, only the times requiring improvement were identified. Therefore, this study aims to construct a system that provides specific feedback after automatically recognizing the areas for improvement, to more effectively support surgical skill education. We expect that this system will reduce the burden on surgeons while enhancing the efficiency of skill acquisition.

2   Method

2.1   Surgical Information

Our study focused on four basic scenes of navigation-guided endoscopic sinus surgery (ESS) (Table 1). All cases involved sinusitis in both nasal cavities, with an expert and a resident each treating one side. According to the expert, the anatomical differences and variations in surgical difficulty among these cases were minimal.

Table 1. Definition of surgical scene and instruments used for measurements. *Only when a patient has nasal polyps.

Surgical scene	Task	Surgical instrument used for measurement	
		Right hand	Left hand
Scene 1*	Removal of nasal polyp	Microdebrider	Endoscope
Scene 2	Removal of the uncinate process		
Scene 3	Removal of the ethmoid bulla	Microdebrider and nasal cutting forceps	
Scene 4	Removal of third basal lamella		

2.2   Acquiring Surgical Log Data

Using an optical 3D position measurement device (Polaris Spectra System; Northern Digital, Inc., Waterloo, ON, Canada), we recorded the 3D position information of the surgical instrument tips, the rotation information of the instrument axes, and the time. The surgical instruments used for information acquisition and analysis in each scene are listed in Table 1. The position information of the instrument tips was obtained as position information on the patient's CT images through point-based registration [9]. These measurements were conducted with the approval of the Ethics Committee of Tokyo Jikei University School of Medicine. Data were excluded when the position coordinates of the surgical instrument were completely outside of the nose, as this was considered to indicate that the instrument had been removed.

2.3   Extraction of Features and Areas for Improvement in Surgical Techniques

Features shown in Table 2 were calculated from the log data, and a Surgical Process Model (SPM) (equations (1) and (2)) was defined to formalize and model the transitions and processes of surgical tasks. In this study, the sampling rate for the SPM was 5 Hz. Using the SPM, we created an average surgical model for experts and individual surgical process models for each resident. By comparing these models with the DTW Algorithm [11], we identified areas with significant differences as surgical technique issues to be improved [15]. The measured data encompassed 39 cases. Individuals with over 300 ESS surgery experiences were classified as experts, while those with fewer than 50 cases were classified as residents. A total of 303 areas were identified as surgical technique issues, which were categorized into the following six types as follows [15]:

Table 2. Definition of surgical feature parameters.

Operation features of the left or right hand	
Velocity (v [mm/s])	Rate of change in the position of the instrument tip
Acceleration (a [mm/s^2])	Rate of change in the velocity of the instrument tip
Jerk (j [mm/s^3])	Rate of change in the acceleration of the instrument tip
Rotation (r [deg/s])	Rate of change in the orientation of the instrument rod
x, y, z	The position coordinates of each instrument, which arranged to achieve symmetry in the nasal septum plane
Bimanual operation feature	
Relative velocity (rv [mm/s])	Difference in the velocity between the endoscope and the instrument
Relative acceleration (ra [mm/s^2])	Difference in the acceleration between the endoscope and the instrument
Relative jerk (rj [mm/s^3])	Difference in jerk between the endoscope and the instrument
Bimanual angle (ba [deg])	Angle between the endoscope rod and the instrument rod
Bimanual distance 1 (bd1 [mm])	Distance between the endoscope tip and the instrument tip
Bimanual distance 2 (bd2 [mm])	Difference between the instrument tip and center-line, which passes through the center of the endoscope lens, parallel to the endoscope rod

1. Unable to capture the surgical instrument at the center of the endoscope.
2. Endoscope and surgical instruments are blurred or interfere with one another.
3. The tips of the endoscope and surgical instrument are very close.
4. Immobility of endoscope or surgical instrument.
5. Variation in treatment (i.e. different) position in the corresponding scene.
6. Insertion and evulsion of the endoscope or the surgical instrument.

$$SPM = <ac_i, ac_2, ..., ac_n > \qquad (1)$$

$$
\begin{aligned}
ac_i = (&v_{R_i}, a_{R_i}, j_{R_i}, r_{R_i}, x_{R_i}, y_{R_i}, z_{R_i} \\
&v_{L_i}, a_{L_i}, j_{L_i}, r_{L_i}, xv_{L_i}, yv_{L_i}, zv_{L_i} \\
&rv_i, ra_i, rj_i, ba_i, bd1_i, bd2_i)
\end{aligned}
\qquad (2)
$$

2.4   Automatic Recognition of Extracted Surgical Issues

The surgical issues identified in Sect. 2.3 only indicate the times when the issues occurred. To automatically determine which of the six types of issues classified in the previous section each issue belongs to, we used machine learning to classify each SPM (i.e. frame). The reason for frame-by-frame learning was due to the existence of issues transitions (e.g., not centered on the screen → instrument tip is close → blurring). Different models were constructed for scenes 1 and 2, and for scenes 3 and 4, because the dimensions of the defined SPMs differ. The classification methods and parameters tested in this study were as follows:

- Support Vector Machine (SVM) (Kernel = RBF)
- Logistic Regression (LR) (`Class_weight` = balanced, `Max_iter` = 200, Solver = newton-cg)
- Naive Bayes Model (NB) (Kernel = Gaussian)
- K-Nearest Neighbors (K-NN) (`N_neighbors` = 5 for Scenes 1 and 2, and 9 for Scenes 3 and 4)
- Random Forest (RF) (`N_estimators` = 500, `Max_depth` = None, `Min_sampl-es_split` = 2, `Min_samples_leaf` = 1, `Max_features` = sqrt)

The parameters for each method were empirically determined through grid search. To create the classification model, we used part of the resident's surgical issue areas extracted in Sect. 2.3 (21 cases). For scenes 1 and 2, 1475 SPMs were used, and for scenes 3 and 4, 3282 SPMs were used. For training, 75% of the data was used, with the remaining 25% used as test data. The training data and test data were randomly divided, with careful consideration to ensure that the same procedural tasks performed by the same residents were not present in both sets as much as possible. Three experts reviewed the annotations of the procedural issues. They watched the extracted videos to determine whether the content fit into any of the improvement categories from 1 to 6. Figure 1 illustrates the overall workflow for detection and recognition as described in Sects. 2.3 and 2.4.

2.5   Software for Presenting Automatically Recognized Surgical Issues

We combined the surgical issues detection method and surgical situation recognition method developed in Sects. 2.3 and 2.4 to construct a system that provides feedback on the evaluation results. The goal was to create software that allows surgeons to identify surgical issues without having to review the entire surgery, thus supporting efficient skill acquisition. As a result of a survey conducted among surgeons regarding the necessary requirements for the display system, the software was required to: "indicate the locations where surgical issues occurred", "display the details of operations at problematic areas", and "provide an overview of issues at a glance". Therefore, the proposed system consists of six modules: (1) surgical timeline, (2) list of issues locations, (3) list of issues

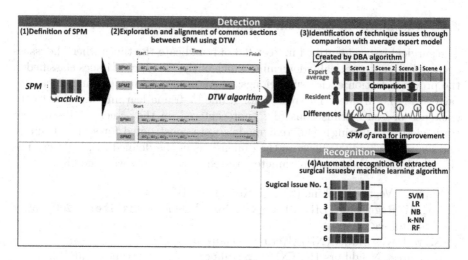

Fig. 1. Pipeline for detection and recognition described in Sects. 2.3 and 2.4.

details, (4) video display of issues segments, (5) proportion of issues time, and (6) ranking of issues in order of frequency. Figure 2 shows the developed software. The issues classification outputs frame-by-frame classification results. For teaching purposes, the predominant issues in the detected area was presented as the representative issues. To evaluate the usefulness of this software, a survey was conducted with surgeons. The survey was designed based on the software quality characteristics outlined in ISO/IEC 9126, focusing on system functionality and usability. The survey participants included 6 surgeons: 3 experts and 3 residents. Participation was voluntary, and the survey followed the principles of the Helsinki Declaration. Responses to each question were rated on a 5-point scale (5: Strongly agree, 4: Somewhat agree, 3: Neutral, 2: Somewhat disagree, 1: Strongly disagree). Additionally, participants were asked to freely describe the good and bad points of the system.

3   Results and Discussion

3.1   Automatic Recognition of Extracted Surgical Issues

The results of comparing SVM, LR, NB, K-NN, and RF are shown in Table 3 and Table 4. For both scene 1, 2, and scene 3, 4, RF produced the best results. For the models of scene 1, 2, the accuracy was 0.98 and the F-value was 0.95. For the models of scene 3, 4, the accuracy was 0.81 and the F-value was 0.80. RF can reduce prediction variance using bagging and is highly robust against noise. It is capable of learning various nonlinear patterns more flexibly while preventing overfitting, which likely led to the good results for this dataset. Overall, the recognition rate for "endoscope insertion/evolusion" was slightly lower, with a tendency to be misclassified as endoscope and instrument blurring or interference" or "endoscope and instrument immobility". The insertion and removal of

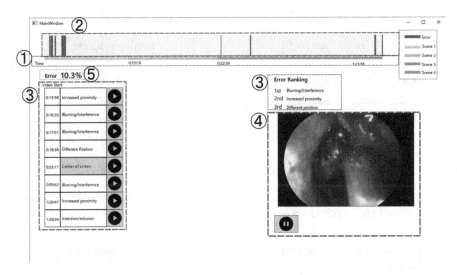

Fig. 2. Example of a software for presenting automatically recognized surgical issue. (1)A bar that segments the scenes is placed at the bottom of the surgical timeline, with (2)red markers above indicating where issues occurred. (3)A list of the surgical issues is displayed in the order they occurred, with a video playback button beside each. (4)Clicking the playback button plays the corresponding surgical video. The selected list item changes background color to indicate selection, and the corresponding surgical issue section on the timeline blinks red. The number on the left end of the list indicates the start time of the video. (5) calculates the proportion of the overall surgery time during which surgical issues occurred. (6) ranks surgical issues by occurrence frequency, prioritizing longer durations if the frequency is the same. (Color figure online)

the endoscope or instruments typically occur due to reasons such as checking the procedure details among the surgical staff, switching instruments, or temporarily pausing the procedure because the view is obstructed by blood. During these moments, the instruments are often in a safe state, such as being powered off, resulting in a noticeably faster retraction speed compared to when performing procedures. This could be a factor contributing to the slight misrecognition as blurring or interference actions. In the field of surgical situation recognition, many methods using deep learning have been proposed, most of which utilize endoscopic video data [1]. Some studies use kinematic data, but most of these studies use data that include both kinematic and video data [13]. Additionally, the kinematic data used is often raw data [4]. There are studies using SVM, 1-NN [17], NB [14], and RF [3,8] for process classification. Since the classification methods tested in this study did not consider temporal elements, methods that consider time series such as HMM or LSTM might yield better results. However, the results of this study suggest that using indicators reflecting the characteristics of surgical skills as features can sufficiently classify surgical situations with machine learning. This research newly achieved recognizing and classifying surgical skill issues extracted by our algorithm, using kinematic features calculated

Table 3. Scene 1 and 2

	Accuracy	macro-F1
SVM	0.84	0.69
LR	0.79	0.69
NB	0.69	0.50
k-NN	0.91	0.85
RF	**0.98**	**0.95**

Table 4. Scene 3 and 4

	Accuracy	macro-F1
SVM	0.62	0.56
LR	0.61	0.60
NB	0.35	0.33
k-NN	0.72	0.69
RF	**0.81**	**0.80**

from kinematic data as input parameters, rather than providing an overarching recognition of the surgical process in a clinical environment.

3.2 Software for Presenting Automatically Recognized Surgical Issues

Figure 3 shows the survey results regarding the software. Negative feedback on the system included comments such as "The meaning of the term 'different positions of the surgical instrument' is unclear, making it difficult to know how to improve". On the other hand, positive feedback highlighted that "the overall error rate being displayed like a score is good", "it is educational as improvement points are immediately clear when reviewing surgical videos", and "it is helpful to be able to quickly review dangerous maneuvers without needing to watch the entire video", suggesting it aids in time-saving and workflow improvement, and increases motivation for review. The somewhat poor responses to questions 1 and 3 are likely due to the unclear meaning of "position of the surgical instrument", which made it difficult to directly link the presented content to improvement methods. Nevertheless, the proposed display system received high overall evaluation scores. Notably, all surgeons believed it would be useful for postoperative review. Previously, reviewing surgeries required watching the entire video from start to finish to identify surgical issues, a time-consuming process. This system enables busy surgeons to review without having to watch the entire procedure, leading to significant time savings. Additionally, comparing these results across cases may help in understanding the progression of surgical skills. However, the current validation was limited by the small number of cases and subjects. More extensive experiments with a larger number of cases and subjects are needed to generalize the results. Previous research on surgical skill training has often focused on assessing and classifying surgeons' skill levels and evaluating the validity of these assessments [2]. Recently, there has been an increase in research examining feedback functions for surgeons, but none have yet achieved widespread practical application. VOA [10] has features for presenting skill evaluation results and viewing instructional videos on improvement points, but it is limited to the VR simulator. Oita-RASOP [12] digitizes evaluations that were previously conducted on paper. While it reduces complexity and facilitates post-operative analysis by digitally storing data, it does not lessen the effort required to attend surgeries or watch surgical videos. Although feedback in higher education is known to be essential for enhancing learning outcomes, its implementation remains challenging. The system developed in this study addresses these challenges by automatically evaluating skills, identifying areas for improvement, and providing feedback in clinical settings. This new proficiency support system offers a solution to feedback-related issues. Our model could highlight specific areas for improvement in surgical techniques, which can prompt attention in subsequent surgeries, leading to efforts toward safer procedures.

	Strongly disagree	Disagree a little	Neither	Agree a little	Strong agree
[Question 1] Did you quickly understand the meaning of the items displayed in the system?	1	2	3	4	5
[Question 2] Did you smoothly display the video of the improved part?	1	2	3	4	5
[Question 3] Did you easily confirm the improvement points (occurrence location and its contents)?	1	2	3	4	5
[Question 4] Do you think this system will be useful when you review after surgery?	1	2	3	4	5
				Average	Expert Resident

Fig. 3. Result of the questionnaire.

4   Conclusion

In this study, we developed a system to automatically classify and present surgical issues to the surgeon based on kinematic data extracted from navigation-guided ESS. By using random forest algorithm, we categorized the surgical issues according to their nature. The verification results confirmed that the system could classify detected surgical issues with high accuracy. Additionally, the system received high ratings from surgeons in a survey, suggesting its usefulness for post-surgery review.

Prospect of Application. Our system can be applied not only to ESS but also to other surgical procedures as a tool for identifying areas for improvement during reviews. This can lead to more efficient support for skill acquisition.

Acknowledgments. This study was funded by JSPS KAKENHI Grant Number 23K17013.

Disclosure of Interests. The authors have no competing interests to declare that are relevant to the content of this article.

References

1. Chen, Y.W., Zhang, J., Wang, P., Hu, Z.Y., Zhong, K.H.: Convolutional-deconvolutional neural networks for recognition of surgical workflow. Front. Comput. Neurosci. **16** (2022). https://doi.org/10.3389/fncom.2022.998096, https://www.frontiersin.org/articles/10.3389/fncom.2022.998096, publisher: Frontiers
2. Dhanakshirur, R.R., Katiyar, V., Sharma, R., Suri, A., Kalra, P.K., Arora, C.: From feline classification to skills evaluation: a multitask learning framework for evaluating micro suturing neurosurgical skills. In: 2023 IEEE International Conference on Image Processing (ICIP), pp. 3374–3378 (2023). https://doi.org/10.1109/ICIP49359.2023.10222868
3. Gonzalez, G.T., et al.: From the dexterous surgical skill to the battlefield-a robotics exploratory study. Military Med. **186**(Supplement_1), 288–294 (2021). https://doi.org/10.1093/milmed/usaa253
4. Hutchinson, K., Reyes, I., Li, Z., Alemzadeh, H.: Evaluating the task generalization of temporal convolutional networks for surgical gesture and motion recognition using kinematic data. IEEE Robot. Autom. Lett. **8**, 5132–5139 (2023). https://doi.org/10.1109/LRA.2023.3292581
5. Langridge, B., Momin, S., Coumbe, B., Woin, E., Griffin, M., Butler, P.: Systematic review of the use of 3-dimensional printing in surgical teaching and assessment. J. Surg. Educ. **75**(1), 209–221 (2018). https://doi.org/10.1016/j.jsurg.2017.06.033, https://www.sciencedirect.com/science/article/pii/S1931720417301836
6. Lu, J., Cuff, R.F., Mansour, M.A.: Simulation in surgical education. Am. J. Surgery **221**(3), 509–514 (2021). https://doi.org/10.1016/j.amjsurg.2020.12.016, https://www.sciencedirect.com/science/article/pii/S0002961020307947
7. Lungu, A.J., Swinkels, W., Claesen, L., Tu, P., Egger, J., Chen, X.: A review on the applications of virtual reality, augmented reality and mixed reality in surgical simulation: an extension to different kinds of surgery. Expert Rev. Med. Devices **18**(1), 47–62 (2021). https://doi.org/10.1080/17434440.2021.1860750, publisher: Taylor & Francis _eprint
8. Madapana, N., et al.: DESK: a robotic activity dataset for dexterous surgical skills transfer to medical robots. In: 2019 IEEE/RSJ International Conference on Intelligent Robots and Systems (IROS), pp. 6928–6934 (2019). https://doi.org/10.1109/IROS40897.2019.8967760, https://ieeexplore.ieee.org/document/8967760/, conference Name: 2019 IEEE/RSJ International Conference on Intelligent Robots and Systems (IROS) ISBN: 9781728140049 Place: Macau, China Publisher: IEEE
9. Maurer, C.R., Fitzpatrick, J.M., Wang, M.Y., Galloway, R.L., Maciunas, R.J., Allen, G.S.: Registration of head volume images using implantable fiducial markers. IEEE Trans. Med. Imaging **16**(4), 447–462 (1997). https://doi.org/10.1109/42.611354

10. Mirchi, N., Bissonnette, V., Yilmaz, R., Ledwos, N., Winkler-Schwartz, A., Maestro, R.F.D.: The virtual operative assistant: an explainable artificial intelligence tool for simulation-based training in surgery and medicine. PLoS ONE **15**(2), e0229596 (2020). https://doi.org/10.1371/journal.pone.0229596, https://journals.plos.org/plosone/article?id=10.1371/journal.pone.0229596, publisher: Public Library of Science
11. Sakoe, H., Chiba, S.: Dynamic programming algorithm optimization for spoken word recognition. IEEE Trans. Acoust. Speech Signal Process. **26**(1), 43–49 (1978). https://doi.org/10.1109/TASSP.1978.1163055
12. Ueda, Y., Kawasaki, T., Inomata, M., Shiraishi, N.: Development of a new feedback system using groupware in surgical technique education focused on laparoscopic surgery. Ann. Med. Surgery **85**(7), 3769 (2023). https://doi.org/10.1097/MS9.0000000000001019
13. Van Amsterdam, B., et al.: Gesture recognition in robotic surgery with multimodal attention. IEEE Trans. Med. Imaging **41**(7), 1677–1687 (2022). https://doi.org/10.1109/TMI.2022.3147640, https://ieeexplore.ieee.org/document/9701436/
14. Weede, O., et al.: Workflow analysis and surgical phase recognition in minimally invasive surgery. In: 2012 IEEE International Conference on Robotics and Biomimetics (ROBIO), pp. 1080–1074 (2012). https://doi.org/10.1109/ROBIO.2012.6491111
15. Yamaguchi, T., Nakamura, R., Kuboki, A., Otori, N.: Clinical study of skill assessment based on time sequential measurement changes. Sci. Rep. **12**(1), 6638 (2022). https://doi.org/10.1038/s41598-022-10502-7, https://www.nature.com/articles/s41598-022-10502-7, publisher: Nature Publishing Group
16. Yamaguchi, T., Nakamura, R., Kuboki, A., Sawano, Y., Ebata, R., Otori, N.: Skill assessment and visualization system for endoscopic sinus surgeryâĂf: a clinical study. J JSCAS **22**(1), 21–32 (2020). https://doi.org/10.5759/jscas.22.21
17. Zappella, L., Béjar, B., Hager, G., Vidal, R.: Surgical gesture classification from video and kinematic data. Med. Image Anal. **17**(7), 732–745 (2013). https://doi.org/10.1016/j.media.2013.04.007, http://www.sciencedirect.com/science/article/pii/S1361841513000522

Quantifying Knee Cartilage Shape and Lesion: From Image to Metrics

Yongcheng Yao[1]($\boxtimes$) and Weitian Chen[2]

[1] UKRI CDT in Biomedical AI, School of Informatics, The University of Edinburgh, Edinburgh, UK
yc.yao@ed.ac.uk

[2] CU Lab of AI in Radiology (CLAIR), Department of Imaging and Interventional Radiology, The Chinese University of Hong Kong, Hong Kong, China
wtchen@cuhk.edu.hk

Abstract. Imaging features of knee articular cartilage have been shown to be potential imaging biomarkers for knee osteoarthritis. Despite recent methodological advancements in image analysis techniques like image segmentation, registration, and domain-specific image computing algorithms, only a few works focus on building fully automated pipelines for imaging feature extraction. In this study, we developed a deep-learning-based medical image analysis application for knee cartilage morphometrics, CartiMorph Toolbox (CMT). We proposed a 2-stage joint template learning and registration network, CMT-reg. We trained the model using the OAI-ZIB dataset and assessed its performance in template-to-image registration. The CMT-reg demonstrated competitive results compared to other state-of-the-art models. We integrated the proposed model into an automated pipeline for the quantification of cartilage shape and lesion (full-thickness cartilage loss, specifically). The toolbox provides a comprehensive, user-friendly solution for medical image analysis and data visualization. The software and models are available at https://github.com/YongchengYAO/CMT-AMAI24paper.

Keywords: knee cartilage lesion · medical application · deep learning

1 Introduction

Osteoarthritis (OA) represents a predominant cause of disability among the elderly demographic, with knee OA being a highly prevalent sub-type of the disease. In light of the global trend towards an aging population, an increase in the burden of OA can be expected. The pathogenesis of knee OA involves deterioration in various knee joint tissues including the articular cartilage, subchondral bone, meniscus, and ligament. Notably, the loss of articular cartilage integrity represents a hallmark feature of knee OA progression. Cartilage morphometrics is a promising tool for deriving biomarkers from magnetic resonance imaging (MRI) or radiograph. The combination of medical image acquisition,

© The Author(s), under exclusive license to Springer Nature Switzerland AG 2025
S. Wu et al. (Eds.): AMAI 2024, LNCS 15384, pp. 162–172, 2025.
https://doi.org/10.1007/978-3-031-82007-6_16

image computing, and visualization has the potential to facilitate knee OA monitoring, pathology research, treatment evaluation, and surgical planning. Despite the advances in semiautomated cartilage lesion quantification [5,17,21,23], automated lesion grading [4,7], and knee joint tissue segmentation [6,10,11,24], a fully automated image analysis application is rarely encountered. To this end, we developed CartiMorph Toolbox (CMT) for automatic shape and lesion analysis. It is a deep-learning-powered cartilage morphometrics solution, from an image to quantitative metrics.

Contribution. CMT consists of deep learning (DL) models for tissue segmentation and registration. We proposed a method for joint template learning and registration, CMT-reg. We implemented and improved the cartilage morphometrics framework, CartiMorph [25], and developed a integrated suite of modules for computing environment configuration, project management, DL model lifecycle management (including training, fine-tuning, evaluation, and inference), and data visualization. The software and models are publicly available[1].

2   Related Work

Deep Segmentation Model. Deep learning has been attracting increasing interesting in medical image segmentation due to its superior performance and learning ability. Advancements in DL-based knee tissue segmentation include the combination of convolutional neural network (CNN) with shape model [1,14], alpha matte [10], and self attention [13]. There is increasing number of medical image segmentation models based on vision Transformer in recent years [12,15]. Most deep segmentation models are trained and optimized for specific tasks. It is desired to have DL models that generalize well on out-of-distribution unseen data. The auto-configuring nnU-Net [9] and the foundation model Med-SAM [16] demonstrate significant generalisability, offering a strong foundation for advanced deep learning applications in medical imaging. We implemented the 3D variant of nnU-Net in CMT.

Deep Registration Model. VoxelMorph [2] represents a successful application of deep learning for medical image registration. Knee image registration models have been developed [3,20,24]. We compared CMT-reg with 2 state-of-the-art (SOTA) algorithms: (i) LapIRN [18], the SOTA method in Learn2Reg [8] challenge, and (ii) Aladdin [3], which achieves SOTA performance in atlas-as-a-bridge alignment.

Cartilage Shape and Lesion Analysis. Shape and lesion analysis of knee cartilage includes the quantification of healthy anatomy and lesion. Methods for cartilage thickness mapping [5,17], semiautomated lesion quantification [22], and subregional parcellation [5,19] have been developed. CartiMorph [25] integrated deep segmentation and registration models in the cartilage morphometrics pipeline, and achieved improvement in thickness mapping, parcellation, and

---

[1] https://github.com/YongchengYAO/CMT-AMAI24paper.

full-thickness cartilage loss (FCL) estimation. In this work, we proposed methods to simplify the CartiMorph framework and yet achieve superior performance in template-to-image registration. Specifically, we used a single CNN for joint template learning and image registration.

3   Methods

3.1   Toolbox Overview

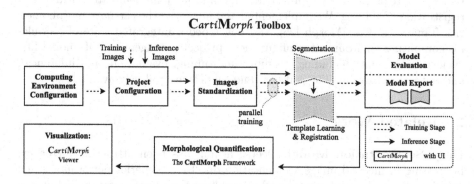

Fig. 1. Structure of CartiMorph Toolbox (CMT).

CMT comprises of modules for computing environment configuration, project configuration, image standardization, DL models management, morphological quantification, and data visualization (Fig. 1). The configurations of data source, data analysis steps, hyper-parameters setting, and figures and metrics visualization are integrated in CMT user interface. The toolbox was developed to address several challenges in achieving fully automated DL applications for cartilage morphometrics.

DL Models Life-cycle Management. The development of DL models involves the configuration of model training environment, data processing, and model evaluation. A user-friendly mechanism for model sharing and fine-tuning is useful for adapting pre-trained models to new domains. A plugin-and-use model inference tool may facilitate the development of DL applications. CMT management the whole life-cycle of DL models (in the toolbox) by providing user interface for models training, fine-tuning, evaluation, inference, and sharing.

Image Standardization. This module consists of image intensity normalization, image re-orientation, and image resampling. It is an important data preprocessing step for DL model training and downstream algorithms. The standard image orientation in CMT is RAS+ where the image dimensions correspond to the right, anterior, and superior directions.

Sub-regional Parcellation. CartiMorph [25] introduced approaches for rule-based cartilage parcellation and regional FLC estimation, which have only been validated on right-side knee images. More importantly, deviation from the standard scanning position could lead to inaccurate partitioning results. We enhanced the parcellation method to accommodate both left and right knee images by flipping the left knee images before and after the algorithm. The robustness against scanning position variation is improved by rigid-body registration to the learned template image.

3.2 DL Models

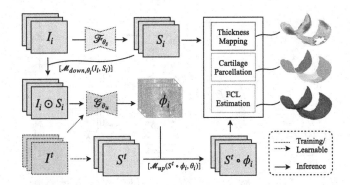

Fig. 2. Deep learning models and quantification algorithms in CMT.

Figure 2 provides an overview of the 2 DL models and image computing algorithms in CMT. A segmentation CNN F_{θ_s} is trained on $\{(\boldsymbol{I}_i, \boldsymbol{S}_i^l)\}_{i=1}^{n_t}$, where $\boldsymbol{I}_i$ is the input image and $\boldsymbol{S}_i^l$ is the ground truth segmentation label. We integrate the template learning and image registration into a single CNN $G_{\{\theta_u, \boldsymbol{I}^t\}}$, which is trained on the masked and optionally down-sampled image $\boldsymbol{I}_i \odot \boldsymbol{S}_i^l$. The down-sampling step aims to accommodate the model on a GPU with limited memory by leveraging spatial redundancy in the dense deformation field ϕ_i. A template image $\boldsymbol{I}^t$ is learned from $G_{\{\theta_u, \boldsymbol{I}^t\}}$ and the corresponding template segmentation mask $\boldsymbol{S}^t$ is constructed via registration. Specifically, we register all training images into the template space and apply the image-to-template deformation field to their ground truth mask; a probability map $\boldsymbol{P}^t$ can therefore be calculated as the average warped mask

$$[\phi_i^{-1}], \phi_i = G_{\{\theta_u, \boldsymbol{I}^t\}}((\boldsymbol{I}_i \odot \boldsymbol{S}_i^l)), \tag{1}$$

$$\boldsymbol{P}^t = \frac{1}{n_t} \sum_{i=1}^{n_t} (\boldsymbol{S}_i^l \circ \phi_i^{-1}), \tag{2}$$

where ϕ_i^{-1} and ϕ_i denotes image-to-template and template-to-image deformation field, respectively; finally, the template mask S^t is obtained by thresholding P^t.

Once F_{θ_s} and $G_{\{\theta_u, I^t\}}$ finish training, the predicted segmentation mask S_i and the deformation field ϕ_i are utilized in subsequent algorithms for cartilage thickness mapping, cartilage parcellation, and FCL estimation. We adopted 3D nnU-Net as the segmentation model and the proposed CMT-reg as the template-learning-and-registration model.

3.3   Joint Template Learning and Registration Model

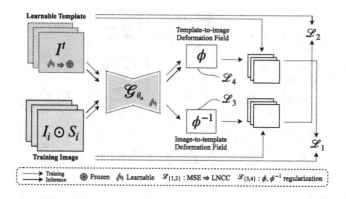

Fig. 3. The proposed joint template learning and registration model, CMT-reg.

Template construction, involving the creation of a representative image from multiple aligned images, is intrinsically tied to image registration. With the advances of deep registration models, methods for template learning have been developed. Common image similarity losses include mean squared error (MSE), cross-correlation (CC), normalized cross-correlation (NCC), local normalized cross-correlation (LNCC). Previous studies [2,25] have demonstrated that LNCC is superior to MSE in image registration task. However, the influence of different loss functions on template image quality remains under-explored. We present the results of template images trained with various losses in Sect. 4.

Based on our observation that the LNCC loss excels in image registration and MSE in template learning, we propose to jointly learn the template and train the registration CNN in a 2-stage strategy (Fig. 3). In the first training stage, both the template and CNN are learnable. In the second stage, the template is frozen while the CNN are trainable. The model is optimized with image similarity losses $\mathcal{L}_{\{1,2\}}$ and deformation field regularization $\mathcal{L}_{\{3,4\}}$. For the image similarity loss, MSE is used in stage 1 and LNCC is used in stage 2.

4   Experiments and Results

4.1   Registration Model Evaluation

In CMT, the FCL estimation algorithm depends on the alignment between the template mask S^t and the model predicted segmentation mask S_i. Combined with mesh processing algorithms, the warped template mask $S^t \circ \phi_i$ is used to reconstruct the intact cartilage surface. The ideal behavior of the registration model is that the warped template mask could cover as much FCL regions as possible without encompassing non-cartilage tissues.

Metrics. We first adopted the conventional evaluation metrics, the Dice similarity coefficient (DSC) and the 95th percentile Hausdorff distance (HD95), to quantify the discrepancy between $S^t \circ \phi_i$ and S_i. Additionally, we measured the relative difference between the surface area of the bone-cartilage interface from $S^t \circ \phi_i$ and that of the manually calibrated pseudo-healthy bone-cartilage interface M_i^{pseudo}: $(A_i - A_i^{\text{pseudo}})/A_i^{\text{pseudo}}$, $A_i^{\text{pseudo}} = \mathcal{O}_{\text{surfArea}}(M_i^{\text{pseudo}})$, where $A_i = \mathcal{O}_{\text{surfArea}}(\mathcal{O}_{\text{surfSeg}}(S^t \circ \phi_i))$, and $\mathcal{O}_{\text{surfSeg}}(\cdot)$ generates the bone-cartilage interface mesh from a 3D mask, $\mathcal{O}_{\text{surfArea}}(\cdot)$ calculates surface area.

Models. We trained variants of LapIRN and Aladdin. Like CMT-reg, Aladdin is a joint template learning and registration model, while LapIRN is solely an image registration model. For LapIRN, we first trained models and used an external template, *CLAIR-Knee-103R*, from the CartiMorph study[2] for template-to-image evaluation. Two variants of LapIRN were trained: (i) LapIRN-diff, a model formulated with the stationary velocity field, and (ii) LapIRN-disp, a model formulated with displacement field. We trained variants of Aladdin under various setting of image similarity loss (MSE, NCC, and LNCC) and evaluation target ($\mathcal{L}_{sim}$: ordinal image similarity loss; $\mathcal{L}_p^i$: pair similarity loss in image space; $\mathcal{L}_p^t$: pair similarity loss in template space).

Implementation Details. CMT requires conda for managing virtual environments. Our implementation of nnU-Net (v1.7.0) was released as a python package, CartiMorph-nnUNet. The proposed CMT-reg is based on VoxelMorph and was released as CartiMorph-vxm. Models were trained with NVIDIA A100 (80G). A window size of 27 was used in LNCC loss for all models. The channel numbers of CMT-reg is $\{[48, 96, 96, 96]^{\text{enc}}, [96]^{\text{neck}}, [96, 96, 96, 96]^{\text{dec}}, [48, 48]^{\text{conv}}\}$, corresponding to the encoder, bottleneck, decoder, and the size-preserving convolutional block, respectively.

4.2   Data

We evaluated the toolbox with the OAI-ZIB dataset that consists of 507 MR images and manual segmentation labels for the femoral cartilage (FC), tibial cartilage (TC), femur, and tibia. We subdivided the tibial cartilage into the medial tibial cartilage (MTC) and lateral tibial cartilage (LTC). Data split is

---

[2] Data from https://github.com/YongchengYAO/CartiMorph.

shown in Table 1, where the same testing set is reserved for model evaluation. The CMT-reg and LapIRN were trained with data split 1, while Aladdin models were trained with data split 2. The Kellgren-Lawrence (KL) grades were employed in stratified random sampling to guarantee the inclusion of cases with varying cartilage lesion severities in both the training and testing sets. Subset 3 includes 12 cases from the testing set, featuring severe cartilage lesions, was utilized to evaluate the models' behavior based on the relative surface area difference.

Table 1. Datasets for model training, testing, and analysis. Dataset 1 and 2 share the same testing set. Dataset 3 is a subset of the testing set, used for analyzing the behavior of registration models.

Data Split	Train (%)	Validation (%)	Test (%)[KL Grade: 0–4, N/A]
#1	404 (80%)	0	103 (20%) [21,12,22,28,15,5]
#2	324 (64%)	80 (16%)	
Subset	**Analysis [KL Grade: 0–4, N/A]**		
#3	12 [0,0,0,6,6,0]		

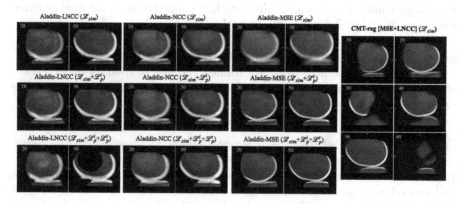

Fig. 4. Learned template images from variants of Aladdin and the proposed model, CMT-reg. Numbers in the upper left corner are indices of sagittal slices.

4.3   Results and Discussion

Template Image Quality. Fig. 4 shows that template images learned from models with MSE loss exhibit greater sharpness compared to those produced with LNCC loss. Additionally, models trained with LNCC loss sometimes produced corrupted images, such as the Aladdin-LNCC ($\mathcal{L}_{sim}+\mathcal{L}_p^i$) model in Fig. 4. This observation informed our model training strategy, wherein we used MSE loss to learn the template image and then switch to LNCC loss for continuing the registration network training. Although Aladdin models achieve high registration accuracy with noisy and blurry template images, we prefer a model that learns a high-quality template, as it can be used in general registration models like LapIRN.

Balanced Registration Models. Table 2 shows that our model is comparable to SOTA models in terms of volume overlap (DSC) and surface distance (HD95). In our application, the desired registration model must achieve a balance between accuracy (evaluated by DSC and HD95) and FCL region coverage (evaluated by relative surface area difference). Table 3 shows our model outperforms Aladdin models and is comparable to LapIRN models in FCL region coverage.

Table 2. Template-to-image registration accuracy.

Model (Loss)	DSC ↑			HD95 ↓ (mm)		
	FC	mTC	ITC	FC	mTC	ITC
Aladdin-LNCC ($\mathcal{L}_{sim}$)	**0.905**	0.816	0.839	**0.58**	**0.92**	0.94
Aladdin-LNCC ($\mathcal{L}_{sim}+\mathcal{L}_p^i$)	**0.905**	0.817	0.839	0.59	**0.92**	0.92
Aladdin-LNCC ($\mathcal{L}_{sim}+\mathcal{L}_p^i+\mathcal{L}_p^t$)	0.904	0.809	0.831	0.64	1.09	1.16
Aladdin-NCC ($\mathcal{L}_{sim}$)	0.904	0.818	0.842	0.59	**0.92**	0.89
Aladdin-NCC ($\mathcal{L}_{sim}+\mathcal{L}_p^i$)	**0.908**	**0.829**	**0.858**	**0.55**	**0.85**	**0.72**
Aladdin-NCC ($\mathcal{L}_{sim}+\mathcal{L}_p^i+\mathcal{L}_p^t$)	0.904	0.819	0.840	0.62	0.99	1.03
Aladdin-MSE ($\mathcal{L}_{sim}$)	0.505	0.368	0.305	3.49	5.69	6.51
Aladdin-MSE ($\mathcal{L}_{sim}+\mathcal{L}_p^i$)	0.889	0.808	0.849	0.65	0.97	**0.76**
Aladdin-MSE ($\mathcal{L}_{sim}+\mathcal{L}_p^i+\mathcal{L}_p^t$)	0.885	0.803	0.841	0.65	0.98	0.82
LapIRN-diff ($\mathcal{L}_{sim}$)	0.855	0.740	0.731	1.09	1.69	2.01
LapIRN-disp ($\mathcal{L}_{sim}$)	0.898	0.806	**0.850**	0.81	1.38	1.28
CMT-reg ($\mathcal{L}_{sim}$)	0.895	**0.821**	**0.850**	0.70	1.10	0.89

Data Visualization. We showcased examples of figures from the visualization module, CartiMorph Viewer (CMV), in Fig. 5. Additionally, CMV displays regional metrics (including volume, thickness, surface area, and FCL), facilitating the direct correlation of qualitative measurements with visual representations.

Table 3. Registration models behavior analysis.

Model (Loss)	$(A_i - A_i^{\text{pseudo}})/A_i^{\text{pseudo}}$ $\downarrow\downarrow$		
	FC	mTC	ITC
Aladdin-LNCC ($\mathcal{L}_{sim}$)	-0.035	-0.115	-0.140
Aladdin-LNCC ($\mathcal{L}_{sim}+\mathcal{L}_p^i$)	-0.029	-0.106	-0.143
Aladdin-LNCC ($\mathcal{L}_{sim}+\mathcal{L}_p^i+\mathcal{L}_p^t$)	-0.026	-0.080	-0.133
Aladdin-NCC ($\mathcal{L}_{sim}$)	-0.031	-0.112	-0.150
Aladdin-NCC ($\mathcal{L}_{sim}+\mathcal{L}_p^i$)	-0.029	-0.098	-0.145
Aladdin-NCC ($\mathcal{L}_{sim}+\mathcal{L}_p^i+\mathcal{L}_p^t$)	-0.032	-0.088	-0.134
Aladdin-MSE ($\mathcal{L}_{sim}$)	-0.203	-0.393	-0.468
Aladdin-MSE ($\mathcal{L}_{sim}+\mathcal{L}_p^i$)	-0.021	-0.079	-0.142
Aladdin-MSE ($\mathcal{L}_{sim}+\mathcal{L}_p^i+\mathcal{L}_p^t$)	**-0.002**	-0.070	-0.129
LapIRN-diff ($\mathcal{L}_{sim}$)	**0.007**	-0.087	-0.134
LapIRN-disp ($\mathcal{L}_{sim}$)	0.040	**-0.047**	**-0.103**
CMT-reg ($\mathcal{L}_{sim}$)	0.036	**-0.048**	**-0.124**

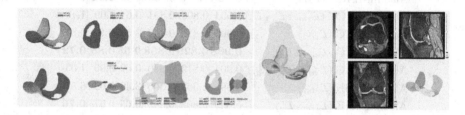

Fig. 5. Examples of data visualization in CartiMorph Viewer (CMV)

5 Conclusion

In this study, we developed the CartiMorph Toolbox (CMT), a medical AI application for knee cartilage morphometrics. The key component, CMT-reg, is a
2-stage joint template learning and registration network. Trained on the public
OAI-ZIB dataset, CMT-reg demonstrated satisfying balance between accuracy
and FCL region coverage. CMT offers an out-of-the-box solution for medical
image computing and data visualization.

Prospect of Application. The toolbox offers an AI solution for medical image
computing, enabling precise quantification of cartilage shape and lesion. It automates the complicated process of model training, inference, and image analysis.
Its potential applications include clinical diagnostics support system, treatment
planning, and research on knee cartilage health.

Acknowledgments. This work was supported by the United Kingdom Research and
Innovation (grant EP/S02431X/1), UKRI Centre for Doctoral Training in Biomedical
AI at the University of Edinburgh, School of Informatics. For the purpose of open

access, the author has applied a creative commons attribution (CC BY) licence to any author accepted manuscript version arising.

Disclosure of Interests. The authors have no competing interests to declare that are relevant to the content of this article.

References

1. Ambellan, F., Tack, A., Ehlke, M., Zachow, S.: Automated segmentation of knee bone and cartilage combining statistical shape knowledge and convolutional neural networks: data from the osteoarthritis initiative. Med. Image Anal. **52**, 109–118 (2019). https://doi.org/10.1016/j.media.2018.11.009
2. Balakrishnan, G., Zhao, A., Sabuncu, M.R., Guttag, J., Dalca, A.V.: VoxelMorph: a learning framework for deformable medical image registration. IEEE Trans. Med. Imaging **38**(8), 1788–1800 (2019). https://doi.org/10.1109/TMI.2019.2897538
3. Ding, Z., Niethammer, M.: Aladdin: joint atlas building and diffeomorphic registration learning with pairwise alignment. In: Proceedings of the IEEE/CVF Conference on Computer Vision and Pattern Recognition (CVPR), pp. 20784–20793 (2022)
4. Dório, M., et al.: Association of baseline and change in tibial and femoral cartilage thickness and development of widespread full-thickness cartilage loss in knee osteoarthritis - data from the osteoarthritis initiative. Osteoarthritis Cartilage **28**(6), 811–818 (2020). https://doi.org/10.1016/j.joca.2020.03.011
5. Favre, J., Erhart-Hledik, J.C., Blazek, K., Fasel, B., Gold, G.E., Andriacchi, T.P.: Anatomically standardized maps reveal distinct patterns of cartilage thickness with increasing severity of medial compartment knee osteoarthritis. J. Orthop. Res. **35**(11), 2442–2451 (2017). https://doi.org/10.1002/jor.23548
6. Gaj, S., Yang, M., Nakamura, K., Li, X.: Automated cartilage and meniscus segmentation of knee MRI with conditional generative adversarial networks. Magn. Reson. Med. **84**(1), 437–449 (2020). https://doi.org/10.1002/mrm.28111
7. Guermazi, A., et al.: Brief report: Partial- and full-thickness focal cartilage defects contribute equally to development of new cartilage damage in knee osteoarthritis: The multicenter osteoarthritis study. Arthritis Rheumatol. **69**(3), 560–564 (2017). https://doi.org/10.1002/art.39970
8. Hering, A., et al.: Learn2reg: comprehensive multi-task medical image registration challenge, dataset and evaluation in the era of deep learning. IEEE Trans. Med. Imaging **42**(3), 697–712 (2023). https://doi.org/10.1109/TMI.2022.3213983
9. Isensee, F., et al.: nnU-Net: self-adapting framework for U-Net-based medical image segmentation. Nat. Methods (2018). https://doi.org/10.1038/s41592-020-01008-z
10. Khan, S., Azam, B., Yao, Y., Chen, W.: Deep collaborative network with alpha matte for precise knee tissue segmentation from MRI. Comput. Methods Programs Biomed. **222**, 106963 (2022). https://doi.org/10.1016/j.cmpb.2022.106963
11. Li, S., Zhao, S., Zhang, Y., Hong, J., Chen, W.: Source-free unsupervised adaptive segmentation for knee joint MRI. Biomed. Signal Process. Control **92**, 106028 (2024). https://doi.org/10.1016/j.bspc.2024.106028
12. Li, X., et al.: SDMT: spatial dependence multi-task transformer network for 3D knee MRI segmentation and landmark localization. IEEE Trans. Med. Imaging **42**(8), 2274–2285 (2023). https://doi.org/10.1109/TMI.2023.3247543

13. Liang, D., Liu, J., Wang, K., Luo, G., Wang, W., Li, S.: Position-prior clustering-based self-attention module for knee cartilage segmentation. In: Wang, L., Dou, Q., Fletcher, P.T., Speidel, S., Li, S. (eds.) Medical Image Computing and Computer Assisted Intervention - MICCAI 2022, pp. 193–202. Springer Nature Switzerland, Cham (2022). https://doi.org/10.1007/978-3-031-16443-9_19

14. Liu, F., Zhou, Z., Jang, H., Samsonov, A., Zhao, G., Kijowski, R.: Deep convolutional neural network and 3D deformable approach for tissue segmentation in musculoskeletal magnetic resonance imaging. Magn. Reson. Med. **79**(4), 2379–2391 (2018). https://doi.org/10.1002/mrm.26841

15. Liu, Q., Xu, Z., Jiao, Y., Niethammer, M.: iSegFormer: interactive segmentation via transformers with application to 3D knee MR images. In: Wang, L., Dou, Q., Fletcher, P.T., Speidel, S., Li, S. (eds.) Medical Image Computing and Computer Assisted Intervention - MICCAI 2022, pp. 464–474. Springer Nature Switzerland, Cham (2022). https://doi.org/10.1007/978-3-031-16443-9_45

16. Ma, J., He, Y., Li, F., Han, L., You, C., Wang, B.: Segment anything in medical images. Nat. Commun. **15**(1), 654 (2024). https://doi.org/10.1038/s41467-024-44824-z

17. Maerz, T., Newton, M., Matthew, H., Baker, K.: Surface roughness and thickness analysis of contrast-enhanced articular cartilage using mesh parameterization. Osteoarthritis Cartilage **24**(2), 290–298 (2016). https://doi.org/10.1016/j.joca.2015.09.006

18. Mok, T.C.W., Chung, A.C.S.: Large deformation diffeomorphic image registration with Laplacian pyramid networks. In: Martel, A.L., et al. (eds.) Medical Image Computing and Computer Assisted Intervention - MICCAI 2020, pp. 211–221. Springer International Publishing, Cham (2020). https://doi.org/10.1007/978-3-030-59716-0_21

19. Panfilov, E., Tiulpin, A., Nieminen, M.T., Saarakkala, S., Casula, V.: Deep learning-based segmentation of knee MRI for fully automatic subregional morphological assessment of cartilage tissues: data from the osteoarthritis initiative. J. Orthop. Res. **40**(5), 1113–1124 (2022). https://doi.org/10.1002/jor.25150

20. Shen, Z., Han, X., Xu, Z., Niethammer, M.: Networks for joint affine and non-parametric image registration. In: Proceedings of the IEEE/CVF Conference on Computer Vision and Pattern Recognition (CVPR) (2019)

21. Williams, T.G., et al.: Anatomically corresponded regional analysis of cartilage in asymptomatic and osteoarthritic knees by statistical shape modelling of the bone. IEEE Trans. Med. Imaging **29**(8), 1541–1559 (2010). https://doi.org/10.1109/TMI.2010.2047653

22. Wirth, W., et al.: Regional analysis of femorotibial cartilage loss in a subsample from the osteoarthritis initiative progression subcohort. Osteoarthritis Cartilage **17**(3), 291–297 (2009). https://doi.org/10.1016/j.joca.2008.07.008

23. Wirth, W., Eckstein, F.: A technique for regional analysis of femorotibial cartilage thickness based on quantitative magnetic resonance imaging. IEEE Trans. Med. Imaging **27**(6), 737–744 (2008). https://doi.org/10.1109/TMI.2007.907323

24. Xu, Z., Niethammer, M.: DeepAtlas: joint semi-supervised learning of image registration and segmentation. In: Shen, D., et al. (eds.) Medical Image Computing and Computer Assisted Intervention - MICCAI 2019, pp. 420–429. Springer International Publishing, Cham (2019). https://doi.org/10.1007/978-3-030-32245-8_47

25. Yao, Y., Zhong, J., Zhang, L., Khan, S., Chen, W.: CartiMorph: a framework for automated knee articular cartilage morphometrics. Med. Image Anal. **91**, 103035 (2024). https://doi.org/10.1016/j.media.2023.103035

RadImageGAN – A Multi-modal Dataset-Scale Generative AI for Medical Imaging

Zelong Liu[1], Peyton Smith[1], Alexander Lautin[1], Jieshen Zhou[1], Maxwell Yoo[1], Mikey Sullivan[1], Haorun Li[1], Louisa Deyer[1], Alexander Zhou[1], Arnold Yang[1], Alara Yimaz[1], Catherine Zhang[1], James Grant[1], Daiqing Li[2], Zahi A. Fayad[1,5], Sean Huver[2], Timothy Deyer[3,4], and Xueyan Mei[1,5(✉)]

[1] BioMedical Engineering and Imaging Institute, Icahn School of Medicine at Mount Sinai, New York, NY, USA
xueyan.mei@icahn.mssm.edu
[2] NVIDIA, Santa Clara, CA, USA
shuver@nvidia.com
[3] East River Medical Imaging, New York, NY, USA
tdeyer@eastriverimaging.com
[4] Department of Radiology, Cornell Medicine, New York, NY, USA
[5] Windreich Department of Artificial Intelligence and Human Health, Icahn School of Medicine at Mount Sinai, New York, NY, USA

Abstract. Deep learning in medical imaging often requires large-scale, high-quality data, or initiation with suitably pre-trained weights. However, medical datasets are limited by data availability, domain-specific knowledge, and privacy concerns, and the creation of large and diverse radiologic databases like RadImageNet is highly resource-intensive. To address these limitations, we introduce RadImageGAN, a multi-modal medical image generator developed by training StyleGAN-XL on the RadImageNet dataset of CT and MRI images and the HyperKvasir dataset of gastrointestinal images. RadImageGAN can generate high-resolution synthetic medical imaging datasets across 12 anatomical regions and 130 pathological classes in 3 modalities. Furthermore, we developed the RadImageGAN-Labeler, which can generate multi-class pixel-wise annotated paired synthetic images and masks for diverse downstream segmentation tasks with minimal manual annotation. Using synthetic auto-labeled data from RadImageGAN can significantly improve performance on four diverse downstream segmentation datasets by augmenting real training data. We find that RadImageGAN can improve model performance and address data scarcity while reducing the resources needed for annotations for segmentation tasks.

Keywords: StyleGAN · Diffusion Model · Medical Image Segmentation

S. Wu et al. (Eds.): AMAI 2024, LNCS 15384, pp. 173–185, 2025.
https://doi.org/10.1007/978-3-031-82007-6_17

1 Introduction

Machine learning has significantly advanced in the field of medical imaging, enhancing diagnostic accuracy, treatment effectiveness, and cost efficiency [1, 2]. These models require extensive volumes of diverse, high-quality data [3], however, collecting and annotating such data is a resource-intensive task limited by privacy and regulatory concerns [4]. RadImageNet, a vast radiological image database with 1.35 million images across CT, MRI, and ultrasound modalities, categorized into 165 pathologic classes across 11 anatomic regions, has recently been developed to address data scarcity [5]. Despite the comprehensive resource it provides, creating such a database demands considerable time and expertise. Traditional methods like transfer learning and basic data augmentation partially address these challenges, but generative techniques like generative adversarial networks (GANs) [6] and diffusion models have begun to offer more effective solutions by creating synthetic datasets that closely mimic real ones, improving data availability and model training [7–9].

Recent studies have demonstrated GAN applications in synthetic data augmentation for liver lesion classification and high-resolution chest radiograph synthesis [10, 11] and aggregated GANs for brain tumor image generation [12]. However, these methods are generally limited to specific modalities, anatomies, and pathologies and often lack semantic segmentation, which could enhance downstream utility. Akbar et al. investigated using progressive GAN and StyleGAN 1–3 for medical image segmentation on BRATS datasets [13] using synthetic data [14–16]. Saragih et al. and Stojanovski et al. utilized Denoising Diffusion Probabilistic Models to create synthetic images, noting improved segmentation performance, although potentially limited by the training dataset size [17–19].

In this study, we propose training StyleGAN-XL [16], which scales StyleGAN to accommodate multi-class, large, unstructured datasets, to produce synthetic radiological images that correspond to the diagnostic classes of RadImageNet and the Hyper-Kvasir dataset. Our goal is to create a versatile multi-class radiologic data generator, "RadImageGAN," capable of generating synthetic, labeled, multi-class medical images. To further enhance RadImageGAN's utility, we have developed a multi-class, pixel-wise label generator for the synthetic images produced by RadImageGAN, titled "RadImageGAN-Labeler." We evaluated the performance of RadImageGAN against DiT [20], a diffusion-based model, on image generation and downstream applications.

2 Methods

2.1 RadImageGAN and RadImageGAN-Labeler

We utilized StyleGAN-XL to develop RadImageGAN for generating high-resolution 512×512 pixel synthetic medical images from the extensive and diverse RadImageNet and HyperKvasir databases, as shown in Fig. 1. StyleGAN-XL, leveraging pre-trained networks and classifier guidance applied to StyleGAN3 [21], excels in synthesizing images from large, varied datasets [16]. This GAN-based method progressively adds synthetic and super-resolution layers during training, enhancing detail as resolution increases from 16×16 to 512×512 pixel. The model development is monitored by the adversarial loss defined in the Projected GAN [22] as:

$$\min(G)\max(Dl) \sum_{l \in L} \left(\mathbb{E}_x \left[logD_l(P_l(x)) \right] + \mathbb{E}_z[\log(1 - D_l(P_l(G(z))))] \right) \qquad (1)$$

where the real image x and its latent code z are mapped by the generator G and the discriminator D in StyleGAN-XL architecture, and $\{D_l\}$ is a set of independent discriminators for different feature projections $\{P_l\}$.

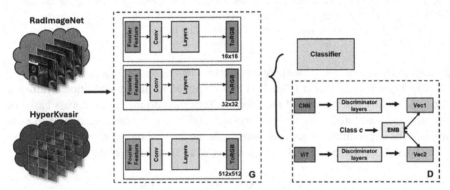

Fig. 1. Development of RadImageGAN. RadImageNet and HyperKvasir databases were utilized to develop the style codes for generator. Within the image synthesis network G, we initially train a model at 16x16 pixel, and then upsample the images for higher resolution using model weights from the previous stage. We have multiple independent discriminators using CNN and ViT architecture

To extend the capabilities of RadImageGAN, we also introduce RadImageGAN-Labeler, based on BigDatasetGAN [23], to provide paired segmentation masks. To segment pixel-wise labels based on RadImageGAN, we develop a feature interpreter functioning as the segmentation decoder. As shown in Fig. 2, the feature interpreter module resizes each layer from the RadImageGAN generator to feature maps and vectors, and then these feature vectors are upsampled by a decoder consisting of convolutional layers and batch normalization layers to generate a pixel-wise segmentation mask. RadImageGAN-Labeler contains an ensemble classifier for segmentation masks, which consists of sequential blocks of the Linear, ReLU and Batch Normalization layers.

2.2 Diffusion Models with Transformers (DiT) and DiT-Labeler

We also apply DiT to develop a synthetic image generator trained on RadImageNet and HyperKvasir datasets. DiT is a Latent Diffusion Model (LDM) [24] that consists of denoising diffusion probabilistic models (DDPMs) with variational autoencoder (VAE) generated latent space [25]. The model development begins with the tokenization of the input image representation, where each image is associated with a timestep and a class label. These tokens are then processed by a sequence of DiT blocks. Each DiT block

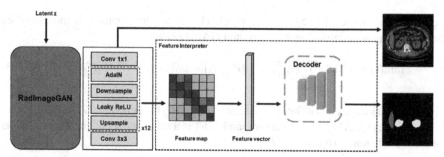

Fig. 2. The architecture of the RadImageGAN-Labeler. The RadImageGAN-Labeler contains a module to extract layer output from RadImageGAN blocks to feature vectors and then applies a segmentation decoder to generate pixel-wise segmentation masks.

is structurally composed of multiple transformer layers, and uniquely incorporates an adaptive layer normalization (adaLN) block designed to handle conditional information dynamically. The adaptive LayerNorm adjusts the normalization process based on timestep and class label, enhancing the model's ability to generate contextually accurate images. The latent diffusion process can sample the latent variable, x_t, from the real data x_0 at timestep t via hyperparameter α_t and Gaussian noise ϵ_t as follows:

$$x_t = \sqrt{\alpha_t}x_0 + \sqrt{1 - \alpha_t}\epsilon_t, \, \epsilon_t \sim \mathcal{N}(0, \mathbf{I}) \tag{2}$$

The DiT model is trained to learn the reverse process that reconstructs an original image from noisy data in timestep. Because DiT contains class label c as extra input information, classifier-free guidance encourages the sampling process to find x with high $\log p(c|x)$ [26]. In addition, we develop a separate pixel-wise segmentation decoder based on MONAI 2D segmentation UNet [27]. The DiT-Labeler employs 5 convolutional layers with kernel sizes of 3x3. The encoder consists of layers with 16, 32, 64, 128, and 256 filters, each downsampled with a stride of 2, and incorporates 12 residual units per convolutional block to facilitate training the segmentation network.

3 Experiments and Results

3.1 Datasets

Upstream Dataset for Generator Developments. RadImageGAN was trained on a specific subset of the RadImageNet database, designated for CT and MR images, which includes 880,314 images across 124 diagnostic labels [5]. Additionally, it was trained on a segment of the HyperKvasir dataset, focused on endoscopy images that are categorized into 6 pathological classes with a total of 5,714 adequately sampled images for training [17]. Ultrasound images were omitted from the original RadImageNet dataset due to their lack of diagnostic labels.

Downstream Datasets for Segmentation Evaluation. The downstream datasets were selected to evaluate the effectiveness of RadImageGAN and DiT in medical imaging segmentation. Four public datasets—BTCV-Abdomen CT [28], CHAOS-MRI T2 [29], Labeled Lumbar Spine MRI [30], and CVC-ClinicDB [31]—were chosen, covering three imaging modalities and various anatomical regions. Specifically, the liver and kidney from BTCV and CHAOS, intervertebral disc (IVD), posterior element (PE), and thecal sac (TS) segmentation from Labeled Lumbar Spine, and polyp segmentation from CVC-ClinicDB were tested as in-domain classes for RadImageGAN.

3.2 Implementation Details: RadImageGAN Generator and DiT Generator

All images were resized to $16 \times 16, 32 \times 32, 64 \times 64, 128 \times 128, 256 \times 256$, and 512×512 pixel resolutions for each respective model training stage. For the development of RadImageGAN, we started with low-resolution outputs at 16x16 pixel and progressively trained to higher-resolution outputs at 512×512 pixel. For the initial 16x16 stage, the stem model was trained from scratch with 10 synthetic layers and 7 head layers. For each resolution increase, the model utilizes the previous stage's model as pre-trained weights with 7 additional head layers. For the final 512×512 stage, only 5 head layers were added, giving 33 head layers in total. For the 16×16 and 32×32 stages, the batch size was set to 2048, and for all higher-resolution stages, the batch size was set to 256. X-axis flip data augmentation was disabled for all stages. The Fréchet Inception Distance (FID) was used to monitor the training process, and the model with the lowest FID score was selected as the pre-trained weights for the next higher-resolution stage. The RadImageGAN was trained using 8 NVIDIA DGX1-A100 GPUs for CT and MRI images, and 8 NVIDIA V100 GPUs for endoscopy images. It took RadImageGAN 7 min to generate 1000 images using one A100 GPU, while DiT required 8 min to generate 1000 images on eight A100 GPUs.

RadImageGAN-Labeler and DiT-Labeler. In this study, 50 synthetic images were manually annotated to train the labelers. During the training of RadImageGAN-Labeler, we utilized the following hyperparameters: a learning rate of 0.0001, a batch size of 4, and 100 training epochs. For DiT-Labeler, we utilized a learning rate of 0.001, batch size of 4, and 200 training epochs.

3.3 Segmentation Baseline Models – NnU-Net, TransUNet, and VIS-MAE

The 2D nnU-Net [32], TransUNet [33], and VIS-MAE [34] models were employed as baseline models for all segmentation tasks and data conditions, due to their state-of-the-art performance in medical image segmentations. For nnU-Net, we applied its default preprocessing mechanism to set up training parameters. While for both TransUNet and VIS-MAE, we applied the recommended default training parameters including learning rate (0.001 for TransUNet and 0.0001 for VIS-MAE) and optimizer (adamW). For the BTCV-Abdomen, CHAOS-MRI, and CVC-ClinicDB datasets, all images were resized to 512x512 pixels, while images from the Labeled Lumbar Spine MRI dataset were resized to 320x320 pixels.

Comparisons between RadImageGAN and DiT. We compare the RadImageGAN model to DiT using the mean FID, sum FID (sFID), inception score (IS), structural similarity index measure (SSIM) and peak-signal-to-noise ratio (PSNR) by randomly sampling 50,000 CT/MR images and 5,714 endoscopy images (total number of Hyper-kvasir dataset with same label distribution) from RadImageGAN and the DiT model respectively. Shown in Table 1, our proposed RadImageGAN model showed better scores, demonstrating the effectiveness of our RadImageGAN generator. Examples from RadImageGAN and DiT are shown in Fig. 3. Representative images and masks generated by RadImageGAN-Labeler and DiT-Labeler are presented in Fig. 4.

Table 1. Synthetic image quality between diffusion model and RadImageGAN.

Models		FID ↓	sFID ↓	IS ↑	SSIM ↑	PSNR ↑
CT/MR	RadImageGAN	**2.60**	9.14	5.00	**0.23**	**11.03**
	DiT	2.95	**5.33**	**5.28**	0.23	10.84
Endoscopy	RadImageGAN	**27.04**	**118.85**	3.51	**0.47**	**11.47**
	DiT	37.08	128.35	**3.95**	0.04	8.00

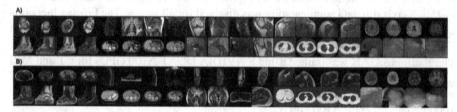

Fig. 3. Representative images produced by the **A)** RadImageGAN and **B)** DiT generators across different sequences, views and contrast.

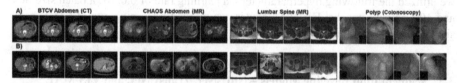

Fig. 4. A) RadImageGAN-Labeler and **B)** DiT-Labeler provide paired synthetic images and masks.

Ablation Studies. To assess RadImageGAN's utility across diverse medical applications, four segmentation tasks and datasets—BTCV, CHAOS, Labeled Lumbar Spine MRI, and CVC-ClinicDB—were selected for their anatomical, modal, and pathological diversity. RadImageGAN and DiT generated synthetic images for specific medical classes, which were then used with RadImageGAN-Labeler and DiT-Labeler to create automatic segmentation masks. The influence of these synthetic images on model training was evaluated through data augmentation strategies using three neural network architectures: nnU-Net, TransUNet, and VIS-MAE. These strategies were implemented across 10 data conditions (DC1 through DC10, as defined in Table 2) to assess effectiveness. The average Dice score and standard deviation, calculated across 5-fold cross validation, were reported. Detailed results of the performances for each data condition and model are summarized in Tables 3 through 6 (R indicates the performance of RadImageGAN-generated synthetic data, while D indicates DiT-generated data).

Table 2. Data conditions for each scenario to evaluate the performance of synthetic data.

Data conditions	Scenarios
DC1	1% real training data
DC2 R/D	1% real training data combined with 99% synthetic data from RadImageGAN or DiT
DC3	10% real training data
DC4 R/D	10% real training data plus 90% synthetic data
DC5	50% real training data
DC6 R/D	50% real training data paired with 50% synthetic data
DC7	100% real training data
DC8 R/D	100% real training data enhanced with 10% synthetic data
DC9 R/D	100% real training data supplemented with 50% synthetic data
DC10 R/D	100% real training data complemented with an equal amount of synthetic data

Table 3. Dice score of models in liver and kidney segmentations on BTCV.

	TransUNet		nnU-Net		VIS-MAE	
	Liver	Kidney	Liver	Kidney	Liver	Kidney
DC1	0.716 ± 0.055	0.516 ± 0.192	0.648 ± 0.067	0.482 ± 0.053	0.632 ± 0.053	0.548 ± 0.058
DC2R	0.678 ± 0.031	0.441 ± 0.080	0.713 ± 0.042	0.645 ± 0.066	0.742 ± 0.039	0.716 ± 0.071
DC2D	0.663 ± 0.032	0.606 ± 0.132	0.574 ± 0.054	0.219 ± 0.070	0.591 ± 0.027	0.341 ± 0.103
DC3	0.774 ± 0.071	0.525 ± 0.129	0.582 ± 0.106	0.582 ± 0.053	0.596 ± 0.180	0.515 ± 0.267
DC4R	0.699 ± 0.070	0.435 ± 0.059	0.678 ± 0.053	0.675 ± 0.063	0.776 ± 0.029	0.768 ± 0.059
DC4D	0.686 ± 0.030	0.628 ± 0.129	0.605 ± 0.057	0.251 ± 0.091	0.622 ± 0.052	0.416 ± 0.115
DC5	0.818 ± 0.059	0.549 ± 0.065	0.823 ± 0.080	0.813 ± 0.100	0.818 ± 0.006	0.868 ± 0.068
DC6R	0.798 ± 0.068	0.530 ± 0.055	0.829 ± 0.057	0.825 ± 0.067	0.835 ± 0.051	0.853 ± 0.046
DC6D	0.858 ± 0.058	0.564 ± 0.063	0.776 ± 0.046	0.675 ± 0.089	0.794 ± 0.084	0.757 ± 0.112

(continued)

Table 3. (*continued*)

	TransUNet		nnU-Net		VIS-MAE	
	Liver	Kidney	Liver	Kidney	Liver	Kidney
DC7	0.801 ± 0.055	0.524 ± 0.028	0.833 ± 0.069	0.832 ± 0.099	0.866 ± 0.040	0.879 ± 0.057
DC8R	0.808 ± 0.060	0.537 ± 0.036	0.834 ± 0.072	0.856 ± 0.071	0.841 ± 0.053	0.871 ± 0.051
DC8D	0.916 ± 0.081	0.588 ± 0.056	0.802 ± 0.057	0.804 ± 0.070	0.834 ± 0.057	0.836 ± 0.069
DC9R	0.810 ± 0.061	0.531 ± 0.051	0.845 ± 0.061	0.854 ± 0.080	0.866 ± 0.045	0.841 ± 0.054
DC9D	0.889 ± 0.089	0.588 ± 0.071	0.813 ± 0.047	0.783 ± 0.061	0.818 ± 0.059	0.805 ± 0.066
DC10R	0.832 ± 0.053	0.527 ± 0.063	0.841 ± 0.051	0.849 ± 0.083	0.845 ± 0.036	0.863 ± 0.054
DC10D	0.904 ± 0.081	0.608 ± 0.106	0.796 ± 0.043	0.738 ± 0.079	0.801 ± 0.075	0.789 ± 0.101

Table 4. Dice score of models in liver and kidney segmentations on CHAOS.

	TransUNet		nnU-Net		VIS-MAE	
	Liver	Kidney	Liver	Kidney	Liver	Kidney
DC1	0.641 ± 0.071	0.504 ± 0.121	0.578 ± 0.089	0.579 ± 0.105	0.593 ± 0.055	0.692 ± 0.037
DC2R	0.626 ± 0.044	0.532 ± 0.072	0.611 ± 0.054	0.676 ± 0.031	0.623 ± 0.03	0.710 ± 0.049
DC2D	0.565 ± 0.068	0.628 ± 0.076	0.471 ± 0.064	0.292 ± 0.075	0.479 ± 0.053	0.507 ± 0.039
DC3	0.655 ± 0.088	0.547 ± 0.069	0.446 ± 0.087	0.394 ± 0.065	0.628 ± 0.059	0.740 ± 0.015
DC4R	0.631 ± 0.071	0.539 ± 0.079	0.548 ± 0.048	0.563 ± 0.042	0.682 ± 0.050	0.779 ± 0.057
DC4D	0.616 ± 0.060	0.576 ± 0.072	0.521 ± 0.074	0.386 ± 0.028	0.545 ± 0.044	0.626 ± 0.044
DC5	0.707 ± 0.083	0.515 ± 0.038	0.692 ± 0.084	0.818 ± 0.062	0.771 ± 0.063	0.875 ± 0.019
DC6R	0.700 ± 0.083	0.527 ± 0.043	0.702 ± 0.076	0.792 ± 0.041	0.735 ± 0.067	0.848 ± 0.048
DC6D	0.711 ± 0.067	0.532 ± 0.050	0.700 ± 0.065	0.742 ± 0.080	0.709 ± 0.044	0.813 ± 0.044
DC7	0.729 ± 0.073	0.532 ± 0.021	0.750 ± 0.067	0.845 ± 0.0423	0.837 ± 0.062	0.918 ± 0.026
DC8R	0.716 ± 0.085	0.535 ± 0.041	0.766 ± 0.070	0.849 ± 0.058	0.773 ± 0.079	0.860 ± 0.027
DC8D	0.748 ± 0.050	0.533 ± 0.026	0.747 ± 0.056	0.836 ± 0.047	0.761 ± 0.100	0.870 ± 0.021
DC9R	0.717 ± 0.087	0.527 ± 0.055	0.763 ± 0.064	0.862 ± 0.017	0.770 ± 0.069	0.855 ± 0.034
DC9D	0.737 ± 0.050	0.523 ± 0.036	0.743 ± 0.053	0.810 ± 0.063	0.761 ± 0.074	0.871 ± 0.033
DC10R	0.723 ± 0.073	0.538 ± 0.051	0.757 ± 0.056	0.857 ± 0.037	0.765 ± 0.077	0.858 ± 0.035
DC10D	0.719 ± 0.053	0.536 ± 0.037	0.760 ± 0.080	0.815 ± 0.022	0.753 ± 0.063	0.872 ± 0.033

4   Discussion and Conclusions

RadImageGAN framework generates synthetic images across multiple imaging modalities and pathologies, demonstrating superior quality over DiT as evidenced by lower FID and higher SSIM and PSNR scores, demonstrating better similarity, contrast and structure, and less noise. This framework achieves optimal performance with a 10% to 50% synthetic-to-real data ratio.

Table 5. Dice score of models in polyp segmentation on CVC-ClinicDB.

	TransUNet	nnU-Net	VIS-MAE
DC1	0.208 ± 0.195	0.377 ± 0.071	0.311 ± 0.087
DC2R	0.708 ± 0.032	0.685 ± 0.089	0.616 ± 0.018
DC2D	0.203 ± 0.053	0.213 ± 0.042	0.285 ± 0.142
DC3	0.808 ± 0.032	0.656 ± 0.076	0.676 ± 0.026
DC4R	0.794 ± 0.037	0.755 ± 0.062	0.707 ± 0.014
DC4D	0.660 ± 0.046	0.503 ± 0.035	0.392 ± 0.757
DC5	0.893 ± 0.037	0.788 ± 0.053	0.879 ± 0.034
DC6R	0.901 ± 0.018	0.830 ± 0.044	0.860 ± 0.018
DC6D	0.889 ± 0.017	0.788 ± 0.015	0.798 ± 0.009
DC7	0.926 ± 0.008	0.798 ± 0.058	0.894 ± 0.012
DC8R	0.928 ± 0.013	0.819 ± 0.044	0.899 ± 0.010
DC8D	0.927 ± 0.010	0.903 ± 0.013	0.878 ± 0.012
DC9R	0.921 ± 0.015	0.832 ± 0.037	0.888 ± 0.011
DC9D	0.915 ± 0.010	0.872 ± 0.018	0.865 ± 0.007
DC10R	0.924 ± 0.011	0.830 ± 0.048	0.894 ± 0.012
DC10D	0.913 ± 0.012	0.832 ± 0.015	0.868 ± 0.016

RadImageGAN-Labeler generates paired pixel-wise segmentation masks from a few manually annotated images and outperforms DiT-Labeler, which struggles with smaller labels like kidneys and polyps when trained with the same data volume. RadImageGAN-Labeler employs a sequential pixel interpreter and captures features during image generation, whereas DiT-Labeler uses a UNet-based decoder and relies on the final image, likely requiring more data for peak performance due to its complex architecture.

Prospect of Application: RadImageGAN can generate high-resolution medical images with corresponding segmentation masks across 130 classes, addressing data scarcity and enhancing patient privacy, with potential applications to improve model performance in medical imaging.

Table 6. Dice score of models in IVD, PE, and TS segmentations on Lumbar Spine MRI.

	TransUNet		
	IVD	PE	TS
DC1	0.931 ± 0.008	0.000 ± 0.000	0.285 ± 0.390
DC2R	0.923 ± 0.001	0.688 ± 0.023	0.779 ± 0.011
DC2D	0.815 ± 0.047	0.655 ± 0.049	0.735 ± 0.040
DC3	0.961 ± 0.002	0.804 ± 0.010	0.879 ± 0.008
DC4R	0.938 ± 0.004	0.729 ± 0.018	0.826 ± 0.009
DC4D	0.959 ± 0.002	0.825 ± 0.009	0.891 ± 0.007
DC5	0.972 ± 0.002	0.871 ± 0.007	0.914 ± 0.005
DC6R	0.969 ± 0.002	0.861 ± 0.008	0.904 ± 0.007
DC6D	0.970 ± 0.002	0.878 ± 0.006	0.918 ± 0.004
DC7	0.974 ± 0.002	0.896 ± 0.007	0.922 ± 0.006
DC8R	0.974 ± 0.002	0.892 ± 0.007	0.921 ± 0.005
DC8D	0.974 ± 0.001	0.896 ± 0.008	0.923 ± 0.004
DC9R	0.973 ± 0.002	0.890 ± 0.008	0.919 ± 0.006
DC9D	0.973 ± 0.002	0.888 ± 0.007	0.921 ± 0.005
DC10R	0.973 ± 0.002	0.888 ± 0.007	0.918 ± 0.006
DC10D	0.972 ± 0.001	0.886 ± 0.007	0.922 ± 0.005
	nnU-Net		
DC1	0.924 ± 0.022	0.852 ± 0.017	0.772 ± 0.036
DC2R	0.919 ± 0.004	0.779 ± 0.008	0.700 ± 0.012
DC2D	0.839 ± 0.054	0.664 ± 0.070	0.738 ± 0.022
DC3	0.967 ± 0.003	0.907 ± 0.010	0.857 ± 0.016
DC4R	0.941 ± 0.002	0.835 ± 0.013	0.776 ± 0.011
DC4D	0.940 ± 0.008	0.826 ± 0.015	0.876 ± 0.009
DC5	0.974 ± 0.001	0.927 ± 0.005	0.899 ± 0.007
DC6R	0.973 ± 0.002	0.924 ± 0.005	0.893 ± 0.007
DC6D	0.972 ± 0.001	0.878 ± 0.009	0.922 ± 0.004
DC7	0.975 ± 0.001	0.929 ± 0.005	0.906 ± 0.007
DC8R	0.975 ± 0.001	0.928 ± 0.005	0.905 ± 0.006
DC8D	0.975 ± 0.001	0.902 ± 0.008	0.929 ± 0.004
DC9R	0.975 ± 0.002	0.927 ± 0.005	0.902 ± 0.008
DC9D	0.974 ± 0.001	0.893 ± 0.008	0.927 ± 0.005

(*continued*)

Table 6. (*continued*)

	TransUNet		
	IVD	PE	TS
DC10R	0.974 ± 0.002	0.926 ± 0.005	0.900 ± 0.008
DC10D	0.971 ± 0.002	0.877 ± 0.011	0.920 ± 0.004
	VIS-MAE		
DC1	0.935 ± 0.002	0.728 ± 0.024	0.829 ± 0.006
DC2R	0.941 ± 0.002	0.755 ± 0.024	0.832 ± 0.011
DC2D	0.903 ± 0.013	0.718 ± 0.027	0.762 ± 0.029
DC3	0.972 ± 0.002	0.887 ± 0.005	0.920 ± 0.006
DC4R	0.968 ± 0.002	0.867 ± 0.010	0.910 ± 0.006
DC4D	0.963 ± 0.002	0.858 ± 0.013	0.904 ± 0.005
DC5	0.976 ± 0.001	0.914 ± 0.006	0.933 ± 0.002
DC6R	0.975 ± 0.001	0.896 ± 0.007	0.925 ± 0.004
DC6D	0.973 ± 0.001	0.894 ± 0.009	0.925 ± 0.005
DC7	0.976 ± 0.001	0.907 ± 0.007	0.930 ± 0.005
DC8R	0.975 ± 0.001	0.906 ± 0.006	0.929 ± 0.004
DC8D	0.975 ± 0.001	0.906 ± 0.006	0.929 ± 0.004
DC9R	0.975 ± 0.001	0.905 ± 0.007	0.928 ± 0.004
DC9D	0.974 ± 0.001	0.903 ± 0.006	0.928 ± 0.004
DC10R	0.975 ± 0.001	0.905 ± 0.006	0.928 ± 0.005
DC10D	0.974 ± 0.001	0.901 ± 0.007	0.927 ± 0.004

Acknowledgement. X.M. is supported by the Eric and Wendy Schmidt AI in the Human Health Program.

Disclosure of Interests. T.D. is the managing partner of RadImageNet LLC. X.M. has been a paid consultant to RadImageNet LLC.

References

1. Esteva, A., et al.: A guide to deep learning in healthcare. Nat. Med. **25**, 24–29 (2019)
2. Sahni, N.R., Stein, G., Zemmel, R., Cutler, D.M.: The potential impact of artificial intelligence on healthcare spending. In: The Economics of Artificial Intelligence: Health Care Challenges. University of Chicago Press (2023)
3. LeCun, Y., Bengio, Y., Hinton, G.: Deep learning. Nature **521**, 436–444 (2015)
4. Greenspan, H., van Ginneken, B., Summers, R.M.: Guest editorial deep learning in medical imaging: overview and future promise of an exciting new technique. IEEE Trans. Med. Imaging **35**, 1153–1159 (2016)

5. Mei, X., et al.: RadImageNet: an open radiologic deep learning research dataset for effective transfer learning. Radiology: Artif. Intell. **4**, e210315 (2022)
6. Goodfellow, I.J., et al.: Generative Adversarial Networks (2014). http://arxiv.org/abs/1406.2661
7. DuMont Schütte, A., Hetzel, J., Gatidis, S., Hepp, T., Dietz, B., Bauer, S., Schwab, P.: Overcoming barriers to data sharing with medical image generation: a comprehensive evaluation. npj Digit. Med. **4**, 1–14 (2021)
8. Shin, H.-C., et al.: Medical Image Synthesis for Data Augmentation and Anonymization using Generative Adversarial Networks (2018). http://arxiv.org/abs/1807.10225
9. Gonzales, A., Guruswamy, G., Smith, S.R.: Synthetic data in health care: a narrative review. PLOS Digit Health **2**, e0000082 (2023)
10. Frid-Adar, M., Klang, E., Amitai, M., Goldberger, J., Greenspan, H.: Synthetic data augmentation using GAN for improved liver lesion classification. In: 2018 IEEE 15th International Symposium on Biomedical Imaging (ISBI 2018), pp. 289–293 (2018)
11. Jang, M., et al.: Image Turing test and its applications on synthetic chest radiographs by using the progressive growing generative adversarial network. Sci. Rep. **13**, 2356 (2023)
12. Mukherkjee, D., Saha, P., Kaplun, D., Sinitca, A., Sarkar, R.: Brain tumor image generation using an aggregation of GAN models with style transfer. Sci. Rep. **12**, 9141 (2022)
13. Baid, U., et al.: The RSNA-ASNR-MICCAI BraTS 2021 Benchmark on Brain Tumor Segmentation and Radiogenomic Classification (2021). http://arxiv.org/abs/2107.02314
14. Usman Akbar, M., Larsson, M., Blystad, I., Eklund, A.: Brain tumor segmentation using synthetic MR images - a comparison of GANs and diffusion models. Sci. Data **11**, 259 (2024)
15. Karras, T., Laine, S., Aila, T.: A Style-Based Generator Architecture for Generative Adversarial Networks (2019). http://arxiv.org/abs/1812.04948
16. Sauer, A., Schwarz, K., Geiger, A.: StyleGAN-XL: Scaling StyleGAN to Large Diverse Datasets (2022). http://arxiv.org/abs/2202.00273
17. Borgli, H., et al.: HyperKvasir, a comprehensive multi-class image and video dataset for gastrointestinal endoscopy. Sci. Data **7**, 283 (2020). https://doi.org/10.1038/s41597-020-00622-y
18. Saragih, D.G., Hibi, A., Tyrrell, P.N.: Using diffusion models to generate synthetic labeled data for medical image segmentation. Int. J. CARS (2024). https://doi.org/10.1007/s11548-024-03213-z
19. Stojanovski, D., Hermida, U., Lamata, P., Beqiri, A., Gomez, A.: Echo from noise: synthetic ultrasound image generation using diffusion models for real image segmentation. In: Kainz, B., Noble, A., Schnabel, J., Khanal, B., Müller, J.P., and Day, T. (eds.) Simplifying Medical Ultrasound, pp. 34–43. Springer, Cham (2023). https://doi.org/10.1007/978-3-031-44521-7_4
20. Peebles, W., Xie, S.: Scalable Diffusion Models with Transformers (2022). https://arxiv.org/abs/2212.09748
21. Karras, T., Aittala, M., Laine, S., Härkönen, E., Hellsten, J., Lehtinen, J., Aila, T.: Alias-Free Generative Adversarial Networks (2021). http://arxiv.org/abs/2106.12423. https://doi.org/10.48550/arXiv.2106.12423
22. Sauer, A., Chitta, K., Müller, J., Geiger, A.: Projected GANs Converge Faster (2021). http://arxiv.org/abs/2111.01007
23. Li, D., et al.: BigDatasetGAN: synthesizing ImageNet with pixel-wise annotations (2022). http://arxiv.org/abs/2201.04684
24. Rombach, R., Blattmann, A., Lorenz, D., Esser, P., Ommer, B.: High-Resolution Image Synthesis with Latent Diffusion Models (2022). http://arxiv.org/abs/2112.10752
25. Kingma, D.P., Welling, M.: Auto-Encoding Variational Bayes (2022). http://arxiv.org/abs/1312.6114
26. Ho, J., Salimans, T.: Classifier-Free Diffusion Guidance (2022). http://arxiv.org/abs/2207.12598

27. Consortium, T.M.: Project MONAI (2020). https://zenodo.org/record/4323059
28. Segmentation Outside the Cranial Vault Challenge (2015)
29. Kavur, A.E., et al.: CHAOS Challenge - combined (CT-MR) healthy abdominal organ segmentation. Med. Image Anal. **69**, 101950 (2021)
30. Sudirman, S.: Label Image Ground Truth Data for Lumbar Spine MRI Dataset (2019). https://data.mendeley.com/datasets/zbf6b4pttk/2
31. Bernal, J., Sánchez, F.J., Fernández-Esparrach, G., Gil, D., Rodríguez, C., Vilariño, F.: WM-DOVA maps for accurate polyp highlighting in endoscopy: validation vs. saliency maps from physicians. Comput. Med. Imaging Graph. **43**, 99–111 (2015)
32. Isensee, F., Jaeger, P.F., Kohl, S.A.A., Petersen, J., Maier-Hein, K.H.: NnU-Net: a self-configuring method for deep learning-based biomedical image segmentation. Nat. Methods **18**, 203–211 (2021)
33. Chen, J., et al.: TransUNet: Transformers Make Strong Encoders for Medical Image Segmentation (2021). http://arxiv.org/abs/2102.04306
34. Liu, Z., et al.: VISION-MAE: a foundation model for medical image segmentation and classification

Ensemble-KAN: Leveraging Kolmogorov Arnold Networks to Discriminate Individuals with Psychiatric Disorders from Controls

Gianluca De Franceschi[1], Inês W. Sampaio[2], Stefan Borgwardt[3,4],
Joseph Kambeitz[5], Lana Kambeitz-Ilankovic[5,6], Eva Meisenzahl[7],
Raimo K. R. Salokangas[8], Rachel Upthegrove[9,10],
Stephen J. Wood[10,11,12], Nikolaos Koutsouleris[13,14,15],
Paolo Brambilla[1,16(✉)], and Eleonora Maggioni[2]

[1] Department of Neurosciences and Mental Health, Fondazione IRCCS Ca' Granda
Ospedale Maggiore Policlinico, Milan, Italy
paolo.brambilla1@unimi.it
[2] Department of Electronics, Information and Bioengineering, Politecnico di Milano,
Milan, Italy
[3] Department of Psychiatry and Psychotherapy and Center for Brain, Behaviour and
Metabolism, University of Luebeck, Luebeck, Germany
[4] Department of Psychiatry, Psychiatric University Hospital, University of Basel,
Basel, Switzerland
[5] Department of Psychiatry and Psychotherapy, Faculty of Medicine and University
Hospital of Cologne, Cologne, Germany
[6] Faculty of Psychology and Educational Sciences, Department of Psychology,
Ludwig-Maximilian University, Munich, Germany
[7] Department of Psychiatry and Psychotherapy, Medical Faculty, Heinrich-Heine
University, Duesseldorf, Germany
[8] Department of Psychiatry, University of Turku, Turku, Finland
[9] Institute of Mental Health and Centre for Human Brain Health, University of
Birmingham, Birmingham, UK
[10] School of Psychology, University of Birmingham, Birmingham, UK
[11] Orygen, Melbourne, Australia
[12] Centre for Youth Mental Health, University of Melbourne, Melbourne, Australia

[13] Department of Psychiatry and Psychotherapy, Ludwig-Maximilian University
Munich, Munich, Germany
[14] Max Planck Institute of Psychiatry, Munich, Germany
[15] Institute of Psychiatry, Psychology and Neuroscience, King's College London,
London, UK
[16] Department of Pathophysiology and Transplantation, University of Milan, Milan,
Italy

Abstract. Machine learning (ML) techniques are crucial for improving
diagnostic accuracy in psychiatry using neuroimaging-based biomarkers.

N. Koutsouleris, P. Brambilla and E. Maggioni—These authors contributed equally to
this work.

Deep learning models like Kolmogorov Arnold Networks (KANs) are particularly promising in this context but struggle with high-dimensional datasets. We propose the Ensemble-KAN (E-KAN) method to overcome these limitations, integrating multiple base learners. Our novel approach aims to advance classification especially when multiple sources of data are available. The E-KAN was tested against traditional ML models in discriminating recent-onset psychosis (ROP) or depression (ROD) from healthy controls using multimodal environmental and neuroimaging data and it underwent a rigorous ablation study to test its effectiveness. Results demonstrate enhanced performance over traditional ML models, highlighting the efficacy of E-KAN models in psychiatric diagnostics. Specifically, our E-KAN achieved an accuracy of 72.5%, outperforming single-KAN models and traditional ML algorithms. This study underscores the potential of E-KAN models in advancing psychiatric research and personalized medicine through improved diagnostic capabilities. The code is available at https://github.com/brainpolislab/E-KAN.

Keywords: E-KAN · Multimodal · Psychiatry · Ensemble machine learning

1 Introduction

Machine learning (ML) and deep learning (DL) techniques are extensively studied to enhance diagnostic accuracy in psychiatry, focusing on neuroimaging-based biomarkers [9,21,27]. Common ML models used in the field are SVM, random forests (RF), and DL models like CNNs [6]. DL models excel in capturing complex features but require large annotated datasets, which are scarce in psychiatry [26]. In addition, most studies to date have used single-modality magnetic resonance imaging, either functional (fMRI) or structural (sMRI), missing the benefits of multimodal approaches that integrate different data types; despite its potential, multimodal integration poses a challenge due to high dimensionality and low sample sizes (HDLSS) [3]. Therefore, even though extensive ML research has been conducted, reliable neuromarkers for psychiatric disorders are still elusive due to the complexity and non-linearity of patterns within this kind of data [9]. Recently, Kolmogorov Arnold Networks (KAN) have shown promising results in non-linear pattern discovery, achieving comparable or better results than multi-layer perceptrons (MLPs) with shallower architectures [17], that are a deep learning gold standard. KANs offer greater interpretability and can train non-linear activation functions, providing also many model inspection tools. However, KANs struggle with large datasets due to the generation of redundant activation functions. To address this issue, we propose a new ensemble method that leverages KANs' strengths and mitigates their limitations in handling high-dimensional data. Ensemble methods can enhance weak learners or efficiently manage large datasets by combining suboptimal model outputs to improve overall performance [7,25]. Our E-KAN approach integrates multiple base learners' predictions and incorporates feature selection to boost performance. Our objectives are: i) Develop an ensemble model to overcome KAN's limitations with HDLSS datasets, and ii) Test its capability to identify patterns differentiating diagnostic classes. In this study, E-KAN was tested using the multi-site PRONIA dataset to classify individuals with recent onset psychosis (ROP) or depression (ROD) from healthy controls (HC) based on environmental and multimodal neuroimaging features.

2   Methods

2.1   Dataset Processing and Harmonization

This study utilized data from the PRONIA European project [22], which aimed to develop prognostic tools for the early diagnosis of psychosis and depression. The sample included 506 individuals from seven research centres, divided into three groups: ROP, ROD and HC. For our classification task, we merged ROP and ROD in a unique patient group (P) to be distinguished from HC by our model. Our subjects are 25 years old on average for each group (HC, P). The male and female subjects (nM, nF) are for HC (nM = 153, nF = 100) and for P (nM = 125, nF = 128). The PRONIA group longitudinally collected clinical and neuroimaging data following standardized protocols described in other works [5]. In our study, only non-augmented data collected at baseline was used; sMRI and fMRI data were processed using the SPM12 [20] software and its CAT12 [10] toolbox to extract brain morphological and functional connectivity features for group classification; more details can be found in [5]. Specifically, the dataset comprised: i) 68 volumetric measures of grey matter in brain regions-of-interest (ROIs) defined by the Hammers atlas [11], ii) 320 nodal strength in absolute value of functional connectivity for each ROI defined by the Dosen-bach atlas [8], iii) 2 demographic variables (age, sex), and iv) 7 environmental variables, such as years of education and information on substance use (nicotine and alcohol consumption). Environmental features were standard scaled, while only neuroimaging features were processed through the following correction pipeline: i) multi-site ComBat Harmonization; ii) biological confounder (age and sex) removal via linear regression; and iii) data standardization as presented in Fig. 1. This pipeline removed site-specific MRI scanner effects and the influence of age and sex confounders based on [23]. The harmonization functions used were implemented using the neurocombat function, available on GitHub [1] and presented in [23]. This pipeline was applied within a 2 times repeated 5-fold cross-validation (CV) framework, estimating all model parameters exclusively in the training set [23]. The diagnostic groups (ROP and ROD) were included in the linear regression model to account for their variance, the corrections were applied to the training and validation set considering only the coefficients of confounders.

2.2   KAN

KANs are based on the Kolmogorov representation theorem [13], which states that every multivariate function, $f(\mathbf{x})$, can be decomposed exactly according to the following equation:

$$f(\mathbf{x}) = f(x_1, \ldots, x_n) = \sum_{q=0}^{2n} \varPhi_q \left(\sum_{p=1}^{n} \phi_{q,p}(x_p) \right) \tag{1}$$

where $\phi_{q,p}$ is an inner univariate function, $\phi_{q,p} : [0,1] \rightarrow \mathbb{R}$, and $\varPhi_q : \mathbb{R} \rightarrow \mathbb{R}$ is another outer function applied to the sum of all inner univariate functions to combine them. This concept has been implemented as a non-linear multivariate function approximator in the form of a multilayer perceptron with arbitrary width and depth, that adjusts learnable B-splines instead of connection weights. According to [17], KANs overcome the depth requirements of neural networks, achieving an optimal function approximation with fewer layers. Moreover, just like artificial neural networks (ANN), KANs can be tuned at the level of the loss function and the number of epochs, called steps, and can be regularized by pruning unnecessary links. It is also possible to tune other parameters, such as the resolution of the spline approximation with a parameter called grid (G) and the order of each polynomial used to model the spline (K). According to [17] this method struggles with the course of dimensionality (COD), also there are still not many publications where this technique has been applied to a high-dimensional dataset. Plus, the analytic equation that can be computed at the end may be hard to interpret, especially if there are many variables to consider. Recently, many studies have proposed improvements upon the original KAN algorithm, by modifying activation functions or even including the KAN within DL networks [4,14]. Compared to state-of-the-art models for tabular data like TabNet [2], which uses an attention mechanism, or Random Forest, based on decision trees, KAN lacks a robust internal feature selection mechanism. However, its decision function approximation, grounded in an exact mathematical approximation theorem, makes it more efficient for input-output relationship modeling given reasonable dimensionality.

2.3   Ensemble-KAN

In this work, we leveraged the non-linear modelling capability of KANs while mitigating the COD by designing a model architecture, a KAN ensemble model. The ensembling technique is often used to improve the accuracy of base learners by combining their prediction capabilities. Inspired by stacking and voting ensemble techniques [7], we propose a KAN ensemble where each KAN is fed with fewer predictors. The proposed model, as described in Fig. 1, consists of a first layer where N single KANs are packed in an ensemble architecture and a final decision layer with a KAN meta-learner. First, data is split into uniform feature subsets to be fed to the N single KAN models. Each subset undergoes a feature selection (FS) stage, which was added to further improve the performance of each single KAN, where k_1 is the hyperparameter that defines the number of selected features from the initial subgroups. Then, before the KAN meta-learner step, a model prediction selection filters the N outputs from the previous layer, with k_2 defining the number of outputs to consider for the final decision. By making $k_2 < N$, the meta-learner prioritizes the selection of the best single-KAN models.

First Feature Selection Step. In the presence of multimodal features, such as sMRI and fMRI ones, mixed feature subsets are fed into the single-KAN models. To create uniform feature subgroups, based on the number of models N, the dataset is first subdivided using the round-robin algorithm, $subgroup\_i \equiv i$ mod N, where each index i, is divided by N giving a quotient and a remainder that is at maximum equal to $N - 1$. Each feature subset is then fed into the first FS step. Embedded FS steps are common in ML algorithms. For example, decision trees use Gini or entropy indexes to choose the best predictors, enhancing predictive performance. Similarly, our model selects predictors for each KAN using a statistical test, following a filter method approach widely used in models dealing with biomarkers [12]. The selection process involves the identification of the k_1 features whose distributions between groups differ the most, using an F-statistic similarity test. Both the k_1 and the kind of statistic test are tunable hyperparameters. To implement this selection, the `SelectKBest()` method from `sklearn` is used.

KAN Base Learners. In this step, each feature subset is fed into one KAN model, which is trained to predict class labels. The hyperparameter N can vary from 2 to a maximum of n_features, where each KAN model would be fed with one feature, in this case $N=n\_features$. Each base learner has as many nodes in the input layer as the number of predictors fed to it, 1 node in the second layer and 2 nodes in the output layer. The single KAN models can be tuned, but in the current application a fixed architecture has been used for all models. The `torch.argmax()` function sets the output to 0 or 1 based on the highest probability. We set the KANs hyperparameters to G = 6, K = 3, and steps = 20. Each KAN base-learner produces a binary prediction for the class labels. This vector is then fed to the next step.

Model Prediction Ranking. At this point, to ease the prediction of the KAN meta-learner, another FS step is added to force the final decision model to select the k_2 most relevant predictions from the ensemble layer. The k_2 hyperparameter allows for the removal of the most inaccurate predictors according to the `SelectKBest()` method. The χ^2 test is used within the filter method for this process.

KAN Meta-learner. The last step of the stacking ensemble is often called meta-learner, and it models the outputs from all the base learners [24]. We have chosen a KAN model to integrate the outputs from the previous N single KANs because of its non-linear modelling framework. It can combine model predictions via linear combinations, ending up in a weighted average that is a common technique, but also highly complex non-linear combinations that are unusual for conventional meta-learners [15,19,24]. The hyperparameters' values of this KAN meta-learner are similar to the base learners (G = 6, K = 3), except for the input size that is set to be as wide as the number of prediction vectors selected, which are at maximum k_2. It also has a regularization parameter $\lambda = 0.0009$ and a learning rate $lr = 0.1$ with steps = 100.

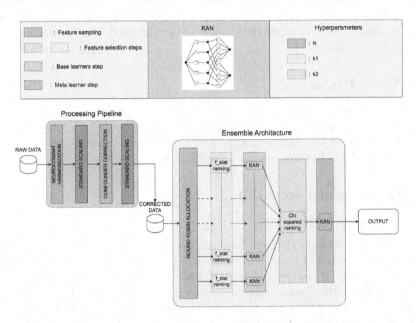

Fig. 1. E-KAN architecture and pipeline. The data first goes through a pre-processing pipeline to mitigate confounding effects and then the proposed E-KAN is applied.

3 Experiments

All the experiments conducted to test the algorithm were run on an i7-14700KF processor with the same dataset for all the comparisons and validation tests. To compile the Python script, VS code with Jupyter Notebook was used.

3.1 Validation Procedures and Comparisons

We performed a comprehensive ablation study on the E-KAN architecture to understand the impact of k_1, k_2, and N on the ensemble structure and identify the best combination for our application. Three separate experiments were conducted, using the F1 score as metrics for comparison: i) we varied k_1 and k_2, keeping $N = 20$; ii) we varied k_1 and N by keeping $k_2 = 4$; iii) we studied how the number of models affected the performance by varying k_2 and N while keeping $k_1 = 4$. Then, we compared the best E-KAN with default SVM, XGB, Adaboost, a fine-tuned TabNet [2], XGB and Random forest with 20 base learners (to see how they perform with fewer base learners), the single-KAN base learner and a deeper KAN having 2 hidden layers with respectively 8 and 4 nodes have been compared, both with $G = 6$, $K = 3$, and steps = 20. For all the tests, repeated stratified cross-validation, consisting of 5 folds repeated 2 times, was performed over the whole dataset. The F1 score, AUC and accuracy metrics average and standard deviation were selected to compare the different models. The hyperparameters configurations of all the models are explicitly defined in the script of our GitHub repository.

3.2   Model Explanation

To explain model prediction, we used two techniques. Since the meta-learner is a KAN, a visual inspection was performed using the `pykan` library [16] to inspect it to see whether it can fuse all the models' predictions. To inspect and compare the whole model behaviour, we used the tools of SHAP [18].

4   Results and Discussion

4.1   Ablation Study

In Fig. 2 it can be seen that the hyperparameter variation affects the model's performance. We found that: i) increasing N improves performance for high k_1 but not for low k_1, therefore the number of base learners is relevant; ii) the single models improve with fewer features as shown by k_1 and k_2 variation effect, so the feature selection step also improves the performance. A t-test of extreme F1 score pairs shows significant differences (p-value < 0.05), highlighting each part's valuable contribution to the final algorithm (Table 1).

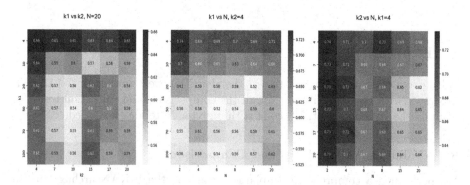

Fig. 2. Impact of hyperparameters variation on the model performances: for each matrix, a different combination of hyperparameters was studied to test the efficacy of the proposed method to improve KAN performances on the dataset, by gradually diminishing or increasing the effect of each step on the algorithm.

Table 1. Significance of performance improvements

Pair	p-value
$(k_1 = 4, k_2 = 4)$ vs $(k_1 = 100, k_2 = 20)$	1.9×10^{-3}
$(k_1 = 4, N = 2)$ vs $(k_1 = 100, N = 20)$	9.39×10^{-5}
$(k_2 = 4, N = 2)$ vs $(k_2 = 20, N = 20)$	1.09×10^{-5}

4.2 Benchmarking

By selecting $k_1 = 4$, $k_2 = 4$, and $N = 8$, our method significantly outperforms a single base learner (p-value $= 3.85 \times 10^{-9}$ for accuracy and p-value $= 1.23 \times 10^{-6}$ for F1 scores with t-test) and is comparable to common ensemble algorithms (RF, XGB), outperforming SVM, TabNet [2], and a deep KAN network. Default XGB with 100 base learners achieves the best performance, suggesting potential improvements for our method through more powerful ensembling techniques like boosting. Overall, our method demonstrates strong performance due to its architecture, designed to enhance the base learners' effectiveness in non-linear pattern discovery (Table 2).

Table 2. Comparison with other models

Classifier	Accuracy	AUC	F1
XGB	0.791($\pm$0.038)	0.790($\pm$0.039)	0.777($\pm$0.046)
XGB(n_estimators=20)	0.774($\pm$0.048)	0.774($\pm$0.048)	0.753($\pm$0.063)
RandomForest	0.742($\pm$0.040)	0.742($\pm$0.040)	0.737($\pm$0.048)
RandomForest(n_estimators=20)	0.699($\pm$0.059)	0.699($\pm$0.059)	0.685($\pm$0.071)
SVM	0.571($\pm$0.046)	0.571($\pm$0.046)	0.544($\pm$0.064)
Adaboost	0.733($\pm$0.035)	0.733($\pm$0.036)	0.721($\pm$0.039)
TabNet [2]	0.683($\pm$0.050)	0.683($\pm$0.050)	0.664($\pm$0.054)
KAN base learner	0.496($\pm$0.059)	0.496($\pm$0.059)	0.465($\pm$0.101)
Deep KAN	0.518($\pm$0.045)	0.516($\pm$0.046)	0.498($\pm$0.232)
E-KAN (our method)	**0.725($\pm$0.035)**	**0.725($\pm$0.035)**	**0.713($\pm$0.044)**

4.3 Model Inspection

By plotting the meta-learner architecture, we can see in Fig. 3 that the final output is given as a non-linear combination of the base-learners' outputs. Furthermore, we can see how each input is relevant for the final output, meaning a complete integration of the model predictions in the final step.

Feature ranking results are illustrated in Fig. 4. It can be seen how the proposed E-KAN method gives higher relevance to environmental features compared

Fig. 3. Meta-learner: Trained meta-learner plot showing four inputs fed to the network, summed and fed to the trained output activation functions.

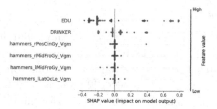

Fig. 4. Shap summary plot: The colormap denotes the magnitude of the feature value, the x-axis denotes the Shapley value, and the y-axis denotes the feature studied. (Color figure online)

to neuroimaging ones to decide the final output. Specifically, the greatest relevance was given to education years, followed by alcohol consumption and grey matter volume in posterior cingulate, midfrontal, and lateral occipital regions. Also, the importance of each feature is not equal for all the subjects, meaning that each prediction is dependent on the combination of subjects' feature values.

5   Conclusion

Our study shows that E-KAN models can significantly improve diagnostic accuracy over standard ML methods using our multimodal HDLSS datasets, though further validation with larger and more complex datasets is needed. The E-KAN model explainability allowed us to identify subject-specific patterns, showing its potential value for precision medicine applications.

Prospects of Application. After proper fine-tuning procedures, E-KAN models can be employed effectively to find complex non-linear relationships among many predictors in diverse precision medicine clinical settings.

Acknowledgments. This study was supported by EU-FP7 project PRONIA (Personalized Prognostic Tools for Early Psychosis Management) under the Grant Agreement n° 602152 (PI: NK). EM was supported by the European Union - NextGeneration EU (PRIN 2022 PNRR, grant n. P20229MFRC); GDF was supported by the Italian Ministry of Health (grant n° GR-2018-12367290). IWS was supported by grants from EBRAINS-Italy, project funded under the National Recovery and Resilience Plan

(NRRP), Mission 4, "Education and Research" - Component 2, "From research to Business" Investment 3.1 - Call for tender n° 3264 of Dec 28, 2021 of Italian Ministry of University and Research (MUR) funded by the European Union - NextGenerationEU, with award number: Project code IR0000011, Concession Decree n° 117 of June 21, 2022 adopted by the Italian Ministry of University and Research, CUP B51E22000150006, Project title "EBRAINS-Italy (European Brain ReseArch INfrastruc-tureS-Italy). PB was partially supported by the Italian Ministry of University and Research (Dipartimenti di Eccellenza Program 2023-2027 - Dept of Pathophysiology and Transplantation, University of Milan), the Italian Ministry of Health (Hub Life Science- Diagnostica Avanzata, HLS-DA, PNC-E3-2022-23683266- CUP: C43C22001630001/MI-0117; Ricerca Corrente 2024) and by the Fondazione Cariplo (grant n° 2019-3416).

Disclosure of Interests. No competing interest to declare

References

1. Sampaio et al., I.W.: neurocombat_pyclasse (2024). https://github.com/inesws/neurocombat_pyClasse
2. Arik, S.Ö., Pfister, T.: Tabnet: attentive interpretable tabular learning. In: Proceedings of the AAAI Conference on Artificial Intelligence, vol. 35, pp. 6679–6687 (2021)
3. Berisha, V., Krantsevich, C., Hahn, P.R., Hahn, S., Dasarathy, G., Turaga, P., Liss, J.: Digital medicine and the curse of dimensionality. NPJ Digital Med. 4(1), 153 (2021)
4. Bozorgasl, Z., Chen, H.: Wav-kan: wavelet kolmogorov-arnold networks. arXiv preprint arXiv:2405.12832 (2024)
5. Buciuman, M.O., et al.: Structural and functional brain patterns predict formal thought disorder's severity and its persistence in recent-onset psychosis: Results from the pronia study. Biological Psychiatry: Cognitive Neurosci. Neuroimaging 8(12), 1207–1217 (2023). https://doi.org/10.1016/j.bpsc.2023.06.001. https://www.sciencedirect.com/science/article/pii/S2451902223001441
6. Colombo, F., Calesella, F., Mazza, M.G., Melloni, E.M.T., Morelli, M.J., Scotti, G.M., Benedetti, F., Bollettini, I., Vai, B.: Machine learning approaches for prediction of bipolar disorder based on biological, clinical and neuropsychological markers: A systematic review and meta-analysis. Neurosci. Biobehav. Rev. **135**, 104552 (2022)
7. Dietterich, T.G.: Ensemble methods in machine learning. In: International Workshop on Multiple Classifier Systems, pp. 1–15. Springer (2000)
8. Dosenbach, N.U., et al.: Prediction of individual brain maturity using FMRI. Science **329**(5997), 1358–1361 (2010)
9. ENIGMA-consortium: About enigma. https://enigma.ini.usc.edu/about-2/
10. Gaser, C., Dahnke, R., Thompson, P.M., Kurth, F., Luders, E., Initiative, A.D.N.: Cat–a computational anatomy toolbox for the analysis of structural mri data. biorxiv, pp. 2022–06 (2022)
11. Hammers, A., Allom, R., Koepp, M.J., Free, S.L., Myers, R., Lemieux, L., Mitchell, T.N., Brooks, D.J., Duncan, J.S.: Three-dimensional maximum probability atlas of the human brain, with particular reference to the temporal lobe. Hum. Brain Mapp. **19**(4), 224–247 (2003)

12. Jović, A., Brkić, K., Bogunović, N.: A review of feature selection methods with applications. In: 2015 38th International Convention on Information and Communication Technology, Electronics and Microelectronics (MIPRO), pp. 1200–1205. IEEE (2015)

13. Kolmogorov, A.N.: On the representation of continuous functions of many variables by superposition of continuous functions of one variable and addition. In: Doklady Akademii Nauk. vol. 114, pp. 953–956. Russian Academy of Sciences (1957)

14. Li, C., Liu, X., Li, W., Wang, C., Liu, H., Yuan, Y.: U-kan makes strong backbone for medical image segmentation and generation. arXiv e-prints pp. arXiv–2406 (2024)

15. Li, Y., Xu, Z., Wang, Y., Zhou, H., Zhang, Q.: Su-net and du-net fusion for tumour segmentation in histopathology images. In: 2020 IEEE 17th International Symposium on Biomedical Imaging (ISBI), pp. 461–465. IEEE (2020)

16. Liu, Z.: pykan repository on github (2024). https://github.com/KindXiaoming/pykan

17. Liu, Z., Wang, Y., Vaidya, S., Ruehle, F., Halverson, J., Soljačić, M., Hou, T.Y., Tegmark, M.: Kan: kolmogorov-arnold networks. arXiv preprint arXiv:2404.19756 (2024)

18. Lundberg, S.M., Lee, S.I.: A unified approach to interpreting model predictions. In: Guyon, I., Luxburg, U.V., Bengio, S., Wallach, H., Fergus, R., Vishwanathan, S., Garnett, R. (eds.) Advances in Neural Information Processing Systems 30, pp. 4765–4774. Curran Associates, Inc. (2017). http://papers.nips.cc/paper/7062-a-unified-approach-to-interpreting-model-predictions.pdf

19. Momeni, A., Thibault, M., Gevaert, O.: Dropout-enabled ensemble learning for multi-scale biomedical data. In: Brainlesion: Glioma, Multiple Sclerosis, Stroke and Traumatic Brain Injuries: 4th International Workshop, BrainLes 2018, Held in Conjunction with MICCAI 2018, Granada, Spain, September 16, 2018, Revised Selected Papers, Part I 4, pp. 407–415. Springer (2019)

20. Penny, W.D., Friston, K.J., Ashburner, J.T., Kiebel, S.J., Nichols, T.E.: Statistical parametric mapping: the analysis of functional brain images. Elsevier (2011)

21. Prata, D., Mechelli, A., Kapur, S.: Clinically meaningful biomarkers for psychosis: a systematic and quantitative review. Neurosci. Biobehav. Rev. **45**, 134–141 (2014)

22. PRONIA-consortium: Pronia-the project. http://www.proniapredictors.eu/pronia/the-project/index.html

23. Sampaio, I.W., et al.: Comparison of multi-site neuroimaging data harmonization techniques for machine learning applications. In: IEEE EUROCON 2023 - 20th International Conference on Smart Technologies, pp. 307–312 (2023). https://doi.org/10.1109/EUROCON56442.2023.10198911

24. Shorfuzzaman, M.: Iot-enabled stacked ensemble of deep neural networks for the diagnosis of covid-19 using chest CT scans. Computing **105**(4), 887–908 (2023)

25. Thomas, G.D.: Machine learning research: four current directions. Artif. Intell. Mag. **18**(4), 97–136 (1997)

26. Walter, M., Alizadeh, S., Jamalabadi, H., Lueken, U., Dannlowski, U., Walter, H., Olbrich, S., Colic, L., Kambeitz, J., Koutsouleris, N., Hahn, T., Dwyer, D.B.: Translational machine learning for psychiatric neuroimaging. Progress Neuro-Psychopharmacology Biological Psychiatry **91**, 113–121 (2019). https://doi.org/10.1016/j.pnpbp.2018.09.014. https://www.sciencedirect.com/science/article/pii/S0278584618304500, promising neural biomarkers and predictors of treatment outcomes for psychiatric disorders: Novel neuroimaging approaches

27. Woo, C.W., Chang, L.J., Lindquist, M.A., Wager, T.D.: Building better biomarkers: brain models in translational neuroimaging. Nat. Neurosci. **20**(3), 365–377 (2017)

SCIsegV2: A Universal Tool for Segmentation of Intramedullary Lesions in Spinal Cord Injury

Enamundram Naga Karthik[1,2(✉)] [iD], Jan Valošek[1,2,3] [iD], Lynn Farner[4] [iD],
Dario Pfyffer[4,5] [iD], Simon Schading-Sassenhausen[4] [iD], Anna Lebret[4] [iD],
Gergely David[4] [iD], Andrew C. Smith[6] [iD], Kenneth A. Weber II[5] [iD],
Maryam Seif[4,7] [iD], Patrick Freund[4,7] [iD], and Julien Cohen-Adad[1,2,8,9] [iD]

[1] Polytechnique Montréal, Montréal, QC, Canada
jan.valosek@polymtl.ca
[2] Mila - Quebec AI Institute, Montréal, QC, Canada
naga-karthik.enamundram@polymtl.ca
[3] Palacký University Olomouc, Olomouc, Czechia
[4] University of Zürich, Zürich, Switzerland
[5] Stanford University School of Medicine, Stanford, CA, USA
[6] University of Colorado School of Medicine, Aurora, CO, USA
[7] Max Planck Institute for Human Cognitive and Brain Sciences, Leipzig, Germany
[8] CHU Sainte-Justine, Université de Montréal, Montréal, QC, Canada
[9] Functional Neuroimaging Unit, CRIUGM, Université de Montréal,
Montréal, QC, Canada

Abstract. Spinal cord injury (SCI) is a devastating incidence leading
to permanent paralysis and loss of sensory-motor functions potentially
resulting in the formation of lesions within the spinal cord. Imaging
biomarkers obtained from magnetic resonance imaging (MRI) scans can
predict the functional recovery of individuals with SCI and help choose
the optimal treatment strategy. Currently, most studies employ manual
quantification of these MRI-derived biomarkers, which is a subjective and
tedious task. In this work, we propose (i) a universal tool for the automatic segmentation of intramedullary SCI lesions, dubbed SCIsegV2, and
(ii) a method to automatically compute the width of the tissue bridges
from the segmented lesion. Tissue bridges represent the spared spinal
tissue adjacent to the lesion, which is associated with functional recovery in SCI patients. The tool was trained and validated on a heterogeneous dataset from 7 sites comprising patients from different SCI phases
(acute, sub-acute, and chronic) and etiologies (traumatic SCI, ischemic
SCI, and degenerative cervical myelopathy). Tissue bridges quantified
automatically did not significantly differ from those computed manually,
suggesting that the proposed automatic tool can be used to derive relevant MRI biomarkers. SCIsegV2 and the automatic tissue bridges computation are open-source and available in Spinal Cord Toolbox (v6.4

E. N. Karthik and J. Valošek—These authors contributed equally to this work.
P. Freund and J. Cohen-Adad—Joint senior authors.

© The Author(s), under exclusive license to Springer Nature Switzerland AG 2025
S. Wu et al. (Eds.): AMAI 2024, LNCS 15384, pp. 198–209, 2025.
https://doi.org/10.1007/978-3-031-82007-6_19

and above) via the `sct_deepseg -task seg_sc_lesion_t2w_sci` and `sct_analyze_lesion` functions, respectively.

Keywords: Spinal Cord Injury · Segmentation · MRI · Deep Learning · Tissue Bridges

1 Introduction

Traumatic and non-traumatic spinal cord injuries (SCI) represent damage to the spinal cord (SC) with severe consequences, including weakness and paralysis in patients [4]. Traumatic SCI arises from sudden physical impacts, such as car accidents or falls, while non-traumatic SCI can be caused by ischemia (ischemic SCI) or chronic mechanical compression of the SC (degenerative cervical myelopathy, DCM) [1,4]. Both traumatic and non-traumatic SCI commonly involve intramedullary lesions, which are critical areas of tissue damage within the SC. Magnetic resonance imaging (MRI) is routinely used to provide information on the extent and the location of these intramedullary lesions [4,5,22]. Importantly, MRI scans can also be used to compute quantitative biomarkers, such as midsagittal tissue bridges [8]. These help in quantifying the amount of preserved SC neural tissue (carrying motor and sensory information to and from the brain) and have been found to predict functional recovery in patients with traumatic and non-traumatic SCI [8,16–18,20,23].

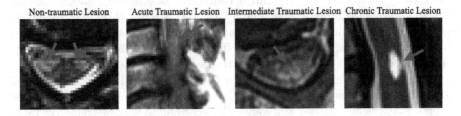

Fig. 1. Representative axial and sagittal T2w MRI scans of the lesion in various SCI etiologies/types.

Identifying MRI biomarkers in SCI automatically is challenging due to the varying size and location of lesions across patients and injury phases. Lesions can evolve from hyper- to hypo-intense depending on the underlying pathological mechanism (Fig. 1), and metal implants in the spine often cause image artifacts [5]. As a result, most studies report biomarkers quantified from manual lesion annotations [8,16–20,23,24], which is a tedious and error-prone task subject to inter-rater variability, making large-scale studies impractical. While two existing studies proposed automatic lesion segmentation in SCI, their methods were developed for specific SCI etiologies: [13] focused on *acute* preoperative traumatic SCI lesions, whereas, [14] introduced `SCIseg`, an open-source model for predominantly chronic, post-operative traumatic and ischemic SCI lesions. However, maintaining multiple etiology-specific models is challenging, highlighting the need for a single, **comprehensive** model for segmenting any kind of SCI lesions. In this regard, our contributions in this work are as follows:

- **Segmentation tool**: We present a comprehensive tool for the automatic segmentation of intramedullary SCI lesions, dubbed `SCIsegV2`. Our model was trained and validated on a heterogeneous, multinational dataset from 7 sites consisting of (i) traumatic SCI (acute preoperative, sub-acute and chronic postoperative) and (ii) non-traumatic SCI (ischemic SCI and DCM).
- **Analysis tool**: We propose a method to automatically compute the mid-sagittal tissue bridges, a predictor of functional recovery in SCI patients.
- **Packaging in open-source software suite**: Both `SCIsegV2` and the automatic tissue bridges computation are open-source and will be integrated into the Spinal Cord Toolbox (SCT) v6.4 and higher.

2   Materials and Methods

2.1   Dataset

We used T2-weighted (T2w) MRI images with heterogeneous image resolutions (isotropic, sagittal, and axial) and magnetic field strengths (1.0T, 1.5T, and 3.0T) from seven sites. The number of patients from each site is as follows: {site 1: ($n = 154$), site 2: ($n = 80$), site 3: ($n = 14$), site 4: ($n = 11$), site 5: ($n = 23$), site 6: ($n = 4$), site 7: ($n = 5$)}. Site 1 contained patients with both traumatic ($n = 97$) and non-traumatic SCI (mainly, DCM) ($n = 57$). Sites 2 & 3 included both preoperative and postoperative traumatic SCI, while sites 4 to 7 included only acute preoperative traumatic SCI. The timing of the MRI examination in relation to injury for traumatic SCI patients from sites 1, 2, and 3 is detailed in Table 1 of [14]. Eight patients from site 1 were followed up with additional MRI examinations, and 40 patients from site 1 had both sagittal and axial T2w images. Patients from sites 1 & 2 were split according to 80-20% train/test ratio. Due to the relatively small size of some datasets, we decided to use sites 3, 5 & 6 entirely for training and kept the patients from sites 4 & 7 as held-out (unseen) test sets to evaluate the model's generalization performance. The model was trained on a total of 281 T2w images and tested on 75 images. The ground truth masks of intramedullary lesions appearing as T2w signal abnormalities were manually annotated by expert raters at individual sites [14]. The SC masks were automatically segmented using the `sct_deepseg_sc` [6] algorithm and manually corrected when necessary.

2.2   SCIsegV2

We used nnUNet [10] as the backbone architecture for the SCI lesion segmentation model. The continuing dominance of nnUNet [9,10] across several open-source challenges has shown that a well-tuned convolutional neural network

(CNN) architecture is robust and continues to achieve state-of-the-art results over novel (and more sophisticated) transformer-based architectures in dense pixel prediction tasks such as image segmentation.

Similar to the recent work building upon the nnUNet framework [11,21], we experimented with its easy-to-tweak trainers for developing SCIsegV2. Specifically, we used: (i) nnUNetTrainer, the default model, and (ii) nnUNetTrainerDA5, the model applying aggressive data augmentation. The augmentation methods in the standard nnUNetTrainer include random rotation, scaling, mirroring, Gaussian noise addition, Gaussian blurring, adjusting image brightness and contrast, low-resolution simulation, and Gamma transformation. In addition to the standard augmentations, nnUNetTrainerDA5 applies additional transforms such as random patch replacement with mean values, sharpening, median filter, gamma correction, and additive intensity gradients. We note that even though the training data is a collection of heterogeneous datasets (acute, chronic traumatic and non-traumatic SCI) from 7 sites, we employed stronger data augmentation to improve generalization across various types of lesions.

The wide spectrum of lesion intensities in different SCI etiologies makes lesion segmentation an extremely challenging task. For instance, lesions in acute SCI are mildly T2w hyperintense and chronic lesions are bright T2w hyperintense (Fig. 1), although typically surrounded by metallic implants causing heavy interference [5]. Therefore, we compared two different training strategies for lesion segmentation: (i) given just the T2w image as the input, the model is trained to segment both the SC and lesions in hierarchical ordering, and (ii) assuming the availability of SC segmentation mask, the model is trained to segment only the lesions, given a 2-channel input consisting of the T2w image concatenated with the SC mask. While the first strategy attempts to implicitly guide the model towards the SC for lesion segmentation, the latter provides an explicit guidance in the form of the input channel.

2.3 Automatic Quantification of Tissue Bridges

The manual measurement of tissue bridges is performed on a single midsagittal slice of a volumetric (3D) T2w MRI image [8,16–20,23,24] (Fig. 2A). The midsagittal slice is defined as the middle slice of all slices where the SC is visible (Fig. 2B). Ventral and dorsal tissue bridges are quantified as the width of spared tissue at the minimum distance from the intramedullary lesion edge to the boundary between the SC and cerebrospinal fluid (Fig. 2C).

To automate the measurement of tissue bridges, we propose a method that computes ventral and dorsal tissue bridges utilizing the lesion and SC segmentation masks. To compensate for different neck positions and, consequently, different SC curvatures, we use angle correction, which adjusts the tissue bridge widths with respect to the SC centerline [7]. The method computes tissue bridges from all sagittal slices containing the lesion, allowing quantification of not only

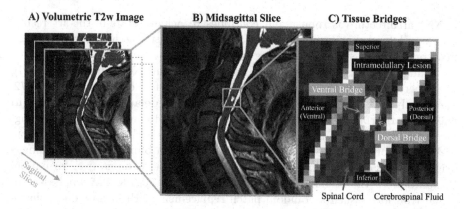

Fig. 2. Illustration of tissue bridges. A) Volumetric T2w image of a spinal cord injury (SCI) with chronic intramedullary lesion. B) Midsagittal slice used to compute the tissue bridges. C) Ventral and dorsal tissue bridges are defined as the width of spared tissue at the minimum distance from the intramedullary lesion edge to the boundary between the SC and cerebrospinal fluid.

midsagittal but parasagittal tissue bridges as well. For the purpose of this study (and to compare against existing manual measurements based on midsagittal tissue bridges), we considered only the midsagittal slice for the automatic measurement of the tissue bridges.

2.4 Experiments

We divided our experiments into 3 categories to investigate the effects of input types, data augmentation strategies and SCI etiology-specific models. All images were preprocessed with right-left, posterior-anterior, inferior-superior (RPI) orientation, resampled to a common resolution ($0.92 \times 0.68 \times 0.92$ mm^3, which is the median of all image resolutions in the training set) and intensity-normalized using Z-score normalization. The model was trained for 1000 epochs with 5-fold cross-validation, using a batch size of 2 and the stochastic gradient descent optimizer with a polynomial learning rate scheduler.

Inputs. We trained 2 different models: (i) a model that segments *both* the SC and lesions given just the T2w image as input (referred to as `single`), and (ii) a model that segments *only* the lesion given a 2-channel input consisting of T2w image and the SC segmentation (referred to as `multi`). As briefly discussed in Sect. 2.2, this experiment is to understand whether providing additional (localization) context in the form of SC segmentation as input would improve the lesion segmentation performance.

Data Augmentation. Given the increasing literature towards unrealistic transformations leading to better test-time performance [2], we compared 2 models with and without aggressive data augmentation to understand which model leads to better generalization on external test sets with acute preoperative SCI images. These are referred to as `defaultDA` and `aggressiveDA`, respectively.

SCI Etiology-Specific Models. This crucial experiment will provide insight into the initial hypothesis, asking whether a comprehensive SCI model is achievable. Toward this end, we compared our `SCIsegV2` model trained on all 7 sites against etiology-specific models individually trained on non-traumatic SCI and acute preoperative SCI data, respectively.

SCIseg. We also evaluate our model against SCIseg [14] which was trained on data from three sites comprising traumatic and ischemic SCI lesions. The model used a three-phase training strategy involving active learning and is available in SCT. Details about the training strategy can be found in [14].

Tissue Bridges. To validate the automatic measurements of the tissue bridges, we compared the method against manual and semi-automatic techniques in 15 individuals with traumatic SCI from site 1. Specifically, we compared the following: (1) **manual** - manual measurement of tissue bridges on manually segmented intramedullary lesions, (2) **semi-automatic** - automatic measurement of the tissue bridges using the proposed method on manually segmented intramedullary lesions, and (3) **fully-automatic** - automatic measurement of tissue bridges using `SCIsegV2` predictions. Statistical analysis was performed using the SciPy v1.10.0. The distribution of the data was assessed with the D'Agostino and Pearson normality test. Subsequently, the Kruskal-Wallis H-test was performed to compare the methods independently for ventral and dorsal bridges.

Evaluation Metrics. We used `MetricsReloaded` [12] and contributed to its development by adding lesion-wise metrics, specifically, lesion-wise sensitivity, positive predictive value, and F_1-score in addition to the existing metrics.

3   Results

Figure 3 shows the test Dice scores averaged across 5 folds for all models described in Sect. 2.4. Starting with the etiology-specific models, we observed that the model trained only on acute preoperative (`AcuteSCI`) data does not perform well on sites 1 and 2 containing non-traumatic and traumatic SCI data. While it performs relatively better on test sets from unseen sites (sites 4 and 7), it does not outperform the `SCIsegV2` models. Likewise, the model trained only on non-traumatic SCI data (`DCM`) performs well on a similar test set but fails in generalizing to acute preoperative SCI of sites 4 and 7.

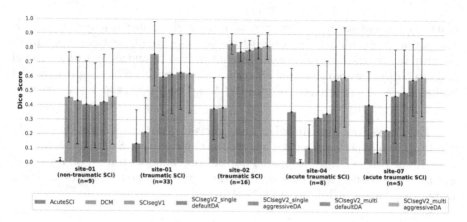

Fig. 3. Comparison of Dice scores for different SCI models. Each bar plot shows the test Dice scores averaged across 5 folds (the error bar represents the standard deviation).

Since `SCIsegV1` [14] was trained on a dataset of 3 sites predominantly consisting of traumatic SCI, it outperforms `SCIsegV2` models in sites 1 and 2. However, we observed that even `SCIsegV1` performs poorly on sites 4 and 7 suggesting that the segmentation of acute preoperative SCI lesions is extremely challenging. Within `SCIsegV2` models, we noted that training with aggressive data augmentation only results in marginal improvements in lesion segmentation performance. However, concatenating the SC segmentation as a second channel along with the input image (resulting in a 2-channel input) showed considerable improvements, especially in acute preoperative images, compared to a single-channel input with just the T2w image.

In Table 1, we present a quantitative comparison of different models using lesion-wise metrics. We noticed that the models' performance depends heavily on the specific SCI phases and etiologies. Except for site 1 (traumatic SCI), `SCIsegV2` outperforms `SCIsegV1` in all other sites. Comparing within the `SCIsegV2` models, one of downsides of the `multi-` models, despite achieving higher Dice scores (Fig. 3), is its dependency on the SC masks as input.

Table 2 shows the comparison of the midsagittal tissue bridges obtained using different methods (manual vs semi-automatic vs fully-automatic; see Sect. 2.4 for details) for 15 patients with traumatic SCI from site 1. For the fully-automatic technique, we used the `SCIsegV2_single_aggressiveDA` model to obtain the lesion segmentations. There was *no* statistically significant ($p > .05$) difference between the bridges computed using different methods.

Table 1. Comparison of lesion-wise metrics for `SCIsegV1` and various `SCIsegV2` models (with **aggressiveDA**) across the 5 testing sites. Metrics correspond to lesion-wise positive predictive value (PPVL), sensitivity (SensL) and F_1ScoreL; higher the value the better (↑). For a given site, bold values in each column represent the best model.

Model	Metric	Test Sites				
		site-01 (DCM)	site-01 (tSCI)	site-02 (tSCI)	site-04 (acuteSCI)	site-07 (acuteSCI)
`SCIsegV1`	(↑) PPVL	**0.63 ± 0.43**	**0.81 ± 0.31**	0.95 ± 0.14	0.37 ± 0.50	0.62 ± 0.50
	(↑) SensL	0.78 ± 0.44	**0.95 ± 0.16**	0.97 ± 0.12	0.55 ± 0.49	0.72 ± 0.49
	(↑) F_1ScoreL	0.67 ± 0.42	**0.84 ± 0.26**	0.95 ± 0.12	0.35 ± 0.47	0.64 ± 0.49
`SCIsegV2 single`	(↑) PPVL	0.55 ± 0.45	0.73 ± 0.33	**0.96 ± 0.13**	0.55 ± 0.50	**0.78 ± 0.36**
	(↑) SensL	0.68 ± 0.49	0.91 ± 0.24	**0.97 ± 0.12**	0.63 ± 0.48	**0.84 ± 0.36**
	(↑) F_1ScoreL	0.59 ± 0.45	0.77 ± 0.28	**0.95 ± 0.12**	0.53 ± 0.49	**0.80 ± 0.35**
`SCIsegV2 multi`	(↑) PPVL	0.61 ± 0.41	0.70 ± 0.36	0.90 ± 0.20	**0.75 ± 0.39**	0.54 ± 0.41
	(↑) SensL	**0.80 ± 0.42**	0.90 ± 0.26	0.97 ± 0.12	**0.90 ± 0.25**	0.80 ± 0.42
	(↑) F_1ScoreL	**0.67 ± 0.40**	0.74 ± 0.32	0.91 ± 0.15	**0.75 ± 0.37**	0.60 ± 0.40

Table 2. Comparison of *ventral* and *dorsal* midsagittal tissue bridges between manual, semi-automatic, and automatic measurements. Values are reported in millimetres.

ID	Manual Lesions & Manual Measurements		Manual Lesions & Automatic Measurements		SCIsegV2 Predictions & Automatic Measurements	
	Ventral	Dorsal	Ventral	Dorsal	Ventral	Dorsal
sub-zh101	0	2.65	0	2.39	0.34	2.39
sub-zh102	2.10	0.83	2.25	0	2.27	0.67
sub-zh104	0	0	0.54	0	0.55	0
sub-zh105	2.70	0	2.38	0.60	2.99	0
sub-zh106	0	0	0	0	0	0
sub-zh107	0	0.76	0	0.67	0	0.65
sub-zh108	1.32	0.52	1.96	0.66	2.03	0.68
sub-zh109	1.13	1.03	0.71	0	1.08	0.73
sub-zh110	0	0.99	0	0	0	0.39
sub-zh112	3.01	0.36	1.70	0.44	2.64	0.44
sub-zh114	0	0	0	0.38	0	0
sub-zh115	0	0	0	2.12	0	0.42
sub-zh116	3.12	0.50	2.38	0	2.49	0.80
sub-zh118	0.40	0	0	0	0	0
sub-zh119	2.93	2.98	1.04	0.50	1.48	0.95

4 Discussion

In this work, we proposed `SCIsegV2`, a DL-based universal tool for the segmentation of intramedullary lesions across different SCI etiologies and phases. We also automated the calculation of midsagittal tissue bridges, a metric representing spared spinal tissue adjacent to the lesion. This metric is relevant as it is associated with functional recovery in individuals with SCI. Both `SCIsegV2` and the automatic tissue bridges computation are open-source and available in Spinal Cord Toolbox (v6.4 and above) via the `sct_deepseg -task seg_sc_lesion_t2w_sci` and `sct_analyze_lesion` functions, respectively.

The heterogeneity in the appearance of intramedullary lesions across different SCI phases (acute, sub-acute, chronic) and etiologies (traumatic SCI, ischemic SCI, DCM) makes lesion segmentation extremely challenging, even for trained radiologists. Relatively low prevalence of traumatic SCI and the need for early surgical intervention [1] result in a low number of preoperative MRI scans, which adds to the difficulty in training a robust automatic segmentation model, that performs well on "real world" clinical data across multiple sites. Moreover, MRI scans of individuals with chronic SCI frequently exhibit image distortions caused by metallic implants, further complicating the segmentation process.

As a way of simplifying the lesion segmentation problem, using the SC mask to explicitly guide the model towards the cord showed improved results on certain etiologies. However, it introduced a dependency on the SC mask to be concatenated to the input image, preventing a smooth transition from the model's automatic predictions to the computation of tissue bridges, which requires both the cord and lesion masks. In contrast, the `SCIsegV2_single` model capable of segmenting both SC and lesions has a higher utility as it is also applicable in scenarios where SC masks are unavailable. Lastly, as the lesion appearance varies substantially across different SCI types, universal models like `SCIsegV2` learn the differences in lesion distributions across etiologies and even outperform etiology-specific models while showing good generalization across sites.

Limitations and Future Work. One limitation of the model is its higher sensitivity to traumatic SCI lesions, as approximately ($\sim 70\%$) of our dataset consists of this population. This skew is due to the relatively low availability of acute preoperative SCI scans. Acquiring additional data in SCI is generally challenging, but is possible with the help of ongoing clinical trials and consortiums for creating large databases for SCI research [3,15]. While this work used a relatively small and unbalanced cohort, we presented a preliminary proof-of-concept toward a universal tool for SCI lesion segmentation. The current literature only quantifies tissue bridges manually, from a single *midsagittal* slice. However, as lesions are 3D blob-like objects, the midsagittal slice might not necessarily contain the largest portions of the lesion and does not consider parasagittally running fiber tracts. Therefore, combining both *parasagittal* and *midsagittal* slices could provide a comprehensive evaluation of the width of the spared tissue bridges.

Prospect of Application. Automatic segmentation of the lesions and spinal cord could mitigate the bottleneck and inter-rater variability associated with manual annotations. Automating the measurements of tissue bridges could provide an objective, unbiased way in guiding rehabilitation decision making and stratifying patients into homogeneous subgroups of recovery in clinical trials.

Acknowledgements. We thank Mathieu Guay-Paquet and Joshua Newton for their assistance with the management of the datasets and the implementation of the algorithm to SCT. We thank Maxime Bouthillier for the help with manual annotations. We thank Dr. Serge Rossignol and the Multidisciplinary Team on Locomotor Rehabilitation (Regenerative Medicine and Nanomedicine, CIHR), and all the patients. The authors would also like to thank the RHSCIR participants and network, including all the participating local RHSCIR sites along with their PIs: Vancouver General Hospital, Foothills Hospital, Royal University Hospital, Toronto Western Hospital, St. Michael's Hospital, Sunnybrook Health Sciences Centre, Hamilton General Hospital, The Ottawa Hospital Civic Campus, Hôpital de l'Enfant Jésus, Hôpital du Sacre Coeur de Montréal, QEII Health Sciences Centre, Saint John Regional Hospital.

Funded by the Canada Research Chair in Quantitative Magnetic Resonance Imaging [CRC-2020-00179], the Canadian Institute of Health Research [PJT-190258], the Canada Foundation for Innovation [32454, 34824], the Fonds de Recherche du Québec - Santé [322736, 324636], the Natural Sciences and Engineering Research Council of Canada [RGPIN-2019-07244], the Canada First Research Excellence Fund (IVADO and TransMedTech), the Courtois NeuroMod project, the Quebec BioImaging Network [5886, 35450], INSPIRED (Spinal Research, UK; Wings for Life, Austria; Craig H. Neilsen Foundation, USA), Mila - Tech Transfer Funding Program, the Association Française contre les Myopathies (AFM), the Institut pour la Recherche sur la Moelle épinière et l'Encéphale (IRME), the National Institutes of Health Eunice Kennedy Shriver National Institute of Child Health and Development (R03HD094577). ACS is supported by the National Institutes of Health - K01HD106928 and R01NS128478 and the Boettcher Foundation's Webb-Waring Biomedical Research Program. KAW is supported by the National Institutes of Health - K23NS104211, L30NS108301, R01NS128478. The Rick Hansen Spinal Cord Injury Registry and this work are supported by funding from the Praxis Spinal Cord Institute through the Government of Canada and the Province of British Columbia. For more information about RHSCIR(9), please visit www.praxisinstitute.org. JV received funding from the European Union's Horizon Europe research and innovation programme under the Marie Skłodowska-Curie grant agreement No 101107932 and is supported by the Ministry of Health of the Czech Republic, grant nr. NU22-04-00024. ENK is supported by the Fonds de Recherche du Québec Nature and Technologie (FRQNT) Doctoral Training Scholarship. The authors thank Digital Research Alliance of Canada for the compute resources used in this work.

Disclosure of Interests. The authors have no competing interests to declare that are relevant to the content of this article.

References

1. Ahuja, C.S., et al.: Traumatic spinal cord injury. Nat. Rev. Dis. Primers **3**(1) (Apr 2017)

2. Billot, B., et al.: Synthseg: segmentation of brain MRI scans of any contrast and resolution without retraining. Med. Image Anal. **86**, 102789 (2023)
3. Birkhäuser, V., et al.: Tasci—transcutaneous tibial nerve stimulation in patients with acute spinal cord injury to prevent neurogenic detrusor overactivity: protocol for a nationwide, randomised, sham-controlled, double-blind clinical trial. BMJ Open **10**(8) (2020)
4. David, G., Mohammadi, S., Martin, A.R., Cohen-Adad, J., Weiskopf, N., Thompson, A., Freund, P.: Traumatic and nontraumatic spinal cord injury: pathological insights from neuroimaging. Nat. Rev. Neurol. **15**(12), 718–731 (2019)
5. Freund, P., Seif, M., Weiskopf, N., Friston, K., Fehlings, M.G., Thompson, A.J., Curt, A.: MRI in traumatic spinal cord injury: from clinical assessment to neuroimaging biomarkers. Lancet Neurol. **18**(12), 1123–1135 (2019)
6. Gros, C., et al.: Automatic segmentation of the spinal cord and intramedullary multiple sclerosis lesions with convolutional neural networks. Neuroimage **184**, 901–915 (2019)
7. Gros, C., et al.: Automatic spinal cord localization, robust to MRI contrasts using global curve optimization. Med. Image Anal. **44**, 215–227 (2018)
8. Huber, E., Lachappelle, P., Sutter, R., Curt, A., Freund, P.: Are midsagittal tissue bridges predictive of outcome after cervical spinal cord injury? Ann. Neurol. **81**(5), 740–748 (2017)
9. Isensee, F., et al.: nnu-net revisited: a call for rigorous validation in 3d medical image segmentation (2024)
10. Isensee, F., et al.: nnu-net: a self-configuring method for deep learning-based biomedical image segmentation. Nat. Methods **18**(2), 203–211 (2021)
11. Ma, J., Li, F., Wang, B.: U-mamba: enhancing long-range dependency for biomedical image segmentation. ArXiv abs/2401.04722 (2024)
12. Maier-Hein, L., et al.: Metrics reloaded: recommendations for image analysis validation. Nature methods, pp. 1–18 (2024)
13. McCoy, D.B., et al.: Convolutional neural Network-Based automated segmentation of the spinal cord and contusion injury: Deep learning biomarker correlates of motor impairment in acute spinal cord injury. AJNR Am. J. Neuroradiol. **40**(4), 737–744 (2019)
14. Naga Karthik, E., Valošek, J., Smith, A.C., et al.: SCIseg: automatic segmentation of intramedullary lesions in spinal cord injury on T2-weighted MRI scans. Radiol. Artif. Intell. **7**(1), e240005 (2025). https://doi.org/10.1148/ryai.240005
15. Noonan, V.K., Kwon, B.K., Soril, L., Fehlings, M.G., Hurlbert, R.J., Townson, A., Johnson, M., Dvorak, M.F.: The rick hansen spinal cord injury registry (rhscir): a national patient-registry. Spinal Cord **50**(1), 22–27 (2011)
16. O'Dell, D.R., Weber, K.A., Berliner, J.C., Elliott, J.M., Connor, J.R., Cummins, D.P., Heller, K.A., Hubert, J.S., Kates, M.J., Mendoza, K.R., Smith, A.C.: Midsagittal tissue bridges are associated with walking ability in incomplete spinal cord injury: A magnetic resonance imaging case series. J. Spinal Cord Med. **43**(2), 268–271 (2020)
17. Pfyffer, D., Huber, E., Sutter, R., Curt, A., Freund, P.: Tissue bridges predict recovery after traumatic and ischemic thoracic spinal cord injury. Neurology **93**(16), e1550–e1560 (2019)
18. Pfyffer, D., et al.: Prognostic value of tissue bridges in cervical spinal cord injury: a longitudinal, multicentre, retrospective cohort study. The Lancet Neurology (2024)
19. Pfyffer, D., Vallotton, K., Curt, A., Freund, P.: Tissue bridges predict neuropathic pain emergence after spinal cord injury. J. Neurol. Neurosurg. Psychiatry **91**(10), 1111–1117 (2020)

20. Pfyffer, D., Vallotton, K., Curt, A., Freund, P.: Predictive value of midsagittal tissue bridges on functional recovery after spinal cord injury. Neurorehabil. Neural Repair **35**(1), 33–43 (2021)

21. Roy, S., et al.: Mednext: transformer-driven scaling of convnets for medical image segmentation. In: International Conference on Medical Image Computing and Computer-Assisted Intervention (2023)

22. Seif, M., David, G., Huber, E., Vallotton, K., Curt, A., Freund, P.: Cervical cord neurodegeneration in traumatic and Non-Traumatic spinal cord injury. J. Neurotrauma **37**(6), 860–867 (2020)

23. Smith, A.C., et al.: Spinal cord tissue bridges validation study: predictive relationships with sensory scores following cervical spinal cord injury. Top. Spinal Cord Inj. Rehabil. **28**(2), 111–115 (2022)

24. Vallotton, K., Huber, E., Sutter, R., Curt, A., Hupp, M., Freund, P.: Width and neurophysiologic properties of tissue bridges predict recovery after cervical injury. Neurology **92**(24), e2793–e2802 (2019)

EHRmonize: A Framework for Medical Concept Abstraction from Electronic Health Records using Large Language Models

João Matos[1], Jack Gallifant[2], Jian Pei[1], and A. Ian Wong[1(✉)]

[1] Duke University, Durham, USA
med@aiwong.com
[2] Massachusetts Institute of Technology, Cambridge, USA

Abstract. Electronic health records (EHRs) contain vast amounts of complex data, but harmonizing and processing this information remains a challenging and costly task requiring significant clinical expertise. While large language models (LLMs) have shown promise in various healthcare applications, their potential for abstracting medical concepts from EHRs remains largely unexplored. We introduce EHRmonize, a framework leveraging LLMs to abstract medical concepts from EHR data. Our study uses medication data from two real-world EHR databases to evaluate five LLMs on two free-text extraction and six binary classification tasks across various prompting strategies. GPT-4o's with 10-shot prompting achieved the highest performance in all tasks, accompanied by Claude-3.5-Sonnet in a subset of tasks. GPT-4o achieved an accuracy of 97% in identifying generic route names, 82% for generic drug names, and 100% in performing binary classification of antibiotics. While EHRmonize significantly enhances efficiency, reducing annotation time by an estimated 60%, we emphasize that clinician oversight remains essential. Our framework, available as a Python package, (Package on PyPI, Repository on GitHub, and Documentation on ReadTheDocs.) offers a promising tool to assist clinicians in EHR data abstraction. EHRmonize has the potential to accelerate healthcare research and improve data harmonization processes.

Keywords: Large Language Models · Electronic Health Records · Chart Abstraction of Medical Concepts · EHRmonize

1 Introduction

The development of machine learning models in healthcare critically depends on large-scale, high-quality data. Electronic Health Records (EHRs) offer a rich source of such data, encompassing structured information generated during routine clinical practice, including vital signs, laboratory values, and clinical interventions [20]. However, the full potential of EHR data remains largely untapped due to significant challenges in data processing. A primary obstacle in leveraging

S. Wu et al. (Eds.): AMAI 2024, LNCS 15384, pp. 210–220, 2025.
https://doi.org/10.1007/978-3-031-82007-6_20

EHR data is the substantial variability in recording practices, both between and within hospital systems [14]. This variability manifests in several ways:

- **Inconsistent Terminology:** The same medical concept may be recorded differently across institutions or even within a single hospital. For example, in medication data, "dextrose 5%" is an intravenous fluid for volume expansion (and the same as "D5W" and the normalized RxNorm concept "glucose 50 mg/ml"), but is different from "D50" and "magnesium sulfate 1 g in d5w", which are medical therapies [16].
- **Local Coding Systems:** Many healthcare institutions use local coding systems, making it difficult to compare/aggregate data across different sources.
- **Evolving Standards:** As medical knowledge and practices evolve, so do the terminologies and coding systems used in EHRs, further complicating long-term data harmonization efforts.

Current approaches to addressing these challenges often rely on manual abstraction (i.e., cleaning, categorization, and/or summarization) of concepts and chart review [21,24]. However, these methods are time-consuming, labor-intensive, and prone to errors [2,13,18]. Moreover, the expertise required for accurate data abstraction is not always available, limiting the accessibility of EHR data for many researchers and potentially hindering progress in healthcare research [22]. Although there is a growing body of literature, most papers fail to be reproducible as the underlying codebases are not always shared [12].

Large Language Models (LLMs) have emerged as a promising technology with the potential to revolutionize various aspects of medicine [4,15]. Their ability to understand and generate human-like text has shown promise in tasks such as note summarization, clinical decision support, and medical education [19]. Furthermore, LLMs have demonstrated significant encoded medical knowledge, as evidenced by their performance on medical question-answering benchmarks [10].

Given these capabilities, *we hypothesize that LLMs can significantly improve workflow efficiency in abstracting medical concepts from EHR data.* By automating the categorization and harmonization of EHR entries, LLMs could potentially address many of the challenges associated with EHR data processing. Ultimately, this could lower barriers to entry for researchers and enabling more widespread use of EHR data in healthcare research and analytics.

In this paper, we introduce EHRmonize, a novel framework that leverages the power of LLMs to automate the cleaning and categorization of medical concepts in EHR data. Our work makes the following key contributions:

- **LLM-based EHR Data Harmonization**: We present a novel approach to using LLMs for abstracting medical concepts in EHR data, addressing the critical need for efficient, scalable data harmonization methods.
- **Curated Dataset:** We provide a curated dataset of medication data from MIMIC-IV [11] and eICU-CRD [17], enabling reproducibility of our findings and facilitating further research in this domain. This labeled dataset is made publicly available[1].

---

[1] Dataset on HuggingFace.

- **Comprehensive Evaluation:** We conduct an extensive evaluation of five state-of-the-art LLMs across various prompting strategies, encompassing two free-text tasks and six binary classification tasks. This evaluation provides insights into the capabilities and limitations of different LLMs in EHR data processing tasks.
- **Open-Source Implementation:** We release `EHRmonize` as an open-source PyPI package, implementing the use cases explored in this study and providing customizable modules for further applications. This contribution aims to foster collaboration and accelerate progress in the field of EHR data science.

By developing tools that automate the categorization and harmonization of EHR entries, `EHRmonize` aims to address critical challenges in EHR data processing, lower barriers to entry for researchers, and ultimately enable more widespread and efficient use of EHR data in healthcare research and analytics. In the following sections, we discuss related work, detail our methodology, present our findings, and discuss this work's implications and future directions.

2   Related Work

The challenge of harmonizing and extracting meaningful information from EHRs has been addressed through various approaches over the years. Traditional methods have included rule-based systems using hard-coded queries for automated data abstraction [20] and cascading architectures for complex classification tasks [5]. While effective for specific use cases, these approaches often lack flexibility and require significant effort to maintain as medical terminologies evolve.

Natural Language Processing (NLP) techniques have been widely applied to unstructured EHR data, with Named Entity Recognition (NER) being a key focus. Ahmad et al. [1] and Durango et al. [6] provide comprehensive reviews of NER techniques applied to clinical text, highlighting successes in identifying medical concepts despite linguistic variability challenges. However, these approaches often struggle with the variability of medical terminology across different EHR systems and require extensive manual input or task-specific fine-tuning, limiting their scalability and generalizability.

Efforts to standardize medical concepts have led to the development of tools like RxNorm [16,23]. While these tools have made significant strides in concept matching across vocabularies, they often require extensive manual review, limiting their scalability. LLMs have opened new avenues for processing extensive medical texts at unprecedented speeds. Liu et al. [15] and Chen et al. [4] discuss the broader potential of LLMs to revolutionize various aspects of healthcare, from clinical decision support to medical education.

However, the application of LLMs in healthcare is not without challenges. Recent studies have highlighted concerns regarding the faithfulness [9] and bias [3] of LLMs in medical contexts. In the domain of medication information processing, Gallifant et al. [8] demonstrated high performance in matching drug brand and generic terms using various LLMs, with GPT-4 achieving near-perfect accuracy. Nevertheless, their work also revealed limitations in handling more complex aspects of medication nomenclature. These findings underscore the need for specialized tools to manage the intricacies of medical drug data, which are crucial for developing comprehensive frameworks for AI-enabled pharmacovigilance and data harmonization [7].

EHRmonize addresses a critical gap in this landscape by focusing on abstraction rather than mere extraction or labeling. We leverage LLMs for automated EHR data harmonization, aiming to capture and standardize higher-level concepts across diverse EHR systems. This approach combines the flexibility of machine learning with the nuanced understanding of medical language demonstrated by LLMs, potentially offering a more scalable and adaptable solution to the challenges of EHR data harmonization.

3   Methods

EHRmonize facilitates EHR data harmonization, addressing multidisciplinary collaboration challenges between data scientists and clinicians (Fig. 1). It comprises two components: corpus generation (SQL-based extraction of relevant text/concepts from EHR databases) and LLM inference (conversion of raw input to standardized classes via few-shot prompting) (Fig. 2).

Context: A multidisciplinary clinical data science team is working with EHRs. The clinicians agreed to include the patients on antibiotics, but exclude patients on anticoagulants. It is necessary to abstract medication and route names as "antibiotics" or "anticoagulants".
Current Workflow, by role:
1. Data Scientist: Queries unique medication names from EHRs and sends them to clinician.
2. Clinician: Maps medications into predefined classes and returns to the data scientist.
Challenge: Step 2 may involve manual labeling of thousands of entries with the help of a clinical expert, which not all teams have access to.
User Story: As a data scientist working with EHR data, I want to automatically abstract medical concepts **as a first pass**, so that collaboration with clinical experts is **more efficient**.

Fig. 1. Example workflow and challenges in multidisciplinary clinical data science.

Tasks: We defined two task types: (1) free-text extraction of generic routes and drug names from raw entries, and (2) binary classification of (drug, route) pairs as antibiotic, anticoagulant, electrolytes, IV fluid, opioid analgesic, or stress ulcer prophylaxis. Data sources were MIMIC-IV [11] and eICU-CRD [17]. MIMIC-IV is a publicly accessible critical care database with de-identified health data from over 70,000 ICU stays from one Boston hospital. [11] eICU-CRD contains high-resolution data from over 200,000 ICU admissions in over 200 U.S hospitals. [17] Preprocessing involved SQL extraction of unique drug-route pairs, selection of top 200 prevalent entries per task, and manual labeling by a physician (AIW).

Labeling: *Generic drug names:* Free-text drug names were translated to the lowercase generic name, matching either the clinical drug component, precise

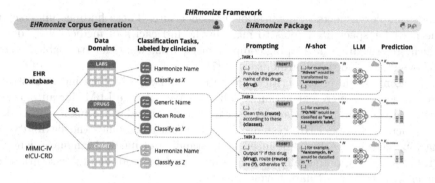

Fig. 2. Overall workflow of `EHRmonize`. Corpus generation from EHRs provides the data that needs categorization, across different domains and tasks, which is then fed to our package that employs LLMs to categorize the entries into predefined classes.

ingredient, or ingredient in RxNorm, a National Library of Medicine system to normalize medications [16]. Salt names (e.g., hydromorphone hydrochloride to hydromorphone) were not included unless the active ingredient was shared across multiple salts (e.g., "metoprolol tartrate" vs. "metoprolol succinate"). Prescription strengths were not included (e.g., "hydromorphone hydrochloride 1 mg" to "hydromorphone"). Concentrations were included for intravenous fluids and dextrose to disambiguate a precise drug (e.g., "normal saline 0.9%" to "sodium chloride 9 mg/ml"; "dextrose 50%" to "glucose 500 mg/ml"). Medications with significant combinations (e.g., "pneumococcal 23-valent polysaccharide vaccine") kept all common RxNorm components but did not include valence. *Generic routes:* Entries were transformed to the lowercase (no abbreviations) RxNorm classification (e.g., "IV" to "injectable product"; "PO/NG" to "oral product"). *Binary classifications:* Six classes were one-hot encoded.

> You are a well trained clinician doing data cleaning and harmonization. You are given a raw drug name and administration route out of the EHR data below, within square brackets such as [drugname, route]. Please output **"1"** if [**"normal saline"**, **"IV"**] is classified as **"IV fluid"**, otherwise **"0"**. "IV fluid" means "intravenous fluid given for the purpose of volume expansion". Consider the following example: An input drug name "sodium chloride 0.9%" and route "IV" would be classified as **"1"**. Please output nothing more than **"1"** or **"0"**.

Fig. 3. One-shot prompting example for the "IV fluid" binary classification task.

Prompting: Prompts included a specific task description, where we instruct the model to act like an experienced clinician, how the output format is expected to be, and how the expected class can be defined. When few-shot prompting was used, a few representative examples were provided (Fig. 3).

LLMs: We assessed five models of 4 different families: Anthropic's Claude-3.5-Sonnet; Meta's Llama3-70B; Mistral's Mixtral-8x7B (via AWS's Bedrock API);

Table 1. Characteristics of the medication entries in the labeled dataset.

Database	N	Free-Text (#Unique)		Binary Tasks(#Positive)					
		GenericRoute	GenericName	Antibiotic	Anticoagulant	Electrolytes	IV Fluids	Opioid Analgesic	Stress ulcer prophylaxis
MIMIC-IV	198	6	83	8	13	17	22	12	8
eICU-CRD	200	5	50	5	7	24	28	22	8

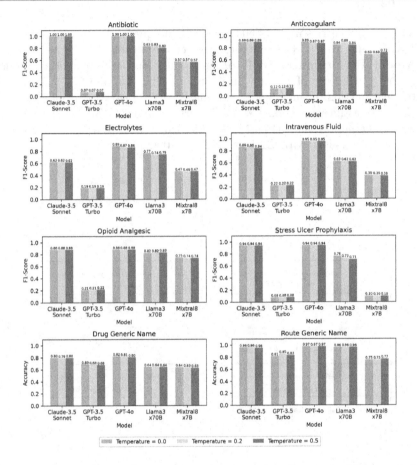

Fig. 4. LLM 10-shot performance across tasks and temperatures (398 samples).

and OpenAI's GPT-3.5-Turbo and GPT-4o. These models were selected due to their good performance in medical and non-medical benchmarks and cost-efficiency ratio. As we use these models "off-the-shelf", all data is considered test data.

Experiments: Besides the five different models, we explored different temperatures (0, 0.2, 0.5) and (0 to 10)-shot prompting. As the objective of `EHRmonize`
is to improve efficiency in data cleaning, the time necessary to do manual annotation and `EHRmonize`'s output review was recorded and compared.

4   Results

We labeled 398 entries from 14,604 and 8,803 unique medication-route pairs in
eICU-CRD and MIMIC-IV databases, respectively (Table 1).

Model Performance: GPT-4o consistently outperformed other models,
achieving an F1-score of 1.00 for antibiotic classification and 0.97 accuracy for
route identification. Claude-3.5-Sonnet matched GPT-4o's performance in several binary classification tasks. GPT-3.5-Turbo, Llama3 70B, and Mixtral 8x7B
showed lower performance (Fig. 4). Generic drug name extraction proved challenging for all models, with GPT-4o achieving 0.82 accuracy.

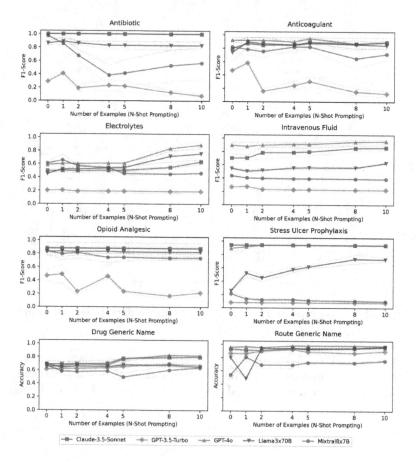

Fig. 5. LLM performance (temp. 0.2) with varying N-shot prompting across tasks.

Table 2. Five exemplary errors for the generic drug task, using GPT-4o with 10-shot.

Input Data	Expected Prediction	Prediction
Magnesium Sulfate	magnesium sulfate	magnesium
Sodium Chloride 0.9%	normal saline	sodium chloride 9 mg/ml
Dextrose 50%	glucose 500 mg/ml	dextrose 500 mg/ml
Metoprolol Tartrate	metoprolol tartrate	metoprolol
Albuterol 0.083% Neb Soln	albuterol 0.83 mg/ml	albuterol

Table 3. Time (in minutes) spent in data annotation and in EHRmonize output review, using GPT-4o with 10-shot prompting.

Database	MIMIC-IV				eICU-CRD			
Task Type	Generic	Route	Binary	**Total**	Generic	Route	Binary	**Total**
Annotation	6:03	3:56	5:53	15:52	4:46	3:40	8:31	16:57
Revision	2:02	0:37	2:27	5:06	2:37	1:11	2:55	6:43
Corrections	10/100	2/100	1/600	13/800	22/100	3/100	1/600	26/800
Savings (%)	66.4%	84.3%	58.4%	**67.9%**	45.1%	67.7%	65.8%	**60.4%**

N-shot Prompting: GPT-4o and Claude-3.5-Sonnet exhibited stable, high performance with increasing examples. Unexpectedly, GPT-3.5-Turbo's performance declined as the number of examples increased, particularly in antibiotic, anticoagulant, and opioid analgesic tasks. Llama3 70B and Mixtral 8x7B maintained intermediate, relatively stable performance (Fig. 5).

Temperature Impact: Variations in temperature up to 0.5 had minimal impact on model performance across tasks.

Efficiency Gains: EHRmonize significantly reduced annotation time, with savings of 67.9% for MIMIC-IV and 60.4% for eICU-CRD (Table 3).

Error Analysis: The errors presented in Table 2, from the "generic drug" task, indicate that the model generally captures the correct concept but struggles with specific details. The errors primarily arise from variations in order, omitted concentrations, or incomplete concepts, as seen in the glucose versus dextrose misclassification. However, the predictions tend to be reasonably close to the true labels, indicating that the model's understanding is not entirely incorrect.

5   Conclusion and Discussion

EHRmonize demonstrates the potential of LLMs to abstract medical concepts from structured EHR data across multiple classification tasks. The framework demonstrated significant efficiency gains, reducing annotation time by approximately 60%. This underscores EHRmonize's potential to *enhance*, rather than *replace*, manual chart review by prepopulating options and allowing clinicians to focus on more complex abstraction tasks.

Several limitations of this study warrant consideration. The dataset, while curated by a well-trained physician and supported by RxNorm materials, is limited in size (398 samples) and focused solely on medication data. Future research should aim to expand the dataset's volume and scope, incorporating other domains such as laboratory results and flowsheet data. Additionally, the current approach to N-shot example selection was deterministic; exploring the impact of example ordering could yield valuable insights into prompt engineering for medical NLP tasks.

Further avenues for improvement include incorporating semantic equivalence in free-text evaluation, implementing batching for enhanced efficiency, exploring retrieval-augmented generation (RAG) methods to extend N-shot examples, and investigating fine-tuning strategies for task-specific optimization. The potential of agentic approaches in managing abstraction workflows and ensuring consistency across outputs also merits exploration. Finally, regular evaluation on periodic data could facilitate the identification of concept drift, allowing the tool to adapt to evolving medical practices and terminologies.

Prospect of Application: EHRmonize, now available as a Python package on PyPI, represents a significant step towards lowering barriers in EHR data research. Improving abstraction efficiency for structured data fields-a task often performed manually-has the potential to accelerate research and enable more comprehensive analyses of EHR data.

Disclosure of Interests. AIW has received funding from NIMHD under U54MD012530. AIW has received support from AWS and CloudForce. All other authors have no competing interests.

References

1. Ahmad, P.N., Shah, A.M., Lee, K.: A review on electronic health record text-mining for biomedical name entity recognition in healthcare domain. In: Healthcare, vol. 11, p. 1268. MDPI (2023)
2. Byrne, M.D., Jordan, T., Welle, T.: Comparison of manual versus automated data collection method for an evidence-based nursing practice study. Appl. Clin. Inform. **4**(01), 61–74 (2013)
3. Chen, S., et al.: Cross-care: assessing the healthcare implications of pre-training data on language model bias (2024). https://arxiv.org/abs/2405.05506
4. Chen, Y., Liu, C., Huang, W., Cheng, S., Arcucci, R., Xiong, Z.: Generative text-guided 3d vision-language pretraining for unified medical image segmentation. arXiv preprint arXiv:2306.04811 (2023)
5. Dai, H.J., Su, C.H., Wu, C.S.: Adverse drug event and medication extraction in electronic health records via a cascading architecture with different sequence labeling models and word embeddings. J. Am. Med. Inform. Assoc. **27**(1), 47–55 (2020)
6. Durango, M.C., Torres-Silva, E.A., Orozco-Duque, A.: Named entity recognition in electronic health records: A methodological review. Healthcare Inform. Res. **29**(4), 286 (2023)

7. Gallifant, J., Celi, L.A., Sharon, E., Bitterman, D.S.: Navigating the complexities of artificial intelligence–enabled real-world data collection for oncology pharmacovigilance (2024)
8. Gallifant, J., et al.: Language models are surprisingly fragile to drug names in biomedical benchmarks (2024)
9. Han, T., Kumar, A., Agarwal, C., Lakkaraju, H.: Towards safe and aligned large language models for medicine. arXiv preprint arXiv:2403.03744 (2024)
10. Jin, D., Pan, E., Oufattole, N., Weng, W., Fang, H., Szolovits, P.: What disease does this patient have? a large-scale open domain question answering dataset from medical exams. CoRR abs/2009.13081 (2020). https://arxiv.org/abs/2009.13081
11. Johnson, A.E.W., et al.: MIMIC-IV, a freely accessible electronic health record dataset. Sci. Data **10**(1), 1 (2023). https://doi.org/10.1038/s41597-022-01899-x. https://www.nature.com/articles/s41597-022-01899-x
12. Johnson, A.E.W., Pollard, T.J., Mark, R.G.: Reproducibility in critical care: a mortality prediction case study. In: Doshi-Velez, F., Fackler, J., Kale, D., Ranganath, R., Wallace, B., Wiens, J. (eds.) Proceedings of the 2nd Machine Learning for Healthcare Conference. Proceedings of Machine Learning Research, vol. 68, pp. 361–376. PMLR, 18–19 Aug 2017. https://proceedings.mlr.press/v68/johnson17a.html
13. Lan, H., Thongprayoon, C., Ahmed, A., Herasevich, V., Sampathkumar, P., Gajic, O., O'Horo, J.C.: Automating quality metrics in the era of electronic medical records: digital signatures for ventilator bundle compliance. Biomed. Res. Int. **2015**(1), 396508 (2015)
14. Lester, C.A., Flynn, A.J., Marshall, V.D., Rochowiak, S., Rowell, B., Bagian, J.P.: Comparing the variability of ingredient, strength, and dose form information from electronic prescriptions with rxnorm drug product descriptions. J. Am. Med. Inform. Assoc. **29**(9), 1471–1479 (2022)
15. Liu, Y., et al.: Summary of ChatGPT-Related research and perspective towards the future of large language models. Meta-Radiology **1**(2), 100017 (2023). https://doi.org/10.1016/j.metrad.2023.100017. https://www.sciencedirect.com/science/article/pii/S2950162823000176
16. National Library of Medicine: Rxnorm technical documentation. https://www.nlm.nih.gov/research/umls/rxnorm/docs/index.html. Accessed 23 June 2024
17. Pollard, T.J., Johnson, A.E.W., Raffa, J.D., Celi, L.A., Mark, R.G., Badawi, O.: The eICU Collaborative Research Database, a freely available multi-center database for critical care research. Scientific Data **5**(1), 180178 (2018). https://doi.org/10.1038/sdata.2018.178. https://www.nature.com/articles/sdata2018178
18. Sauer, C.M., Chen, L.C., Hyland, S.L., Girbes, A., Elbers, P., Celi, L.A.: Leveraging electronic health records for data science: common pitfalls and how to avoid them. The Lancet Digital Health **4**(12), E893–E898 (2022). https://doi.org/10.1016/S2589-7500(22)00154-6. https://doi.org/10.1016/S2589-7500(22)00154-6, open AccessPublished:September 22, 2022
19. Thirunavukarasu, A.J., Ting, D.S.J., Elangovan, K., Gutierrez, L., Tan, T.F., Ting, D.S.W.: Large language models in medicine. Nat. Med. **29**(8), 1930–1940 (2023). https://doi.org/10.1038/s41591-023-02448-8. https://www.nature.com/articles/s41591-023-02448-8
20. Valencia Morales, D.J., et al.: Validation of automated data abstraction for sccm discovery virus covid-19 registry: practical ehr export pathways (virus-peep). Front. Med. **10**, 1089087 (2023)
21. Vassar, M., Matthew, H.: The retrospective chart review: important methodological considerations. J. Educ. Eval. Health Professions **10** (2013)

22. Wang, S., McDermott, M.B.A., Chauhan, G., Hughes, M.C., Naumann, T., Ghassemi, M.: Mimic-extract: A data extraction, preprocessing, and representation pipeline for MIMIC-III. CoRR abs/1907.08322 (2019). http://arxiv.org/abs/1907.08322

23. Waters, R., Malecki, S., Lail, S., Mak, D., Saha, S., Jung, H.Y., Imrit, M.A., Razak, F., Verma, A.A.: Automated identification of unstandardized medication data: a scalable and flexible data standardization pipeline using rxnorm on gemini multicenter hospital data. JAMIA Open 6(3), ooad062 (October 2023). https://doi.org/10.1093/jamiaopen/ooad062

24. Yin, A.L., et al.: Comparing automated vs. manual data collection for covid-specific medications from electronic health records. Int. J. Med. Inform. 157, 104622 (2022)

Evaluating the Impact of Pulse Oximetry Bias in Machine Learning Under Counterfactual Thinking

Inês Martins[1,2(✉)], João Matos[3,4], Tiago Gonçalves[1,2], Leo A. Celi[4], An-Kwok Ian Wong[3], and Jaime S. Cardoso[1,2(✉)]

[1] Faculty of Engineering, University of Porto, Porto, Portugal
{ines.a.martins,jaime.cardoso}@inesctec.pt
[2] Institute for Systems and Computer Engineering, Technology and Science, Porto, Portugal
[3] Duke University, Durham, USA
[4] Massachusetts Institute of Technology, Cambridge, USA

Abstract. Algorithmic bias in healthcare mirrors existing data biases. However, the factors driving unfairness are not always known. Medical devices capture significant amounts of data but are prone to errors; for instance, pulse oximeters overestimate the arterial oxygen saturation of darker-skinned individuals, leading to worse outcomes. The impact of this bias in machine learning (ML) models remains unclear. This study addresses the technical challenges of quantifying the impact of medical device bias in downstream ML. Our experiments compare a "perfect world", without pulse oximetry bias, using SaO_2 (blood-gas), to the "actual world", with biased measurements, using SpO_2 (pulse oximetry). Under this counterfactual design, two models are trained with identical data, features, and settings, except for the method of measuring oxygen saturation: models using SaO_2 are a "control" and models using SpO_2 a "treatment". The blood-gas oximetry linked dataset was a suitable testbed, containing 163,396 nearly-simultaneous SpO_2 - SaO_2 paired measurements, aligned with a wide array of clinical features and outcomes. We studied three classification tasks: in-hospital mortality, respiratory SOFA score in the next 24 h, and SOFA score increase by two points. Models using SaO_2 instead of SpO_2 generally showed better performance. Patients with overestimation of O_2 by pulse oximetry of $\geq 3\%$ had significant decreases in mortality prediction recall, from 0.63 to 0.59, $P < 0.001$. This mirrors clinical processes where biased pulse oximetry readings provide clinicians with false reassurance of patients' oxygen levels. A similar degradation happened in ML models, with pulse oximetry biases leading to more false negatives in predicting adverse outcomes.

Keywords: Bias · Machine Learning · Medical Devices · Pulse Oximetry

© The Author(s), under exclusive license to Springer Nature Switzerland AG 2025
S. Wu et al. (Eds.): AMAI 2024, LNCS 15384, pp. 221–230, 2025.
https://doi.org/10.1007/978-3-031-82007-6_21

1   Introduction

Machine learning (ML) has the potential to revolutionize healthcare, promising increased objectivity in decisions, enhanced health system efficiency, and better overall health outcomes [2]. However, effective deployment of ML applications in healthcare is happening at a slower pace than expected. Obermeyer and colleagues' seminal work in 2019 [16] raised concerns about the risk of bias in health ML, highlighting that an algorithm widely used in U.S. hospitals was less likely to refer Black people than White people (with similar illnesses) to more personalized treatment programs. These inconsistencies were attributed to the fact that the model was based on health care cost, instead of actual illness [16].

However, understanding the causality and underlying factors driving downstream unfairness in ML models for healthcare is challenging due to significant confounding variables. Despite this complexity, addressing these issues is crucial for mitigating biases and improving model performance. Medical devices, such as pulse oximeters, thermometers, and sphygmomanometers, may introduce similar inconsistencies in model results due to calibration flaws [4]. These devices are routinely used to collect vital signs to support clinical decision-making, especially in the Intensive Care Unit (ICU), where patients are more unstable [18].

Pulse oximeters estimate arterial oxygen saturation by measuring light absorption at two light wavelengths (660nm - red and 940nm - infrared) of oxyhemoglobin and deoxyhemoglobin in capillary blood. However, this physical principle can be independently affected by skin tone [7,12]. Moreover, it is known that oximeters' original validation was not performed on a diverse population [15]. Literature provides evidence that these devices measure the blood oxygen saturation differently across subpopulations [15,20]. Sjoding et al. [20] found that Black patients experienced nearly triple hidden hypoxemia cases compared to White patients when using pulse oximetry measurements (SpO_2) instead of arterial oxygen saturation in arterial blood gas (SaO_2). These discrepancies were associated with inequities in oxygen therapies, subsequently higher organ dysfunction scores, and increased mortality rates among subpopulations [22]. And still, existing devices are likely to keep being used in a myriad of environments while no better devices are developed and regulated [5].

Although the impact of pulse oximetry bias on patient outcomes is well-documented, its effect on downstream ML models using these biased measurements remains unknown. This study aims to address the question: *How can we assess whether a model's performance and fairness are affected by a feature encoding racial bias?* Utilizing counterfactual thinking and the pulse oximetry use case, we aim to develop a framework to evaluate the impact of medical device bias on downstream ML tasks. The main contributions of this paper are:

- **Counterfactual approach:** We introduce a novel methodological framework that leverages counterfactual thinking to analyze the impact of medical device bias on downstream machine learning performance and fairness across subgroups;

- **Comprehensive evaluation:** We conduct a wide array of experiments using the pulse oximetry bias use case, across three different clinical prediction tasks, and two different ML models. We utilize the blood-gas linked dataset (BOLD) [14] as a test-bed, including data from MIMIC-III [10], MIMIC-IV [9], and eICU-CRD [17].

Our work can be extended to other medical devices and databases, providing a useful approach for researchers examining algorithmic bias in health ML. The code developed in this study is publicly available in a GitHub repository[1].

2   Methodology

2.1   Counterfactual Approach

We designed our experiments to compare a "perfect world", where pulse oximetry bias does not exist - a measure that SaO_2, the blood-gas reading, can provide - to the "actual world", where pulse oximetry bias affects certain subgroups of patients - as measured by SpO_2. Under this counterfactual design, the former can be interpreted as a "control", and the latter as the "treatment". In a ML setting, this necessitates keeping all other variables ("confounders") - train and test split; remaining features; classification task; and evaluation metric - the same for both groups, ensuring that the device used to measure arterial O_2 saturation is the sole varying factor (Fig. 1).

Finding "counterfactuals" in real-world data is particularly challenging in the medical domain because no two patients are inherently the same, making it difficult to account for confounding factors. Therefore, we employed BOLD - a blood-gas and oximetry linked dataset - where SaO_2 and SpO_2 are paired per patient. As each patient of this dataset has both measures nearly simultaneously, we can control for all other variables and assess the impact of pulse oximetry bias for each patient, in terms of ML performance.

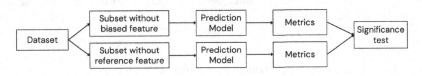

Fig. 1. Assessment of the impact of medical device bias on downstream ML.

2.2   Dataset

BOLD was created by harmonizing three Electronic Health Record databases (MIMIC-III, MIMIC-IV, eICU-CRD), comprising ICU stays of U.S. patients [14]. It contains paired pulse oximetry readings (SpO_2) and preceding arterial blood

---

[1] https://github.com/InesAMar/PulseOxBias.

gas measurements (SaO_2), acquired within a 5-minute interval. Pairs with values between 70% and 100% are included. Patient characteristics, vital signs, laboratory values, and Sequential Organ Failure Assessment (SOFA) scores [11] are time-aligned with the SaO_2 sample. To augment our sample size for this study, we extended BOLD beyond the first pair of measurements per hospitalization, to include all possible pairs.

2.3   Feature Selection and Preprocessing

The respiratory SOFA (rSOFA) score was computed by the difference between the overall SOFA score and the sum of the remaining individual scores (coagulation, liver, cardiovascular, central nervous system and renal). Features with clinical relevance were manually selected by a physician author (AIW) [8, 21, 23]. These included demographics: age and sex; comorbidities; vital signs: blood pressure, heart rate, respiratory rate, and temperature; laboratory test values: albumin, anion gap, bicarbonate, blood urea nitrogen, creatinine, glucose, hemoglobin, lactate, platelet count, potassium, red blood cell count, red cell distribution width, and sodium; and SOFA scores: overall, respiratory, and cardiovascular. Missing vital signs and laboratory values were imputed as the mid-point of the normal range [1, 13].

2.4   Machine Learning

Predictions were performed at the time of a (SpO_2, SaO_2), based on past features as described above and targeting outcomes in the next 24 h. A stratified 10-fold cross-validation strategy (to divide between train and test sets) was performed to evaluate the model's consistency across folds and improve the robustness of the results. This approach ensures that no patient would simultaneously be in both splits. Three binary classification tasks were studied: in-hospital mortality, future rSOFA score (1 if $\geq$ 1 point, 0 otherwise), and future increased SOFA score (1 if increasing by at least two points [19], 0 otherwise). Logistic regression (LR) and XGBoost classifier were fit and assessed. Their performance was evaluated with the area under the receiver operating curve (AUROC), recall, F1-score, and accuracy.

2.5   Disparity Axes and Statistical Inference

The aforementioned evaluation metrics were computed across different subgroups of patients, according to different disparity axes:

- **Race and ethnicity:** grouped into the following categories: "Asian", "Black", "Hispanic or Latino", "White" and "Other or Unknown". This variable is used as a surrogate for skin tone, the hypothesized root cause of bias [7].
- **Magnitude of Bias:** grouped into four non-overlapping bins: < -3%, between -3% and 0%, between 0% and 3%, and $\geq$ 3%. This is a marker for patients who actually have faulty pulse oximetry readings and, therefore, are "at risk" (or not).

Table 1. Patient Characteristics of the Study Cohort (IQR, Interquartile Range).

	Asian	Black	Hispanic or Latino	Other	White
n	605	3397	1448	2823	25979
Sex Female, n (%)	253 (41.8)	1613 (47.5)	661 (45.6)	1142 (40.5)	11251 (43.3)
Age, median [IQR]	66.0 [54.0,78.0]	61.0 [51.0,71.0]	67.5 [53.0,78.0]	65.0 [52.0,75.0]	67.0 [57.0,77.0]
In-Hospital Mortality, n (%)	115 (19.0)	589 (17.3)	280 (19.3)	501 (17.7)	4528 (17.4)
Hidden Hypoxemia, n (%)	15 (2.5)	129 (3.8)	40 (2.8)	71 (2.5)	722 (2.8)
Comorbidity Score, median [IQR]	4.0 [2.0,6.0]	4.0 [2.0,6.0]	4.0 [2.0,6.0]	4.0 [2.0,6.0]	4.0 [2.0,6.0]
SOFA Past Overall 24hr, median [IQR]	5.0 [2.0,8.0]	5.0 [3.0,8.0]	5.0 [3.0,8.0]	6.0 [3.0,8.0]	5.0 [3.0,8.0]
SOFA Future Overall 24hr, median [IQR]	4.0 [2.0,7.0]	5.0 [3.0,8.0]	5.0 [3.0,7.0]	5.0 [3.0,8.0]	5.0 [3.0,7.0]
N pairs (per hosp. adm.), median [IQR]	2.0 [1.0,5.0]	2.0 [1.0,5.0]	2.0 [1.0,6.0]	2.0 [1.0,5.0]	2.0 [1.0,5.0]

- **Hidden Hypoxemia (HH):** defined as having $SaO_2 < 88\%$ and $SpO_2 \geq 88\%$ [22]. This represents patients who are most affected by pulse oximetry bias.

Two-sided paired t-tests were performed to compare the performance of the SpO_2 vs. SaO_2 models, fold by fold.

3   Results

3.1   Dataset Description

The extended version of BOLD contained 163,396 pairs, representing 34,252 patients described in Table 1. Positivity rates for the classification tasks revealed class imbalances: in-hospital mortality at 24.0%; future rSOFA score at 41.6%; and SOFA score increase at 23.8%.

3.2   Experiments

Different Model Architectures: The two model architectures had similar results, but XGBoost generally outperformed LR. Only XGBoost results will be presented in detail.

Across Racial Groups: By clustering the results across race and ethnicity groups, several situations were identified as significantly different by the

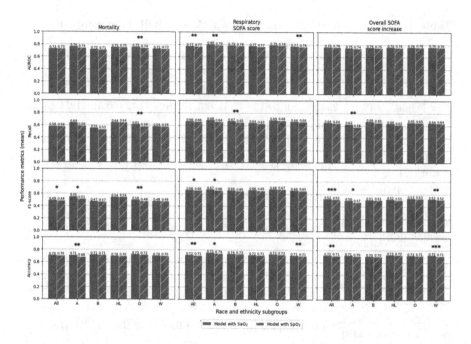

Fig. 2. Mean value of the XGBoost performance metrics across race and ethnicity subgroups. Significant differences between SpO_2 and SaO_2 models are identified with: "*", for p-values ≤ 0.05; "**", for p-values ≤ 0.01; or "* * *", for p-values ≤ 0.001. A: Asian; B: Black; HL: Hispanic or Latino; O: Other; W: White.

XGBoost model, as shown in Fig. 2. For example, Asian patients had a degradation from 0.55 to 0.51 in F1-Score ($P < 0.05$), when using SpO_2 as a feature, a trend that was verified across metrics and tasks for these patients.

Across Magnitude of Bias: Figure 3 represents the bias effect on XGBoost prediction performance when disparities were divided into four bins, according to the difference between SpO_2 and SaO_2 values. Accuracy is significantly higher in the SaO_2 model when SpO_2 underestimates O_2, and vice-versa. On the other hand, recall is significantly higher in the SaO_2 model when SpO_2 overestimates O_2, and vice-versa. Differences in performance are exacerbated by higher disparities.

Across HH Groups: Results show that accuracy is significantly lower and recall is significantly higher to the SaO_2 model in patients with HH (Fig. 4). These findings agree with the ones above. In the class 0 group, significant differences were associated with higher performance of the SaO_2 model, which is in line with the results from the full cohort (Fig. 2).

The aforementioned trends are consistent across tasks, where groups that are more "at risk" exhibit ML performance degradation in models using SpO_2, as opposed to SaO_2. AUROC results often present marginal differences in performance. However, the model with SaO_2 usually attains higher values. Results

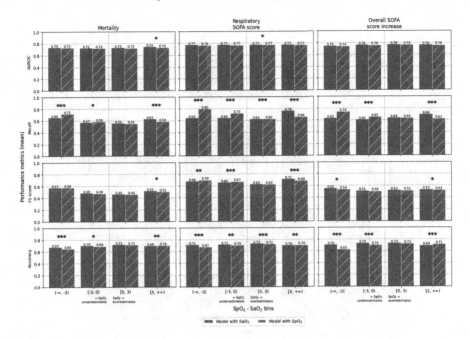

Fig. 3. Mean value of the XGBoost performance metrics across disparity groups. Significant differences between SaO_2 and SpO_2 models are identified with: "$*$", for p-values ≤ 0.05; "$**$", for p-values ≤ 0.01; or "$* * *$", for p-values ≤ 0.001.

in Figs. 2, 3 and 4 can be significantly different where the means appear equal because the performance metrics means were rounded to 2 decimal places.

4   Discussion and Conclusion

This work presents a counterfactual approach to quantify the impact of medical device bias in ML performance. Empirically applied to the pulse oximetry use case, we compare two otherwise identical ML models, differing only in their use of either unbiased SaO_2 (blood-gas) data or biased SpO_2 (pulse oximetry) data. By isolating the method of O_2 measurement, we directly target the quantification of bias. Evaluated using BOLD (N = 163,396), we conducted experiments on three binary classification tasks.

In our ML tasks, the positive classes correspond to adverse health outcomes, while the negative class represents a less sick population. O_2 overestimation by SpO_2 ($[3, +\infty)$ disparity group in Fig. 3) may increase correct predictions for the negative class, contributing to higher accuracy. However, this also leads to a decrease in the correct predictions for the positive class and, consequently, in recall. Misidentifying positive cases due to biased measurements from medical devices could exacerbate disparities in healthcare diagnoses and treatment access. HH was higher for Black patients - 3.8% (see Table 1), suggesting that models with SpO_2 would have worse performance. Although differences were verified, they were not statistically significant. An additional analysis would have

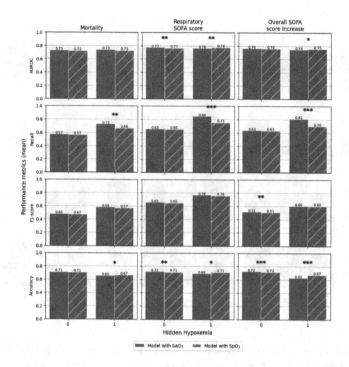

Fig. 4. Mean value of the XGBoost performance metrics between patients with consistent SaO_2 and SpO_2 values (above or equal to 88%) - class 0 - and the ones with hidden hypoxemia - class 1. Significant differences between SaO_2 and SpO_2 models are identified with: "$*$", for p-values ≤ 0.05; "$**$", for p-values ≤ 0.01; or "$***$", for p-values ≤ 0.001.

to be performed across race and ethnicity groups. The experiments across racial and ethnic groups did not show systematic differences in the remaining groups, as expected. In fact, using race and ethnicity as a disparity axis is debatable, as it is often considered a "social construct", and herein used an imperfect surrogate for skin tone, the hypothesized root cause of bias [7]. The analyses across the degree of bias and HH present more occurrences of ML performance degradation.

Overall, our results mirror clinical scenarios where biased pulse oximetry readings provide clinicians with false reassurance of patients' oxygen levels. A similar degradation happened in ML models, with bias leading to more false negatives in predicting adverse outcomes. These results reinforce previous reports in the literature [6,22], suggesting that biased pulse oximetry readings not only lead to adverse outcomes and inequities in healthcare diagnoses but have the potential to exacerbate existing disparities if blindly fed to ML models.

The developed framework has the potential to be a valuable tool for advancing more just ML solutions in healthcare, revolving around bias and fairness. Its inherent counterfactual approach enhances the transparency and explainability of performance degradation across patient subgroups. Besides, our framework is easy to understand and use, as shown by our experiments with pulse oximetry data across three different clinical prediction tasks and two different machine learning algorithms. It brings a faster and more interesting approach for researchers dealing with algorithmic bias in health ML. Additionally, given that this methodology is agnostic to the task and device, it can be easily applied to other use cases, such as temporal thermometry, which has also been found to exhibit racial bias due to similar underlying physical mechanisms (infrared light) being independently affected by skin pigmentation [3].

Our framework presents several limitations, as it depends on the availability of both a faulty and a gold-standard measurement. While BOLD provided a suitable test-bed, this may not be the case for all measurements from medical devices. Moreover, BOLD retrospectively aligns blood-gas and oximetry data, leveraging the vast amounts of information in Electronic Health Records, but this process can introduce errors and noise. Future work should explore the applicability of the presented methods in other settings to further validate their utility and versatility, potentially outside of healthcare, and investigate the integration of these methodologies in post-deployment AI. Naturally, we also expect this framework to contribute towards developing solutions to mitigate the effect of medical device bias in ML models within a real-world clinical setting.

Prospect of Application: Hospital systems should consider similar approaches before algorithm deployment. Further use cases need to be identified, as not all sources of bias allow for a counterfactual approach. It would be interesting to continue the study on medical devices that rely on light sensors, more specifically infrared light, such as temporal thermometers.

Acknowledgements. This work has received funding from the Portuguese Foundation for Science and Technology (FCT) through the Ph.D. Grant "2020.06434.BD".

Disclosure of Interests. The authors have no competing interests in the paper.

References

1. Laboratory reference ranges in healthy adults. https://emedicine.medscape.com/article/2172316-overview?form=fpf. Accessed 12 June 2024
2. Balagopalan, A., et al.: Machine learning for healthcare that matters: reorienting from technical novelty to equitable impact. PLOS Digit. Health **3**(4), e0000474 (2024)
3. Bhavani, S.V., Wiley, Z., Verhoef, P.A., Coopersmith, C.M., Ofotokun, I.: Racial differences in detection of fever using temporal vs oral temperature measurements in hospitalized patients. JAMA **328**(9), 885–886 (2022)
4. Charpignon, M.L., et al.: Critical bias in critical care devices. Crit. Care Clin. **39**(4), 795–813 (2023)
5. Dempsey, K., Lindsay, M., Tcheng, J.E., Wong, A.K.I.: The high price of equity in pulse oximetry: a cost evaluation and need for interim solutions. medRxiv (2023)
6. Fawzy, A., et al.: Racial and ethnic discrepancy in pulse oximetry and delayed identification of treatment eligibility among patients with COVID-19. JAMA Intern. Med. **182**(7), 730–738 (2022)

7. Hao, S., et al.: Utility of skin tone on pulse oximetry in critically ill patients: a prospective cohort study. medRxiv (2024)
8. Hempel, L., Sadeghi, S., Kirsten, T.: Prediction of intensive care unit length of stay in the MIMIC-IV dataset. Appl. Sci. **13**(12), 6930 (2023)
9. Johnson, A.E., et al.: MIMIC-IV, a freely accessible electronic health record dataset. Sci. Data **10**(1), 1 (2023)
10. Johnson, A.E., et al.: MIMIC-III, a freely accessible critical care database. Sci. Data **3**(1), 1–9 (2016)
11. Jones, A.E., Trzeciak, S., Kline, J.A.: The sequential organ failure assessment score for predicting outcome in patients with severe sepsis and evidence of hypoperfusion at the time of emergency department presentation. Crit. Care Med. **37**(5), 1649–1654 (2009)
12. Jubran, A.: Pulse oximetry. Crit. Care **19**(1) (2015)
13. Matos, J., Struja, T., Gallifant, J., Charpignon, M.L., Cardoso, J.S., Celi, L.A.: Shining light on dark skin: pulse oximetry correction models. In: 2023 IEEE 7th Portuguese Meeting on Bioengineering (ENBENG), pp. 211–214. IEEE (2023)
14. Matos, J., et al.: Bold: blood-gas and oximetry linked dataset. Sci. Data **11**(1), 535 (2024)
15. Moran-Thomas, A.: How a popular medical device encodes racial bias. Boston Rev. **8**(5), 2020 (2020)
16. Obermeyer, Z., Powers, B., Vogeli, C., Mullainathan, S.: Dissecting racial bias in an algorithm used to manage the health of populations. Science **366**(6464), 447–453 (2019)
17. Pollard, T.J., Johnson, A.E., Raffa, J.D., Celi, L.A., Mark, R.G., Badawi, O.: The eICU collaborative research database, a freely available multi-center database for critical care research. Sci. Data **5**(1), 1–13 (2018)
18. Sauer, C.M., Chen, L.C., Hyland, S.L., Girbes, A., Elbers, P., Celi, L.A.: Leveraging electronic health records for data science: common pitfalls and how to avoid them. Lancet Digit. Health **4**(12), E893–E898 (2022). https://doi.org/10.1016/S2589-7500(22)00154-6, Open Access, Published: 22 September 2022
19. Singer, M., et al.: The third international consensus definitions for sepsis and septic shock (sepsis-3). JAMA **315**(8), 801–810 (2016)
20. Sjoding, M.W., Dickson, R.P., Iwashyna, T.J., Gay, S.E., Valley, T.S.: Racial bias in pulse oximetry measurement. N. Engl. J. Med. **383**(25), 2477–2478 (2020)
21. Sun, Y., He, Z., Ren, J., Wu, Y.: Prediction model of in-hospital mortality in intensive care unit patients with cardiac arrest: a retrospective analysis of MIMIC-IV database based on machine learning. BMC Anesthesiol. **23**(1), 178 (2023)
22. Wong, A.K.I., et al.: Analysis of discrepancies between pulse oximetry and arterial oxygen saturation measurements by race and ethnicity and association with organ dysfunction and mortality. JAMA Netw. Open **4**(11), e2131674–e2131674 (2021)
23. Zhang, Y., Hu, J., Hua, T., Zhang, J., Zhang, Z., Yang, M.: Development of a machine learning-based prediction model for sepsis-associated delirium in the intensive care unit. Sci. Rep. **13**(1), 12697 (2023)

Normative Modeling with Focal Loss and Adversarial Autoencoders for Alzheimer's Disease Diagnosis and Biomarker Identification

Songlin Zhao[1], Rong Zhou[1], Yu Zhang[2], Yong Chen[3], and Lifang He[1(✉)]

[1] Department of Computer Science and Engineering, Lehigh University, Bethlehem, PA, USA
lih319@lehigh.edu
[2] Department of Bioengineering, Lehigh University, Bethlehem, PA, USA
[3] Department of Biostatistics, Epidemiology and Informatics, University of Pennsylvania, Philadelphia, PA, USA

Abstract. In this paper, we introduce a novel normative modeling approach that incorporates focal loss and adversarial autoencoders (FAAE) for Alzheimer's Disease (AD) diagnosis and biomarker identification. Our method is an end-to-end approach that embeds an adversarial focal loss discriminator within the autoencoder structure, specifically designed to effectively target and capture more complex and challenging cases. We first use the enhanced autoencoder to create a normative model based on data from healthy control (HC) individuals. We then apply this model to estimate total and regional neuroanatomical deviation in AD patients. Through extensive experiments on the OASIS-3 and ADNI datasets, our approach significantly outperforms previous state-of-the-art methods. This advancement not only streamlines the detection process but also provides a greater insight into the biomarker potential for AD. Our code can be found at https://github.com/soz223/FAAE.

Keywords: Normative modeling · Focal loss · Adversarial learning · Autoencoder · Alzheimer's Disease

1 Introduction

Alzheimer's Disease (AD) is a progressive neurodegenerative disorder characterized by brain dysfunction, presenting significant challenges in both diagnosis and treatment due to individual heterogeneity. Early and accurate detection of AD is crucial for effective patient management and treatment planning. Traditional diagnostic methods primarily rely on clinical assessments and neuroimaging techniques, which can be time-consuming and subjective. To address these challenges, there is an increasing trend toward developing automated, data-driven methods for AD diagnosis and biomarker analysis.

S. Wu et al. (Eds.): AMAI 2024, LNCS 15384, pp. 231–240, 2025.
https://doi.org/10.1007/978-3-031-82007-6_22

Normative modeling is a powerful statistical framework for clinical assessments that compares individual deviations against a normative range derived from a healthy control (HC) population [12]. This method captures variability by comparing with a standard reference model, elucidating disease heterogeneity and uncovering abnormalities. Given the imbalanced nature of medical data [23], where models often bias toward larger groups, normative modeling effectively avoids this by using only one group for training. Recent advancements in deep learning, especially autoencoders (AEs), have further advanced normative modeling. Various methods have been proposed, such as [1,2,8,10,14,15,18,21,24].

Drawing on insights from previous studies [15,21], we leverage recent developments in the use of adversarial autoencoders (AAEs) for normative modeling. Adversarial learning enhances AEs by aligning the aggregated posterior with the prior, thus minimizing divergence between the model's prior and posterior for improved accuracy. Despite these advances, a notable challenge in existing models is their reduced effectiveness in learning from complex samples, particularly in contexts with uneven data distribution, where some data samples are inherently easier for the model to learn, while others pose significant challenges due to their complexity. This discrepancy often leads to adversarial learning models focusing on simpler patterns that are easier to replicate, neglecting the intricate and complex patterns in the more difficult samples. Additionally, the emphasis on minimizing divergence between the model's prior and posterior can result in reduced sensitivity to these nuanced variations, thereby affecting the model's overall ability to adapt and generalize effectively across varied data samples. This situation highlights the critical need for innovative approaches that can effectively address these specific challenges in normative modeling.

In this paper, we introduce a novel normative modeling approach that leverages focal loss and adversarial autoencoders (FAAE) to enhance the detection of AD. By combining these elements, our approach effectively focuses training on challenging cases, preventing easy examples from dominating the training process. We present the results of our extensive testing on the OASIS-3 and ADNI, which are comprehensive and widely used datasets in AD research. Our findings indicate that FAAE-based normative model significantly outperforms previous state-of-the-art methods in AD detection in terms of AUROC (Area Under the Receiver Operating Characteristic Curve score) and sensitivity scores. By analyzing the contrast in deviation plots for AD compared to HC, we can gain a deeper understanding of disease heterogeneity, offering a promising framework for clinical diagnosis and biomarker discovery. This strategic integration bridges the gap between existing methods and the untapped potential of focal loss in normative modeling, setting a new precedent in the field.

2   Materials and Methods

2.1   Dataset Collection and Processing

In this study, we use fMRI data from Open Access Series of Imaging Studies 3 (OASIS-3) [9] and Alzheimer's Disease Neuroimaging Initiative (ADNI) [13]

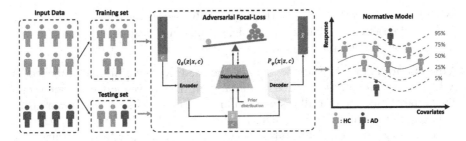

Fig. 1. An overview of our proposed FAAE.

databases. OASIS-3 comprises a total of 1497 samples with 21 AD samples and 1476 HC samples, and ADNI comprises a total of 579 samples with 141 AD samples and 438 HC samples.

For both OASIS-3 and ADNI datasets, we follow the standard procedures to preprocess each sample using the fMRIPrep pipeline [3], including intensity nonuniformity correction, skull stripping, spatial normalization, FSL-based segmentation, boundary-based registration, slice-time correction, susceptibility distortion correction, resampling in both original and standard spaces, and motion artifact removal using ICA-AROMA. To handle data collected from multiple periods, we treated the data for each 100-day interval as a sample, assuming no significant change during that period. Data acquisition during a 6-minute session (164 volumes) employs a 16-channel head coil scanner (TR $= 2.2$ s, TE $= 27$ ms, FOV $= 240 \times 240$ mm, FA $= 90°$).

In order to generate regional features for each sample, we first average the voxel-level BOLD time series into 100 regions-of-interest (ROIs) for each time point based on the Schaefer-100 parcellation [17]. These averaged time series are then further averaged over time points to create ROI-based input features. Following [15,21], we incorporate key demographic variables including age, gender, and intracranial volume (ICV) as covariates to control their potential impact on the results. Utilizing the same preprocessing steps results in a 22-dimensional covariate vector for each sample.

2.2   Normative Modeling

Overview. Figure 1 presents an overview of our proposed FAAE architecture and process for normative modeling. In the training phase, the model is trained only on the HC group, thus constructing a normative range of healthy brain patterns in each brain region. In the testing phase, we calculate a thorough evaluation of each patient's deviation from the established normative range, facilitating precise identification of AD and its associated ROIs.

We use an autoencoder as our model architecture. The backbone module establishes a normative range by training with a dataset of healthy control (HC) individuals. The encoder condenses features into a latent representation, while the decoder reconstructs the input from this latent space, enabling the model to understand healthy brain patterns. An adversarial focal loss discriminator is then integrated to enhance the model's sensitivity in detecting complex AD cases. Below, we detail each module.

Autoencoder. In this study, we employ the conditional variational autoencoder (CVAE) as the foundational architecture for our normative modeling framework. This type of autoencoder allows us to influence the model's reconstruction using demographic variables such as age, gender, and ICV. Moreover, it is capable of generating a probabilistic latent space representation, which is crucial for effectively capturing the inherent variability and uncertainty prevalent in the data for normative modeling.

Our model architecture consists of three primary components: the encoder, the latent distribution, and the decoder. The encoder compresses high-dimensional data into a compact, low-dimensional latent space. The latent distribution focuses on understanding the data's distribution through its mean (μ) and variance (σ), which define the probabilistic contours of the latent space. These parameters are essential for generating new data samples, useful for augmenting datasets, especially in cases of rare conditions or imbalanced datasets common in normative modeling. In our study, we use standard random sampling within the latent space to facilitate this generative process as follows:

$$\mathbf{z} = \boldsymbol{\mu} + \boldsymbol{\sigma} \odot \boldsymbol{\varepsilon}, \quad \boldsymbol{\varepsilon} \sim \mathcal{N}(0,1). \tag{1}$$

where $\mathbf{z}$ is the latent representation obtained from the encoder and $\odot$ denotes the element-wise product. This sampling strategy is instrumental in maintaining the balance between data representation accuracy and the flexibility needed for effective normative modeling. Subsequently, the decoder reconstructs the data back to its original high-dimensional form, starting from this probabilistically encoded latent representation. Through this intricate process of encoding, probabilistic modeling in the latent space, and decoding, our model architecture ensures that the most salient features of the data are preserved and accurately represented. The objective function can be formulated as:

$$L_{\mathrm{CVAE}} = \mathbb{E}[\log P_\phi(\mathbf{x}|\mathbf{z},\mathbf{c})] - KL(Q_\theta(\mathbf{z}|\mathbf{x},\mathbf{c})||P_\phi(\mathbf{z}|\mathbf{c})), \tag{2}$$

where $\mathbf{x}$ represents the input features and $\mathbf{c}$ the confounding variables. The functions $Q_\theta(\mathbf{z}|\mathbf{x},\mathbf{c})$, $P_\phi(\mathbf{x}|\mathbf{z},\mathbf{c})$, and $P_\phi(\mathbf{z}|\mathbf{c})$ correspond to the encoder, decoder, and prior distribution, respectively, with ϕ and θ denoting their parameters. The term $\mathbb{E}[\log P_\phi(\mathbf{x}|\mathbf{z},\mathbf{c})]$ measures the reconstruction error, indicating how closely the output matches the input data. The term Kullback-Leibler (KL) divergence, $KL(Q_\theta(\mathbf{z}|\mathbf{x},\mathbf{c})||P_\phi(\mathbf{z}|\mathbf{c}))$, assesses the accuracy of the distribution $Q_\theta(\mathbf{z}|\mathbf{x},\mathbf{c})$.

Adversarial Focal-Loss Discriminator. Building on the insights from prior studies [15,21], we integrate adversarial learning into the CVAE-based framework described above. This combination enhances the model's reconstruction loss by incorporating the perceptual-level representation capabilities of the discriminator, a key component in adversarial learning.

In adversarial learning, the system has two components: the discriminator and the generator. The discriminator distinguishes between samples from the prior distribution and the CVAE's latent distribution. The generator (also the decoder) produces samples to fool the discriminator. This interaction improves the quality and accuracy of the generated samples. The objective function can be expressed as follows:

$$L_{\text{Adv}} = \mathbb{E}[\log D(\mathbf{z}|\mathbf{c})] + \mathbb{E}[\log(1 - D(Q_\theta(\mathbf{z}|\mathbf{x}, \mathbf{c})))], \qquad (3)$$

where $D(\mathbf{z}|\mathbf{c})$ is the discriminator, and $Q_\theta(\mathbf{x}|\mathbf{z}, \mathbf{c}))$ is the generator, which in this particular case, acts as the encoder role.

Recent research [11] indicates that discriminators in adversarial learning may sometimes struggle with hard samples, which are particularly challenging for the model to learn. This can impact the model's ability to adapt and generalize effectively across diverse data samples. To address this issue, we introduce focal loss into the adversarial objective function. Focal loss modifies the standard cross-entropy loss by adjusting the weighting of samples within the loss function, offering significant advantages for handling imbalanced datasets and effectively targeting hard-to-learn samples [4]. To elaborate, the focal loss is mathematically defined as follows:

$$FL(p) = \begin{cases} -\alpha(1 - p)^\gamma \log(p), & y = 1 \\ -(1 - \alpha)p^\gamma \log(1 - p), & y = 0 \end{cases} \qquad (4)$$

where p denotes the predicted probability of the true label. The parameter α serves as a scaling factor, while γ is employed to amplify the focus on learning from hard samples, where the model is more likely to make errors. Leveraging this formulation in Eq. (4), we adapt the adversarial learning loss to take the following form:

$$\begin{aligned} L_{\text{AdvFL}} = \; & \mathbb{E}\left[-\alpha(1 - D(\mathbf{z}|\mathbf{c}))^\gamma \log D(\mathbf{z}|\mathbf{c})\right] \\ & + \mathbb{E}\left[-(1 - \alpha)(D(Q_\theta(\mathbf{z}|\mathbf{x}, \mathbf{c})))^\gamma \log(1 - D(Q_\theta(\mathbf{z}|\mathbf{x}, \mathbf{c})))\right]. \end{aligned} \qquad (5)$$

This extension to the adversarial learning framework integrates the principles of focal loss, optimizing our model's focus on the more challenging samples encountered while training our one-class normative model on the HC group. Specifically, the parameter α plays a key role in balancing the weights of the discriminator and generator, thus minimizing the bias towards prevalent healthy patterns. Meanwhile, γ increases the model's sensitivity to subtle variations, a crucial aspect for identifying early-stage or less apparent anomalies. This approach enhances the model's ability to discern nuanced deviations, which is key for effective normative modeling in medical applications.

Final Loss. Combining Eqs. (2) and (5), the total loss for training our FAAE model is expressed as follows:

$$L_{\text{FAAE}} = L_{\text{CVAE}} + L_{\text{AdvFL}}. \qquad (6)$$

Deviation Metric. We employ the standard mean square error (MSE) as a performance function to compute the deviation between the input data and the reconstructed output, defined as: $D_{\mathrm{MSE}} = \frac{\|\mathbf{x}-\hat{\mathbf{x}}\|_2^2}{n}$, where $\hat{\mathbf{x}}$ represents the reconstruction of the input data $\mathbf{x}$ as generated by the decoder, and n denotes the dimension of $\mathbf{x}$, which is set to 100 in this study.

3   Experiments and Results

Experimental Settings. We split the data into a training set, comprising 80% of the randomly selected HC samples, and a test set, consisting of the remaining HC samples and all AD samples. We follow the same setting as [21] to normalize the training and test sets, as well as neural network architectures, and standard parameter settings. To ensure robust results, we employ bootstrap resampling, repeating the process 30 times and reporting the average results.

Competing Methods. To evaluate our proposed FAAE, we conduct comparisons with five deep normative modeling methods: vanilla AE [1], VAE [7], CVAE [19], ACVAE [21], and AAE [16]. Each method represents a unique normative modeling approach. For these methods, we utilize their publicly available codes and apply the same parameter settings as our experiments to ensure a fair and consistent comparison.

Evaluation Metrics. Measures of performance included the area under the receiver operating characteristic (AUROC), sensitivity, and specificity, which are commonly used in disease diagnosis. A highly sensitive test ensures that patients with the disease are correctly identified, while a highly specific test ensures that patients without the disease are accurately excluded. The AUROC score combines both sensitivity and specificity, providing a single metric that reflects the overall diagnostic performance of a test. A higher AUROC score indicates better discrimination between patients with and without the disease.

Table 1. Testing performance comparison of different models.

Methods	OASIS-3 AUROC	Sensitivity	Specificity	ADNI AUROC	Sensitivity	Specificity
AE	58.83 ± 2.21	55.24 ± 13.67	61.03 ± 11.29	65.70 ± 2.50	66.60 ± 5.08	66.93 ± 5.76
VAE	61.54 ± 1.82	65.71 ± 5.55	56.47 ± 5.40	59.36 ± 2.61	55.46 ± 2.10	**72.39 ± 3.52**
CVAE	62.81 ± 1.26	68.10 ± 5.65	56.64 ± 3.42	62.11 ± 1.17	56.60 ± 7.40	72.39 ± 8.16
ACVAE	64.64 ± 2.53	64.76 ± 17.97	61.46 ± 13.84	**67.82 ± 0.98**	67.38 ± 1.74	64.41 ± 1.51
AAE	55.94 ± 3.05	44.76 ± 21.53	69.15 ± 20.47	64.57 ± 2.65	60.43 ± 10.35	**72.46 ± 9.65**
FAAE	**68.56 ± 3.98**	**70.00 ± 12.06**	61.76 ± 11.99	66.15 ± 1.17	**72.20 ± 5.30**	60.50 ± 4.74

Results. Table 1 shows the performance of six comparison methods on both OASIS-3 and ADNI datasets. From the results, we can observe that our method

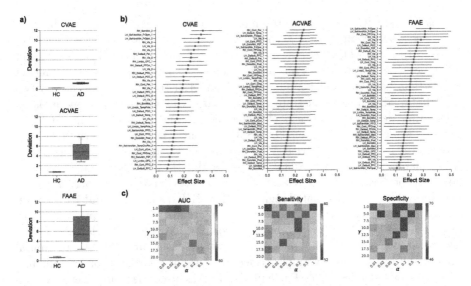

Fig. 2. (a)–(b) Observed mean deviation and effect size of HC vs. AD on OASIS-3 for top-3 methods, respectively. (c) Parameter sensitivity on OASIS-3.

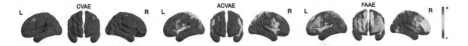

Fig. 3. Comparative analysis of average regional-deviation values of AD across top-3 methods on OASIS-3 dataset.

significantly outperforms other methods in terms of sensitivity, while also achieving higher or comparable AUROC scores. In most medical applications, high sensitivity is crucial as it minimizes false negatives, thereby reducing the risk of missing disease cases.

Notably, FAAE demonstrates a marked improvement in sensitivity compared to adversarial learning-based methods like ACVAE and AAE. While adversarial learning typically yields higher specificity in AD detection, as evidenced by AAE's top scores, it significantly falls short in sensitivity. This shortfall is likely due to a bias towards easy samples in adversarial learning, which is especially prevalent in datasets with a dominant healthy class. Confirming our hypothesis, FAAE shows enhanced sensitivity, underscoring the role of focal loss in effectively classifying minority cases in imbalanced datasets. Another observation is that although AAE has high specificity, their sensitivity is low. The reason behind this is that AAE applies adversarial learning on an imbalanced dataset, which leads to overfitting.

Moreover, we use OASIS-3 as an example to illustrate our analysis of model performance and regional brain impacts. Figure 2(a) shows the deviation boxplots for top-3 methods in the test set, which indicates that FAAE can better distinguish HC and AD. Furthermore, we investigate the impact of different brain regions by computing 95% confidence intervals for the effect size differences between HC and AD, where an interval not containing 0 indicates a significant difference. Figure 2(b) shows our method identifies more regions with significant effects than baseline models, indicating its superior robustness and sensitivity.

Additionally, we demonstrate regional variations for the top-3 methods by calculating deviations between expected norms and observed values in AD. Figure 3 shows the results on OASIS-3. Regions with higher deviations indicate a stronger association with AD. Notably, FAAE identifies critical areas like LH_Default_PFC_5 (prefrontal cortex) and RH_Cont_PFCmp_1 (medial posterior prefrontal cortex), consistent with previous studies [6,20,22], and uncovers additional AD-related regions such as RH_Default_pCunPCC_2 (precuneus posterior cingulate cortex), RH_Cont_PFCl_2 (lateral prefrontal cortex), and RH_Cont_Cing_1 (cingulate cortex). On the ADNI dataset, FAAE also identifies critical brain regions such as LH_Default_PFC_6 (prefrontal cortex) and RH_Cont_PCFmp_2 (medial posterior prefrontal cortex), aligning with previous studies [5,6]. Particularly, FAAE discovers somatosensory dysfunction in RH_SomMot_5 (primary somatosensory cortex). These findings, highlighting both known and novel regions linked to AD, could be crucial for identifying potential biomarkers in Alzheimer's research.

Parameter Analysis. Figure 2(c) demonstrates the parameter sensitivity analysis of FAAE with respect to the focal loss parameters α and γ on OASIS-3. The results reveal stable AUROC performance across most settings, with a noticeable increase in AUROC values at higher γ levels, particularly $\gamma = 15$ and $\gamma = 17.5$ combined with specific α values. Sensitivity to α and γ is evident, with higher detection rates of actual AD cases at increased γ, especially at $\gamma = 15$ and $\alpha = 0.2$. This underscores the importance of carefully balancing α and γ to optimize the model for medical diagnostics.

Sample Size Analysis. We investigate the effect of varying HC sample sizes in the training set. Table 2 presents the performance of our FAAE model on the ADNI dataset. All training samples are sampled from the 80% HC as in the experimental setting. Generally, increasing the number of HC samples in the training data enhanced model performance initially, but this improvement stabilized as the sample size continued to grow. For instance, AUROC improves from 65.98 ± 2.36 with 200 samples to 70.04 ± 1.86 with 1000 samples, with no significant improvement beyond that. Specificity follows a similar trend. Sensitivity increases from 65.20 ± 5.02 with 200 samples to 70.57 ± 4.06 with 600 samples, then slightly decreases to 68.35 ± 4.60 at 1400 samples.

Table 2. Performance as a function of the number of training samples.

Metrics	200	400	600	800	1000	1200	1400
AUROC	65.98 ± 2.36	67.73 ± 2.45	68.91 ± 3.12	69.05 ± 2.23	70.04 ± 1.86	69.85 ± 1.32	70.01 ± 1.59
Sensitivity	65.20 ± 5.02	65.39 ± 4.95	70.57 ± 4.06	70.71 ± 5.67	68.79 ± 4.88	68.32 ± 5.92	68.35 ± 4.60
Specificity	62.79 ± 3.66	64.84 ± 3.23	62.31 ± 4.72	60.91 ± 5.92	64.82 ± 3.55	64.73 ± 5.96	65.29 ± 5.05

4   Conclusions

This paper introduces an innovative normative modeling approach for Alzheimer's Disease (AD) diagnosis and biomarker identification. Our method combines an adversarial focal loss discriminator with an autoencoder framework, improving the detection of complex AD cases. By establishing a normative model based on healthy controls, we estimate neuroanatomical deviations in AD patients. Extensive validation on the OASIS-3 and ADNI datasets demonstrates that our approach significantly outperforms existing methods in AD detection, enhancing clinical sensitivity. Future research could expand this work by integrating multimodal data and advanced brain network analysis for a more comprehensive understanding and improved diagnostic precision.

Prospect of Application: Our FAAE-based normative modeling approach enhances AD diagnosis and biomarker discovery. It aids early detection, personalized treatment, and diagnostic interpretation in clinical settings. In research, it uncovers novel disease mechanisms, improving patient outcomes and advancing the understanding of neurodegenerative diseases.

Acknowledgments. This work is partially supported by the NSF grants (MRI-2215789, IIS-2319451), NIH grants (R21EY034179, R21AG080425, R21MH130956, R01MH129694), and Lehigh's grants under Accelerator (S00010293), CORE (001250), and FIG (FIGAWD35).

Disclosure of Interests. The authors have no competing interests to declare that are relevant to the content of this article.

References

1. Chamberland, M., et al.: Detecting microstructural deviations in individuals with deep diffusion MRI tractometry. Nat. Comput. Sci. **1**(9), 598–606 (2021)
2. Chen, X., Konukoglu, E.: Unsupervised detection of lesions in brain MRI using constrained adversarial auto-encoders. arXiv preprint arXiv:1806.04972 (2018)
3. Esteban, O., et al.: fMRIPrep: a robust preprocessing pipeline for functional MRI. Nat. Methods **16**(1), 111–116 (2019)
4. Gao, F., Zhu, J., Jiang, H., Niu, Z., Han, W., Yu, J.: Incremental focal loss GANs. Inf. Process. Manag. **57**(3), 102192 (2020)
5. Grady, C.L., McIntosh, A.R., Beig, S., Keightley, M.L., Burian, H., Black, S.E.: Evidence from functional neuroimaging of a compensatory prefrontal network in Alzheimer's disease. J. Neurosci. **23**(3), 986–993 (2003)
6. Jobson, D.D., Hase, Y., Clarkson, A.N., Kalaria, R.N.: The role of the medial prefrontal cortex in cognition, ageing and dementia. Brain Commun. **3**(3), fcab125 (2021)
7. Kingma, D.P., Welling, M.: Auto-encoding variational Bayes. arXiv preprint arXiv:1312.6114 (2013)
8. Kusner, M.J., Paige, B., Hernández-Lobato, J.M.: Grammar variational autoencoder. In: International Conference on Machine Learning, pp. 1945–1954. PMLR (2017)

9. LaMontagne, P.J., et al.: Oasis-3: longitudinal neuroimaging, clinical, and cognitive dataset for normal aging and Alzheimer disease. MedRxiv pp. 2019–12 (2019)

10. Lawry Aguila, A., Chapman, J., Janahi, M., Altmann, A.: Conditional VAEs for confound removal and normative modelling of neurodegenerative diseases. In: Wang, L., Dou, Q., Fletcher, P.T., Speidel, S., Li, S. (eds.) MICCAI 2022. LNCS, vol. 13431, pp. 430–440. Springer, Cham (2022). https://doi.org/10.1007/978-3-031-16431-6_41

11. Liu, C., Dong, X., Potter, M., Chang, H.M., Soni, R.: Adversarial focal loss: asking your discriminator for hard examples. arXiv preprint arXiv:2207.07739 (2022)

12. Marquand, A.F., Rezek, I., Buitelaar, J., Beckmann, C.F.: Understanding heterogeneity in clinical cohorts using normative models: beyond case-control studies. Biol. Psychiat. **80**(7), 552–561 (2016)

13. Mueller, S.G., et al.: The Alzheimer's disease neuroimaging initiative. Neuroimaging Clin. **15**(4), 869–877 (2005)

14. Pinaya, W.H., Mechelli, A., Sato, J.R.: Using deep autoencoders to identify abnormal brain structural patterns in neuropsychiatric disorders: a large-scale multisample study. Hum. Brain Mapp. **40**(3), 944–954 (2019)

15. Pinaya, W.H., et al.: Using normative modelling to detect disease progression in mild cognitive impairment and Alzheimer's disease in a cross-sectional multi-cohort study. Sci. Rep. **11**(1), 15746 (2021)

16. Pinaya, W.H., et al.: Normative modelling using deep autoencoders: a multi-cohort study on mild cognitive impairment and Alzheimer's disease. bioRxiv pp. 2020–02 (2020)

17. Schaefer, A., et al.: Local-global parcellation of the human cerebral cortex from intrinsic functional connectivity MRI. Cereb. Cortex **28**(9), 3095–3114 (2018)

18. Schlegl, T., Seeböck, P., Waldstein, S.M., Schmidt-Erfurth, U., Langs, G.: Unsupervised anomaly detection with generative adversarial networks to guide marker discovery. In: Niethammer, M., et al. (eds.) IPMI 2017. LNCS, vol. 10265, pp. 146–157. Springer, Cham (2017). https://doi.org/10.1007/978-3-319-59050-9_12

19. Sohn, K., Lee, H., Yan, X.: Learning structured output representation using deep conditional generative models. In: Advances in Neural Information Processing Systems, vol. 28 (2015)

20. Wang, K., et al.: Altered functional connectivity in early Alzheimer's disease: a resting-state fMRI study. Hum. Brain Mapp. **28**(10), 967–978 (2007)

21. Wang, X., Zhou, R., Zhao, K., Leow, A., Zhang, Y., He, L.: Normative modeling via conditional variational autoencoder and adversarial learning to identify brain dysfunction in Alzheimer's disease. In: 2023 IEEE 20th International Symposium on Biomedical Imaging, pp. 1–4. IEEE (2023)

22. Wang, Z., et al.: Differentially disrupted functional connectivity of the subregions of the inferior parietal lobule in Alzheimer's disease. Brain Struct. Funct. **220**, 745–762 (2015)

23. Wicaksana, J., Yan, Z., Cheng, K.T.: FCA: taming long-tailed federated medical image classification by classifier anchoring. arXiv preprint arXiv:2305.00738 (2023)

24. Wolleb, J., Bieder, F., Sandkühler, R., Cattin, P.C.: Diffusion models for medical anomaly detection. In: Wang, L., Dou, Q., Fletcher, P.T., Speidel, S., Li, S. (eds.) MICCAI 2022. LNCS, vol. 13438, pp. 35–45. Springer, Cham (2022). https://doi.org/10.1007/978-3-031-16452-1_4

One-Shot Medical Video Object Segmentation via Temporal Contrastive Memory Networks

Yaxiong Chen[1,2], Junjian Hu[1], Chunlei Li[3], Zixuan Zheng[3], Jingliang Hu[3], Yilei Shi[3], Shengwu Xiong[1,2], Xiao Xiang Zhu[4], and Lichao Mou[3(✉)]

[1] Wuhan University of Technology, Wuhan, China
[2] Shanghai Artificial Intelligence Laboratory, Shanghai, China
[3] MedAI Technology (Wuxi) Co. Ltd., Wuxi, China
`lichao.mou@medimagingai.com`
[4] Technical University of Munich, Munich, Germany

Abstract. Video object segmentation is crucial for the efficient analysis of complex medical video data, yet it faces significant challenges in data availability and annotation. We introduce the task of one-shot medical video object segmentation, which requires separating foreground and background pixels throughout a video given only the mask annotation of the first frame. To address this problem, we propose a temporal contrastive memory network comprising image and mask encoders to learn feature representations, a temporal contrastive memory bank that aligns embeddings from adjacent frames while pushing apart distant ones to explicitly model inter-frame relationships and stores these features, and a decoder that fuses encoded image features and memory readouts for segmentation. We also collect a diverse, multi-source medical video dataset spanning various modalities and anatomies to benchmark this task. Extensive experiments demonstrate state-of-the-art performance in segmenting both seen and unseen structures from a single exemplar, showing ability to generalize from scarce labels. This highlights the potential to alleviate annotation burdens for medical video analysis. Code is available at https://github.com/MedAITech/TCMN.

Keywords: video object segmentation · one-shot learning · medical imaging · memory network · temporal contrastive learning

1 Introduction

Video object segmentation is pivotal for efficiently processing complex medical video data and empowering accurate analysis. Precise segmentation of varying tissue regions and lesions facilitates early and accurate diagnosis of lesion characteristics. Furthermore, tracking lesions during surgical procedures aids surgeons in localization, enabling more effective treatment.

J. Hu—Work done during an internship at MedAI Technology (Wuxi) Co. Ltd.

© The Author(s), under exclusive license to Springer Nature Switzerland AG 2025
S. Wu et al. (Eds.): AMAI 2024, LNCS 15384, pp. 241–251, 2025.
https://doi.org/10.1007/978-3-031-82007-6_23

Yet medical video object segmentation faces key data and annotation challenges. While pioneering works have explored lesion and nerve segmentation from ultrasound and endoscopy [1,2], acquiring sizable labeled medical video data places high burden on domain experts. Semi-supervised approaches [3,4] reduce annotations but still rely on class-specific features, limiting generalization to unseen classes.

To surmount the above limitations, we introduce one-shot medical video object segmentation—accurately separating foreground and background throughout a video sequence given a first frame annotation. Our goal is not only to segment known objects, but, crucially, to generalize to segment new classes without any fine-tuning or re-training.

The essence of video object segmentation lies in exploiting dynamic cues within video frames to propagate mask information across the sequence. In the one-shot setting, a mask annotation is provided for the first frame, offering a valuable foreground localization cue to leverage for subsequent unlabeled frames. Recent video object segmentation methods employ memory networks to model inter-frame dependencies. [5] pioneers the integration of memory networks into this task. [6] refines affinity calculations to improve propagation. [7] compresses stored representations with a recurrent embedding module. By computing spatiotemporal attention between query pixels and past frames, these memory-augmented models determine pixel-wise foreground likelihoods.

Prevailing memory-based approaches primarily emphasize feature storage and retrieval, without adequately modeling the temporal context between frames. This may overlook crucial inter-frame dependencies that encode video dynamics. We propose to incorporate contrastive learning into the memory framework to explicitly optimize the storage and use of temporal information. Our core insight is that embeddings of frames belonging to the same semantic class should exhibit proximity that decays with increasing temporal distance; that is, the learned embeddings have greater proximity within the memory when from adjacent timesteps, while displaying more divergence for distant timesteps. To realize this idea, we propose a temporal contrastive memory network for video object segmentation. Our model comprises four main components—an image encoder, a mask encoder, a temporal contrastive memory bank, and a decoder. The image and mask encoders learn image and mask representations of each frame, respectively. Both representations are stored in the memory bank. To model intricate video dynamics, we devise a temporal contrastive loss within the memory bank which aligns feature representations of adjacent frames in the memory while pushing apart those from distant frames. This enhances inter-frame relationship modeling. The decoder fuses encoded image features and memory readouts to predict segmentations.

To benchmark one-shot video object segmentation in medical imaging, we introduce a multi-modal, multi-organ dataset compiled from colonoscopy and cardiac ultrasound videos across four sources: ASU-Mayo [10], CVC-ClinicDB [8], HMC-QU [11], and CAMUS [9]. Our key contributions are:

- We formulate and investigate the task of one-shot segmentation in medical videos.
- We assemble a diverse medical video dataset, establishing a benchmark for this problem.
- We propose a temporal contrastive memory network. Extensive experiments demonstrate state-of-the-art performance in segmenting both seen and unseen anatomical structures or lesions from a single exemplar.

2 Methodology

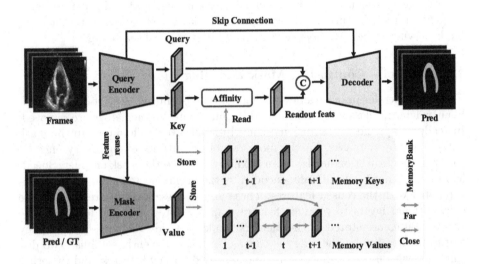

Fig. 1. Overview of our proposed model for one-shot medical video object segmentation. Our model consists of four main components: an image encoder, a mask encoder, a temporal contrastive memory bank, and a decoder. We feed the first frame and its corresponding mask annotation into the image encoder and mask encoder, respectively, to generate key and value feature maps. These are stored in the memory bank as initial memories. For subsequent frames, we input them into the image encoder to generate new key features and utilize the memory bank to produce segmentations. Concurrently, we feed the predicted segmentations to the mask encoder to generate new value features, which, along with the newly generated key features, are stored in the memory bank as updated memories. Our designed memory bank optimizes the memory information through temporal contrastive learning. This process is repeated until the entire video is segmented.

Our objective is to segment the remaining frames of a video sequence, given the annotation of the initial frame. As depicted in Fig. 1, the proposed framework comprises four key components: a query encoder, a mask encoder, a memory bank, and a mask decoder. Notably, to leverage relevant historical frame information during the segmentation process of subsequent frames, we construct a continuously updated memory bank. This memory bank serves as a repository for features extracted from both the query encoder and the mask encoder, facilitating the propagation of temporal cues. In the following sections, we provide a comprehensive elucidation of each component.

2.1 Query Encoder

The query encoder leverages a modified ResNet-50 [13] architecture, where the classification head and the final convolutional stage are omitted. Subsequently, we extend the network by appending two independent projection heads. Consequently, the query encoder takes single video frames as input and generates pairs of query and key feature maps as outputs. The latter are cached in the memory bank, serving as new memory keys to facilitate temporal reasoning.

2.2 Temporal Contrastive Mask Encoding

The mask encoder in our framework employs a customized ResNet-18 [13] backbone, where the classification head and the final convolutional stage are removed. Instead, we append two additional convolutional layers. The input to the mask encoder is object masks. Furthermore, we reuse outputs of the query encoder (prior to the projection heads) as an auxiliary input to the mask encoder. Specifically, object masks are initially encoded by the backbone and subsequently concatenated with the reused features. These joint representations are fed into the convolutional layers to produce feature maps, denoted as value features. The value features are stored in the memory bank alongside the corresponding key features generated by the query encoder. Thus, we efficiently establish two distinct sets within the memory bank: one allocated for key features, and the other for value features.

The quality of memory values in the memory bank has a direct impact on the segmentation of subsequent frames. Therefore, we further incorporate temporal contrastive learning into our framework. Specifically, for the value set $\mathcal{V}$, our hypothesis is that adjacent memory values in time exhibit stronger semantic similarity. This is because objects in consecutive video frames typically have similar shapes and appear in similar backgrounds, hence their encoded features should have similar representations. On the contrary, for distant memory values in time, we expect that their feature representations are relatively dissimilar. This design enables our model to effectively utilize temporal information for memory.

To utilize the information of previous frames to assist in the segmentation of the current frame, we employ a simple yet efficient method for retrieving relevant information from the memory bank. Specifically, we use an evaluation model based on negative squared Euclidean distance [25] to match memory keys in the memory bank with key feature maps of the current frame obtained from the query encoder. This calculation involves performing pixel-level computations on feature maps to generate a similarity matrix. Finally, by the simple matrix multiplication of memory values and softmax-normalized similarity matrix, we obtain readout feature maps for the query frame.

2.3   Mask Decoder

The readout features are concatenated with query features. This concatenated representation is then fed into the mask decoder to predict segmentation masks. Specifically, the mask decoder comprises interleaved convolutional and upsampling layers, followed by a softmax operation.

2.4   Overall Loss

To enhance the quality of memory values stored in the memory bank, we propose a novel temporal contrastive loss:

$$\mathcal{L}_{\text{tc}} = \sum_{t=1}^{|\mathcal{V}|} \frac{(1 - \text{sim}(\boldsymbol{v}_{t-1}, \boldsymbol{v}_t)) + (1 - \text{sim}(\boldsymbol{v}_t, \boldsymbol{v}_{t+1}))}{1 - \text{sim}(\boldsymbol{v}_{t-1}, \boldsymbol{v}_{t+1}) + \epsilon}, \tag{1}$$

where $\text{sim}(\boldsymbol{a}, \boldsymbol{b}) = \boldsymbol{a}^{\text{T}}\boldsymbol{b} / \|\boldsymbol{a}\| \|\boldsymbol{b}\|$ denotes the cosine similarity between vectors $\boldsymbol{a}$ and $\boldsymbol{b}$, and $\boldsymbol{v}_t$ represents the t-th memory value in the memory bank. A small value ϵ is added to the denominator to prevent division-by-zero errors in practice. We use bootstrapped cross entropy (BCE) [24] as the supervised loss:

$$\mathcal{L}_{\text{bce}} = \frac{1}{|\mathcal{D}|} \sum_{\boldsymbol{y}_i \in \mathcal{D}} \{\hat{\boldsymbol{y}}_i < \eta\} \mathbf{H}(\boldsymbol{y}_i, \hat{\boldsymbol{y}}_i), \tag{2}$$

where $\mathcal{D}$ is the set of frames in a video, excluding the first frame. $\hat{\boldsymbol{y}}_i$ is the predicted segmentation mask of the i-th frame, and $\boldsymbol{y}_i$ is the corresponding ground truth mask. $\mathbf{H}(\cdot)$ denotes cross entropy loss. We only calculate the loss for pixels with probabilities less than a threshold η to prevent over-training on easy samples. The overall loss function of our model is:

$$\mathcal{L} = \alpha \mathcal{L}_{\text{bce}} + \beta \mathcal{L}_{tc}, \tag{3}$$

where α and β are two coefficients balancing the two loss terms.

3   Experiments

3.1   Experimental Settings

Datasets. We conduct experiments on four public medical video datasets. The first is the ASU-Mayo colonoscopy video dataset, containing 10 negative videos from normal subjects and 10 positive videos from patients. We use the positive videos, consisting of 5,402 video frames in total, with 3,799 frames containing polyps, for our experiments. The second dataset is CVC-ClinicDB, comprising

29 colonoscopy videos, totaling 612 frames, all of which contain polyps. The third dataset is HMC-QU, containing 109 apical-4-chamber (A4C) view echocardiography videos with left ventricle wall segmentation masks. The final dataset is CAMUS, containing 500 patient samples, each including apical-2-chamber (A2C) and A4C echocardiography videos with segmentation masks for left ventricle wall, left ventricle, and left atrium. The first three datasets, i.e., ASU-Mayo, CVC-ClinicDB, and HMC-QU, are divided into training and test sets with an 8:2 ratio. The training sets from the three datasets are then combined and used to train models. It is worth noting that, to validate models' generalization capabilities, we use the CAMUS dataset, which contains two classes not present in training videos.

Evaluation Metrics. We employ three widely used metrics, Jaccard index $\mathcal{J}$ [12], contour accuracy $\mathcal{F}$, and *Dice*, to evaluate the performance of models. $\mathcal{J}$ is defined as the intersection-over-union of an estimated segmentation mask and the corresponding ground truth. $\mathcal{F}$ is defined by treating a mask as a set of closed contours and computing a contour-based F-measure.

Implementation Details. Our experiments are conducted on a single 24 GB NVIDIA GeForce RTX 4090 GPU with the Adam optimizer using PyTorch. Following previous practices [5–7], we first pre-train models on static image datasets [14–16] with synthetic deformation and then use real video data for main training. We use randomly cropped 384×384 patches and a batch size of 16 during pre-training. A batch size of 8 is adopted during main training. In addition, following a training strategy present in [5,6], we sample 3 temporally ordered frames from a training video by randomly skipping 0-5 frames. During inference, we designate every fifth frame as a memory frame. Given the relatively short duration of video sequences in the dataset, we opt not to impose a fixed limit on the size of memory bank. Instead, the memory bank capacity is determined by available resources on the target inference platform.

3.2   Comparison with State-of-the-Art Methods

To evaluate the performance of our method, we extensively compare it with state-of-the-art approaches, including STCN [6], AOT [22], DeAOT [21], RDE [7], AFB-URR [19], JOINT [18], RPCM [17], XMem [23], and Cutie [20]. To ensure a fair and unbiased comparison, we obtain the segmentation results of all competing methods through their publicly available implementations.

Quantitative Comparison. For performance on test sets with seen classes, Table 1 reports numerical results. It can be seen that our method outperforms competing approaches on every dataset. As for testing on unseen classes, experimental results can be found in Table 2, where our method achieves the second-best results on the left ventricular category and the best results on the left atrial category. On average, the proposed model surpasses competitors.

Table 1. Quantitative evaluation of the proposed method and other approaches on the ASU-Mayo, CVC-ClinicDB, and HMC-QU datasets for one-shot medical video object segmentation. "Mean" denotes the average performance across the three datasets.

Methods	ASU-Mayo			CVC-ClinicDB			HMC-QU			Mean		
	$\mathcal{J}$	$\mathcal{F}$	Dice	$\mathcal{J}$	$\mathcal{F}$	Dice	$\mathcal{J}$	$\mathcal{F}$	Dice	$\mathcal{J}$	$\mathcal{F}$	Dice
AFB-URR	62.23	70.02	68.98	77.22	68.07	85.64	86.59	98.91	92.76	75.34	79.00	82.79
STCN	68.58	76.97	77.30	82.72	77.76	89.27	89.94	99.38	94.66	80.41	84.70	87.08
AOT	67.29	75.24	75.57	77.03	65.38	85.18	77.49	94.55	87.25	73.93	78.39	82.67
JOINT	70.08	77.71	78.79	77.27	67.07	86.01	84.36	97.65	91.44	77.24	79.00	85.41
DeAOT	70.68	79.79	79.56	74.24	64.89	82.89	77.11	94.55	87.00	74.01	79.86	83.15
RPCM	58.49	62.72	66.15	62.07	48.95	73.73	38.13	52.47	51.05	52.90	54.71	63.64
RDE	61.89	69.00	70.49	77.18	70.66	85.53	87.65	98.94	93.36	75.57	79.53	83.13
XMem	67.58	76.12	76.15	82.74	76.46	89.58	90.41	99.38	94.92	80.24	83.99	86.88
Cutie	61.89	69.32	67.99	66.74	56.58	74.88	72.21	87.99	83.61	66.74	70.96	75.49
w/o $\mathcal{L}_{tc}$	70.52	79.48	79.48	84.16	77.77	90.57	90.25	**99.50**	94.83	81.64	85.58	88.30
Ours	**71.34**	**80.13**	**80.36**	**84.82**	**80.61**	**90.75**	**90.50**	99.47	**94.98**	**82.22**	**86.74**	**88.70**

Table 2. Quantitative evaluation of the proposed method and competing approaches on two unseen classes, left ventricle and left atrium, from the CAMUS dataset.

Methods	Left Ventricle			Left Atrium			Mean		
	$\mathcal{J}$	$\mathcal{F}$	Dice	$\mathcal{J}$	$\mathcal{F}$	Dice	$\mathcal{J}$	$\mathcal{F}$	Dice
AFB-URR	66.65	39.61	77.55	51.83	30.32	63.50	59.24	34.97	70.52
STCN	75.98	54.72	84.91	72.46	57.24	81.12	74.22	55.98	83.02
AOT	79.09	**61.02**	86.44	63.64	40.89	74.31	71.37	50.96	80.38
JOINT	62.22	29.65	75.00	53.87	24.66	66.03	58.04	27.16	70.52
DeAOT	78.73	53.05	87.75	51.60	32.10	61.12	65.17	42.57	74.43
RPCM	54.89	26.44	69.01	44.44	21.53	58.09	49.67	23.98	63.55
RDE	20.64	26.75	29.23	21.14	27.36	29.55	20.89	27.05	29.39
XMem	72.27	37.98	83.16	80.34	57.68	88.70	76.30	47.83	85.93
Cutie	**82.59**	56.36	**90.31**	72.67	49.87	82.46	77.63	53.11	86.39
w/o $\mathcal{L}_{tc}$	80.06	56.46	84.91	73.80	57.24	81.12	76.93	55.98	83.02
Ours	81.56	58.55	89.35	**83.10**	**66.37**	**90.33**	**82.33**	**62.46**	**89.84**

Qualitative Comparison. Figure 2 visually presents the qualitative performance of our model on different classes. The first two rows show segmentation results on classes that the model has learned, while the last two rows show results on classes that the model has not seen before. Notably, our model shows good segmentation performance even in these unseen classes, confirming that it learns objectness cues rather than class-specific features.

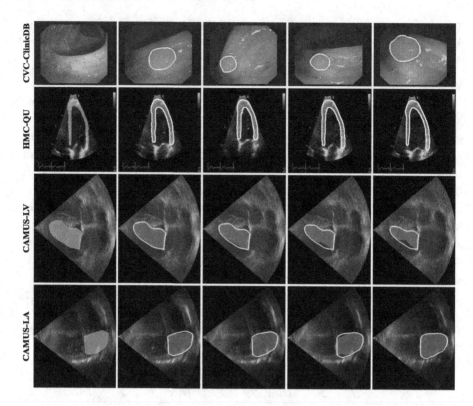

Fig. 2. Qualitative results. The first two rows show segmentation results on classes that our model has learned during training, while the last two rows show results on classes that the model has not seen during training. The green masks indicate annotation masks of the first frames within videos. The red masks represent predicted segmentation masks obtained by our model on subsequent frames, and white lines indicate the corresponding ground truth contours for these frames. (Color figure online)

3.3 Ablation Study

To verify the effectiveness of key components of our model, we conduct extensive ablation experiments on four datasets. We take a model without the temporal contrastive loss as the baseline. Upon incorporating this loss, our model witnesses improvements of 0.58%, 1.16%, and 0.4% in average $\mathcal{J}$, $\mathcal{F}$, and $Dice$, respectively, for the seen classes, and notable gains of 5.40%, 6.48%, and 6.82% for the unseen classes.

4   Conclusion

In this paper, we introduce the task of one-shot video object segmentation for medical videos and propose a temporal contrastive memory network to address the key challenges associated with limited annotations. We conduct extensive experiments on our diverse, multi-source medical video benchmark, demonstrating that our approach achieves state-of-the-art performance. By leveraging a contrastive memory mechanism, our model can accurately segment both seen and unseen anatomical structures or lesions from only the first frame's annotation. This highlights our method's potential to significantly alleviate laborious annotation efforts required for understanding medical videos. In future work, we plan to explore enhancements to memory banks, focusing on optimizing memory sizes and developing a dynamic selection strategy for memory frames. These improvements aim to increase the applicability of our method across diverse scenarios.

Prospect of Application: The proposed method can serve as an interactive, intelligent medical video annotation tool. Users need only provide annotation for the first frame, after which the model generates segmentation masks for subsequent frames, significantly reducing annotation burdens for clinicians. Furthermore, experiments demonstrate the generalizability of this approach.

Acknowledgements. This work is supported in part by the National Key Research and Development Program of China (2022ZD0160604), in part by the Natural Science Foundation of China (62101393/62176194), in part by the High-Performance Computing Platform of YZBSTCACC, and in part by MindSpore (https://www.mindspore.cn), a new deep learning framework.

Disclosure of Interests. The authors have no competing interests to declare that are relevant to the content of this paper.

References

1. Lin, J., et al.: Shifting more attention to breast lesion segmentation in ultrasound videos. In: International Conference on Medical Image Computing and Computer Assisted Intervention, pp. 497–507 (2023)
2. Peng, S., Zhao, P., Ye, Y., Chen, J., Chang, Y., Zheng, X.: Spinal nerve segmentation method and dataset construction in endoscopic surgical scenarios. In: International Conference on Medical Image Computing and Computer Assisted Intervention, pp. 597–606 (2023)
3. Ni, H., Xue, Y., Ma, L., Zhang, Q., Li, X., Huang, S.X.: Semi-supervised body parsing and pose estimation for enhancing infant general movement assessment. Med. Image Anal. **83**, 102654 (2023)
4. Wu, H., Liu, J., Xiao, F., Wen, Z., Cheng, L., Qin, J.: Semi-supervised segmentation of echocardiography videos via noise-resilient spatiotemporal semantic calibration and fusion. Med. Image Anal. **78**, 102397 (2022)
5. Oh, S.W., Lee, J.Y., Xu, N., Kim, S.J.: Video object segmentation using space-time memory networks. In: IEEE/CVF International Conference on Computer Vision, pp. 9226–9235 (2019)
6. Cheng, H.K., Tai, Y.W., Tang, C.K.: Rethinking space-time networks with improved memory coverage for efficient video object segmentation. In: Advances in Neural Information Processing Systems, pp. 11781–11794 (2021)

7. Li, M., Hu, L., Xiong, Z., Zhang, B., Pan, P., Liu, D.: Recurrent dynamic embedding for video object segmentation. In: IEEE/CVF Conference on Computer Vision and Pattern Recognition, pp. 1332–1341 (2022)

8. Bernal, J., Sánchez, F.J., Fernández-Esparrach, G., Gil, D., Rodríguez, C., Vilariño, F.: WM-DOVA maps for accurate polyp highlighting in colonoscopy: Validation vs. saliency maps from physicians. Comput. Med. Imaging Graph. **43**, 99–111 (2015)

9. Leclerc, S., et al.: Deep learning for segmentation using an open large-scale dataset in 2D echocardiograph. IEEE Trans. Med. Imaging **38**, 2198–2210 (2019)

10. Tajbakhsh, N., Gurudu, S.R., Liang, J.: Automated polyp detection in colonoscopy videos using shape and context information. IEEE Trans. Med. Imaging **35**, 630–644 (2016)

11. Degerli, A., Kiranyaz, S., Hamid, T., Mazhar, R., Gabbouj, M.: Early myocardial infarction detection over multi-view echocardio-graphy. Biomed. Sig. Process. Control **87**, 105448 (2024)

12. Everingham, M., Van Gool, L., Williams, C.K., Winn, J., Zisserman, A.: The pascal visual object classes (VOC) challenge. Int. J. Comput. Vision **88**, 303–338 (2010)

13. He, K., Zhang, X., Ren, S., Sun, J.: Deep residual learning for image recognition. In: IEEE Conference on Computer Vision and Pattern Recognition, pp. 770–778 (2015)

14. Wang, Y., Feng, M., Wang, D., Yin, B., Ruan, X.: Learning to detect salient objects with image-level supervision. In: IEEE Conference on Computer Vision and Pattern Recognition, pp. 136–145 (2017)

15. Shi, J., Yan, Q., Xu, L., Jia, J.: Hierarchical image saliency detection on extended CSSD. IEEE Trans. Pattern Anal. Mach. Intell. **38**, 717–729 (2015)

16. Zeng, Y., Zhang, P., Zhang, J., Lin, Z., Lu, H.: Towards high-resolution salient object detection. In: IEEE/CVF International Conference on Computer Vision, pp. 7234–7243 (2019)

17. Xu, X., Wang, J., Li, X., Lu, Y.: Reliable propagation-correction modulation for video object segmentation. In: AAAI Conference on Artificial Intelligence, pp. 2946–2954 (2022)

18. Mao, Y., Wang, N., Zhou, W., Li, H.: Joint inductive and transductive learning for video object segmentation. In: IEEE/CVF International Conference on Computer Vision, pp. 9670–9679 (2021)

19. Liang, Y., Li, X., Jafari, N., Chen, J.: Video object segmentation with adaptive feature bank and uncertain-region refinement. In: Advances in Neural Information Processing Systems, pp. 3430–3441 (2020)

20. Cheng, H.K., Oh, S.W., Price, B., Lee, J.Y., Schwing, A.: Putting the object back into video object segmentation. arXiv preprint arXiv:2310.12982 (2023)

21. Yang, Z., Yang, Y.: Decoupling features in hierarchical propagation for video object segmentation. In: Advances in Neural Information Processing Systems, pp. 36324–36336 (2022)

22. Yang, Z., Wei, Y., Yang, Y.: Associating objects with transformers for video object segmentation. In: Advances in Neural Information Processing Systems, pp. 2491–2502 (2021)

23. Cheng, H.K., Schwing, A.G.: XMem: long-term video object segmentation with an Atkinson-Shiffrin memory model. In: Avidan, S., Brostow, G., Cissé, M., Farinella, G.M., Hassner, T. (eds.) ECCV 2022. LNCS, vol. 13688, pp. 640–658. Springer, Cham (2022). https://doi.org/10.1007/978-3-031-19815-1_37

24. Cheng, H.K., Tai, Y.W., Tang, C.K.: Modular interactive video object segmentation: interaction-to-mask, propagation and difference-aware fusion. In: IEEE/CVF Conference on Computer Vision and Pattern Recognition, pp. 5559–5568 (2021)
25. Frey, B.J., Dueck, D.: Clustering by passing messages between data points. Science **315**, 972–976 (2007)

Data-Efficient Radiology Report Generation via Similar Report Features Enhancement

Yanfeng Li[1], Jinghan Sun[2], and Liansheng Wang[1,2]($\boxtimes$)

[1] Department of Computer Science at School of Informatics, Xiamen University,
Xiamen, China
liyanfeng@stu.xmu.edu.cn, lswang@xmu.edu.cn
[2] National Institute for Data Science in Health and Medicine, Xiamen University,
Xiamen, China
jhsun@stu.xmu.edu.cn

Abstract. The utilization of Artificial Intelligence in automatically generating radiology reports presents a promising solution for enhancing the efficiency of the diagnostic process and reducing human error. However, existing methods require training on large datasets of image-report pairs, which are often scarce. Moreover, the accuracy of reports generated with limited paired data significantly diminishes. To address these challenges, this study introduces a data-efficient method that integrates the retrieval of similar reports with text fusion enhancements to tackle the scarcity of image-report pairs and generate accurate radiology reports. Our method is compared with several state-of-the-art approaches, showing advancements on the MIMIC-CXR and IU X-ray benchmarks with the same limited data pairs. It achieves near-optimal results on MIMIC-CXR and comparable results on IU-Xray, highlighting not only its effectiveness and potential to improve radiological diagnosis with fewer image reports but also its ability to generate more accurate reports. By enhancing cross-modal feature interaction and demonstrating higher diagnostic accuracy, this work contributes to the fields of clinical medicine and artificial intelligence.

Keywords: Radiology report generation · Similar reports retriever · Textual features enhancement · Transformer

1 Introduction

Automated radiology report generation using deep learning is transforming medical imaging diagnostics. Traditionally, radiologists manually examine radiology images, identify issues, and write reports, which is time-consuming and requires expertise. AI advancements now allow automated systems to analyze images and generate reports swiftly, improving diagnostic accuracy and efficiency. This technology reduces radiologists' workloads, and lowers human errors, positioning it as a pivotal area of research in clinical medicine and AI.

© The Author(s), under exclusive license to Springer Nature Switzerland AG 2025
S. Wu et al. (Eds.): AMAI 2024, LNCS 15384, pp. 252–262, 2025.
https://doi.org/10.1007/978-3-031-82007-6_24

In recent years, report generation has been significantly influenced by image captioning [4,11,15,23,26], achieving great progress [2,3,9,17,21]. However, there are still two main challenges to be addressed in report generation. Firstly, due to patient privacy concerns and the substantial human resources required for medical data collection, radiology image-report data pairs are rarer compared to natural image-text data pairs [27]. The existing works [12,24] rely too heavily on a large number of image and report pairs, which do not align with the reality of scarce medical data. Besides, while Massachusetts General Hospital provides the largest dataset MIMIC-CXR [10] currently used for report generation, training with the entire dataset is computationally intensive and time-consuming. Although Zhang et al. [27] have conducted semi-supervised learning studies, their method using additional unpaired images for training is not in a data-efficient manner. Therefore, training an effective report generation model on limited paired datasets is more realistically significant. Secondly, generating accurate and effective radiology reports is hard, especially in data-limited situations. Although there are studies on image captioning in data-efficient contexts [1,14], they focus solely on natural language generation metrics, whereas report generation tasks prioritize clinical efficacy metrics. Unlike the significant variability in image captioning, authentic reports in report generation are based on semi-structured templates. Excluding key diagnostic terms, reports for different patients are still similar, which can inflate natural language generation metrics. Therefore, generated reports must have the capability to identify key pathological conditions depicted in the images. This means clinical efficacy metrics should matter more than language evaluation metrics. Moreover, class imbalance in medical data also hinders the model's ability to identify anomalies.

To address these challenges, we propose a data-efficient method based on similar reports retriever and textual features enhancement to augment the generation of radiology reports. Our method utilizes a smaller number of image-report pairs for training and employs a significant number of reports as a retrieval library for similar reports. Specifically, our method leverages the Cross-Modal Memory (CMM) module as an interactive component to align visual and textual features. Existing CMM-based methods [2,21] focus on optimizing cross-modal feature alignment. However, when data pairs become scarce, these methods struggle to effectively align cross-modal features. Our method prioritizes input optimization before alignment, utilizing additional similar features to enhance input and aid in feature alignment. Based on this insight, we introduce a pretrained similar reports retriever for retrieving similar reports [22,25] in order to alleviate data scarcity and class imbalance. Further, we propose a textual features enhancement module based on cross-attention [20], which fuse the similar report with the authentic report, resulting in enhanced text fusion features for cross-modal feature alignment. The experiment shows that, under the same conditions of limited paired data, our method outperforms several state-of-the-art methods to some extent on the widely used MIMIC-CXR and IU X-Ray benchmark datasets, proving its effectiveness.

Our work contributes primarily in two ways: a) We introduce a similar reports retriever and a textual features enhancement module, which indirectly enhances the interaction of cross-modal features by enriching textual features, thereby producing better radiology reports. b) We demonstrate superior performance over several state-of-the-art methods on two extensively used benchmark datasets with fewer image-report pairs, validating the effectiveness of our method.

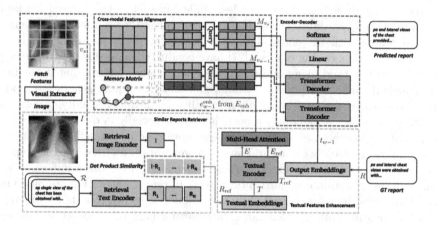

Fig. 1. The overall architecture of our model.

2   Method

Problem Setting. Our research is conducted within a smaller subset compared to the original dataset. A certain ratio of the dataset contains paired image and report data, while the remaining portion is unpaired. Our objective is to generate more accurate reports with the smallest possible value of ratio.

In the report generation task, given a 2D radiology image I with a source visual sequence $V = \{v_1, \ldots, v_s, \ldots, v_S\}$ and a corresponding target textual sequence (report) $T = \{t_1, \ldots, t_w, \ldots, t_W\}$. Here, $v_s \in \mathbb{R}^d$ represents features extracted by the visual extractor, S denotes the total number of extracted feature patches and d denotes the dimension of visual features; $t_w \in \mathbf{TKN}$, where W denotes the number of tokens in the report, and $\mathbf{TKN}$ represents the vocabulary set of all tokens. The entire process of the report generation task can be described by the following chain rule: $p(T|V) = \prod_{w=1}^{W} p(t_w|t_1, \ldots, t_{w-1}, V)$.

Method Overview. Figure 1 displays the overall architecture of our method. The overall architecture process can be briefly described as follows: An image is input into the visual extractor to extract visual features. Then, the most similar report retrieved through the image and the authentic report undergo feature fusion to enhance textual features. Next, cross-modal features are mapped to a memory matrix for alignment. Finally, a report is generated through an encoder-decoder. The following subsections describe the four main modules: Visual Extractor, Similar Reports Retriever, Text-enhanced Cross-modal Memory, and Encoder-Decoder.

Visual Extractor. For a radiology image I, visual features V are extracted using a pre-trained visual encoder. The image is divided into equal-sized patches, and features are extracted from each patch. These features are then concatenated in rows to create a feature sequence. This sequence of features serves as the input for subsequent modules. The process can be formalized as $V = \{v_1, \ldots, v_s, \ldots, v_S\} = f_v(I)$, where f_v denotes the visual extractor, $v_s \in \mathbb{R}^d$, and S represents the number of patches.

Similar Reports Retriever. To find reports semantically similar to the target report and thereby enhance its textual features, we follow the work of CLIP [18] and CXR-CLIP [25], utilizing the pre-trained model of CXR-CLIP as the backbone of our retrieval module, and conducted similar reports retrieval based on this foundation. Specifically, within a retrieval set of N radiology reports $\mathcal{R} = \{\mathcal{R}_1, \ldots, \mathcal{R}_N\}$, we seek to identify the report R_{ref} that best matches the semantic features of a given radiology image I, excluding the target report itself. This process can be expressed: $R_{\text{ref}} = f_{\text{srr}}(I, \mathcal{R}) = \arg\max_{\mathcal{R}_i \in \mathcal{R}} \cos(f_v^{\text{clip}}(I), f_t^{\text{clip}}(\mathcal{R}_i))$. Here, $f_{\text{srr}}(\cdot)$ represents the similar reports retriever, $f_v^{\text{clip}}(\cdot)$ represents the visual encoder within the retriever, $f_t^{\text{clip}}(\cdot)$ represents the text encoder within the retriever, and $\cos(\cdot)$ represents cosine similarity calculation.

Text-enhanced Cross-modal Memory. Memory technology enables the association of diverse features through key-value mapping, essential for tasks like report generation that involve both visual and textual features. By leveraging memory technology, potential shared associations between radiology images and reports can be unearthed, allowing the model to be trained in a unified manner and to learn the commonalities between cross-modal features. We employ Cross-modal Memory (CMM), based on the work of Chen et al. [2], to map potentially associated visual and textual features into a unified feature representation space.

Given visual features $V = \{v_1, \ldots, v_S\}$ extracted from image I and text embeddings $T = \{t_1, \ldots, t_W\}$ extracted from report R, these are input into the CMM module to obtain corresponding memory vectors $\{M_{v_1}, \ldots, M_{v_s}, \ldots, M_m\}$ and $\{M_{t_1}, \ldots, M_{t_w}, \ldots, M_m\}$. Here, $t_w \in \mathbb{R}^d$, $M_{v_s} \in \mathbb{R}^d$, $M_{t_w} \in \mathbb{R}^d$, W denotes the maximum number of text tokens, m denotes the number of memory vectors.

Textual Features Enhancement. To mitigate information loss when obtaining memory for target report text embeddings, we enhance the target report's text embeddings to retain as much original information as possible, enabling more effective cross-modal memory retrieval. Our method leverages similar reports retrieved by a similar reports retriever to augment the target report, as these similar reports share common features with the target image matched by the target report. We use a multi-head attention mechanism to align key information and capture semantic associations between the target and similar texts. This allows simultaneous attention to different levels and aspects of semantic information in both texts. Specifically, given a target report R and a similar report R_{ref}, we tokenize and convert them into word embeddings, resulting in $T = \{t_1, \ldots, t_W\}$ and $T_{\text{ref}} = \{t_1^{\text{ref}}, \ldots, t_W^{\text{ref}}\}$. These embeddings are then encoded into corresponding textual features, allowing both texts to be represented in the same feature space. This encoding process can be expressed as

$$E = \{e_1, \ldots, e_D\} = f_{\text{encoder}}^{\text{tfe}}(T), E_{\text{ref}} = \{e_1^{\text{ref}}, \ldots, e_D^{\text{ref}}\} = f_{\text{encoder}}^{\text{tfe}}(T_{\text{ref}}). \quad (1)$$

Here, $f_{\text{encoder}}^{\text{tfe}}(\cdot)$ denotes the textual features enhancement process's text encoder, $e_d \in \mathbb{R}^d$, and D represents the number of encoded features.

The obtained textual features are then input into a multi-head attention module, where the calculation process for the multi-head attention mechanism can be expressed: $\{Q_h, K_h, V_h\} = \{EW_h^Q, E_{\text{ref}}W_h^K, E_{\text{ref}}W_h^V\}$, $A_h = \text{softmax}\left(\frac{Q_h K_h^T}{\sqrt{d}}\right)$. Here, $W_h^Q, W_h^K, W_h^V \in \mathbb{R}^{d \times (d/H)}$ are trainable parameter matrices, $A^h \in \mathbb{R}^{D \times D}$ represents the attention weight matrix of the h-th head, H denoting the number of heads, and $h = 1, \ldots, H$. Finally, the enhanced textual features can be obtained: $E_h^{\text{enh}} = A_h V_h$, $E_{\text{enh}} = \text{concat}(E_1^{\text{enh}}, \ldots, E_H^{\text{enh}})$, where $E_{\text{enh}} \in \mathbb{R}^{D \times d}$.

Cross-modal Features Alignment. With the enhanced textual features E_{enh}, we can align cross-modal features. Cross-modal feature alignment acts as a bridge connecting visual and textual features, unifying them in the same feature space. Specifically, cross-modal alignment requires a memory matrix $M = \{M_1, \ldots, M_m\}$ as a medium for interaction between different modalities, with M_i representing the i-th memory vector. CMM applies multi-thread alignment to align visual and textual features. Multi-thread alignment aims to find the closest memory vectors for mapped visual and textual features, reducing cross-modal discrepancy. First, mappings for visual features, textual features, and memory vectors are performed, which can be expressed: $v_s^{\text{map}} = W_v v_s$, $t_s^{\text{map}} = W_t e_w^{\text{enh}}$, $k_i = W_M M_i$. Here, W_v, W_t, W_M are trainable mapping matrices. Then, by calculating distances, we can find the set of x most relevant memory vectors for the mapped visual and textual features, expressed: $D_v = \frac{v_s^{\text{map}} k_i^T}{\sqrt{d}}$, $D_t = \frac{t_s^{\text{map}} k_i^T}{\sqrt{d}}$. For visual features, the set of x most relevant memory vectors can be represented as $\{k_{v_1}, \ldots, k_{v_x}\}$. Next, we can use k_{v_i} to find the corresponding memory vector M_{v_i} in the memory matrix and calculate the corresponding value vector $v_{v_i} = M_{v_i} W_{\text{value}}$. Furthermore, we can calculate the memory vector weights w and the memory output r for visual features, expressed:

$$w_{v_i} = \frac{\exp(D_{v_i})}{\sum_{j=1}^{x} \exp(D_{v_j})}, \quad r_{v_i} = \sum_{i=1}^{x} (w_{v_i} v_{v_i}). \quad (2)$$

Similarly, we can perform the same process for textual features to obtain the memory output r_{t_i}. Notably, this process uses enhanced textual features to further improve the expression of textual semantics, thereby obtaining semantic information more closely related to visual features.

Encoder-Decoder. Our model uses the Transformer architecture, a widely used and effective encoder-decoder for sequence-to-sequence tasks. Initially, the source sequence, i.e., the visual corresponding memory $\{M_{v_1}, \ldots, M_{v_S}\}$, is input into the encoder: $\{Q_1, \ldots, Q_K\} = f_{\text{encoder}}(M_{v_1}, \ldots, M_{v_S})$, where f_{encoder} represents the encoder. Subsequently, the intermediate results obtained from the encoder, along with the textual corresponding memory $\{M_{t_1}, \ldots, M_{t_W}\}$, are input into the decoder for generating the final report. The decoding process can be expressed as $G_w = f_{\text{decoder}}(M_{t_1}, \ldots, M_{t_{w-1}})$, where f_{decoder} represents the decoder, and G_w denotes the text token generated at time step w. Ultimately, repeat the above process until the report is fully generated.

3 Experiments

Datasets and Evaluation Metrics. We used two extensively acknowledged chest X-ray datasets, MIMIC-CXR [10] and IU X-Ray [5], to evaluate our model's performance. MIMIC-CXR is the largest public X-ray dataset, with over 370,000 images from about 65,000 patients and 200,000 radiology reports. Following Chen et al. [3]'s work, we used their train, validation, and test set divisions, sampling the training data by set ratios to optimize our model's training. IU X-Ray dataset comprises around 7,470 X-ray images and 3,955 radiology reports. IU X-Ray dataset features highly structured reports detailing patient demographics, clinical observations, and diagnostic conclusions. Following Jin et al. [9], we used the entire IU X-Ray dataset as a test set to assess models trained on MIMIC-CXR. This choice was influenced by two factors: the limitations of test set splits used by Chen et al. [3] for disease-aware evaluation, and the challenge of uneven disease category distribution exacerbated by their smaller training set size and sampling of image-report pairs.

The effectiveness of our method is evaluated using clinical efficacy (CE) metrics, BERT scores, and natural language generation (NLG) metrics. CE metrics, encompassing precision, recall, and F1 scores, are calculated following the translation of reports into 14 disease category labels using CheXbert [19], facilitating an assessment of our model's clinical relevance. NLG metrics, such as BLEU4 [16], METEOR [7], ROUGE-L [13], alongside the Bert Score [28], are employed to evaluate the comprehensive quality of generated reports.

Implementation Details. Our model's visual extractor is based on a ResNet-101 [8] pre-trained on ImageNet [6], extracting 512-dimensional visual features for each patch. For the CMM module, we set the number of threads to 8 and the count of the most relevant memory vectors to 32. The dimension of the memory matrix and the number of memory vectors N are both initialized randomly to 512 and 2048, respectively. The learning rates for the visual extractor and encoder-decoder are set to 1×10^{-4} and 5×10^{-5}, respectively. The model is trained under cross-entropy loss using the Adam optimizer, with a learning rate decay of 0.8 per epoch. The beam size is set to 3. The model is trained in 30 epochs with a batch size of 16, using two RTX 2080Ti GPUs.

Comparisons with Prior Research. We compared our method with several state-of-the-art approaches on the MIMIC-CXR and IU X-Ray datasets. To simulate the limited availability of image-report pairs in medical contexts, we only used 25% of the MIMIC-CXR dataset. Subsequently, we retrained our method and comparative models on this reduced dataset obtained through random sampling. Table 1 presents the results, evaluating metrics such as CE, Bert Score, and NLG. On the MIMIC-CXR dataset, our method demonstrated overall superiority across various metrics, except for METEOR where it narrowly trailed the top-performing M2KT by 0.0008. Notably, our method excelled in CE metrics, particularly in F1 and Recall, where it outperformed competitors by approximately 0.02. Furthermore, evaluations on the IU X-Ray dataset showed our method's ability to generalize across different datasets. It excelled in F1 and Recall in CE metrics and performed best in METEOR among NLG metrics.

Table 1. The results of the comparative experiments between our method and prior research on the IU X-Ray and MIMIC-CXR datasets. The best values are highlighted in bold and the second best values are underlined. The annotation "*" indicates that the improvement of our method over the compared method is significant ($p < 0.01$).

Dataset	Model	CE Metrics			Bert Score	NLG Metrics		
		F1	Precision	Recall		BLEU4	METEOR	ROUGE-L
IU X-Ray	R2Gen [3]	0.1363*	0.2286	0.1422*	0.6819*	0.0843*	0.1424*	0.2873*
	R2GenCMN [2]	0.1452*	**0.2433**	0.1499*	0.6889*	0.0920	0.1525*	0.2985*
	XProNet [21]	0.1141*	0.1927	0.1204*	**0.6999**	**0.0986**	0.1565*	**0.3172**
	M2KT [24]	0.0869*	0.1392*	0.0755*	0.6471*	0.0526*	0.1542*	0.2424*
	Ours	**0.1603**	0.1957	**0.1713**	0.6904	0.0877	**0.1582**	0.3023
MIMIC-CXR	R2Gen [3]	0.2019*	0.3013*	0.1936*	0.6684*	0.0955*	0.1312*	0.2728*
	R2GenCMN [2]	0.2053*	0.2861*	0.2085*	0.6659*	0.0983*	0.1328*	0.2701*
	XProNet [21]	0.1828*	0.3115*	0.1769*	0.6673*	0.0944*	0.1287*	0.2727*
	M2KT [24]	0.0900*	0.1796*	0.0851*	0.6399*	0.0939*	**0.1388**	0.2614*
	Ours	**0.2149**	**0.3246**	**0.2143**	0.6717	**0.1035**	0.1380	**0.2767**

Ablation Analysis. We conducted two ablation studies to demonstrate the effectiveness of our introduced modules, namely Similar Reports Retriever (SRR) and Textual Features Enhancement (TFE). For SRR, we employed the entire training set of MIMIC-CXR as a retrieval library for similar reports, and validated its effectiveness by randomly pairing reports for subsequent use in TFE as a control. For TFE, we utilized SRR to retrieve the most similar report for unused images in the full dataset, using it as a pseudo-report for model training as a form of data augmentation. From Table 2, it is evident that in the TFE ablation study, our method is leading on both datasets across all metrics, which proves the effectiveness of the TFE module. In the SRR ablation study, our method achieved overall leadership on MIMIC-CXR, except for Bert Score. On IU X-Ray, although it only gained an advantage in METEOR among the NLG metrics, it led in all CE metrics, demonstrating that our method focuses more on the clinical features of the conditions. Furthermore, we selected a sample image and inputted it into multiple models (including our method, two models from ablation experiments, and R2GenCMN) to gather generated reports for comparative analysis. As depicted in Fig. 2, our method can identify more relevant content from the actual report compared to other models, suggesting its capability to produce more accurate reports. Overall, our method has demonstrated its effectiveness.

Table 2. The results of the ablation experiments on the IU X-Ray and MIMIC-CXR datasets. The best values are highlighted in bold.

Dataset	Model	CE Metrics			Bert Score	NLG Metrics		
		F1	Precision	Recall		BLEU4	METEOR	ROUGE-L
IU X-Ray	Ours (SRR + TFE)	**0.1603**	**0.1957**	**0.1713**	0.6904	0.0877	**0.1582**	0.3023
	Random Pairs + TFE	0.1127	0.1938	0.1231	**0.6943**	**0.0985**	0.1520	**0.3049**
	SRR + Pseudo Pairs Feeding	0.0391	0.0269	0.0714	0.6782	0.0861	0.1483	0.2816
MIMIC-CXR	Ours (SRR + TFE)	**0.2149**	**0.3246**	**0.2143**	0.6717	**0.1035**	**0.1380**	**0.2767**
	Random Pairs + TFE	0.1926	0.2626	0.2041	**0.6721**	0.0994	0.1325	0.2742
	SRR + Pseudo Pairs Feeding	0.0082	0.0043	0.0714	0.6595	0.0739	0.1077	0.2564

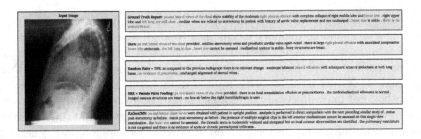

Fig. 2. An example report generated on the MIMIX-CXR dataset by various models, highlighting words common to both the generated and Ground Truth reports in red. (Color figure online)

Ratios Exploration. We explored the impact of different ratios on the scarcity of image report pairings. Using R2GenCMN as a baseline, we tested ratios of 25%, 50%, and 75%, which denote the availability of paired data in the training set, with the remainder unpaired by default. Table 3 shows the CE metrics, Bert Score, and NLG metrics results at these ratios for both datasets. At a 75% ratio, our method performed comparably across metrics, with notable achievements in F1 scores on both datasets. As the ratio decreased, our method excelled further: at 50%, it outperformed all metrics on both datasets; at 25%, it showed superior performance on most metrics for IU X-Ray and all metrics for MIMIC-CXR. These findings underscore the effectiveness of our method under limited image report pairings, highlighting its data-efficient capabilities.

Table 3. The results of the ratios exploration experiments compared with R2GenCMN on the IU X-Ray and MIMIC-CXR datasets. The best values are highlighted in bold.

Dataset	Ratio	Model	CE Metrics			Bert Score	NLG Metrics		
			F1	Precision	Recall		BLEU4	METEOR	ROUGE-L
IU X-Ray	75%	R2GenCMN	0.1585	0.2921	**0.1592**	**0.7057**	**0.1024**	**0.1694**	**0.3293**
		Ours	**0.1598**	**0.3357**	0.1510	0.6994	0.0970	0.1607	0.3157
	50%	R2GenCMN	0.1235	0.2059	0.1339	0.6960	0.0963	0.1604	0.3127
		Ours	**0.1443**	**0.2519**	**0.1428**	**0.7130**	**0.1077**	**0.1729**	**0.3396**
	25%	R2GenCMN	0.1452	**0.2433**	0.1499	0.6889	**0.0920**	0.1525	0.2985
		Ours	**0.1603**	0.1957	**0.1713**	0.6904	0.0877	**0.1582**	**0.3023**
MIMIC-CXR	75%	R2GenCMN	0.2277	**0.3261**	**0.2328**	0.6737	**0.1066**	**0.1425**	**0.2824**
		Ours	**0.2282**	0.3212	0.2256	**0.6760**	0.1047	0.1399	0.2786
	50%	R2GenCMN	0.1638	0.2552	0.1803	0.6659	0.0931	0.1268	0.2702
		Ours	**0.1945**	**0.3086**	**0.1988**	**0.6728**	**0.1026**	**0.1385**	**0.2779**
	25%	R2GenCMN	0.2053	0.2861	0.2085	0.6659	0.0983	0.1328	0.2701
		Ours	**0.2149**	**0.3246**	**0.2143**	**0.6717**	**0.1035**	**0.1380**	**0.2767**

4   Conclusion

This work proposed a data-efficient method for generating radiology reports. By adopting a cross-modal memory mechanism to align visual and textual features, and integrating a similar reports retriever with a text fusion enhancement module, our method outperforms several state-of-the-art methods on the MIMIC-CXR and IU X-Ray datasets with limited data pairs. This demonstrates that our method not only effectively mitigates limitations from image-report scarcity but also producing effective and accurate radiology reports in data-limited cases. This work can inform future research on improving radiology report generation, especially in scenarios with limited data pairs availability.

Prospect of Application: This work introduces a data-efficient technology for automated generation of radiology image reports, particularly beneficial for low- to middle-income countries and small to medium-sized healthcare facilities where paired data is generally scarce.

Acknowledgments. This work was supported by National Natural Science Foundation of China (Grant No. 62371409).

Disclosure of Interests. The authors have no competing interests to declare that are relevant to the content of this article.

References

1. Chen, J., Guo, H., Yi, K., Li, B., Elhoseiny, M.: VisualGPT: data-efficient adaptation of pretrained language models for image captioning. In: CVPR, pp. 18030–18040 (2022)
2. Chen, Z., Shen, Y., Song, Y., Wan, X.: Cross-modal memory networks for radiology report generation. In: ACL (2022)
3. Chen, Z., Song, Y., Chang, T.H., Wan, X.: Generating radiology reports via memory-driven transformer. In: EMNLP (2020)
4. Cornia, M., Stefanini, M., Baraldi, L., Cucchiara, R.: Meshed-memory transformer for image captioning. In: CVPR, pp. 10578–10587 (2020)
5. Demner-Fushman, D., et al.: Preparing a collection of radiology examinations for distribution and retrieval. JAMIA $23(2)$, 304–310 (2016)
6. Deng, J., Dong, W., Socher, R., Li, L.J., Li, K., Fei-Fei, L.: Imagenet: a large-scale hierarchical image database. In: CVPR, pp. 248–255. IEEE (2009)
7. Denkowski, M., Lavie, A.: Meteor 1.3: Automatic metric for reliable optimization and evaluation of machine translation systems. In: Proceedings of the Sixth Workshop on Statistical Machine Translation, pp. 85–91 (2011)
8. He, K., Zhang, X., Ren, S., Sun, J.: Deep residual learning for image recognition. In: CVPR, pp. 770–778 (2016)
9. Jin, H., Che, H., Lin, Y., Chen, H.: PromptMRG: diagnosis-driven prompts for medical report generation. In: AAAI, vol. 38, pp. 2607–2615 (2024)
10. Johnson, A.E., et al.: MIMIC-CXR, a de-identified publicly available database of chest radiographs with free-text reports. Sci. Data $6(1)$, 317 (2019)
11. Li, J., Li, D., Xiong, C., Hoi, S.: Blip: bootstrapping language-image pre-training for unified vision-language understanding and generation. In: ICML, pp. 12888–12900. PMLR (2022)
12. Li, M., Lin, B., Chen, Z., Lin, H., Liang, X., Chang, X.: Dynamic graph enhanced contrastive learning for chest x-ray report generation. In: CVPR, pp. 3334–3343 (2023)
13. Lin, C.Y.: Rouge: a package for automatic evaluation of summaries. In: Text Summarization Branches Out, pp. 74–81 (2004)
14. Lu, Y., Guo, C., Dai, X., Wang, F.Y.: Data-efficient image captioning of fine art paintings via virtual-real semantic alignment training. Neurocomputing 490, 163–180 (2022)
15. Luo, Y., et al.: Dual-level collaborative transformer for image captioning. In: AAAI, vol. 35, pp. 2286–2293 (2021)
16. Papineni, K., Roukos, S., Ward, T., Zhu, W.J.: BleU: a method for automatic evaluation of machine translation. In: ACL, pp. 311–318 (2002)
17. Qin, H., Song, Y.: Reinforced cross-modal alignment for radiology report generation. In: ACL, pp. 448–458 (2022)
18. Radford, A., et al.: Learning transferable visual models from natural language supervision. In: ICML, pp. 8748–8763. PMLR (2021)
19. Smit, A., Jain, S., Rajpurkar, P., Pareek, A., Ng, A.Y., Lungren, M.P.: ChexBERT: combining automatic labelers and expert annotations for accurate radiology report labeling using BERT. In: EMNLP (2020)
20. Vaswani, A., et al.: Attention is all you need. In: NeurIPS, vol. 30 (2017)
21. Wang, J., Bhalerao, A., He, Y.: Cross-modal prototype driven network for radiology report generation. In: Avidan, S., Brostow, G., Cissé, M., Farinella, G.M., Hassner, T. (eds.) ECCV 2022. LNCS, vol. 13695, pp. 563–579. Springer, Cham (2022). https://doi.org/10.1007/978-3-031-19833-5_33

22. Wang, Z., Wu, Z., Agarwal, D., Sun, J.: MedClip: contrastive learning from unpaired medical images and text. In: EMNLP (2022)
23. Yang, M., et al.: Multitask learning for cross-domain image captioning. IEEE TMM **21**(4), 1047–1061 (2018)
24. Yang, S., Wu, X., Ge, S., Zheng, Z., Zhou, S.K., Xiao, L.: Radiology report generation with a learned knowledge base and multi-modal alignment. Med. Image Anal. **86**, 102798 (2023)
25. You, K., et al.: CXR-CLIP: toward large scale chest x-ray language-image pretraining. In: Greenspan, H., et al. (eds.) MICCAI 2023. LNCS, vol. 14221, pp. 101–111. Springer, Cham (2023). https://doi.org/10.1007/978-3-031-43895-0_10
26. Yu, L., Zhang, J., Wu, Q.: Dual attention on pyramid feature maps for image captioning. IEEE TMM **24**, 1775–1786 (2021)
27. Zhang, K., et al.: Semi-supervised medical report generation via graph-guided hybrid feature consistency. IEEE TMM (2023)
28. Zhang, T., Kishore, V., Wu, F., Weinberger, K.Q., Artzi, Y.: BERTscore: evaluating text generation with BERT. In: ICLR (2019)

Author Index

Printed in the United States
by Baker & Taylor Publisher Services